Moodle 1.9 for Second Language Teaching

Engaging online language-learning activities using the Moodle platform

Jeff Stanford

[PACKT]
PUBLISHING

BIRMINGHAM - MUMBAI

Moodle 1.9 for Second Language Teaching

Copyright © 2009 Packt Publishing

First published: October 2009

Production Reference: 1141009

Published by Packt Publishing Ltd.
32 Lincoln Road
Olton
Birmingham, B27 6PA, UK.

ISBN 978-1-847196-24-8

www.packtpub.com

Cover Image by Parag Kadam (paragvkadam@gmail.com)

Credits

Author
Jeff Stanford

Reviewers
Andy Baker

Clive Wright

Acquisition Editor
David Barnes

Development Editor
Swapna V. Verlekar

Technical Editor
Mithun Sehgal

Indexer
Hemangini Bari

Editorial Team Leader
Abhijeet Deobhakta

Project Team Leader
Priya Mukherji

Project Coordinator
Leena Purkait

Proofreader
Chris Smith

Graphics
Nilesh Mohite

Production Coordinator
Shantanu Zagade

Cover Work
Shantanu Zagade

About the Author

Jeff Stanford is a free-lance educational technologist. He discovered Moodle five years ago, and has remained an ardent fan ever since. He now does regular consultancy work, helping teachers make the most of online learning possibilities. To get away from the computer, he also does training consultancy work for organizations like Anglia Assessment, Fintra, Pearson, and the British Council now and then. He is an Associate tutor in Applied Linguistics for the University of Leicester and a teacher trainer on Cambridge ESOL courses. He also runs a web hosting service and advises on setting up and running Drupal and Moodle websites. You can reach him via `http://moodleflair.com` and `http://moodleforlanguages.co.uk`.

I would like to thank my reviewers, Helena Gomm, Malcolm Griffiths, Constanze Eichelbaum, and Maria Stanford, who provided a great deal of constructive feedback on the book. I owe Helena a particular debt of gratitude: if she hadn't coaxed me into writing an article for ETP on Moodle, Packt Publishing's David Barnes wouldn't have come across me and the book would never have been written. I would also like to thank Anthony Gaugham, Tim Francis, and Sue Morris for their helpful comments on some of the chapters.

Thanks must go to Packt Publishing for their impressive patience and support throughout this project.

And finally, I'd like to thank the hundreds of teachers I've worked with who've provided me with feedback and comments that have been so valuable in the writing of this book.

About the Reviewers

Andy Baker is Head of ICT at Bishop Challoner Catholic College in Birmingham. He has a strong interest in innovation, particularly in education, and feels that technology, if used effectively, is fundamental in motivating learners to learn.

When he's not teaching, Andy likes to spend quality time with his wife Vicci and daughters Francesca and Grace.

Andy lives in Worcestershire, England, and can be reached at abaker@iteach.uk.com.

Clive Wright has been a senior teacher in charge of e-learning as well as a secondary schools advisor working with educational establishments and leading on, amongst other things, the use of Information and Communication Technology in the classroom. He has had extensive experience leading teacher training on the use of new technologies in education. Clive believes that technology can engage and excite young people in their education, enhancing their learning as well as making the learning experience more enjoyable and thereby more effective. He is director of a website software company nomumbojumbo (nomumbojumbo.com), and he also works with schools setting up Moodle environments and providing Moodle training. Clive lives in the medieval Cathedral city of Lichfield in England with his wife Rebecca and four children Ellie, Beth, Hannah, and Will. He can be contacted on cwright@iteach.uk.com.

Table of Contents

Preface

That word "Moodle" keeps cropping up all over the place—it's in the newspapers, on other teachers' tongues, in more and more articles. Do you want to find out more about it yourself and learn how to create all sorts of fun and useful online language activities with it? Your search ends right here.

This book demystifies Moodle and provides you with answers to your queries. It helps you create engaging online language-learning activities using the Moodle platform. It has suggestions and fully working examples for adapting classroom activities to the Virtual Learning Environment.

The book starts with examples based on what you need for your language teaching and shows which bits of Moodle you need to make them. As such, it isn't a comprehensive guide to Moodle, but it aims to provide relevant information for language teachers. There is no one way to organize a language course. It depends on the level and age of students, the language learning goals, and learning style preferences, amongst other things. But most language courses include a focus on the skills of speaking, listening, reading, and writing, and also offer support for vocabulary, pronunciation, and grammar. This book has taken those areas as its starting point.

Most of this book is a recipe book, a how-to book. In it you'll see activities that you'd find in a typical language-teaching syllabus and learn how you can produce these on Moodle. You'll be provided with step-by-step instructions to copy examples and then adapt them according to your own teaching situation. Most of the activities are ordered so that each chapter starts with easier activities. The ease of setup for each activity is indicated by a star system. Now and then you'll be referred to other chapters where an example already exists.

The non-recipe chapters are guides for setting up Moodle (Chapter 2), using Moodle for Assessment (Chapter 9), making your Moodle site look good (Chapter 11), and helping prepare students to use Moodle (Chapter 12).

What this book covers

Chapter 1, *What Does Moodle Offer Language Teachers?* outlines the key features of Moodle that make it such an excellent tool for language teaching. It relates Moodle to **communicative language teaching** syllabuses and provides an outline of the whole book.

Chapter 2, *Getting Started with Moodle* provides an overview of the administration features you'll need to have in place before you begin. We'll consider the importance of roles, groups, and outcomes, as well as the add-ons that are worth including to make the most of Moodle for language teaching.

Chapter 3, *Vocabulary Activities* looks at a variety of activities that help students to learn words. It considers how Moodle can help students review and recycle vocabulary, and looks at the different ways of keeping vocabulary records.

Chapter 4, *Speaking Activities* makes much use of the add-on NanoGong recorder to illustrate activities that look at pronunciation, intonation, fluency, stress, and participation in discussions.

Chapter 5, *Grammar Activities* is very much at home in Moodle. It's possible to create a wide range of activities for presenting grammar, providing noticing activities, controlled practice using grammar, and keeping grammar records.

Chapter 6, *Reading Activities* focuses on how you can use Moodle to motivate students to read and interact with texts. There's also an activity on extended reading.

Chapter 7, *Writing Activities* shows how helpful Moodle can be for collaborative work on drafts, for adding graphics and organizing writing in effective ways.

Chapter 8, *Listening Activities* looks at the different ways you can present recordings and gives examples of different task types.

Chapter 9, *Assessment* considers the gradebook and its many uses. The wide range of possibilities is potentially overwhelming. The chapter provides some clear paths through it, and shows how you can use Moodle statistics to improve your assessment activities.

Chapter 10, *Extended Activities* considers activities that are longer than those already covered, longer in terms of the activity duration and longer to set up, but definitely worthwhile for language teaching.

Chapter 11, *Formatting and Enhancing Your Moodle Materials* provides some guidelines for making your language learners' experience more effective by checking the quality of text, images, and audio. It also considers the importance of clear navigation paths.

Chapter 12, *Preparing Your Students to Use Moodle* provides some guidelines for making Moodle part of your students' learning timetable.

Chapter 11 and Chapter 12 are not part of the actual book, but you can download them from Packt's website.

Chapter 11 is available at `http://www.packtpub.com/files/6248-Chapter-11.pdf`, and Chapter 12 is available at `http://www.packtpub.com/files/6248-Chapter-12.pdf`.

What you need for this book

To follow this book, you need access to a Moodle site where you have been registered. You'll need to work with your Moodle administrator or have administration access yourself to do the set-up work. You'll also need administrative access to do things like override permissions on set-up pages when you're setting up activities. Also helpful is an enthusiasm for learning, teaching, and using the Web to reach out and make a difference in your students' lives.

Conventions

In this book, you will find a number of styles of text that distinguish between different kinds of information. Here are some examples of these styles, and an explanation of their meaning.

Code words in text are shown as follows: "He takes `{:SHORTANSWER:~=a#well done! ~%20%an#nearly right!}` picture of Amy on his phone and sends it to Roxy."

New terms and **important words** are shown in bold. Words that you see on the screen, in menus or dialog boxes for example, appear in the text like this: "First, let's make sure we're in editing mode. To do that, click on the **Turn editing on** button. We always need to do that if we want to add a resource or an activity."

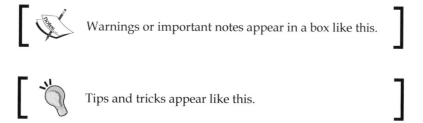

[Warnings or important notes appear in a box like this.]

[Tips and tricks appear like this.]

Reader feedback

Feedback from our readers is always welcome. Let us know what you think about this book—what you liked or may have disliked. Reader feedback is important for us to develop titles that you really get the most out of.

To send us general feedback, simply send an email to feedback@packtpub.com, and mention the book title via the subject of your message.

If there is a book that you need and would like to see us publish, please send us a note in the **SUGGEST A TITLE** form on www.packtpub.com or email to suggest@packtpub.com.

If there is a topic that you have expertise in and you are interested in either writing or contributing to a book, see our author guide on www.packtpub.com/authors.

Customer support

Now that you are the proud owner of a Packt book, we have a number of things to help you to get the most from your purchase.

Errata

Although we have taken every care to ensure the accuracy of our content, mistakes do happen. If you find a mistake in one of our books—maybe a mistake in the text or the code—we would be grateful if you would report this to us. By doing so, you can save other readers from frustration and help us to improve subsequent versions of this book. If you find any errata, please report them by visiting http://www.packtpub.com/support, selecting your book, clicking on the **let us know** link, and entering the details of your errata. Once your errata are verified, your submission will be accepted and the errata added to any list of existing errata. Any existing errata can be viewed by selecting your title from http://www.packtpub.com/support.

Piracy

Piracy of copyright material on the Internet is an ongoing problem across all media. At Packt, we take the protection of our copyright and licenses very seriously. If you come across any illegal copies of our works, in any form, on the Internet, please provide us with the location address or website name immediately so that we can pursue a remedy.

Please contact us at copyright@packtpub.com with a link to the suspected pirated material.

We appreciate your help in protecting our authors, and our ability to bring you valuable content.

Questions

You can contact us at questions@packtpub.com if you are having a problem with any aspect of the book, and we will do our best to address it.

1
What Does Moodle Offer Language Teachers?

Imagine the things you do in a school—putting up timetables, presenting syllabuses, having discussions, presenting videos of new materials, organizing tests, collecting marks, providing feedback to students, guiding students to do their own learning, building a library… Moodle can do all these things and much, much more.

What is Moodle?

I just googled "Moodle" and got over 18 million hits. Moodle is one of the fastest growing free, open source **VLEs (Virtual Learning Environment)** around at the moment. It is also commonly referred to as an **LMS (Learning Management System)** or a **CMS (Course Management System)**. There are already thousands of registered Moodle sites, as you can see on the Moodle site: `http://moodle.org/stats/`.

Just in case some of those terms are new to you:

- **Open source** means that the code is available by licensing agreement and that you can customize it and redistribute it (`http://opensource.org`). These have been powerful factors in the development of open source software for a wide range of free or low-cost software.
- A **VLE** is a way of providing a teaching and learning environment online.

Here are some of the things that make Moodle particularly attractive to all teachers:

- Easy to use—you don't need any programming knowledge
- Access to resources via the Web
- Interaction between learners and tutors
- Collaboration between learners
- Independent learning pathways
- Learner tracking
- Feedback on tasks
- Secure environment
- Automatic backup

There are some myths that Moodle is difficult, unsupported, and will eventually charge users, but these are all calmly deflated at `http://docs.moodle.org/en/Top_10_Moodle_Myths`.

Assumptions

Most of this book is a recipe book, a "how-to" book. In it, I'll take activities that you'd find in a typical language-teaching syllabus and show how you can produce these on Moodle. I'll provide step-by-step instructions for you to copy examples and then adapt them according to your own teaching situation. Most of the activities are ordered so that each chapter starts with easier activities. The ease of setup for each activity is indicated by a star system. Now and then you'll be referred to other chapters where an example already exists.

The non-recipe chapters are guides for setting up Moodle (Chapter 2, *Getting Started with Moodle*), using Moodle for assessment (Chapter 9, *Assessment*), making your Moodle site look good (Chapter 11, *Formatting and Enhancing Your Moodle Materials*), and helping prepare students to use Moodle (Chapter 12, *Preparing Your Students to Use Moodle*).

I'm making a few assumptions:

- You have basic computer skills
- You have Moodle up and running
- You are not necessarily familiar with Moodle's basic features
- You want examples of how you can cover your language teaching syllabus using Moodle
- You don't want to master all aspects of Moodle

- You are not necessarily the Moodle administrator, but have access to the administrator
- You have some experience of teaching
- You want to transfer **constructivist, communicative language teaching** methodology to Moodle.

In case you're not familiar with these concepts, **constructivism** is based on the idea that individuals learn new things (construct knowledge) through experience by comparing new things to what they already know. They do this by solving realistic problems, often in collaboration with other people. Moodle was built on this approach, and many of the core activities lend themselves well to this type of learning. Communicative language teaching tries to help learners become competent language users in real contexts. There's more about this later in this chapter.

Who is this book for?

One of the advantages of a recipe-book approach is that all sorts of people connected to language teaching will find it useful. If you are a teacher, you can dip into it to find a quick solution for an activity you want to create. If you are a course planner, you can review the whole book to build up your own language course. These are some of the people I had in mind when writing:

- School language teachers who run at least part of their courses on computers
- Private language teachers who want to run their own online language school
- Established teachers of English or other languages
- New teachers who want clear examples of communicative language teaching and testing in use
- Teacher trainers who want to guide teachers in the use of this powerful system
- Teachers who have been using Blackboard or another powerful commercial VLE and want to set up their own open source system
- Course planners and ICT support staff who want to understand the ICT needs of language teachers better

An important point here is that there's no single way of using Moodle for language teaching. I've come across teachers who use it mainly as a repository of materials and find the indexing facilities of the Database module useful for that. Module, by the way, is Moodle's word for an activity. Other teachers use it to create supplementary quizzes for the work they do in class. They find the gradebook, which provides an overview of all their students' marks, useful. Other teachers make Moodle the base of their course, even though they have face-to-face sessions, because Moodle is a neat way of keeping important course elements in one place and tracking learner use and progress. It's also a good way of preparing for classes and reflecting on them afterwards. Finally, Moodle can be used as a totally online course with no face-to-face meeting at all.

You might find I'm stating the obvious sometimes, but most hints are included because there were minor hiccoughs when teachers trialed the materials. On the other hand, some readers might feel phased by mention of formats they've never heard of, such as XML or WAV. If that's the case, don't worry! These are usually extra bits of information that some teachers will find useful to make their lives easier or improve the Moodle activities. Not understanding them—or not wanting to understand them—won't stop you from creating the activities.

Why another book on Moodle?

So what's the difference between this book and any other book on Moodle? There's an increasingly large number of books about Moodle on the market. General introductions to Moodle, such as *"Moodle Teaching Techniques"*, *William Rice, Packt Publishing* and *"Moodle 1.9 E-Learning Course Development"*, *William Rice, Packt Publishing*, go through key Moodle modules methodically and then offer examples. This book takes the opposite approach: it starts with examples based on what you need for your language teaching and shows which bits of Moodle you need to make them. As such, it isn't a comprehensive guide to Moodle, but it aims to provide relevant information for language teachers. There is no one way to organize a language course. It depends on the level and age of students, the language learning goals, and learning style preferences, amongst other things. But most language courses include a focus on the skills of speaking, listening, reading, and writing, and also offer support for vocabulary, pronunciation, and grammar. This book has taken those areas as its starting point.

Moodle's popularity has led to the development of hundreds of add-on modules. The list is available at `http://moodle.org/mod/data/view.php?id=6009`. A useful service a book like this can offer is recommending which add-on modules are worth getting. For example, a VLE for language learning without a speak and record facility would be incomplete. I've chosen a simple sound recorder called NanoGong. Why? Because it is supported for Moodle 1.9; it's very easy to install and works well on a variety of browsers. You can also set up Moodle activities without NanoGong, simply by recording directly onto the computer, but you'd lose the advantage of being able to manage your recordings inside Moodle. There's a useful discussion of available recorders at `http://metamedia.typepad.com/metamedia/listen-up-audio-in-moodle.html`.

Voice recording in future versions of Moodle

It's uncertain whether NanoGong will work with Moodle 2.0, but a similar recording plug-in is being developed for it (see http://docs.moodle.org/en/GSOC/2009). Meanwhile, NanoGong is probably the simplest choice.

As well as providing an overview of core Moodle modules, Chapter 2, *Getting Started with Moodle* will take you through all the add-on modules you'll need for this book. The reasons for choosing them are the same in each case:

- Ease of use
- Available support
- Suitability for language learning

It is important to remember that add-on modules may not work with future updates of Moodle, but I've chosen ones which look likely to receive continued support. All the examples in this book work with Moodle 1.9.5.

Sometimes I've recommended an alternative to the core modules, simply because they are better for language teaching. For example, Moodle has core Blog and Wiki modules, but they don't work with NanoGong, the recording tool, whereas the Open University versions named OUblog and OUwiki do work.

Assessment

There are also some aspects of assessment in Moodle which have a specific language-teaching slant in this book:

- Moodle allows you to provide detailed feedback to your students on specific areas of language performance. So you can give separate marks on areas such as grammar, fluency, and pronunciation, for example. You do this by setting up rating scales for each type of activity. In Moodle speak, categories for assessment are called **Outcomes** (see Chapter 2, *Getting Started with Moodle* for more information).

- Moodle also allows us to create marking scales which relate specifically to language work. One example of this would be the use of the language achievement evaluation scales set by the Council of Europe's Common European Framework. (http://www.coe.int/T/DG4/Linguistic/ CADRE_EN.asp). We can customize scales to suit our school or institution.

- Many Moodle activities can be assessed. All the marks can be collected in an online gradebook. Moodle also provides some basic statistics which teachers can use to see how well their tests are working, and to improve them if necessary.

- There is also an add-on ordering task for the Quiz module. This lets students practice ordering the words in a sentence, sentences in a paragraph, and paragraphs in a text, and putting a sequence of events in chronological order.

Making Moodle look good

The success of any activity also depends on how good it looks. Chapter 11, *Formatting and Enhancing Your Moodle Materials* takes a look at some basic things you can do to make your Moodle site look better and, therefore, more attractive to your students.

Communicative Language Teaching

The book is firmly rooted in a communicative approach to language learning. It therefore tries to make the student the center of the learning experience wherever possible. It looks at ways of encouraging interaction, making materials engaging and effective, and of encouraging reflection and self-improvement on the part of the language learner and the teacher.

A PDF by Jack Richards (http://tinyurl.com/cltarticle) gives a good overview of the status quo of various approaches to communicative language teaching.

In the article *"Understanding and Implementing the Clt (Communicative Language Teaching) Paradigm"*, George M. Jacobs and Thomas S. C. Farrell, RELC Journal, Vol. 34, No. 1, 5-30 (2003), the authors highlight some of the key features of CLT. As the following table shows, Moodle accommodates these features well.

Key features of CLT (based on Jack Richards, 2006, and Jacobs and Farrell, 2003)	Moodle features which support CLT
Learner autonomy: Giving learners greater choice over their own learning, both in terms of the content of learning and processes they might employ. The use of small groups is one example of this, as well as the use of self-assessment.	<ul><li>Customization of learners' home pages if **My Moodle** is turned on</li><li>Using questionnaires and polls (Choice module) to allow learners to influence curriculum</li><li>Use of wikis for learners to determine processes</li><li>Group and groupings feature for dividing students</li></ul>

Key features of CLT (as per Jack Richards, 2006, and Jacobs and Farrell, 2003)	Moodle features which support CLT
The social nature of learning: Learning is not an individual, private activity, but a social one that depends upon interaction with others.	• Interaction is built into Chat, Forum, and Wiki modules. • Assignment and Workshop modules allow collaborative writing.
Curricular integration: The connection between different strands of the curriculum is emphasized, so that English is not seen as a stand-alone subject but is linked to other subjects in the curriculum. Text-based learning reflects this approach, and seeks to develop fluency in text types that can be used across the curriculum. Project work in language teaching also requires students to explore issues outside of the language classroom.	HTML pages with hyperlinks and webquests are good examples of how Moodle can be linked to the outside world.
Focus on meaning: Meaning is viewed as the driving force of learning. Content-based teaching reflects this view, and seeks to make the exploration of meaning through content the core of language learning activities.	It's easy to incorporate authentic spoken and written texts into Moodle and activities based on them.
Diversity: Learners learn in different ways and have different strengths. Teaching needs to take these differences into account, rather than try to force students into a single mold. In language teaching, this has led to an emphasis on developing students' use and awareness of learning strategies.	• Learners can go at different speeds. • Learners can be grouped according to interests, level, and needs. • Teachers can help learners use the glossary to build their own records. • The Journal module allows learners and teachers to reflect on learning processes and make changes as a result.
Thinking skills: Language should serve as a means of developing higher-order thinking skills, also known as critical and creative thinking. In language teaching, this means that students do not learn language for its own sake but in order to develop and apply their thinking skills in situations that go beyond the language classroom.	• Wide range of tasks is possible. Chapter 6, *Reading Activities* shows how Bloom's taxonomy can be used to foster higher-order thinking tasks. • The Webquest module is a good place to develop critical evaluation skills.

Key features of CLT (based on Jack Richards, 2006, and Jacobs and Farrell, 2003)	Moodle features which support CLT
Alternative assessment: New forms of assessment are needed to replace traditional multiple-choice and other items that test lower-order skills. Multiple forms of assessment (for example, observation, interviews, journals, portfolios) can be used to build a comprehensive picture of what students can do in a second language.	Moodle offers traditional tests as well as journals and add-on portfolios.
Teachers as co-learners: The teacher is viewed as a facilitator who is constantly trying out different alternatives; that is, learning through doing. In language teaching, this has led to an interest in action research and other forms of classroom investigation.	• The Workshop and Questionnaire modules make it easy to get learner feedback. • Teachers can also monitor the popularity of different activities by tracking student use.

Age and level of students

Moodle can work for learners of all ages. The examples in this book show how young learners, adolescents, and adults can use Moodle. Clearly, you will need to adapt the example activities for your particular students. Make sure they have the content and tasks that they are likely to enjoy and find useful.

If you are creating tasks for pre-adolescents, you might find it useful to use this book in conjunction with *Moodle 1.9 for Teaching 7-14 Year Olds: Beginner's Guide, Mary Cooch, Packt Publishing*, which offers some useful guidelines on things to look out for with this age group.

It is important when working with learners of all ages that you have:

- Learning pathways
- Instructions
- Materials
- Duration of activities
- Cognitive complexity of tasks

As for language level, it's possible to create simple low-level tasks, or quite difficult ones.

You'll need to consider whether the whole site is written in the target language. This is probably only appropriate for higher level learners. It may be more effective for lower level learners if you frame the activities in a language they understand better.

You can include the option for learners to change the language for the headings and help files, though help files are not available in all languages. You may need to check with your Moodle administrator that the appropriate language pack is installed. By clicking on the language selector in the top right-hand corner of the screen, users can change to the language of their choice. Contact your Moodle administrator if the languages you want are not there.

Add-on modules are unlikely to have help files and instructions for all languages. If you find that help files are not available in a language you need, you could write to the authors via the `moodle.org` website, or write them yourself. One of the great things about this open source software is that you can make your own contributions to it. Your Moodle administrator should be able to help you install your new files.

You can also edit existing help files by going to **Site Administration | Language | Language editing**.

What languages can you teach using Moodle?

All the examples in this book are of **ESOL (English as a Second or Other Language)**. However, Moodle can by used to teach a vast variety of languages. All the instructions in this book are in English, but for lower-level learners you may wish to consider changing the base language to the students' first language (L1) and providing instructions in the L1, too.

The official Moodle site offers several support sections for non-English language use:

- `http://moodle.org/course/` is a directory of Moodle forums in many languages
- `http://moodle.org/course/view.php?id=31` is a forum for language teaching
- `http://download.moodle.org/lang16/` provides a range of language packs, which you'll need to change instructions and labels to other languages

Suggested approach to using the book

The introduction to each chapter gives an overview of the whole chapter. So it's worth reading first.

Several reviewers have suggested that a good way to approach the activities in each chapter is to skim through the whole activity first to get a feel for it and then to create the activity step by step in your Moodle course.

Try to make yourself familiar with Chapter 2, *Getting Started with Moodle*. There is frequent reference to it throughout the book. It contains key information on setting up Moodle modules and add-on modules, using extra programs, combining Moodle with other programs, and advice on things such as uploading images and other files or embedding audio and video in Moodle. Happy Moodling!

2

Getting Started with Moodle

One of the great things about Moodle is that the Moodle forums on the main Moodle site `http://moodle.org` are packed with useful discussions and resources. If you have a problem or a question, it's pretty likely that someone else will have had the same problem, and will have started up a discussion and found a solution. However, a common bit of feedback I get from teachers is that there is simply *too much* helpful information on the site, and they don't know where to start. One of my aims in this chapter, then, is to identify administrative functions that are particularly useful for language teachers and present them in a simple, clear way. But don't let this stop you from exploring the forums and help files on the `moodle.org` site where you can look for Moodle docs—these are useful help documents which are accessible from many of your Moodle site pages via the **Moodle Docs** link. You'll see the link at the bottom of the page, usually.

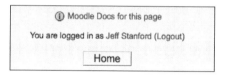

And if there isn't a **Moodle Docs** link at the bottom of the page on your Moodle site, there might be a useful support file indicated by the ⓘ icon.

This chapter is divided into four parts:

Part 1	This gives an overview of the makeup of Moodle. It's essential reading if you don't know Moodle well.
Part 2	This identifies key site administration "how-tos", which you'll need to set up to get your Moodle course, or courses, working. You will find this section useful as a reference for the whole book, as it deals with key information.
Part 3	This lists non-essential add-ons.
Part 4	Here you'll find some design principles for setting up your courses.

Part 1: Overview of Moodle

Installing Moodle

I'm assuming you already have Moodle installed and are familiar with the basics.
The activities in this book are based on Version 1.9.5. There are various possibilities
if you don't have it installed:

- Ask your IT support person.

- Go to `http://download.moodle.org/` and download it yourself. The
  support pages on this site are well written. You will need a domain name and
  a server to host it on. Make sure you have at least PHP 4.3, MySQL 4.1.16, or
  Postgres 8 on your server too. If possible, get the latest versions of each
  of these.

- If you don't want to, or can't do it yourself, you could approach
  a Moodle hosting company. I've put up a list of some of these on the
  `http://moodleflair.com/` site.

- Pick up one of Packt's other books on Moodle, such as *Moodle E-Learning
  Course Development* (`http://www.packtpub.com/learning-moodle-1-9-
  course-development/book`), which has a full commentary on installation.

- If you just want to try out Moodle on your own Windows machine, you
  could download portable Moodle from `http://sourceforge.net/
  projects/portablemoodle`. There is a Mac version available at
  `http://download.moodle.org/macosx/`.

Topography of a Moodle site

So what does Moodle look like? Well, there's a front page which is like an outer shell.
The next layer down is a course which is a bit like a classroom—all the activities
relating to one group of students can be found there.

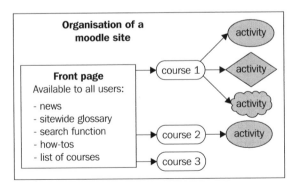

Which browser?

Moodle works well in most browsers, but if you have trouble viewing some pages, it's worth checking out another one. For example, some of the add-on programs we'll be looking at later don't always work in Firefox.

Topography of a Moodle site: Front page

Front pages typically have site news and a list of available courses. From the front page, users can go directly to their course or click on one of the other items.

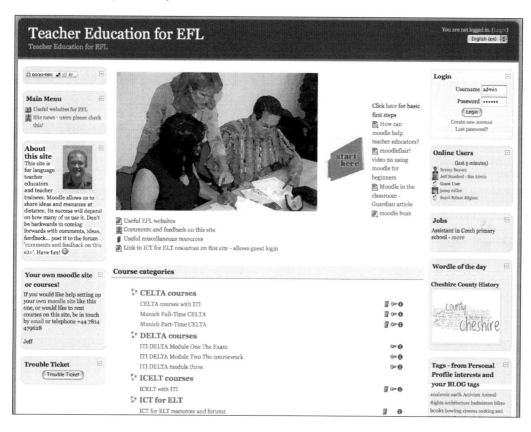

As you can see, there are three columns. The thin outer columns contain **blocks**, which give useful information and other useful functions such as a **Main Menu**, a **Login** box, a list of **Online Users**, and **Blog tags**—keywords from users' blogs. We'll take a closer look at the range of blocks available later in this chapter. The central area is typically used as a news area, and can give a list of courses, organized into **Course categories**, which users can click on. If there is a key icon to the right of the course name, it is password protected. You'll set the enrolment key when you create a course. You can also add or change enrolment keys later.

Topography of a Moodle site: Course page

If you click on **ICT for ELT resources and forums** on the front page, you'll get to a course. In fact, a course in Moodle is an area that can house anything you want it to: forums, a set of materials, or a sequence of activities.

Courses can be organized by topic, week, or social events. Before you set up your course, spend a while deciding how you'd like to organize your course. If you want to make activities available for specific periods, the weekly organization will work well. If you want to create your own topics, as in the screenshot above, then organize your course by topics. The social format looks a bit like a blog site and highlights recent forum postings.

You'll notice that next to each activity, under the **Topic outline**, there is an icon which identifies which module it is. Before we go though setting up a course, here is a list and brief description of the core blocks and core modules which are referred to in this book and which are automatically installed in your Moodle.

Moodle overview: Core blocks

The blocks are the boxes you can see in the left- and right-hand columns. They are mainly used to provide information about course users, send messages, or show course menus. Though, as you'll see later in this chapter, there are many other uses. Once a course has been created, teachers can click on the **Turn editing on** button and activate any of the blocks in the table below. Most of them are not mentioned in the activities in this book, but nevertheless have useful functions. Blocks can be moved around the page by clicking on the **Turn editing on** button and pressing the *up*, *down*, and *across* arrows. If your administrator turns on AJAX and JavaScript, **Site Administration | Appearance | AJAX and Javascript**, you can move blocks around simply by dragging on the title bar with the mouse—that's **Participant Pix** in the following screenshot—and moving the block up, down, or across. This screenshot shows the **Particpant Pix** block being dragged upwards:

Core blocks

Block name	Description
Activities	Lists the activities that are available to students.
Admin bookmarks	Visible only to teachers and administrators. This allows them to create useful bookmarks of pages they visit frequently. For example, students' activity logs.
Administration	Displays a menu of key course settings, such as **Settings**, **Assign Roles**, **Groups**, **Backup**, and **Files**.
Blog Menu	A list of blog postings.
Blog Tags	This is a word cloud of tagged words from users' blogs. The more often a word is tagged, the bigger it gets in the cloud.

Block name	Description
Calendar	
	Allows entries at user, course, and site level. User-level entries can only be seen by the persons who entered them; course-level entries only by course users; site-level entries by all site users. There is a tool for downloading the calendar to your desktop calendar. Entries automatically appear when you set up time-bound activities. See the end of this chapter for a guide to using the calendar.
Course/Site Description	An HTML box which allows you to post text, images, video and audio. The label will be **Course/Site Description.**
Courses	List of courses available on the site.
Global Search	Will search all the site content, and can be useful if you have a very large site. You'll need to set it up first by logging as an administrator—**Site Administration	Miscellaneous	Experimental**. Then activate the global search engine by checking the **enableglobalsearch** box. You can access the **Global Search** settings via the link in **Administration	Modules	Blocks**. Note: this only works if you have at least PHP 5 installed on your server.
HTML	An HTML box which allows you to post text, images, video, and audio. You can also embed videos from other websites, like YouTube, if your school firewall permits this. See the end of this chapter for workarounds and for detailed guidance on embedding.
Latest News	Displays the headlines from the latest news forum items.
Login	Displays a login box.
Main Menu	Displays a menu of the activities available on the course.

Block name	Description
Messages	Messages No messages waiting Messages...
	Displays **Messages** information box and provides a link to the message centre.
Online Users	Displays a list of all users who have been actively online within the last 5 minutes.
Random Glossary Entry	Displays a random entry from a chosen glossary. Is useful for a "word of the day" feature, for example.
Remote RSS Feeds	Enables users to see feeds from other websites. For example, BBC news. Can provide automatic links to useful sources of reading material.
Search Forums	Will search all forum postings for a given word. Students must have access to the forum to be able to see the post.
Site Administration	Key site settings: this is covered in detail in this chapter.
Tags	**Tags - from Personal Profile interests and your BLOG tags** academic earth Activism Animal Rights architecture Art Athletics badminton bikes **books** bowling cinema cooking cooking and breathing. **dancing design** dog
	Same idea as blog tags, but the tagged words come from the **interests** entry in user profiles. Users can edit their profiles by clicking on their name in the top right-hand corner of the screen once they've enrolled and logged on.
Upcoming Events	Displays calendar events which are due soon on the course.

Moodle overview: Add-on blocks

There are two add-on blocks in this book. As with add-on modules, which we'll look at later, the installation instructions are available as `readme.txt` files on the download page: `http://moodle.org` | **Downloads** | **Modules and plugins**.

Personal glossary

This is a great way of encouraging autonomous learning. It allows students to create their own word lists in different languages. It also comes with a quiz which allows students to test themselves. Note that you'll have to turn the **My Moodle** feature on for this to work. (See below).

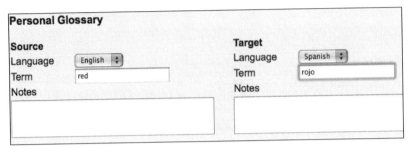

Exabis E-portfolio

This is an excellent means of showcasing documents on a course. Possible language uses are:

- Resumes
- Project presentations
- Discussion documents

Documents can be presented as a hyperlinked scheme, and can be viewed within Moodle or through an external link. See Chapter 10, *Extended Activities* for an example.

Moodle overview: Core modules

Here is a brief overview of the core modules, all of which appear in activities throughout the book. Modules are Moodle-speak for interactive activities. You add them by turning editing on once you're on a course page. Then you click on **Add a resource...** or **Add an activity....** Some of them are very easy to set up, such as Chat, Choice, Forum, and Journal. Others will take a bit more concentration and time to set up. I've indicated the ease of setup with a star system for each activity.

Ease of setup

*	Quite simple—quick and straightforward
**	Moderately difficult
***	Fairly complex

The activities in each chapter are generally organized so that the easier ones come first.

Core modules

Module name	Description
Assignment	Students can submit an assignment online or via an attachment. Instructions for the assignment are posted in the activity description.
Book	Provides a way of organizing web pages into three levels of importance. For example, Main topics and subtopics.
Chat	A simple Chat module like MSN without the bells and whistles. Allows you to save chat transcripts.
Choice	A simple polling activity to gather votes for and against something. It's a good way of catching learners' attention, and can be used for voting on whether something is grammatically correct or as a fun quiz where students have to vote on what they think someone is saying in a recording they hear.
Database	A highly customizable, searchable database. Good for setting up lists of websites and repositories of work, for example.
Forum	Please post comments, questions, suggestions, requests or anything else related to the site here. Thanks - Jeff (webmaster) **Add a new discussion topic** | Discussion	Started by	Replies	Last post
---	---	---	---
Missing messages	Kathryn HENDERSON	2	Jeff Stanford - Site Admin Tue, 23 Jun 2009, 02:05 PM
audio button	Jeff Stanford - Site Admin	0	Jeff Stanford - Site Admin Tue, 23 Jun 2009, 02:04 PM
Moodle in action	Mary Maddison	1	Jeff Stanford - Site Admin Tue, 23 Jun 2009, 02:02 PM
Asking for help	Shirley Liu	1	Jeff Stanford - Site Admin Tue, 23 Jun 2009, 01:51 PM	 Forum is an activity that allows a group of Moodle users to ask and answer questions. Users click on the **Discussion** topic and they can read and reply to messages written by other users. Students can be given more or fewer powers to run discussions.
Glossary	A database shell which makes it easy to set up lexical glossaries, searchable lists of grammar entries, FAQs, and encyclopedia entries.

Module name	Description
Hot Potatoes quiz	

> **Here are some words for 'hello' in other languages. Match the word to the language!**
>
> Match each pair, and then click the Check button.
>
> Check
>
> Hola — Spanish
> Bonjour — French
> Privet — Russian
> Sawat dii Khrap — Thai
> Ahoj —
>
> Check
>
> <= | Index | =>

	Allows you to import quizzes made in Hot Potatoes, a well-developed, free quiz program. See http://hotpot.uvic.ca/ for downloads and tutorials. If you have little time on your hands, this is a very easy way to start including quizzes in your Moodle. See the end of this chapter for more information.
Journal	Private pages. Good for keeping diaries and reflective comments. Only the student and teachers have access.
Label	Not really a module, but a useful device for setting out clear labels on your course page.
Lesson	A branched lesson. Users answer one question and are directed to subsequent questions depending on their answer. For example, if they get the first question wrong, they can redo it or go to an easier one. These are a bit tricky to set up, but are popular with students.
Quiz	Variety of task types which can be organized into a question bank.
Wiki	Web pages which can be edited by all users. Wikipedia is the best-known example. These are good for collaborative work, such as joint writing projects and task planning.
Workshop	Similar to Assignment, but submitted work can be peer reviewed before final submission. Teachers can present model assignments for students to assess before they write their own assignments.

Moodle overview: Add-on modules

This book uses twelve add-on modules and one add-on question type for Quiz. You don't need to add them to use the book, but I've chosen them because they help with language practice, and some of them, like NanoGong, make it much easier to record your voice and students' voices on Moodle web pages. The activities in the book always indicate whether an add-on module is used or not.

Here's a list and description of the add-on modules. The installation instructions are available as `readme.txt` files on the download page: `http://moodle.org` | **Downloads** | **Modules and plugins**. You'll need to get your administrator to download and install them. I've asterisked the ones I think are particularly useful for language teaching.

Add-on module	Description
FLV	This is a fairly sophisticated Flash player. While the Mediacenter (below) plays whatever you upload or point it to in a simple, attractive way, FLV has much greater choice of input type and allows you to edit the set-up page in ways which are useful for language learning. For example, you can turn sound off, remove the control panel, and change the screen size. You can link to YouTube videos and other video files on the Internet. You can also link to the user's web cam if it is turned on.
Lolipop ELP	 This allows students to use the Language On Line Portfolio Project, which is documented at `http://www.webcef.eu/?q=node/88`. The Moodle add-on allows students to self-assess themselves using Common European Framework "can-do" statements for different language skills. They can also set language learning goals and submit evidence of learning for teachers to check.
* Mediacenter (Inwicast)	 This allows teachers to create a very neat podcast center inside their Moodle. It does the same job as iTunes university does. More information at `http://www.inwicast.com/en/`.
Moodle Mindmap	This is a simple multi-layer mindmapping program. It doesn't allow you to embed images, audio or hyperlinks, but is useful for brainstorming writing projects and for developing vocabulary.
Mobile Quiz	This allows teachers to download quiz questions to students' mobile phones. This could be the way to motivate your students to do test questions!
* NanoGong	 If you select just one add-on, make it this one. NanoGong is very easy to set up and to use. It allows you to record directly into Moodle and playback on Moodle. It doesn't work in all modules, but it does work in useful ones like Book, Web page, and Database. Go to `http://gong.ust.hk/` for download for instructions and more information. Don't forget to agree to **trust this certificate** the first time you use it.

Add-on module	Description
OUblog	The key difference between the Moodle Blog and the OUblog is that you can embed video on the OUblog.
OUwiki	Like the OUblog, this add-on allows you to embed video.
* Questionnaire	This is a customizable survey which can be very useful for getting feedback or opinions on various aspects of the course, or for getting students to write their own surveys and practice asking questions. You could also change the permissions so that students can write their own questions. See the *Accounts* section (in a bit) on roles and permissions.
Reader	This allows you to set up an extended reading program and then test students on the books afterwards. You can select your own readers and make your own quizzes.
Stamp collection	Stamps are tokens which you can give to students as a reward for their performance in Moodle assignments. This may be particularly appealing to younger learners.
* WebQuest	This is a structured web investigation. It's excellent for guiding students to do knowledge quests or sharpen their critical evaluation skills.
* Ordering task type for quiz	This is very useful for language learners: it adds one question type to the core Quiz module. It allows students to order parts of a whole. For example, words within a sentence, sentences within a paragraph, or a chronological succession of events.

Part 2: Site administration how-tos

You'll need to work with your Moodle administrator or have administration access yourself to do the set-up work covered in this chapter. You'll also need administrative access to do things like override permissions on set-up pages when you're setting up activities. Override permissions means you can allow users to do additional things, like managing files. You can, of course, disallow them to do certain things.

If you're impatient to start trying out Moodle, the key how-to sections are the first six:

- How to create and manage users
- How to create and manage courses
- How to set up activities
- How to upload files to Moodle
- How to upload images to Moodle

Once you've opened a course, you can get going, and then come back to this section later. But it's worth reviewing all the sections at some point, as they will influence your Moodle site a lot.

To access the administration menu, go to your Moodle site home page, and find the **Site Administration** menu (screenshot below). If your administrator doesn't allow access to these pages, you need them to set up courses and users for you.

We won't cover every setting, just the ones that particularly relate to language teaching. You'll still need to check the other settings to make sure they're what you want.

How to create and manage users

Authentification

Site Administration | Users | Authentification | Manage Authentification

Here you can choose how new users get accepted—or authenticated—by the system.

Manage authentication			
Active authentication plugins			
Name	**Enable**	**Up/Down**	**Settings**
Manual accounts			Settings
No login			Settings
Email-based self-registration	👁		Settings
CAS server (SSO)	👁		Settings

Spammers!

The key thing to know is that if you enable email-based self-registration, you leave the site open to spammers. So it may be better to add and authenticate new users yourself (see the next section).

Accounts

Site Administration | Users | Accounts | Add a new user

Here you can create new users for your Moodle courses. This allows us to avoid the need for email-based self-registration, which can leave the system open to spam attacks.

Site Administration | Users | Accounts | Upload users

If you have a large number of new users, it'll save you time if you prepare a list in a text file and import it. The text file will look something like this:

username, password, firstname, lastname, email, course1

John1, password1, John, Odeh, John@yahoo.com, English1

Annamaria1, password2, Annamaria, Smith, annamaria@yahoo.com, English1

Elizabeth1, password3, Elizabeth, Abel, elizabethabel@yahoo.com, English2

Julia2, password4, Julia, Roberts, jroberts@gmail.com, English2

The first line contains the user profile field names. Each field should be separated by a comma or a semicolon, but only use one separator. When you import the file, you will need to select the separator you used in the **CSV (Comma Separated Values)** delimiter drop-down menu. If your names include diacritics or non-English characters, make sure you choose the appropriate **Encoding**. **UTF-8** is the standard for English.

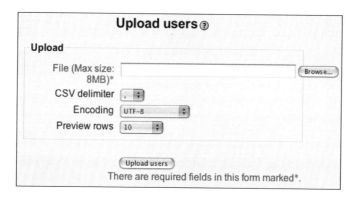

User profile fields

Users | Accounts | User profile fields

Here you can add fields to the user profile. This personalizes your Moodle site and can help students to get to know each other better. Examples:

- Text area for hobbies
- Text area for favorite films/books
- Menu of choices for school houses
- Menu of choices for your country's states (US), departments (France), counties (UK)
- Unique ID numbers
- Wishlists

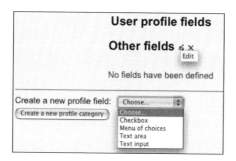

Defining roles

Site Administration | Users | Permissions | Define roles

A **role** is a set of permissions to do things on your Moodle site. The default **Roles** are as follows:

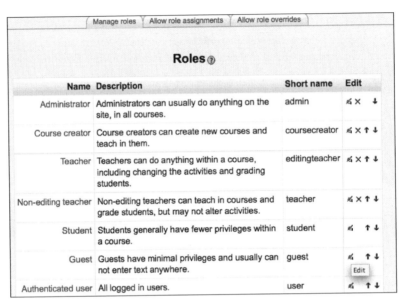

You can explore the permissions for each role by clicking on the role name. The default permissions may be fine, but you might well find there are other things you'd like teachers or students to be able to do. You can either edit the role or you can click on the **Add a new role** button and create a new role with its own set of permissions. For example, you could create a role called "superstudent", which allows students to edit certain pages. Once you've clicked on the name, you'll be presented with a long list of permissions.

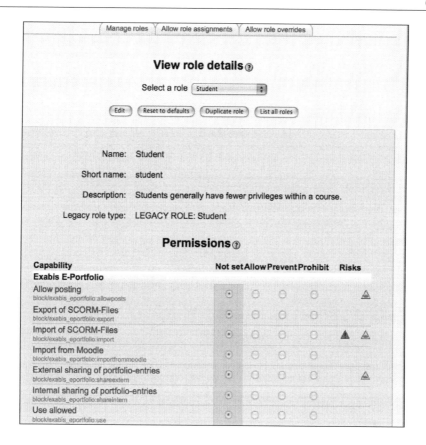

Click on **Edit** to amend the permissions. Here are just a few examples of changes you might want to make for language students:

- Allow **Book | Book editing** if you want students to create their own books.

- Allow **Forum | Add news** if you want students to be responsible for their own news forum.

- Disallow **Glossary | Rate entries** if the feature is abused.

- Disallow **Stamps | View others' stamps** if you don't want students to see how many reward stamps their peers have.

Don't forget to click on **Save changes** when you have finished.

It's worth noting that you can override permissions for a given role for individual modules. To do that, go to the set-up page for the course module, and choose **Locally assigned roles**.

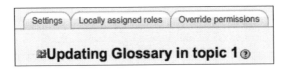

System roles

Site Administration | Users | Permissions | Assign system roles

Here you can give someone a role which is valid for the whole site. It's a good place to set up course creators and teachers. If you don't want a user to have this role on the whole of the site, you can allocate roles on the course page.

How to create and manage courses

Site Administration | Add/edit courses

This is where you can create new courses. In Moodle, **course** is a loose term for an area of the site that is partitioned off. It could be an actual language course, or it may be a collection of resources, or you might be using it as a blogging area or for various forums. You can create categories for your courses by clicking on **Add a new category**. For example, you might like to create categories for different languages and levels. You can choose to hide a course by clicking the eye icon opposite the course name. Only users with the capability to view hidden courses, such as teachers, will be able to access hidden courses. When you first add a course, you'll notice that the default category is "miscellaneous". To change this for new courses, edit the miscellaneous category, by clicking on the edit icon in the **Edit** column.

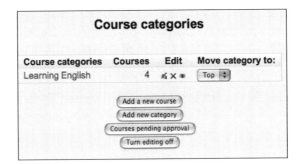

Once you have created a course, you need to edit the course settings.

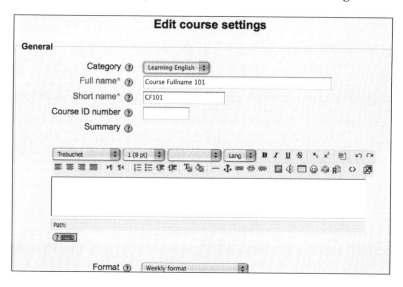

Settings	Details
Category	Make sure your course is in the category you want it to be in. You can always change this later by clicking on the settings button on your course. If you need a new category, you'll need to go back to **Site Administration | Add/edit courses**.
Full name	Choose the clearest name you can. So, for example, "French level 1" would be better than just "French", unless you only have one French course.
Short name	This is the name that will appear in the breadcrumb at the top of the page. So for "French level 1", the short name could be "Frlev1", for example.
Course ID number	If your school has a course code, you could put it here. You could also leave this blank. This field is not shown to students.
Summary	Write a brief description of the course. This can later be seen by users who click on the course block and want an overview of all courses available. It's an HTML box, so you can include images and even an audio introduction.
Format	There's a choice of six formats. Most teachers choose one of the following: <ul><li>**Social format**—which bases the course around a forum.</li><li>**Topics format**—which organizes the course into topic sections, as in the image above.</li><li>**Weekly format**—which organizes the course week by week with a clear start date and a finish date. Each week consists of activities.</li></ul>
Number of weeks/ topics	You can choose between **1** and **52** weeks or topics. If you choose as many as **52**, you will have a long scrolling page, but you do have the option to hide noncurrent weeks or topics.

Settings	Details
Course start date	If you set a start date, the course will not be visible to students until this date.
Hidden sections	You can opt to make hidden sections invisible or just collapsible. You will be able to hide sections by clicking on the right-hand corner of each section. N.B. Sometimes teachers think they have lost sections, when, in fact, they are just hidden.
News items to show	If you select weeks or topics format, a special forum called **News** will appear. It's a good place to post notices for all students to see. By default, all students are subscribed to this forum, and will receive your notices by email. You can choose to display between **0** and **10** items. If you choose **0**, the news box won't appear at all.
Show grades	Many of the activities allow you to give grades. By default, the grades are visible via the grades button on the course page. You can elect to hide the grades by selecting **No** here.
Show activity reports	An activity report shows students' access and contributions to the activities on a course. It's often useful for students to see this, so that they can monitor their own activity. The main reasons for turning it off are because of the extra load it has on the server, thereby slowing it down, or if there's no student interest in them, turning it off will declutter the course menu.
Maximum upload size	This is the maximum file size for files uploaded by students. If the biggest size is not big enough, you'll have to ask the administrator to change the PHP setting. Note that the maximum upload sizes can be varied for each activity on the activity set-up pages.
Is this a meta course?	Making the course a metacourse allows you to enroll students from one or more existing courses, which will save you time. If you select **yes**, you'll be taken to a screen that allows you select the other courses you wish to enroll students from.
Default role	You'll probably choose **student** as the default role. But imagine you have a teachers' course where you exchanged ideas. It would then be useful to make the default role **teacher**.
Course enrollable	Here you can decide whether the course is available now and, if not, what the start and end dates will be.
Enrolment duration	This stipulates the period from the start date in which students are still allowed to enroll.
Enrolment expiry notification	
Notify	This determines whether you, the teacher, will receive notice that a student's enrolment period is about to expire.
Notify students	This determines whether students concerned will receive notice that their enrolment period is about to expire.
Threshold	If you have specified an enrolment duration, this setting determines the number of days notice given before students are unenrolled from the course.

Settings	Details
Groups	This allows you to divide students into groups for some or all activities on a course. If you choose a setting here, it will be the default setting for the whole course. When you set up activities, you'll find a **Groups** option under **Common module settings** on the main set-up page for each activity. The groups setting gives you a choice between: • **No groups** • **Separate groups**—groups work separately and can't see each other's work • **Visible groups**—groups work separately but can see each other's work To populate the groups you'll need to go to the **course page | Administration | Groups**. Once there, you can name the groups and select students for them. There's also an auto-create button which selects students randomly. The groups that you create will be available on each module that allows grouping. Teachers viewing those activities can choose a group to watch. There are nine possible permutations for viewing and editing rights, as summarized in this table.

Wiki types

There are three wiki types: Teacher, Groups, Student. In addition, like any activity, the wiki has the Moodle group modes: "No Groups" "Separate Groups" and "Visible Groups". This leads to the following matrix of nine possibilities:

	No Groups	Separate Groups	Visible Groups
Teacher	There is only one wiki which only the teacher can edit. Students can view the contents.	There is one wiki for every group which just the teacher can edit. Students can view the wiki of their group only.	There is one wiki for every group which just the teacher can edit. Students can view the wikis for all groups.
Groups	There is only one wiki. The teacher and all students can view and edit this wiki.	There is one wiki per group. Students can view and edit the wiki of their own group only.	There is one wiki per group. Students can change the wiki of their own group only. They can view the wikis for all groups.
Student	Every student has their own wiki which only they and their teacher can view and edit.	Every student has their own wiki, which only they and their teacher can edit. Students can view the wikis of other students in their group.	Every student has their own wiki, which only they and their teacher can edit. Students can view the wikis of all other students in the course.

Unless the group mode has been forced by the course settings, it can be set with the groups icons on the course home page after the wiki has been created.

• A teacher can always edit every wiki in the course

Force	This ensures that the group mode you selected applies to all activities on a course. This is very handy if you have different cohorts using the same course and you want to keep them apart from each other.
Availability	Here you can decide whether the course is available or not. This will not override the course start date (above) if you have set it.

Settings	Details
Enrolment key	This is a password for the course. If you set a key, a key icon will appear by the name of the course on the front page, and students will not be able to enter the course without the key.
	You can also set a group enrolment key. Then anyone who enrolls on the course using that key will also automatically be made a member of the group. To do that, you should first set a course enrolment key and then, when you create a group, add a group enrolment key.
Guest access	A **guest** is someone who has not enrolled on Moodle. If they haven't enrolled, they won't be able to submit work in the activities.
Do not allow guests	This is a common setting if you want to keep your students' work private.
Allow guests without the key	This is sometimes useful if you want to allow temporary access to a course to guests.
Allow guests with the key	This allows temporary access, but is good for restricting the number of outsiders who can see the course.
Force language	Here you can choose the default language for your rubrics and menus. The choice in the drop-down window depends on which language packs you have installed.
Role renaming	The default names are: <ul><li>Administrator</li><li>Course creator</li><li>Teacher</li><li>Non-editing teacher</li><li>Student</li><li>Guest</li><li>Authenticated user</li></ul> You might want to change teacher to tutor, student to trainee, etc. Note that the underlying role stays the same. An authenticated user is someone who is enrolled on Moodle, but not necessarily on a course. The role enables them to post to blogs and discussion forums on the front page.

Enrolment key

If students forget the enrolment key, Moodle gives the first letter as a hint. Make sure that the first letter of the course enrolment key is the same as the first letter of each group enrolment key.

Course request

Site Administration | Course request

Do you want your Moodle site users to be able to request new courses? If it's appropriate in your teaching context, it might be a useful way of getting feedback and developing your site. Authenticated users—that is, all users with a logon—will see the **Course request** button at the bottom of the list of courses on their course page. You can set up email notification of any course requests teachers make. You can then approve or reject them by going to the list of courses block where you will see a **Courses pending approval** button.

Short name	Full name	Requested by	Summary	Reason for course request	
cfb	chinese for beginners	Jill Smith	basics of chinese language	I want to learn Chinese	Approve	Reject

Courses pending approval
You are logged in as Jeff Stan
mfl ▸ **Courses pending approval**

If you click on **Approve**, you will immediately be taken to the course settings editing page for the new course that you have approved. By default, the person who requests the course will become the teacher for the new course. If you don't want students to have the ability to become teachers in their own new courses, you can edit the student user permissions (see the section on this earlier).

Backups

This is not a specifically language-teaching point, but do remember to set up automatic backups for your site. Think of all that hard work you're putting into your site! There is a wide range of options of what you can back up and when. Don't be put off if you get an "error message" like this:

```
Summary
========================================================
 Courses: 10
 OK: 0
 Skipped: 0
 Error: 0
 Unfinished: 10

 Some of your courses weren't saved!!

 Please take a look at your backup logs in:
 http://moodleflair.com/moodle/admin/report/backups/index.php
```

It's often not an error and just means that there were no changes to your course contents within the last month. See `http://docs.moodle.org/en/Backup_FAQ` for more information on this.

You can also do a manual backup at any time by going to the course home page: **Administration | Backup**.

 A good way of cloning a course is to do a course backup, then to click on **Restore**. During the restore process, you can opt to restore to a new course, which will be your new, duplicate course.

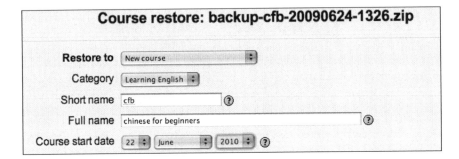

How to set up activities

Each activity starts with a set-up page with an impressive set of variables which help you control the way the activity is used. They are fairly generic, but let's take Quiz as an example and look at some of the variables in detail. To get to the set-up page for any activity, click on **Turn editing on**. Then select **Add an activity...** from the drop-down menu.

Quiz settings

The important thing to remember with the set-up page is that you are setting variables that relate to the whole activity. There are often more adjustments for different parts of the activity that you'll come to once you've completed the set-up page. The Quiz module is a good example of this. Think of the quiz as a shell or framework for the quiz questions that you'll add later:

Settings	Details
Name	This is not the name of the question but of the collection of questions which might be new or existing ones. Good names might be **week 1 test** or **verb revision test 3**.
Introduction	Here we can put some useful information for students, like **This test will practice language we covered in week one of your course**.
Timing	This is where we can decide when the test is available to students. We can also set how long students have to do the test and what the lapse between first and second attempts and between later attempts will be. This is good if you want students to revise a bit more before they retake the test. If you set a time limit, then a "time remaining clock" will appear on the student's test page.

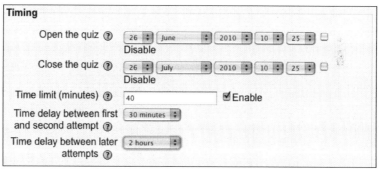

Display	There are useful variables here for deciding whether to shuffle the questions in our quiz and to shuffle options within a question. We can also set the number of questions appearing on each page.

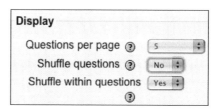

In the above example, only five questions per page will be shown to students. The questions will always come in the same order, because **Shuffle questions** is set to **No**. Distracters within questions will be shuffled because **Shuffle within questions** is set to **Yes**.

Settings	Details
Attempts	Here we can decide how many attempts we want students to be able to make. If you limit the number of attempts, students will see an information box that tells them how many attempts they will have. If we select **Yes** for **Each attempt builds on the last**, students will see the results of their previous attempt. That can be a good way to help them learn. The **Adaptive mode** is also useful in that it allows students to reattempt a question immediately. A penalty is usually subtracted from their score for doing this though. The penalty is set in the next option. 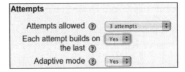
Grades	If we allow multiple attempts in the previous option, then we have a choice of which score to accept. It's important to make your scoring policy transparent to students. <ul><li>**Highest grade** is the best score for any attempt</li><li>The **Average grade** is the average of all attempts</li><li>**First attempt** is the grade for the first attempt</li><li>**Last attempt** is the grade for the last attempt</li></ul>  You can also decide whether or not to apply penalties. If this is not a formal test, you may want to remove penalties to increase student feel-good factor. You can also decide how many decimal digits appear in the grades. Some learners find it easier to understand their score if there are no decimal digits.
Review options	The default is for students to be able to review all types of feedback available after the attempt, while the quiz is still open and after it closes. The feedback is generally very useful for students to see, but there are circumstances where you might remove this access, for example, if you have students taking a more formal test and you don't want them to share answers until the test is over. In that case, you would just check the **Review options** in the third column. 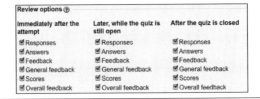

Settings	Details
Quiz security	The following options are not foolproof, but they help create a more secure environment. If you select **Show quiz in a "secure" window**, a new window opens, some mouse actions are prevented and some keyboard commands are prevented. Students can no longer copy and paste, for example.

This is what students will see in their "secure" window if they try to copy.

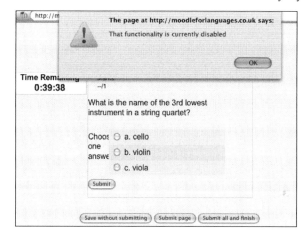

"Require password" means that students can't enter the quiz without this password. You can also restrict access to the quiz by stating which network addresses can have access. If you want to know a computer's network address, go to http://find-my-ip-address.net/. Students who try to access the quiz from unauthorized computers will get the following error message:

Settings	Details
Common Module Settings	This relates to groups settings. There's information about groups earlier in this chapter.
Overall feedback	Here we can provide the general feedback that students will get for their overall scores on the quiz. N.B. This is not feedback on individual quiz questions, which you set when creating the question.

Overall feedback ⑦

Grade boundary	100%
Feedback	Excellent
Grade boundary	90%
Feedback	Very good
Grade boundary	80%
Feedback	Good start!
Grade boundary	70%
Feedback	Not bad!
Grade boundary	60%
Feedback	You're on the right track, but it's worth revising and redoing this.
Grade boundary	0%

Add 3 more feedback fields

How to upload files to Moodle

There are several reasons for uploading files to Moodle. Maybe you want to make them available as a download for students via a course page resource. Maybe you created a Hot Potatoes quiz and need to upload it. Maybe you want students to create and upload web pages they have made, so that you can create a class book (see Chapter 7, *Writing Activities* for an example of this). Sometimes teachers get a bit confused by the process, so here's a run through:

1. Go to **Administration | Files** on your course page or, if you are on an activity set-up page, click on **upload file** in your course activity (for example, Hot Potatoes) if required. This will open a new window.

Maximizing the new window

Sometimes the new window is quite small and you can't see all the options. Don't forget you can click on the green button at the top-left (Mac) or top-right (Windows) of your machine to maximize the size of the window.

2. Click on **Upload a file**.

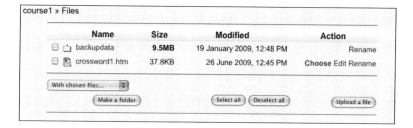

3. Now click on **Browse....**

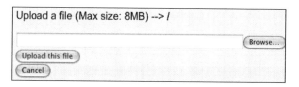

Select the file you want from your computer. Then click on **Upload this file**. If you want to use the file in an activity you're creating, click on **Choose** in the **Action** column. It will then appear in your activity set-up page. Here's an example of a Hot Potatoes crossword which has been uploaded to the Moodle Hot Potatoes set-up page:

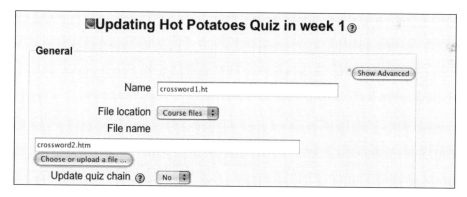

4. If you need to create a new folder in the course files, click on **Make a folder**.

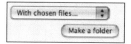

Then complete the details. For example, to create a folder called **recordings**, write:

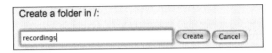

Afterwards, click on the folder in the files list to choose files or add files.

How to upload images to Moodle

When editing text in a web page, forum posting, glossary entry, or database entry, we often want to add images. The page we're editing usually looks like this:

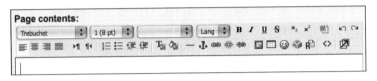

Let's imagine we want to insert a picture of a dog. This is what happens when we click on the **Insert Image** icon in the editing menu. We'll need to import the picture from our computer. Of course, as we're well organized, we'll make sure it goes into an appropriately named folder.

This is the **Insert Image** dialog box. Write the folder name **animals**, and click on **Create folder**.

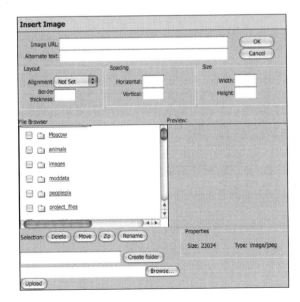

Now click on our newly created folder, **animals**. Click on **Browse...** to select the image file on our computer. Let's upload a picture of a dog. Click on **Upload** in the dialog box. The file will now appear in the Moodle directory. Now click on the dog picture file in the Moodle directory and fill in the details for the image.

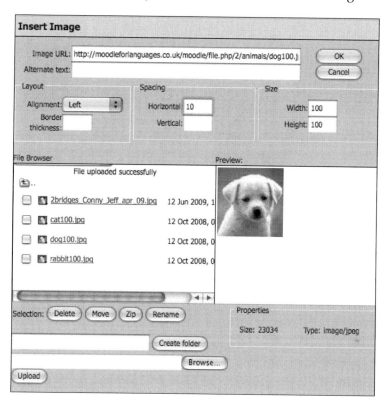

We need to include the following details to improve the picture layout:

Alternate text	These are the words users will see when they hover their mouse cursors over the image.
Layout	Choose **Left** if we want the image to the left of the text, **Right** if we want it to the right, etc. If we choose nothing, the image will appear on a separate line to the text.
Spacing	The number refers to the number of pixels between the image and the text. I've chosen **10** to have a small space and improve layout. A pixel is just one of the smallest dots that we can see on our computer screen.

Click on **OK,** and the image now appears in the definition box.

  Files section

All images are stored and also accessible via the **Files** section on the course page.

How to set up a grading system

General settings

Site Administration | Grades | General settings

The grade book is often a key part of language courses, since the results of students' work in the Quiz, Assignment, and Lesson modules are recorded here. Make a point of going through the following areas to ensure you have the right settings.

Grade category settings

Site administration | Grades | General settings

Graded roles	This controls who appears in the gradebook, which is a list of all scores for quizzes and assignments. If you have created extra roles (see roles, earlier in this part) and want those roles to appear in the gradebook, make sure you check the roles here.
Enable outcomes	Outcomes are ways of providing more feedback on specific areas of competence. In a language context, they could be things like grammar, fluency, or organization. Outcomes are linked to one of the scales that you generate on the site (see below for information on scales). Make sure this setting is on if you want to use outcomes. They will then be available in many of the modules.

Grade display type

Site Administration | Grades | Grade item settings

You have a choice of **Real**, **Percentage** or **Letter**. **Real** is the actual grade out of whatever total you set. **Percentage** is that score converted into a percentage. **Letter** is that score represented as a letter. (see *Letters* in a bit).

Scales

Site Administration | Grades | Scales

Scales are a way of evaluating students' performance. You can use the numerical scale that comes with Moodle, or you can create your own to fit in more closely to your particular teaching context. Here are some examples:

Name of scale	Scale ratings
Award 1	Refer, Pass, Merit, Distinction
Award 2	Fail, Pass after resubmission, Pass
Clarity	Not clear, OK, Quite clear, Very clear
Numerical grade	1, 2, 3, 4, 5, 6
Mistakes	Too many mistakes for this to be easy to read, Quite difficult to read because of the mistakes, Some careless mistakes, Just a few mistakes, No mistakes

These can be applied to written or spoken work. They can also be applied to contributions to forums where you might want to comment on quality.

Forum	Not sure what you're getting at, thanks for your contribution, great post

For consistency's sake, make sure each rating starts with a capital letter and that the punctuation is exactly as it appears in the above table.

To create your own scale, click on **Add a new scale**.

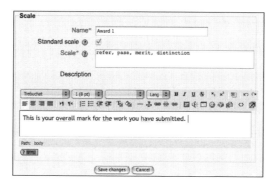

Give the scale a suitable name. Enter the scale you want.

Entering scales
Make sure the steps are in increasing order and are separated by commas.

Give the scale a description so that students (and other teachers) know what you're referring to. Don't forget to click on **Save changes**. Your scale will now be available throughout the site. N.B. Once it has been used, you can no longer delete it.

Outcomes

Site Administration | Grades | Outcomes

This is where you can create outcomes as mentioned earlier. Click on **Add a new outcome**.

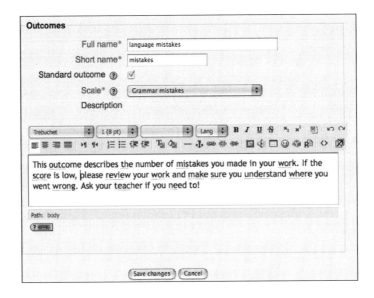

Give the outcome a full name and a short name. Check **standard outcome** if you want the outcome to be available site-wide. Next, select the scale you want to use. In the earlier example I've selected a newly-made mistakes scale for my mistakes outcome. Finally, write a description which will help students understand the outcome and take action if necessary.

Letters (grade letters)

In **Grade display type**, mentioned earlier, you had the option of displaying letters instead of percentages. This is the page where you can set letter equivalents for grades. For example:

A = 90% to 100%

B = 80% to 89%

etc.

You might find a letter system works better for subjectively-marked assignments, such as essays, where it's difficult to give an exact percentage.

How to edit labels and instructions

Language settings

Site Administration | Language | Language settings

Default language: This is the language of the instructions and menus that students will automatically see. You might want to change it to one that students more readily understand.

Language editing

Site Administration | Language | Language editing

This setting allows you to edit labels and instructions for different modules and blocks. Click on **Edit words or phrases**. Choose the block or module file you want to edit. Change the text in the appropriate box. Then click on **Save changes**. It is unlikely you'll want to change anything, but occasionally there are spelling errors or instructions you'd like to make clearer. Also, you could provide bilingual instructions for key areas.

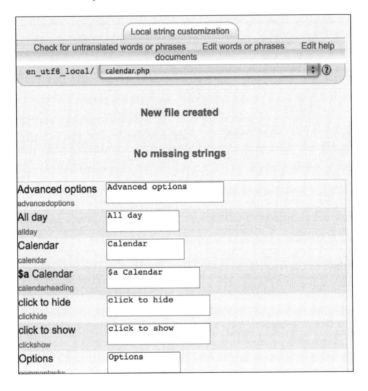

Language packs

Site Administration | Language | Language packs

Make sure you have the language pack you need for the language you are teaching from or to. To add a new language pack, click on the language in the right-hand column, and then click on **Install selected language pack**.

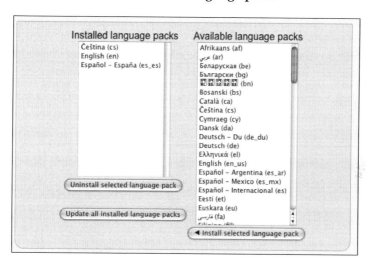

How to manage modules

Site Administration | Modules | Activities | Manage activities

Here you can see the list of modules currently available. I suggest that you go through the list and hide the ones you're unlikely to use by clicking on the eye icon. You can always show them again letter. The Database module is hidden in the following screenshot:

Activity module	Activities	Version	Hide/Show	Delete	Settings
Assignment	8	2007101511	👁	Delete	Settings
Book	6	2008081402	👁	Delete	Settings
Chat	4	2007101509	👁	Delete	Settings
Choice	4	2007101509	👁	Delete	
Database	4	2007101513	⌣	Delete	Settings

The less clutter you have on your site, the easier your users (both teachers and students) will find it to use. It's also a good idea to check that the settings are appropriate. For example, the default for the Forum module is to include the writer's email address, but you might want to override that to preserve the users' privacy. The glossary settings may also need tweaking. Perhaps you'd like to be able to create an RSS feed from them, for example. You can also create automatic hyperlinks to the glossary from elsewhere on the site. So, for example, if a student is reading a story on a Moodle web page and comes across an unknown word which is hyperlinked, they can click on the word and go directly to the glossary entry for that word. This is an excellent tool for language learners.

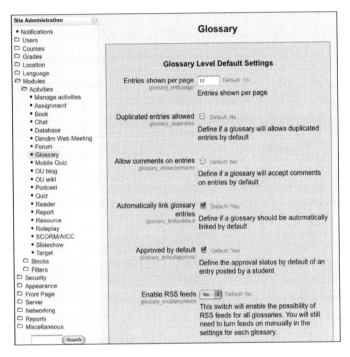

How to manage blocks

Site Administration | Modules | Blocks | Manage blocks

As with modules, it's worth checking the settings for the core blocks to make sure they're appropriate for your course.

One block that may need your attention is the **RSS feeds** block; by default, only administrators can add feeds. Maybe you'd like teachers to be able to. Maybe students, too! This is another example of how versatile Moodle can be. See the next section for help with enabling RSS feeds.

How to manage sticky blocks

Site Administration | Modules | Blocks | Sticky blocks

You can configure certain blocks to appear on all instances of courses and/or all instances of My Moodle—these are called **sticky blocks**. **My Moodle** is a personalized home page which students can customize themselves. Having this freedom to edit blocks often increases student motivation, which is just what we want. Here are some examples of blocks that you might want to convert to sticky blocks:

- **Online users**: Allowing users to see who else is online and get in touch via the message facility.

- **RSS feeds**: Moodle has its own aggregator which allows students to follow RSS feeds: these could be announcements from you via Twitter, or stories from foreign language websites, for example. This setting allows feeds to be shown on Moodle pages. You need to add site-wide RSS feeds to make RSS feeds available to students on their My Moodle pages.

- **My Moodle preview/Twitter**: The My Moodle section, coming in a bit, gives you a preview of a My Moodle page. Using Twitter with Moodle is covered at the end of this chapter.

How to set up remote RSS feeds

Site Administration | Modules | Blocks | Remote RSS Feeds

To add a feed, click on **Add/Edit Feeds**.

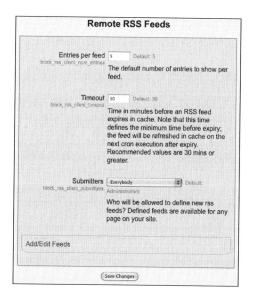

Now copy the RSS feed link from the site you want to track into the box **Add a news feed URL**. If you want other teachers and students to be able to access your feeds, you also need to click on shared feed when you add the feed.

There are lots of ideas for sources of RSS feeds in the RSS feed activity in Chapter 7, *Writing Activities.*

Click on **Validate feed** to make sure the feed is working. If you get a **Congratulations!** message, click on the **Add** button. See Chapter 7, *Writing Activities* for help with adding an RSS feed block to your course.

How to manage filters

Site Administration | Modules | Filters | Manage filters

Several of the activities in this book make use of multimedia plugins, such as Flash and NanoGong. You'll need to make sure that the filters are enabled here. If you don't enable filters for mp3 files, MOV files, etc., students won't be able to watch these media on the Moodle site. Note that there is no filter for WAV audio files, so you'll need to convert them to MP3 files before you try to upload them onto your Moodle site. The recording program, Audacity, allows you to convert easily via its **Export** command in the **File** menu. There's a longer section on Audacity later in this chapter if you need it.

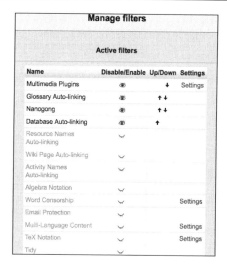

How to control the HTML editor

Site Administration | Appearance

There are many ways you can change the appearance of your Moodle site. The best thing to do is work through the list and experiment. It's worth paying particular attention to the language-learning needs of your students with the following:

HTML editor | Hide buttons

Site Administration | Appearance | HTML editor

If you have learners who don't want such a broad range of editing tools, you can hide some of the editing buttons here. This is particularly useful for first-time users who may prefer simpler interfaces at first.

There may be buttons you don't need on the menu, such as the **x2** buttons (for super- and sub-script). Simply check them and then save the changes. Then the editing menu on your activity set-up pages will look a bit less cluttered.

On the same page, you can change the font faces available, or change the default size—maybe you'd like something bigger for your students. You can even change the background color of the HTML windows from white if you want to spice up your pages.

How to manage tags

Site Administration | Appearance | Manage tags

Tags can be a great way of highlighting vocabulary. As teacher/administrator you can set up official tags on this page. When you or your students write a blog, they can select one of your tags. From this page you can see all the tags that have been created on your Moodle site. If any of them are misspelled, you can correct them. You can also see how many times each tag has been used.

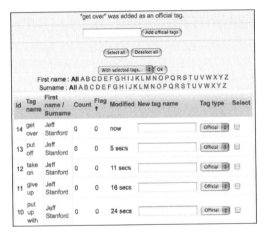

How to control My Moodle

Site Administration | Appearance | My Moodle

If you check this, non-administrative users will be forced to go to their own homepage when they log on. They'll get a reminder of tasks they still have to do, and they can choose which blocks appear. The **Hello everybody!!** message in the next screenshot is an HTML block where the students can write anything they want, put up links, images, embed videos, or add audio. They can also add their own avatar. If you make RSS feeds available for the whole site, they can also be added here. All the above are covered in later sections of this chapter.

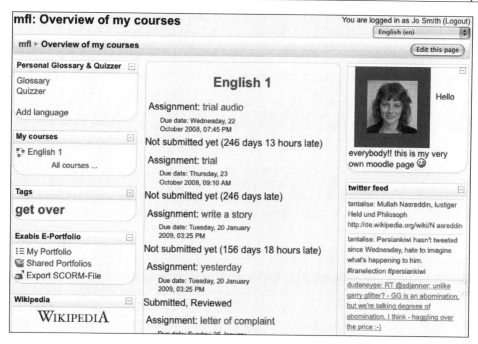

One small point about adding images, though: student users cannot upload images directly from their computers via their **Insert Image** box. But a simple workaround is to click on the **Insert Image** icon and then copy the URL from a social networking site, or a photo site like Flickr (`http://www.flickr.com/`) or Picasa (`http://picasa.google.com/`), and paste that into the **Image URL** box.

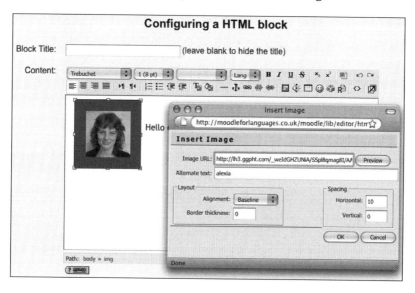

How to enable users to add RSS feeds

Site Administration | Server | RSS

If you want teachers to be able to add RSS feeds to courses and students to be able to add RSS feeds to their My Moodle pages, you need to make sure this is enabled.

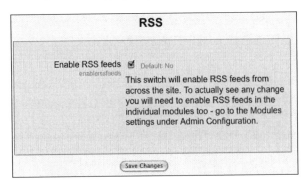

How to set up a course calendar

As the overview earlier shows, calendars can provide a useful function in course management. Here's how to add one to your course.

1. Turn editing on.
2. Go to the **Blocks** menu.
3. Select **Add Calendar**.

4. Click on the month—**September 2009** in this case. That will take you to the calendar entry page.

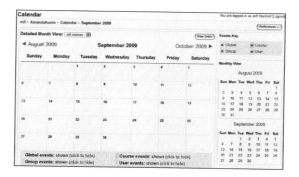

5. First, click on **Preferences...** to set things like the first day of your week.
6. Click on **New Event** to create a new entry.

   ○ **User events** can only be seen by individual users
   ○ **Course events** can be seen by every user in all groups on a course
   ○ **Site events** can be seen by all users on the site

   Choose carefully!

7. Fill in the details on the following screen.

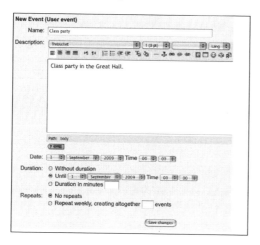

Make sure you fill in the **Until** section. After you've saved your changes, you'll notice that you have the option of exporting your calendar to your desktop calendar.

8. Back on the course page, the calendar entry will be highlighted on the calendar on the course page.

How to create a Flash audio player

We can include MP3 recordings on Moodle web pages. These will appear as simple players. It's well worth learning how to this, so that we can provide listening material for our students.

To create your player:

1. Make the recording. Audacity is a good, free program for doing this. Save the file as an MP3. There's a section on Audacity later in this chapter.

2. Open up a Moodle web page on your course. The easiest way to do this is to go to a course page, then turn editing mode on.

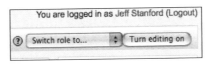

Editing button

You'll find the editing button in the top right-hand corner of your screen.

3. Next, click on **Add a resource...**, and choose **Compose a webpage**.

4. Write a link word; for example, **recording**. Highlight that word by dragging the cursor across it.

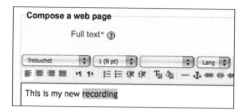

5. Now insert a link to the audio file by clicking on the chain icon in the menu 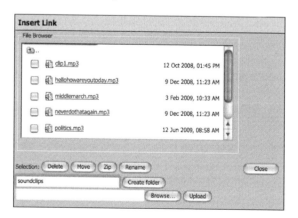.

6. In the **URL** box, write down the link to your audio file. Give the link a title.

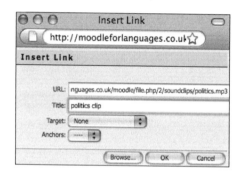

If we don't know the file location, we can either browse to a file on our computer, or link to a Moodle file which we have already uploaded.

It's good practice to make a separate folder for different categories of files. After you click on **Browse...**, you'll see this:

7. Choose a suitable name for your new folder, and then click on **Create folder**.

8. Now click on your newly-created folder.

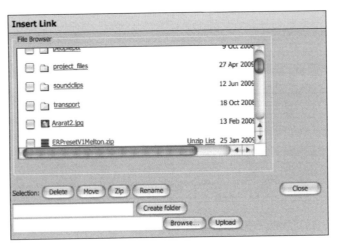

9. Click on **Browse...** to select the audio file on your computer.

10. Click on **Upload this file**. If the maximum file size is too low for your audio file, ask your administrator to increase it by adjusting the php.ini file.

11. Click on the file you've uploaded and we'll be taken back to the web page **Insert Link** dialog box.

12. Click on **OK**.

13. Toggle to the HTML view of your page (<> in the menu), and remove the word **recording** from between the <a>....</a> tags in the HTML.

   This is what it looks like before:

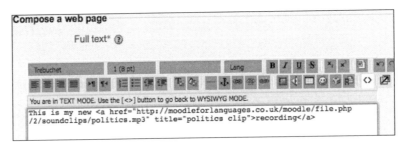

And this is what it looks like after:

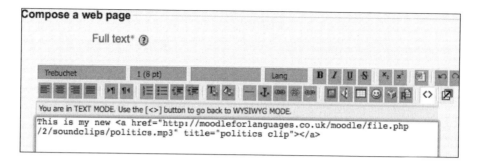

14. Now click on **Save and display** at the bottom of the page. Our recording is now available via the Moodle player.

How to import glossary entries

To save inputting time, you could also think about importing wordlists from other sources into your Moodle glossaries. They will need to be in XML format. So see the *XML file creator* section in this chapter or ask your Moodle administrator if you need help.

There's also a glossary exchange on the official Moodle site: `http://moodle.org/mod/glossary/view.php?id=2739`. Here you can benefit from other people's hard work, by downloading their glossaries. This could also be a useful adjunct to your vocabulary work in Chapter 3, *Vocabulary Activities*. If you produce a glossary that you would like to share with others, you can upload it here, too. Note that if you follow the glossary exchange link, you'll have to click on **Create new account** link on the `moodle.org` site and then enroll on the `moodle.org` **Glossary Exchange** course to access the glossaries.

Once your new account is confirmed, go to `http://moodle.org/course/`, and choose **Moodle Exchange** and then **Glossary Exchange**. In the Moodle **Glossary Exchange**, click on the XML files next to the entries to download the glossary you want.

That will download the glossary to your computer. Then go to a glossary you have set up in Moodle, and click on **Import entries** in the top right hand corner:

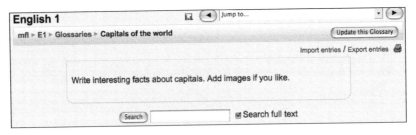

Then browse to the saved XML file to import it.

Click on **Open** or **Save**, depending on your operating system. You'll then get a confirmation that looks something like this:

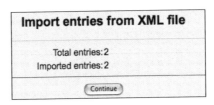

How to download videos from YouTube

It's sometimes useful to download videos from YouTube so that you can edit them for teaching purposes. You can do this in several ways:

- Copy the video URL, and paste it on KEEPVID at `http://keepvid.com/`. When you click **Download**, you will be provided with a link to save the video as an FLV file.
- Firefox users can install a YouTube video converter. Open Firefox, and go to **Tools | Add-ons** to search for the extension. It downloads all embedded objects on a web page, including the video clips. Once you've installed the add-on, the YouTube page will include this **Download Video As** button.

Once you have downloaded your video, you can edit it in Movie Maker (Windows) or iMovie (Mac). This is useful if you want to chunk a longish video in preparation for teaching. Afterwards, you will have to upload the chunked versions to YouTube and embed each chunk separately in your Moodle page.

How to display other websites within your Moodle site

It might be useful to show another website within your Moodle. For example, you might want to use the BBC's **Day in pictures** as a basis for a forum discussion. To do that, click on **Add a resource...**, and select **Compose a web page**. Then click on the toggle HTML icon <> in your HTML editing panel and insert the following code. Swap the URL between the inverted commas in the first line with the URL you want to show.

```
<iframe src =" http://news.bbc.co.uk/2/hi/in_pictures/8130538.stm"
                                  width="100%" height="1000">
  <p>Your browser does not support iframes.</p>
</iframe>
```

That would display the following:

Don't forget that a lot of schools censor websites, so make sure the URL is an allowed site. It is also good practice to acknowledge the source of the website, if it is not clear what it is.

How to avoid spam

A word of warning from Martin Dougiamas, the founder of Moodle:

One of the most common security issues on Moodle sites is profile spam. This is a problem on sites with the combination of these two settings:

- **Email authentication** is enabled, allowing people to self-create an account on the site
- The admin setting **forceloginforprofiles** is disabled, allowing anyone to see and link to user profiles

The problem with these settings is that spammers can create a page on the Moodle site, which they can fill with links and pictures of porn and other nasty stuff. This in turn comes up in Google searches for those things, and is used to boost ratings to porn sites or hacking sites designed to take over your personal computer. Note that this content is designed for people using search engines, and is usually not available from within the Moodle site itself (since spammers don't join any courses), so users and administrators are usually not even aware that their site is having this problem.

To help stop this, go to **Site Administration | Users | Authentification | Manage Authentificaton**, and disable **Email authentication** if is not needed, and if it can't be disabled, then **forceloginforprofiles** should definitely be enabled. You can alter settings at **Site Administration | Security | Site Policies**.

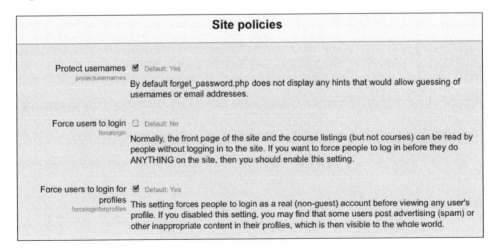

There is also a Captcha feature available, which also helps reduce spamming. You can enable that at **Site Administration | Users | Authentificaton | Email-based Authentification**. The Captcha feature forces users to enter the words they see to complete the authentification process. You'll need to get your Moodle administrator to make sure you have a PHP cURL extension for this to work.

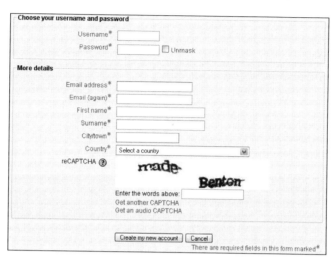

Part 3: Some useful external programs and resources

You can do many of the activities in this book without additional programs. However, the following programs and resources, arranged in alphabetical order, can help enrich your Moodle service:

Assessment	Reminder service
Audio	Scheduling service
Avatars	Screencasts
Directories of websites	Twitter
Firewalls	Video
Hot Potatoes	Widgets
HTML	Word processors
International accent marks and diacritics	XML file creator

Assessment

If you'd like to find out more about assessment, there are several books for beginners that could be helpful:

- *"Language Testing" (Oxford Introduction to Language Study ELT), Brian Heaton, Oxford University Press*
- *"Writing English Language Tests" (Longman Handbooks for Language Teachers), J. B. Heaton, Longman Pub Group*
- *"Language Test Construction and Evaluation" (Cambridge Language Teaching Library), J. Charles Alderson, Caroline Clapham, Dianne Wall, Cambridge University Press*
- *Cambridge Language Assessment series (Cambridge University Press)*
  - *"Assessing Reading", J. Charles Alderson*
  - *"Assessing Writing", Sara Cushing Weigle*
  - *"Assessing Listening", Gary Buck*
  - *"Assessing Speaking", Sari Luoma*
  - *"Assessing Grammar", James E. Purpura*

Websites relating to assessment

Dr Glen Fulcher's site provides a wide range of videos, articles, and links on language testing: `http://languagetesting.info`.

If you'd like to review how to write multiple choice items, try out `http://pareonline.net/getvn.asp?v=4&n=9`.

Audio

Audacity is a free program, available for download from `http://audacity.sourceforge.net/`. The site has extensive support pages that will help you install and use the program. The help pages also offer some foreign language tutorials on installation and use. To save audio files as MP3 files, you'll need to make sure you also download a lame driver. The file you need—`lame_enc.dll`—is available from `http://lame.buanzo.com.ar/`.

Here are some of the attractive features of Audacity:

- Easy to use—click on red to record, brown to stop, green to play. Then navigate to **File | Save** to save your file.

- Allows you to record from the Internet.

- Control recording quality by changing the sample rate and bit rate. See Chapter 11, *Formatting and Enhancing Your Moodle Materials* for more information on this.

- Multiple tracks allowing you to record voice plus music plus other background sounds, for example. In the following screenshot, there is a track for Jeff's voice, background music and bird sounds. To create a new track, you can click on the red record button, import a file (**File | Import)**, or you can copy and paste a track from another project.

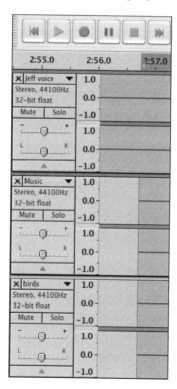

- Ability to change pitch without changing the tempo. This is useful if you have no one to record a dialog with and want to simulate two people, one with a higher voice and one with a lower voice. (See Chapter 4, *Speaking Activities*, *Activity 5* for an example of this). In this screenshot, the pitch has been lowered by 9 semitones from an **F#** note to an **A**.

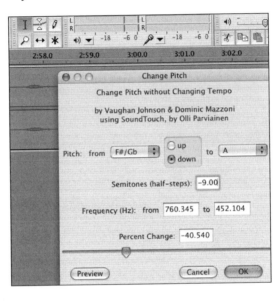

- Ability to slow the tempo without changing the pitch. To do that, select the track you want to change by highlighting it with a mouse. Then choose **Effect | Change tempo**. Drag the **Percent Change** pointer down to make it slower and up to make it faster.

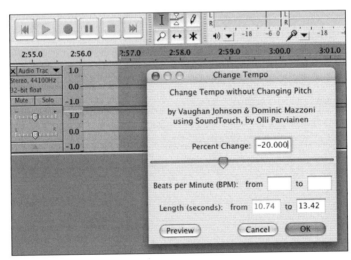

- Ability to add more than one track. For example, the Podcast in Chapter 5, *Grammar Activities*, *Activity 1* could start with clips of music. You could record voice on track one and music on track two.

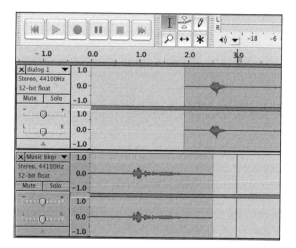

You could also use the fade out feature to make the sound peter out just before the voice comes in. To do that, use your mouse to select the part of the recording where you want the fade out. Then select **Effect | Fade** from the menu.

Some free and handy sound clips can be found at the following sites:

- `http://www.findsounds.com` (sound clips, sound effects)
- `http://www.freeaudioclips.com`
- `http://www.archive.org/audio/etree.php`
- `http://en.wikipedia.org/wiki/Wikipedia:Free_sound_resources`
- `http://www.freesound.org/whatIsFreesound.php`
- `http://www.magnatune.com` (independent music to download)
- `http://odeo.com` (audio and video files)
- `http://soundsnap.com` (sound library—sound effects and loops)
- `http://musopen.com` (classical music)

You and your students can use these to add spice and interest to your Moodle productions!

Avatars

If you have younger children using your Moodle site, they might enjoy using speaking avatars which are available from various sites. For example, http://www.voki.com/create.php. Many adults enjoy these, too, as they help personalize presentations.

You could either create an avatar of yourself so that children hear and see your avatar instead of you, or you can help students make their own avatars.

Once you've created your avatar, simply embed the code Voki gives you into an HTML page on the Moodle site. It works on the following HTML pages: HTML blocks, labels on course home pages, web pages, and books. Here's how you'd add an avatar for a block.

1. On your course home page, click on **Turn editing on**.

2. In the drop-down blocks menu, add an **HTML block**.

3. In the new HTML block, click on the hand edit button ✎ to configure your HTML block. Click on the HTML toggle icon ◇.

4. Copy and paste the code from the Voki site: it will look something like this:

   ```
   <script language="JavaScript" type="text/javascript"
   src="http://vhss-d.oddcast.com/voki_embed_functions.php"></
   script><script language="JavaScript" type="text/javascript">AC_
   Voki_Embed(200,267,"1c368800a939f9214fcce867fd8d07dd",1421611,
   1, "", 0);</script><BR><a href="http://www.voki.com/"><b>Get a
   Voki now!</b></a><BR><BR>
   ```

5. Click on **Save**.

Directories of websites

RSS feeds

Here are a few podcast directories:

- `http://www.podcast411.com/page2.html`
- `http://www.rssmountain.com/directory_category.php`

Once you're confident in this area, you could consider projects that result in your or your students own weekly podcasts. For example, school news, or a weekly drama serial. See Chapter 4, *Speaking Activities*, *Activity 5* for an example of this.

Websites

This URL contains Time Magazine's 50 best websites. It could be a useful source of materials on your course.

`http://www.time.com/time/specials/2007/completelist/0,29569,1809858,00.html`

There is a glossary of useful EFL websites on `http://teachereducation.org.uk`, which may also be useful. As with so many directories, it will take you to yet more directories.

Firewalls

Many schools set up firewalls which stop teachers and students from using popular sites like YouTube. One way round this is to download the video from the video site and then upload it to your Moodle.

Several sites offer a video download service. Here are some I've used:

- `http://www.teflclips.com/?page_id=10`
- `http://kissyoutube.com`
- `http://javimoya.com/blog/youtube_en.php`
- `Edublogs.tv`

They allow you to download YouTube videos as Flash videos, which you can then embed in your Moodle page. Make sure that **Site Administration | Modules | Filters** is set to allow Flash videos.

If you need to convert your file from an FLV file to a SWF Flash file, you can do that online at `http://media-convert.com/convert/`.

The easiest way to show your video on Moodle is to use the SWF activity module, available for download at `http://code.google.com/p/moodle-swf/`.

Hot Potatoes

Hot Potatoes is a free quiz program, which you can download from `http://hotpot.uvic.ca/`. You can make attractive tests such as cloze tests, crosswords, matching exercises, and multiple-choice. It's easy to include images, video, and audio in your questions, too. There are versions for Windows and Mac computers, and you'll find lots of examples and support on the website. The big advantage of using Hot Potatoes, rather than the native Moodle Quiz module, is that it's much easier to use. The main advantage of using the Moodle Quiz module is that you get better statistics on your questions and it may well fit better into the layout of your Moodle. Also, it makes it much less easy for students to cheat by clicking on the back button, which is a feature of Hot Potatoes.

The way Hot Potatoes works with Moodle is that you prepare your quiz in Hot Potatoes, then save it in the same folder as any associated files, like images or sound. You then create a Hot Potatoes activity in Moodle and import your saved Hot Potatoes quiz into a course files folder. You'll need to upload the associated files into the same course file separately.

The Windows version of Hot Potatoes also allows you to save your Hot Potatoes quiz as a SCORM file, which bundles all the files in the activity. You can then import the SCORM file directly into your course home page via **Add an Activity... | SCORM/AICC**.

The only drawback is that you'll lose some of the Moodle Hot Potatoes gradebook features, but you will have a fully-functioning stand-alone activity.

Hot Potatoes crossword

In Chapter 3, *Vocabulary Activities*, there's an example of how you'd make a crossword in Hot Potatoes and import it into Moodle.

HTML

Learning some basic HTML to edit your pages

In case you want to understand and control your web pages a little better, this site introduces you to some basic HTML and gives you chance to try out your code: `http://www.w3schools.com/html/html_primary.asp`. You can also check out:

- `http://www.htmlprimer.com/`
- `http://www.goodellgroup.com/tutorial/`

KompoZer

Students can create a variety of pages within Moodle—for example, in forums, wikis, and assignments, but they do not have permissions to create stand-alone web pages on course pages. Since these pages are fun and useful for students to create as a way of practicing language, it's worth helping them to make them by using a dedicated web-page program. Completed web pages can then be uploaded by students to the course files folder (see uploading files in this chapter) and used by the teacher to display in the Book module.

A simple way of helping students create web pages is to use a free **WYSIWYG (What You See Is What You Get)** program like KompoZer, which is available for Windows and Mac at `http://kompozer.net/download.php`. Once you've downloaded the program, it's a good idea to follow the tutorial in the **Help** menu. There are three key things to remember when you save your web page:

- Create a separate folder for files relating to one web page.
- Anything you insert into the web page, such as images or sound files, must be kept in that folder, or they won't appear on the web page.
- The web page size is limited by the maximum upload limit for your Moodle. Ask your administrator if you need to increase it.

There's an example of how to create a book using student web pages in Chapter 7, *Writing Activities*.

Images

Chapter 11, *Formatting and Enhancing Your Moodle Materials* gives some suggestions on improving your digital images and points to `http://myimager.com`, which has a useful collection of online image editing tools. First of all, you'll need to produce some images. The best source is often your own camera.

The following sites offer collections of ready-to-use free images.

- `http://web.uvic.ca/hcmc/clipart`
- `http://www.openclipart.org`
- `http://www.sxc.hu/`
- `http://www.grsites.com/`
- `http://en.wikipedia.org/wiki/Public_domain_image_resources`
- `http://www.shutterstock.com/`
- `http://www.smugmug.com/`
- `http://media.photobucket.com/`

If you need to edit images to make them more suitable for Moodle, Google's Picasa does a basic job very well. It's available free from `http://picasa.google.com`.

Paint program

If you have younger learners, you might find it useful to get them to paint computer images to decorate their texts. Windows machines come with a Paint program. There are several free paint programs for Mac listed at `http://www.wikihow.com/Find-a-Paint-Program-for-Your-Mac`.

International accent marks and diacritics

The *starr* site provides a good overview of programs and keyboard shortcuts that you can use to include accent marks and non-English scripts in Moodle: `http://www.starr.net/is/type/kbh.html`.

If you need phonemic alphabet, try `http://www.chass.utoronto.ca/~rogers/fonts.html`.

Reminder service

Most Moodle modules currently do not provide an email reminder service. It might be worth using a website like *remember the milk* (`https://www.rememberthemilk.com/`) or *Memo to Me* (`http://www.memotome.com`) to remind yourself and/or your students to do tasks. You can write the reminders in the foreign language, which is another, maybe novel, way of getting students to practice language. Do make sure the service you select can reproduce the language script that you want to use.

Google calendars automate SMS or email (`http://www.google.com/calendar`). Free!

Scheduling service

Sometimes you might find that you need to agree with your students on a good time for getting together for a chat session, or what an appropriate deadline is for a piece of work. The free scheduling service offered by Doodle (`http://www.doodle.com/`) is excellent for this purpose.

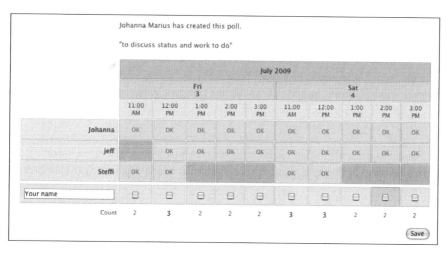

Screen capture

`http://www.jingproject.com/`	Screen image and video capture for Mac/Windows
`http://skitch.com`	Versatile way of capturing images from the screen for quick use in Moodle and all sorts of other places (Mac)
`http://capture-me.softonic.de/mac`	Capture Me (Mac)
`http://www.techsmith.com/screen-capture.asp`	Snagit (Windows)

Screencasts

If your users are likely to have any problems getting to grips with Moodle, consider using the wide range of movies or screencasts that explain the basics. Here's a list of some sites that offer Moodle screencasts:

- `http://human.edublogs.org/moodle-tutorials-2-minute-moodles/`
- `http://www.moodletutorials.org/`
- `http://video.google.com/videosearch?q=moodle#`

Or you could do a search for Moodle movies on `http://youtube.com`.

Alternatively, you could make your own movie tutorials for your site. You'll need screen-recording software such as:

- Jing (`http://www.jingproject.com/`), for Mac and Windows, which is free
- CamStudio (`http://camstudio.org/`), for Windows and Mac OS 10.5.6 or later
- Adobe Captivate 4 (`http://www.adobe.com/products/captivate/ productinfo/product-demos/screen-recording-software/`)
- ScreenFlow (`http://screenflow.en.softonic.com/mac`), for Mac

If your students are at a sufficient high level, you can produce these videos in the language they are learning.

Twitter

Twitter is a micro-blogging tool which is a fun and useful way to engage students. The way it works is that you follow other people's twitter feeds and they can follow yours. In an educational context, you could use this to send messages in a foreign language, or remind students of tasks. It's straightforward to set up an account at `http://www.twitter.com`.

If you combine twitter with an RSS feed, students can see your twitter feeds in an RSS block. See the section on RSS feeds for more help with this.

Right-click on the RSS feed link to copy the link, which will look something like this:

```
https://twitter.com/statuses/friends_timeline/11120032.rss
```

Sometimes the twitter feed  on the twitter site doesn't work on Moodle. There's an easy workaround. Go to `http://freemyfeed.com/`. Then enter the RSS feed for your twitter, which you'll find at the bottom of the twitter page. That will generate a new feed, which does work in Moodle! Here's what a Moodle twitter feed might look like:

Change your tweet feed

On your twitter home page, at `http://twitter.com`, search for a twitter tag you want to include in your feed and then copy the RSS link. For example, if you search for "Michael Jackson", all the tweets in your stream will contain those words.

Video

Movie Maker

This free program from Microsoft is automatically installed on Windows machines. Providing you have a webcam attached to your computer, you can record directly into it. This can be very useful when illustrating sounds and body language, for example. It also allows you to edit up to two tracks, and add titles and transition effects. You can then upload your file to your Moodle site, or if that's problematical, you can use a free video hosting site, which allows you to embed the video on your Moodle pages. See **Video hosting** in this chapter for more information.

If you can't find Movie Maker on your machine, you can search for it on `http://www.microsoft.com`. There are helpful tutorials at `http://www.microsoft.com/windowsxp/using/moviemaker/default.mspx`.

iMovie

This free program from Apple is automatically installed on Macs. If it's not there, you can download it from `http://support.apple.com/downloads/`. Like Movie Maker, it allows you to make recordings, create multiple tracks, visual effects, and voiceovers. There are helpful tutorials at `http://www.apple.com/support/imovie/`.

Jake Ludington's Media Blab

Here you will find helpful tutorials on downloading and editing YouTube videos (`http://tinyurl.com/edityoutube`).

Mashable

This is a useful guide to online video tools and resources (`http://mashable.com/2007/06/27/video-toolbox/`).

Video hosting

`http://youtube.com` and `http://teachertube.com` are two of many sites that offer free video hosting. To upload videos, you'll need to create an account. The process for uploading is then clearly signposted. Once you have uploaded your video, you can embed the video in one of your Moodle HTML pages. Note that embedding may not work in Moodle Blog and Wiki pages. First, copy the embed code. This is clearly signposted on the YouTube and TeacherTube sites.

Copy the code onto your clipboard. Open your HTML page on Moodle. Click on the HTML toggle button ⟨⟩. Paste the code. The flash video is now embedded in your site. Don't forget to check copyright if you are not using your own video.

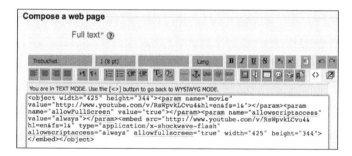

Once the page is saved, we'll be able to see the embedded video.

Subtitles

`http://www.overstream.net` enables you to add subtitles to existing YouTube videos, which can be useful for lower-level language learners.

Widgets

Widgets are add-on tools that you can use in Moodle HTML blocks to enhance your pages. Here are a few examples:

- `http://moodle.org` | **Downloads** | **Modules and plugins** — search for "wikipedia block". This creates a Wikipedia search box on your Moodle page.
- `http://dictionary.cambridge.org/linktous.asp` — online version of Cambridge Advanced Learner's Dictionary.
- `http://www.wolframalpha.com/` — a website that draws on multiple sources to answer user queries about a variety of topics.
- `http://www.google.com/ig/directory` — directory of more widgets you can add.

Word processors

You will probably find it useful to prepare documents on a word processor. If you don't already have one like Word installed, there are open source, free alternatives, such as Open Office, which you can download from `http://download.openoffice.org/`. Word-processed documents (text, spreadsheet, presentations, and PDFs) can be used as attachments to Moodle pages.

XML file creator

If you have a large number of entries that you want to import into a glossary, it's quicker to make an XML file and import it. Here's one, simple process you can follow. It uses a converter created by Yasu Imao, which can be downloaded from: `http://moodleflair.com/moodle/files/glossaryXMLconverter_html4.zip`. You'll need to have a Moodle Glossary up and running. Make a note of the categories you've set up.

Instructions

1. Prepare a tab-separated text document: concept (1st column), definition (second column), category (third column—optional), and keyword (fourth column—optional). For example:

   cow   farmyard animal   animals   cow

   You can do that in any word processor. Make sure your categories match existing categories in your Moodle Glossary.

2. Copy and paste the above into the HTML page mentioned earlier.

   Click on the convert button at the bottom of the page. An XML version will appear in the right-hand panel.

3. Copy and paste the resultant XML into a text editor. If you don't have one, TextWrangler is a good, free text editor, available from `http://www.barebones.com/products/textwrangler/download.html` for both Windows and Mac machines. You may need to adjust the encoding in the preferences section of the menu to accommodate the characters of the language you are writing in.

4. Save the file as a text file.

5. Open your existing Moodle glossary. Click on **Import entries** in the top right-hand corner.

Part 4: General design principles for creating a good Moodle course

It's likely that the activities you choose will be determined by the language syllabus you're teaching to. A good online course follows the principles of a good face-to-face course. Here are 10 reminders which might be handy.

Ten principles of a good Moodle course

Structure	Make sure your course and the activities are clearly structured, so that it's clear what is happening at any particular stage.
Audience	Make sure the course and activities are appropriate for your students.
Goal	Remind yourself why you've set the activity. With so many goodies available in Moodle, it's easy to fall into the trap of doing something because it's there rather than because it's useful and interesting.
Memorable	Try to make the materials interesting and memorable by providing stimulating topics and attractive materials.
Review	Remember to proof your materials. Also, get feedback from students and other teachers with a view to improving the materials. Make this a regular part of every activity and make sure you act on it.
Collaboration	Make collaboration between learners, and teachers and learners, a feature of your courses where possible.
Repetition	Remember that it will help learners' long-term memory if you recycle materials regularly. Make sure that new language is featured in several activities within your course.
Variety	Try to incorporate a variety of activities into your course.
The right activity at the right time	Remember to include some open-ended activities which get students thinking. Doing nothing but a battery of quizzes with fixed answers (closed activities) could be quite soul-destroying. Students often enjoy a sequence of open and closed activities.
Be available	There's nothing more frustrating for users trying to get used to a new learning system if help is not on hand. Make sure students know how to get the support from you that they need from the start.

Moodle course design: Do's and don'ts

With course design still in mind, here's my take on a list of do's and don'ts, which you can find on the `http://moodle.org` site.

Don't let Moodle overwhelm you	Start small. That way teachers and students won't feel intimidated by Moodle. Little by little you can expand your operation—together.
Don't dominate discussions	When you're using the Chat or Forum modules, prompt your students, but let them feel they're in charge.
Don't assume that the coolness of Moodle will inspire or motivate your students	It's easy to be impressed by the vast range of features available on Moodle. And it's easy to think that because you put a lot of time into producing activities students should enjoy them. But it isn't necessarily so. Be ready to accept positive and negative feedback and to act on it.
Don't violate copyright laws	It's tempting to include pictures, images, and sound that you find easily on the Internet. But check you have permission. Remember that students will assume that materials you use are legally there.
Don't forget to check users' profiles	Two reasons for doing this: If you have open enrolment, spammers might find a way into your site, and you'll need to root out undesirable messages. Also, sometimes students write inappropriate texts, which you might want to check.
Don't be afraid to experiment	Set up a course to experiment with and try out all the activities. It's a good way to learn and prepare yourself for your real courses.
Don't be distracted by shiny stuff	Starting off with Moodle is a little bit like being a child in a toyshop. There are so many shiny things to take hold of. I suggest you be modest. Take what you need. Don't overwhelm yourself, your teachers, or your students.

3
Vocabulary Activities

When I ask students what aspect of languages they most like learning, they often reply: "vocabulary". That is closely followed by "speaking" and "pronunciation". The reason they give is almost always something like: "Because it makes me feel rich", "It helps me to do things in the language", "I can express my moods better", "It means I can get what I want". Clearly, vocabulary has an important role. This chapter demonstrates just some of the ways we can use Moodle to help students learn, practice, and review their vocabulary.

Students usually have their preferred way of learning vocabulary. Apart from simply doing a vocabulary-gap-fill or vocabulary-matching exercises (*Activities 11 and 12*) several times—which could get tedious if done in excess—they can refer to glossaries, or even better, build their own glossaries (*Activities 1 and 10*). It's not too difficult to enhance these activities by adding annotations, recordings, pictures, and translations to help process the words and make them easier to remember. There's also a personal glossary (*Activity 8*), which allows students to add their own vocabulary and test themselves using it.

There are several ways we can use Moodle to make vocabulary learning fun by getting students to use vocabulary and play with it. The examples we'll look at in this chapter include a "word of the day" feature (*Activity 2*); rating the usefulness of words in a glossary (*Activity 4*), and running polls (*Activity 6*) in which students can vote on words. *Activity 3* introduces the comment feature and shows how we can provide feedback on students' glossary definitions.

A key element in the success of our vocabulary teaching has to be regular vocabulary work. That means we need variety. The other activities in this chapter demonstrate ways of incorporating vocabulary learning into our regular teaching. For example, *Activity 7* shows how to analyze vocabulary from a chat session transcript and *Activity 5* demonstrates how we can create vocabulary tags and word clouds from students' blogs. Another thing we can do regularly is turn on automatic linking in the glossary and then add new words we want to define for an upcoming reading text, so that when students have difficulty they can click on a link that takes them to a glossary definition.

We'll start off by building a glossary. That's easy to do, and it's a good way of getting something up and running quickly. The activities are then graded according to the complexity of the setup. The last four activities use the Lesson and Quiz modules and will require more time and patience if you haven't set them up before. Just make sure you have a good hour to work through the model activities the first time. Once you're used to them, they'll become second nature. If you want to set up a quiz activity quickly, use *Hot Potatoes (Activity 9)*, as it's easier and quicker to set up than the Moodle version.

Mindmapping is another way of building vocabulary. There is an add-on module, called Mindmap, which does this. See Chapter 7, *Writing Activities, Activity 5* for an example.

Activity 1: Setting up a class glossary

Aim: Build a collection of useful, searchable vocabulary items

Moodle modules: Glossary

Extra programs: None

Ease of setup: *

Making vocabulary lists is nothing new for most students. So what's different about Moodle's Glossary? Well, for a start, it's easy to set up, and is a good activity to start with. Much of the default setup won't even need changing. The big advantage of the Moodle Glossary is that we can manipulate our wordlists. We can sort them by author, category, and entry. We can enhance our glossary with other media, such as images and audio and video recordings. Glossary entries, called "concepts" in Moodlespeak, can then be automatically linked to other texts. So if our students are reading a text in Moodle with a potentially unknown word in it, we can create an entry in the glossary for that word. They then have an automatic link from the difficult word in the text to the glossary entry.

To sum up, glossaries are good to use for vocabulary lists, because:

- They help us keep an easily-accessible, permanent record
- They are searchable
- They can be categorized
- They can be sorted by author, category, and word
- We can auto-link words from texts in our courses to the glossary, so that students can look up difficult words easily
- We can include recordings of words
- We can enable the "comments" feature, which allows students to comment on words, ask questions, provide examples, etc.
- We can import glossaries saved as XML files to save time

In this activity we are going to make a simple wordlist. It will have three categories: Animals, Transport, and Sports. The next screenshot shows what it will look like with the first three entries. Notice that we can provide a description of the purpose of the glossary at the top. Most of the tabs are self-explanatory. The three icons that appear after each definition are for editing the entries. More on that later.

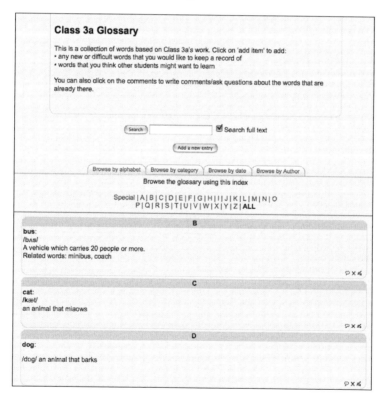

Here's how to do it

1. First, let's make sure we're in editing mode. To do that, click on the **Turn editing on** button. We always need to do that if we want to add a resource or an activity.

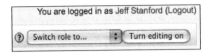

Editing button

The editing button is in the top right-hand corner of the screen.

2. Next, select the **Add an activity...** option.

3. Choose **Glossary**.

4. We'll now come to the set-up page for our glossary. Complete the introductory page following the screenshots and instructions below:

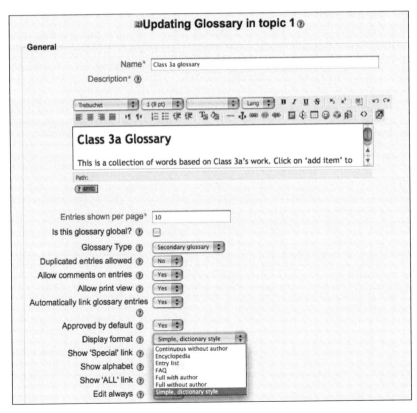

> **Online help**
> Click on the ⓘ button to get help online.

Pay attention to the following in particular. All the other settings are optional:

Settings	Details
Name	This name will appear on the main course page.
Description	This description will help all users—that's other teachers as well as students—to see what the purpose of the glossary is. We can also include some instructions to students on how to use it.
Is this glossary global?	Uncheck this. We only want course members for this particular course to be able to add to and access this glossary.
Glossary Type	Make this a **Secondary glossary**. We can then add it to a main glossary later if we want to. Each course can have one main glossary and any number of secondary glossaries. We can export entries from secondary glossaries to the main glossary.
Allow comments on entries	**Yes**. We want students to be able to add comments or ask questions.
Allow print view	This is generally useful, so check it. It produces a print button which generates a simple printable list of our words. Of course, we might not want to encourage unnecessary printing. In which case, don't check it!
Automatically link glossary entries	This means that words appearing in the glossary will be linked from any texts we produce on our course—not attachments, though. Let's choose **Yes**. We can change the setting later, if we don't like it.
Approved by default	Do we want to be able to check/edit/censor students' contributions before they enter the glossary? Let's click **Yes** to approve by default.
Display format	We can customize the way a user can browse a glossary. Browsing and searching are always available, but as we can see in the screenshot above there are seven display options. Let's choose simple, dictionary style for now.

5. Click on **Save and display** at the bottom of the page. Our glossary is now ready to use.

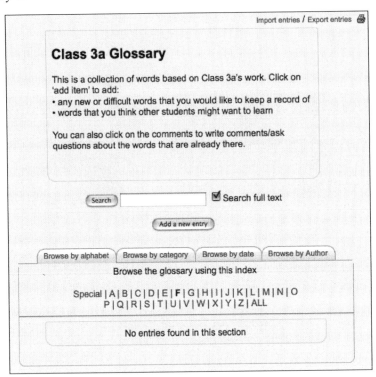

If we don't want our students to be able to add entries to the glossary, we should click on the **Override permissions** tab at the top of the set-up page.

The default allows students to add entries. Click on **Student** to change that permission.

Override permissions in Activity module: Class 3a glossary ⊚

Roles	Description	Overrides
Administrator	Administrators can usually do anything on the site, in all courses.	0
Course creator	Course creators can create new courses and teach in them.	0
Teacher	Teachers can do anything within a course, including changing the activities and grading students.	0
Non-editing teacher	Non-editing teachers can teach in courses and grade students, but may not alter activities.	0
Student	Students generally have fewer privileges within a course.	0
Guest	Guests have minimal privileges and usually can not enter text anywhere.	0
Authenticated user	All logged in users.	0
superstudent	student plus ability to manage slideshows	0

At the bottom of the list of permissions, click on the **Prevent** checkbox next to **Create new entries**. Make the changes you want to, and then click on **Save changes**.

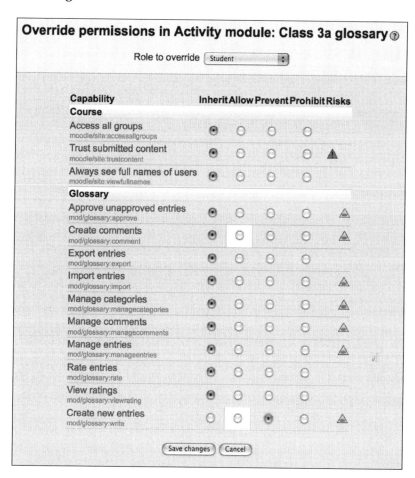

We can add words to the glossary by clicking on **Add a new entry**. Before we do that, though, let's add a few categories.

Adding categories

6. We're going to add three categories to our glossary: Animals, Transport, and Sports. We can add more later, if necessary. First, make sure we're still on the main glossary page.

7. Click on **Browse by category**.

8. Now click on **Edit categories**.

9. Next, click on **Add category**. Now add the categories to our list one by one, following the instructions on the page. We can always edit the list later, if we need to change the spelling or amend the categories.

10. Now let's add our first word to the glossary. Click on **Add a new entry**.

11. Complete the page with a vocabulary entry. Let's take our "dog" example.

    ○ Under **Concept**, write the word **dog**.

    ○ Under **Definition**, include the text we want. For example: **An animal that barks.**

    ○ Choose an appropriate **Category**.

    ○ Choose **Keywords** that relate to the entry. Students will be able to search for entries via these keywords.

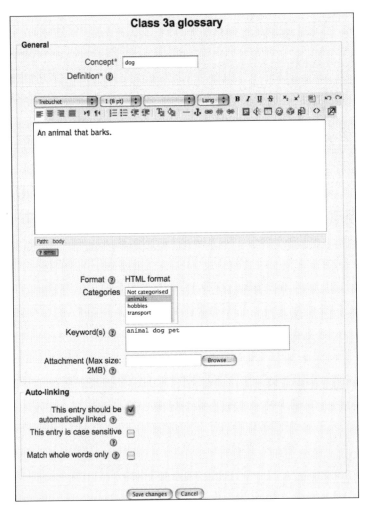

12. Click on **Save changes**. Our first entry is now ready.

13. We can edit glossary entries by clicking on the edit icon ✎, which you can see in the following screenshot.

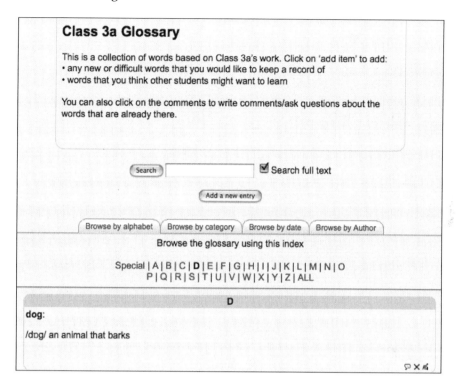

Editing icons/Enhancing image definition

To add comments, click on 💬. To delete the entry, click on ✗.

While editing the definition, we can also click on the image icon 🖼 to insert an image. See Chapter 2, *Getting Started with Moodle* for help with inserting images.

Other ideas

Import glossaries from a text editor into the glossary:

If we have a list of say 20 words or more, we might find it quicker to write them in a text editor first. We can then import them into our glossary via an XML editor. See Chapter 2, *Getting Started with Moodle* for details on how to do this.

Include audio recordings in the glossary:

Following the procedure in Chapter 2, *Getting Started with Moodle* we can also add mini-players in the definition box. We could add, for example, recordings of:

- The word alone
- The word in context
- A brief commentary of the word
- The word with a translation

Unfortunately, NanoGong doesn't work for recording voice in Glossary entries.

Get students to produce illustrations for words using a paint program:
Students, especially younger ones, love making computer pictures. They could upload them into their definitions.

Activity 2: Using a Glossary to create a "word of the day" feature

Aim: Help motivate students by providing random individual words

Moodle modules: Glossary and Block

Extra programs: None

Ease of setup: *

It's good to be able to provide a fun element to language learning when we can. One element of surprise we can introduce easily is a "word of the day". When students open the course page, they'll be rewarded with a new word, its definition, and a link to the glossary.

This is relatively simple to set up. It provides students with a surprise word, either every day or every time they refresh the page, depending on the settings. The word comes from one of the glossaries we'll need to have set up first. We can include links back to the glossary. Images and sounds placed at the top of the definition box also show in the word of the day. The finished **word of the day** block will look like this:

N.B. We need to have a working glossary first. It can be a main glossary (usable on the whole site) or a secondary glossary (only usable on one course).

Here's how to do it

1. Click on **Turn editing on** in the top right-hand corner. Go to the **blocks** column, which is usually on the right.

2. From the drop-down menu, choose **Random Glossary Entry**.

    A new block with the **Random Glossary Entry** will appear.

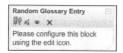

3. Edit the **Random Glossary Entry**.

    Click on the editing icon ✍ and we'll see the following:

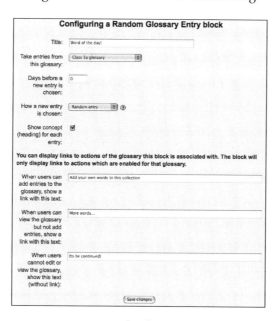

Follow these instructions to configure the block.

Settings	Details
Title	Give the **Random Glossary Entry** block the title—**Word of the Day!**.
Take entries from this glossary	Choose the glossary we want to access words from. In this case it's the glossary called **Class 3a glossary**.
Days before a new entry is chosen	Set this to **1**, so that a new word (glossary entry) appears once a day.
Show concept (heading) for each entry	Check this. We want our word—called a **concept** by Moodle—to appear at the top of the new block.

4. Click on **Save changes**. We can now see the word of the day block in action.

Other ideas
Make a glossary of something else that's interesting. For example, web sites, pictures, poems, lyrics, anecdotes, historical facts, news … the list is endless.

Activity 3: Using comments in the Glossary module for students to comment on keywords

Aim: Getting students to reflect on keywords

Moodle modules: Web page and Glossary

Extra programs: None

Ease of setup: *

Another way of engaging students is to give them the opportunity to comment on words in the glossary. This is good for several reasons:

- It helps them to process the word and so understand it and use it better
- It can be fun and interesting
- It can help teachers see if students have understood the word

In this activity we're going to focus students' attention on the vocabulary they will need for a reading text taken from the novel *Around the World in 80 days* by Jules Verne. You could use any text. By getting students to sort vocabulary and comment on it, we hope they will remember it better and appreciate the text that generated the vocabulary better.

There are various criteria we can give for selecting words to comment on.
For example:

- Words you like
- Words you think are useful
- Words you want to understand
- Words you want to practice using

In the following example we'll look at words students want to practice using. This is what their comment box with a practice sentence might look like at the end:

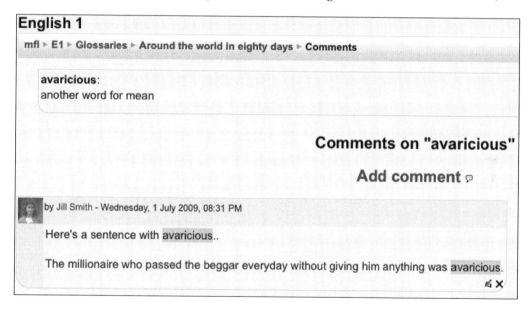

At the top of the box is the keyword **avaricious**, below it is its definition, and below them a comment.

Here's how to do it

1. Let's select a text we want to use. This could be a text you wrote, or a copyright-free piece of literature, or copyrighted material that we have permission to use. In this case I've chosen a description of the character Phileas Fogg from the novel *Around the World in 80 days* by Jules Verne, available from `http://www.gutenberg.org/files/103/103.txt`.

2. Now we need to copy the text into a Moodle web page. To do that, go to your course page. Click on **Turn editing on** in the top right-hand corner.

3. Click on **Add a resource...**, and choose **Compose a web page** from the drop-down menu.

4. Complete the page like this:

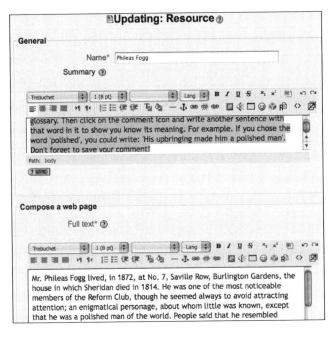

Settings	Details
Name	Give the text an appropriate name.
Summary	This is a good place to write the instructions for the task. We could write the following for example: **This is a description of Phileas Fogg, who travelled around the world in 80 days in Jules Verne's novel.** **Your task is to click on one of the underlined words. That will take you to the glossary. Then click on the comment icon and write another sentence with that word in it to show you know its meaning. For example. If you chose the word 'polished', you could write: 'His upbringing made him a polished man'. Don't forget to save your comment!**
Compose a web page	Paste the full text into this box.
Window	Choose **Same window**.

5. Click on **Save and display**.

6. Next, we need to make a list of keywords from that text. Let's limit it to twenty words. And let's choose potentially difficult words for students, like:

   ○ enigmatical

   ○ noticeable

   ○ polished

   ○ sage

   ○ deliberations

7. Make a glossary entry for each of those words. We could call the glossary **Around the world in eighty days**. We can either define the words in the target language or the students' first language. (See *Activity 1* in this chapter for more information on setting up a glossary.) Let's choose **English** for now.

   Make sure that **Auto-linking** is on for each entry. You'll find the option at the bottom of the page where you're entering a new word.

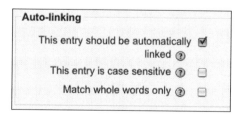

Once the glossary is finished, return to the text on Phileas Fogg and we'll see that each of the glossary entries we wrote is now highlighted.

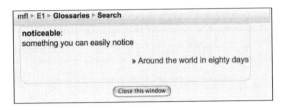

Let's click on the first of those words, **noticeable**. This is what we'll see:

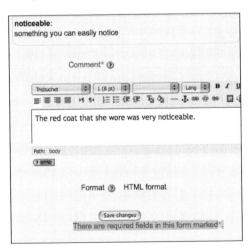

We see the keyword and its definition. There's also a link to the whole glossary.

8. Now comes the interesting part. Tell students to read the text and choose five of the twenty highlighted words. Students should click on each word individually. That will take them to the glossary entry for that word. Then they should click on the glossary link.

9. If necessary, they should search for the word they chose again. They should now click on the comments icon 🗩 and write a comment.

In this example, students are asked to provide a new sentence that uses the same word. They could write a sentence like:

Once students have written their comments, encourage them to read each other's. They can even comment on the comments. The more students write, the more they are processing the vocabulary.

Automatic linking

Don't forget to make sure the automatic linking to glossary filter is on. Go to **Admin** | **Modules** | **Filters** to turn it on.

Activity 4: Using the rating facility to provide feedback on students' definitions

Aim: Prompt students to improve their definitions

Moodle modules: Glossary

Extra programs: None

Ease of setup: *

Feedback … students love it. So do teachers. Most of us want to know how well we're doing.

There are lots of ways of providing feedback in Moodle. In this activity we get students to write definitions of new words in a glossary. Then we give feedback by using the glossary rating facility. This will give them a chance to improve on the definitions, and will help them to understand the words better. The rating facility uses a fixed scale which will provide a preformed comment on students' words. It will help them decide how much they need to rewrite them. In the following example, Jill Smith has written a definition of **put up with** and got a rating of **good basic definition**. She knows that she needs to add detail to make it better.

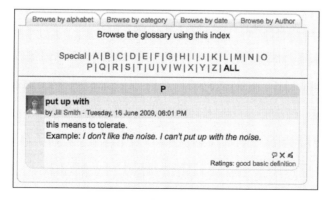

We could add more detail by adding comments to the students' definitions. We'll need to set up a glossary and allow ratings and comments for this activity.

Here's how to do it

Here we will first define a rating scale, then set up a glossary activity for students, and finally rate students' entries based on the activity.

Rating scale

1. First we'll create a rating scale. See Chapter 2, *Getting Started with Moodle* for help with this. Remember that you'll need administrator permissions to do this. Ask your Moodle Administrator, if in doubt.

   Let's call our scale **definitions**, so that it's easily recognizable.

   Let's use descriptors such as the following. We can always change them later.

   - **Sorry but this is wrong**
   - **there's something in this**
   - **nearly right**
   - **good basic definition**
   - **very good definition**

Glossary

2. Set up a glossary activity for the students to add their words to. *Activity 1* in this chapter has instructions on this. We should make sure we:

   - Allow students to add entries
   - Allow students to edit their own entries
   - Allow comments

○   Choose the **Definitions** scale that we produced as rating scale

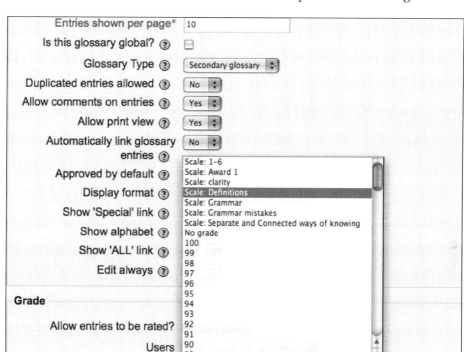

3. Now we need to get students to define words. Give students a list of words to define. In this case they'll be phrasal verbs like:

    ○   Put up with

    ○   Put up

    ○   Put somebody out

It's helpful to give them an example. We could write something like this.

Put somebody out:
This is when we disrupt someone's plans or routine.

4. They should now add their entries to the glossary.

Settings	Details
Concept	Write the word they are defining.
Definition	Write a simple definition of the word.
Auto-linking	No. This is not necessary for this exercise.

Rating students' entries

5. Open the glossary with students' definitions in it. You won't be able to rate anything until students have actually added some definitions.

6. Click on the **Rate...** drop-down menu for one of the definitions, and choose the rating that's appropriate.

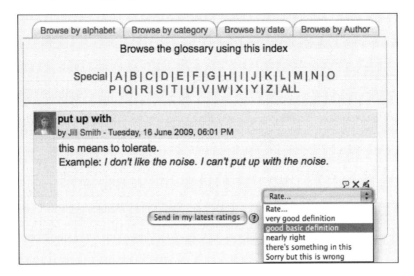

This is a **good basic definition**. So let's choose that rating. Note that we're rating students' definitions and not their comments. Sometimes teachers open the comments box and try to rate that by mistake.

7. Click on **Send in my latest ratings**.

8. Get students to check our ratings and review their definitions if necessary. Students who get this rating know that they are correct, but haven't provided much detail.

Activity 5: Using tags to highlight vocabulary and link to example stories

Aim: Help students process meaning by creating stories based on keywords

Moodle modules: Block and Blog

Extra programs: None

Ease of setup: *

There's nothing like telling a story to make language come alive. The context endows the words with more meaning, makes them easier to remember, and makes the whole process of language learning more enjoyable.

One way of doing this in face-to-face classes is for students to take a word or a group of words and create a short story from them. This Moodle activity does the same thing. It has the advantage that the stories are available to be viewed by the other students in the class. Also, in the variation we're about to create, we'll produce definitions of the vocabulary that students will use in their stories. At the end of the activity, students will be able to access the stories and/or definitions via a tag cloud block on the course page.

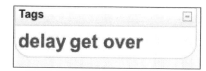

Preparation

1. First, we prepare the key words which we want students to use in their stories.

    For example, if we're teaching English, we may want students to practice some phrasal verbs.

    - Put up with
    - Give up
    - Take on
    - Put off
    - Get over

Administration

2. Next, we need to make official tags out of those words.

   To do that, go to the **Site Administration menu** on the home page for your web site. Don't confuse this with your course page. You can find the home page by clicking on the breadcrumb in the top-left-hand corner of the page. In the following breadcrumb, you'd click on **mfl** to get to the site home page.

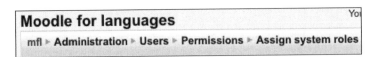

Moodle for languages   Yo

mfl ▸ **Administration** ▸ **Users** ▸ **Permissions** ▸ **Assign system roles**

Access to administration pages

Don't forget that you'll need to be a site administrator to do this. If you're not, ask your Moodle administrator to give you access.

Click on **Appearance**, and then click on **Manage tags**.

3. In the **Add official tags** box, write the first phrasal verb. Then click on the **Add official tags** button.

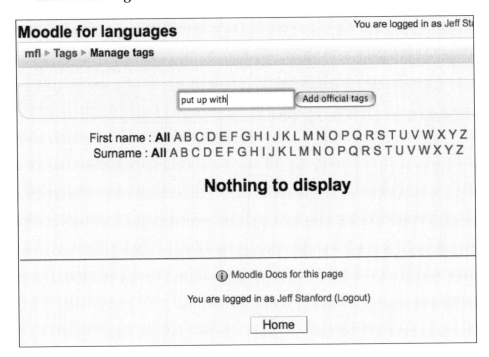

That phrase will then join the list of official tag words. The final list of tags will look like this:

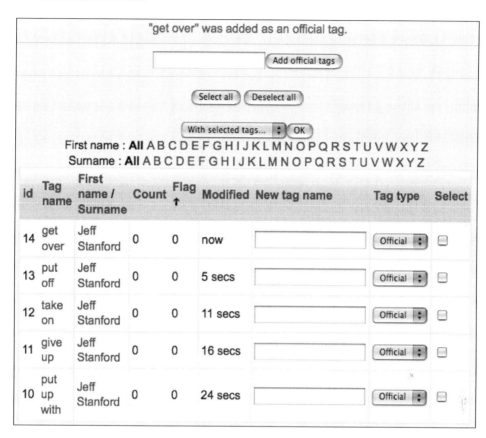

4. Now we're going to provide a definition for each phrase. To do that, we click on a keyword in the **Tag name** column. Let's start with **get over**.

5. Then click on **Edit this tag**.

   We can see the phrase in the **Tag name** box. In the description box below, write a definition of the phrase that we want our students to see. We can also put audio, images, or video here, if we want. At the bottom of the page, we can also add **Related tags**. A related tag for **get over** could be **overcome**, for example.

6. When we're done, we can click on **Update**.

7. Click on **Manage tags** to see a list of all your tags. Repeat the definition process from Step 3 above for all the phrases.

Activity

8. Now we need to tell our students they should write a short story in their blogs, which includes one of the phrases. To do that they should:

   ○ Click on the **Name** (which they will see in the top right-hand corner of the course page or the start page).

   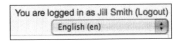

   ○ Click on **Blog**.

   ○ Click on **Add a new entry**.

   ○ Give the blog entry a name related to the phrase they choose.

   ○ Write their story in the **Blog entry body** box. They can include pictures, sound, and video, if they want. They can even embed YouTube videos. (See Chapter 2, *Getting Started with Moodle* for help with this.)

- Under **Tags**, they should choose the phrase their story is about. This is important, because the phrase will then appear in the tag clouds on the course page. When they have finished, they should click on **Save changes**.

In this example, Jill has chosen the phrasal verb **get over** for her story.

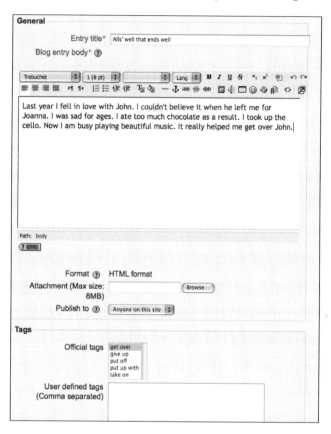

Result

9. Now we need to go to the course page. Make sure we **Turn editing on**. Add the **Tags block**.

We can now see all the keywords we've identified as official tags.

10. Click on one of the words in the **Tags** block.

Now we will see both the definition we wrote and the stories that students wrote.

---

get over

Add "get over" to my interests | Flag as inappropriate | Edit this tag

We use 'get over' to mean that we are not affected by something as much as we were before. For example: Last week I lost my purse. I was upset at first, but now I have got over it.

Related tags: overcome

Recent blog entries with this tag

- Alls' well that ends well - Jill Smith, Wednesday, 17 June 2009, 08:24 AM

See all blogs with this tag...

Activity 6: Using polls to vote on the meaning of words

Aim: Focus students' attention on a keyword in a fun way

Moodle modules: Choice

Extra programs: Recording program (optional)

Ease of setup: *

If we turn language learning into fun, students often forget that they're learning. One way of doing that with Moodle is to use the Choice module. Students vote for a meaning of a word and can compare their answers to their peers'. It will work best if you get all your students involved. Let's take a look at two variations of this activity.

Variation 1: Defining a word

In this first variation, we get students to focus on a word that has been particularly difficult or we suspect will be difficult. Students will see the word and have to choose which definition they think is the right one. Once several students have answered, the graphic display will illustrate their results like the following:

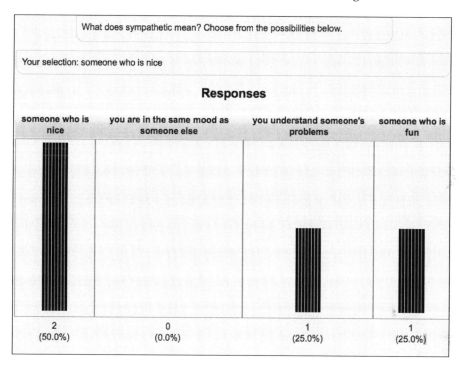

Here's how to do it

1. On the course page, click on **Turn editing on**. Go to the **Add an activity...** drop-down menu and add **Choice.**

2. Fill in the settings page. Copy the settings in the screenshot. If a setting isn't mentioned in the following table, then it's optional.

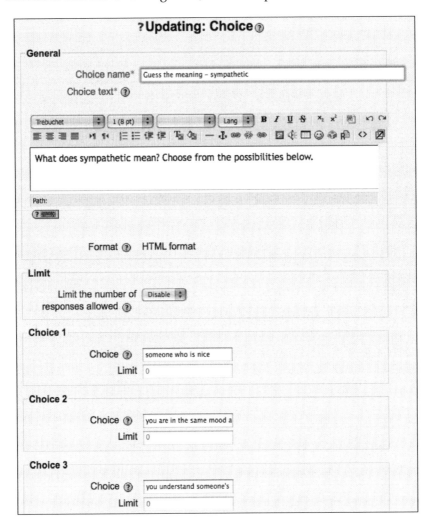

Settings	Details
Choice name	Write an appropriate title for the activity. Let's call this **Guess the meaning - sympathetic**.
Choice text	Write a simple question for students to answer. I've written: **What does sympathetic mean? Choose from the possibilities below**.
Choice 1	Under **Choice**, write **someone who is nice**.
Choice 2	Under **Choice**, write **you are in the same mood as someone else**.
Choice 3	Under **Choice**, write **you understand someone's problems**.
Choice 4	Under **Choice**, write **someone who is fun**.
Display mode	If we have a lot of students, we can go for **horizontal**. If we have few, then **vertical** would be appropriate.

3. Click on **Save and display**. The poll is ready to use. Students click on the activity and then choose the answer.

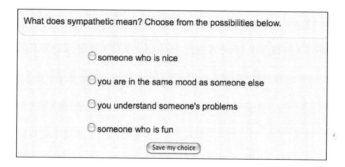

Other variations

Other variations of this could be to include supportive images, or to get students to listen to a sound clip and respond to it in some way. For example:

- Guessing a word based on the definition
- Voting on what they think they heard
- Voting on the emotion they think they heard
- Giving a definition and getting students to vote on the word which is being defined

Downloading results

After the poll closes (based on your **Until** date in Step 2 above), you can download the results in ODS (Open Office), Excel, or text format to use for presentation purposes. The download gives you all the data in text form.

Activity 7: Using a chat session transcript to analyze vocabulary errors

Aim: Help students analyze language errors generated by an online chat

Moodle modules: Chat plus optional use of Wiki and Forum

Extra programs: Optional use of word processor or Audacity

Ease of setup: **

Chatting online is an increasingly common activity. Lots of students use MSN, Yahoo, ICQ, etc. to type out a dialog. This is a great way to practice using language fluently, and can be adapted for a number of purposes. For example:

- Students rehearse a role-play
- Students and the teacher discuss an issue
- Students ask the teacher questions about a given topic or issue
- The teacher tells a story which students can ask questions about

The chat activity allows us to keep a transcript of any online discussion, which we can then review. We can draw students' attention to the errors through error analysis exercises. Reflecting on these errors may help them avoid similar errors later.

Chats usually work better if the teacher is present to moderate. Typical problems might be:

- Students go off track
- They get stuck because they need your guidance
- They don't follow chat-room etiquette that you've agreed on

Netiquette

See *"Moodle Teaching Techniques"*, William Rice, Packt Publishing for suggestions on etiquette.

It is useful for the teacher to mix open questions and closed questions to get students involved.

The more participants in the chat, the less they will be able to contribute. Make sure that participants' roles are clear before they start.

Here's how to do it

1. Set up a chat session. To do that, click on **Turn editing on**, which is on the main course page.

2. Click on **Add an activity....** Choose **Chat** from the drop-down menu.

3. Fill in the settings page. Copy the settings in the screenshot. If a setting isn't mentioned below, it's optional.

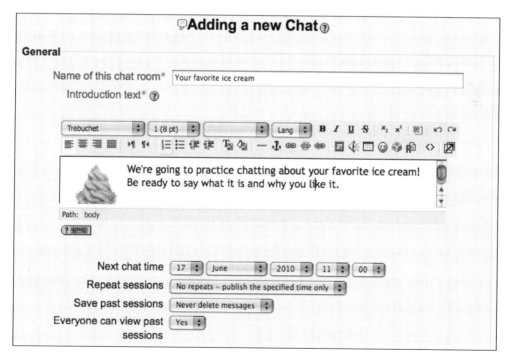

Settings	Details
Name of this chat room	Enter an appropriate name.
Introduction text	This will tell the students what they'll be chatting about. We can include pictures by clicking on the image icon in the edit menu. Let's write **We're going to practice chatting about your favorite ice cream! Be ready to say what it is and why you like it.**.
Next chat time	Chose the date and time of the chat session. Students will see this scheduled time when they click on the activity.
Save past sessions	Let's choose **Never delete messages** so that we always have access to the chat transcript.

Click on **Save and Display**. The chat session is now ready to use. Students click on the chat activity and chat in just the same way they would with other chat rooms. They type their message at the bottom of the screen and then hit the Return button.

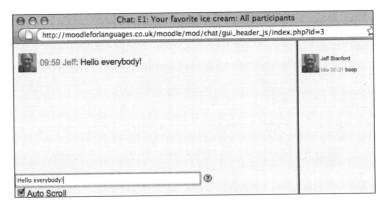

4. After the chat session has finished, re-open the chat activity. Click on **View past chat sessions**. Find the chat session whose transcript you want to view. Click on it to see that session.

Can't see the chat session

Sometimes teachers try this module out by chatting to themselves—an understandable way of getting to know the activity. But, be careful, because Moodle will only save the chat session if at least two people participated in it.

5. We can now copy-paste the session into a variety of other programs. The following are some examples:

Review 1: Review errors in a word processor

In this variation, we give students a print-out of the chat transcript, which helps them try to work out correct versions of their mistakes by themselves.

Here's how to do it

1a. First of all, go to the past chat session mentioned in Step 4 above. Click on **File | Print** from your browser window. You can then give students handouts in class to work on. Refer to Step 3 below to see what it might look like.

1b. Alternatively, we can copy-paste the dialog into a word processor. We can then upload the word processor file to our Moodle course. It's easy to do this by selecting the text with your mouse, then clicking on the right-hand button of your mouse and choosing **Copy**.

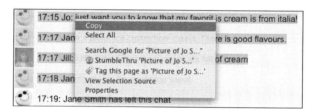

2. Then paste it into a word processor document. To paste, click on the right-hand button of your mouse and choose **Paste**.

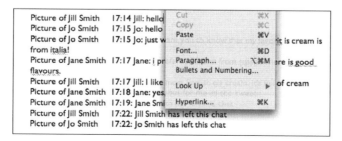

We'll need to edit the text a bit to tidy it up. Include instructions at the top that tell students to try to correct the errors.

3. This is what the word-processed page could look like:

ICE CREAM DIALOG – correcting your errors

INSTRUCTIONS

1. Cover the corrections in the left hand column.
2. Look at the words in bold in the dialog.
3. Try to correct them.
4. Then compare your answer to the corrected version.

Dialog	Correction
17:14 Jill: hello	
17:15 Jo: hello	
17:15 Jo: just want you to know that my **favorit** is cream is from **italia!**	favourite Italy
17:17 Jane: **i** prefer ice cream from **russia**, **There is good flavours**.	Russia. They have nice flavors. (US spelling)
17:17 Jill: **I like most English eis** cream. **it's** full of cream	I like English ice cream most. It's full of cream
17:18 Jane: yes, but for me **its** too sweet.	

---

4. Don't forget to **Save** the file on your computer.

5. To upload a document to our Moodle course page, go to the **Add a resource...** drop-down menu on the course page, and choose **Link to a file or web site**.

6. Give the link a name, and then click on **Choose or upload a file...** to browse to the file we've saved.

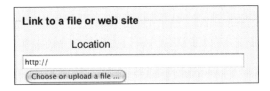

See Chapter 2, *Getting Started with Moodle* if you need more help with uploading files.

7. Click on **Save and display** when the file is uploaded. The file is now ready for the students to access.

Giving the students the answers straightaway will encourage them to become more independent, which is one of the key features of communicative language teaching, as mentioned in Chapter 1, *What does Moodle offer language teachers?*. They may need to come back to you for an explanation of the corrections.

Review 2: Review errors in a wiki

This is similar to the word processing error review above, but in a wiki, students have the chance to work together to try to correct errors.

Here's how to do it

1. Set up a wiki session. To do that, click on **Turn editing on**, which you'll find on the course page.

2. Click on **Add an activity....** Add a **Wiki**.

3. Fill in the settings page. Copy the settings in the screenshot. Make sure you click on the **Show Advanced** button so that you can see all the following options.

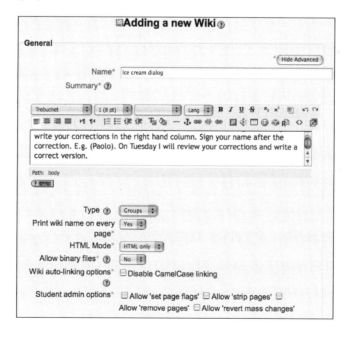

Settings	Details
Name	Enter an appropriate name. Let's write **Ice cream dialog**.
Summary	This will tell the students what to do. Let's write this: **The transcript of your ice-cream dialogue is here. Read through it and try to write your corrections in the right hand column. Sign your name after the correction. E.g. (Paolo). On Tuesday I will review your corrections and write a correct version..**
Student admin options	Don't check any of these.

See Chapter 2, *Getting Started with Moodle* if you need help with Common module settings and groups.

4. Click on **Save and display**.

5. We now have a ready-to-use wiki in front of us. Let's create a table in the wiki with two columns. To do that, we click on the table icon ▦ in the edit menu.

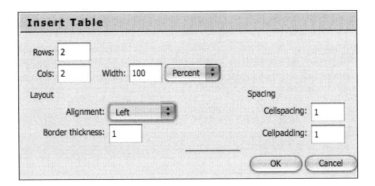

6. Click on **OK**.

7. Give the columns labels. Now copy-paste the transcript from the chat session into the left-hand column of the wiki. This is what we'll get:

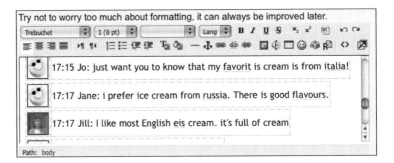

We can now edit the text a little, by deleting the icons. Then it will look like this:

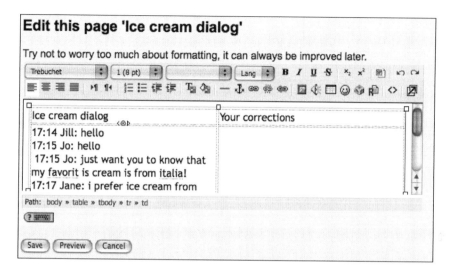

8. Click on **Save**. Students can now access the wiki in the same way, writing their corrections to the dialog in the right-hand column.

Review 3: Review errors by comparing to a teacher recording

This variation gives students the opportunity to compare their dialog to a more natural version recorded by the teacher and a colleague, which they can listen to on a Moodle forum.

Here's how to do it

1. Print out the chat transcript. To do that, from your browser window, click on **File | Print**.

2. Make a note of the unnatural passages.

3. Prepare to record a more natural version of the dialog.

4. Upload both the transcript and the recording to a forum posting. To do this, follow the instructions in Chapter 4, *Speaking Activities, Activity 1*. Our forum introduction will look like the following.

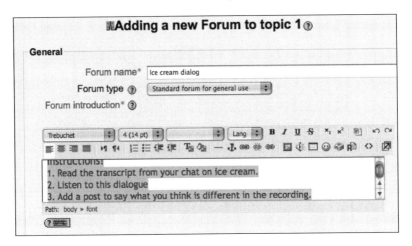

5. This is what students will see:

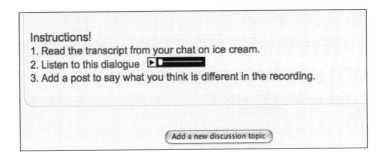

Activity 8: Using a Personal Glossary to set up simple individual vocabulary lists

Aim: Help students set up simple personal vocabulary lists

Moodle modules: Personal Glossary (add-on)

Extra programs: None

Ease of setup: *

The activities in this chapter have so far been organized by us, the teachers. But as students we often like to take responsibility for our own vocabulary learning. One way of doing this is to set up a simple add-on, called Personal Glossary, which lets students create their own simple word lists in any number of languages. There is also a simple test feature: a useful feature for revising key vocabulary. Don't forget this is an add-on. So you'll have to get your administrator to download it from the Moodle site and install it on your server. See Chapter 2, *Getting Started with Moodle* for help with this.

Here's how to do it

1. On the front page, go to **Administration | Modules | Blocks | Manage blocks**.

2. Make sure that **Personal Glossary & Quizzer** is not hidden. Click on the eye icon to open it if it is shut.

| People | 6 | 2007101509 | | | Delete |
| Personal Glossary & Quizzer | 2 | 2007052000 | | | Delete |

3. To switch on **My Moodle**, on the front page, go to **Administration | Appearance | My Moodle**. Check the box **Force users to use My Moodle**.

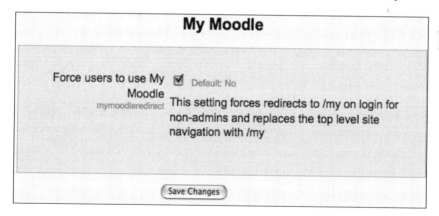

Click on **Save Changes**.

Instructions for students

4. When students log on, they will now come to their **My Moodle** page. The first time they go there, they'll see a blank page.

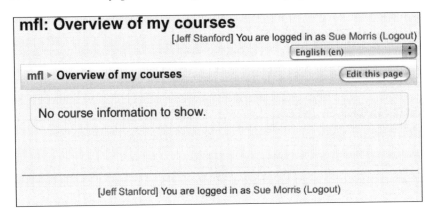

They should click on the **Edit this page** button in the top-right-hand corner. A **Blocks** menu now appears, and they can now add the **Personal Glossary and Quizzer** page.

Can't see My Moodle

We teachers cannot see this page unless we log on as students. To do that, go to the participants' list on the course page. Click on a student's name. Then select **Log in as**. You'll be taken straight to the **My Moodle** page. If there's no participants' list on the course page, click on **Turn on editing**, go to the **Blocks** menu at the bottom of the right-hand column, and add a **People block**.

Students can add any other blocks they want, too. The HTML block, for example, allows them to design any web page they want, with text, audio, video, images.

The new personal glossary page looks like this:

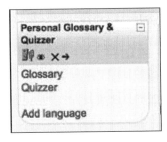

5. Students should click on **Glossary**.

6. Next, they should define the languages they want to use. To do that, they need to click on the **Add language** button. This can be whatever language the student wants to work with. They should then click on **Add**.

7. When the languages are added, students should click on **Glossary** to add some words. For example:

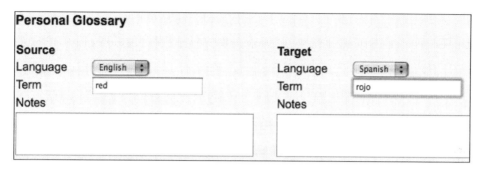

Remind them to change the **Target Language** as appropriate.

They should then click on **Save** for each word they add.

As soon as there are words in the list, students can use the **Quizzer** to test their memory.

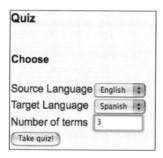

It will look something like this:

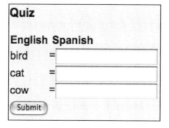

Once students compete the answers and click on **Submit**, they'll get their results. For example:

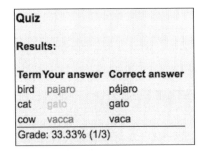

With a result like that, I'm obviously going to have to practice my Spanish spelling!

Activity 9: Creating a crossword in Hot Potatoes

Aim: Help students practice vocabulary

Moodle modules: Hot Potatoes (Moodle)

Extra programs: Hot Potatoes (external program)

Ease of setup: **

Hot Potatoes is a free, easy-to-use quiz-making program, and is ideal for setting up quick quizzes to review or test students. It can be used for reviewing other skills as well. It is great for testing or reviewing grammar, reading, and listening, as well as vocabulary. In this activity we're going to look at an activity not available in Moodle, JCross, which produces crosswords. It's also easier to use than Moodle's Quiz module on the whole.

Here's how to do it

1. Download the Hot Potatoes program onto your computer. See Chapter 2, *Getting Started with Moodle* for more information on this.

2. Open the Hot Potatoes program and choose **JCross**.

3. We are immediately presented with a crossword grid, which we fill in as we wish.

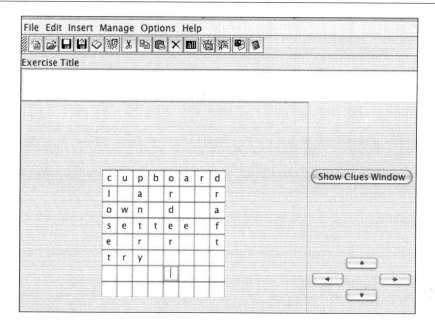

4. Click on **Show Clues Window**. Then we write in the clues we want.

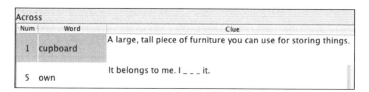

5. Next we click on **Export** and **Create Standard V6 page**.

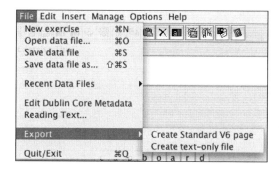

6. Now we're going to import the crossword into Moodle. Make sure Moodle is showing the **Hot Potatoes** activity.

Go to **Site Administration** | **Activities** | **Manage Activities**.

If the eye in the **Hide/Show** column is shut, click on it to open it.

Activities

Activity module	Activities	Version	Hide/Show	Delete	Settings
Assignment	8	2007101511	👁	Delete	Settings
Book	5	2008081402	👁	Delete	Settings
Chat	3	2007101509	👁	Delete	Settings
? Choice	3	2007101509	👁	Delete	
Database	4	2007101513	👁	Delete	Settings
Dimdim Web Meeting	2	2005031000	👁	Delete	Settings
Flash Card Set	1	2008051100	👁	Delete	
Forum	15	2007101512			Settings
Game	4	2009010502	👁	Delete	
Glossary	10	2007101509	👁	Delete	Settings
Glossary Cardbox	2	2006042900	👁	Delete	
Hot Potatoes Quiz	0	2007101511	👁	Delete	Settings

7. Let's go back to our course page. Click on **Turn editing on**, and choose **Hot Potatoes Quiz** from the drop-down menu.

8. Now we complete the set-up page for the Hot Potatoes quiz. Click on **Choose or upload a file...** to upload the new crossword from our computer. See the section on uploading files if you have problems with this.

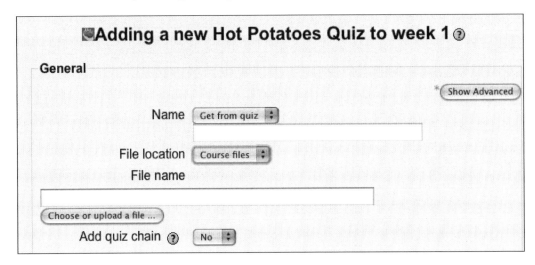

[132]

Settings	Details
Add quiz chain	If we choose **Yes**, this becomes part of a chain of Hot Potatoes quizzes that have identical settings. If we choose **No**, this will be a stand-alone quiz.
Display	Let's choose **best** for **Output format** to get the highest quality version available.

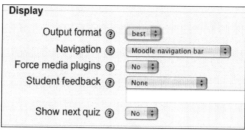

For Navigation we have a choice between:

- **Moodle navigation bar**, which is the standard top bar.

- **Moodle navigation frame**, which puts the standard bar in a separate frame at the top of the quiz.

- **Embedded IFRAME**, which puts the Moodle navigation bar in the same bar as the quiz.

- **Hot Potatoes Navigation buttons**, which provides Hot Potatoes' own navigation buttons.

- **A single 'give up' button**, which students can click on to leave the test. The other navigation elements aren't present when we choose this.

- **None**, which means no navigation aids at all. Students are returned to Moodle on completion of the quiz.

Let's choose the first one, so that Hot Potatoes fits into Moodle as seamlessly as possible.

If we choose **yes** for **Force media plugins**, the quiz will override any other settings we have, and will allow Hot Potatoes to use media with the following extensions: **avi, mpeg, mpg, mp3, mov, wmv**. These are different types of audio recording formats and, are only useful if our Hot Potatoes quiz includes recordings, which it doesn't. So let's uncheck **Force media plugins** for now.

Reports	If we choose **Yes** for **Enable click reporting**, Moodle will store records of every request for a hint that the student makes. This can be useful for teachers trying to identify which were the difficult items in a quiz.

9. Click on **Save and display** and we now have the crossword working in our Moodle.

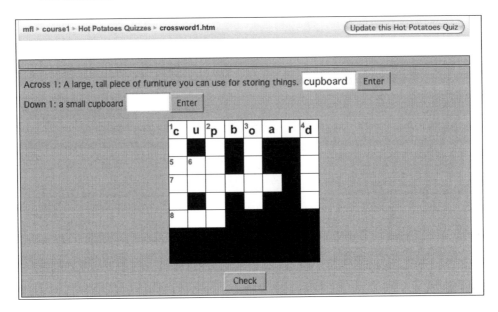

Activity 10: Using a Database to set up categorized vocabulary lists

Aim: Help students set up personal vocabulary lists

Moodle modules: Database

Extra programs: None

Ease of setup: ***

So far we've looked at several ways of building vocabulary lists. In *Activity 1* we built a simple class glossary. In *Activity 8* we set up a personal glossary for users to use independently. The personal glossary is simple to set up and easy to use, but there may be times when we'd like a more sophisticated personal glossary. That's what this activity will set up. The database allows us to build and customize vocabulary repositories for each student.

The reason this activity has come nearer the end of the chapter is because it's slightly more complex to set up. A simpler but more comprehensive solution will arrive if group mode gets added to the Glossary module, but that doesn't exist at the time of this writing.

This is what we're aiming for. The result looks clean and simple.

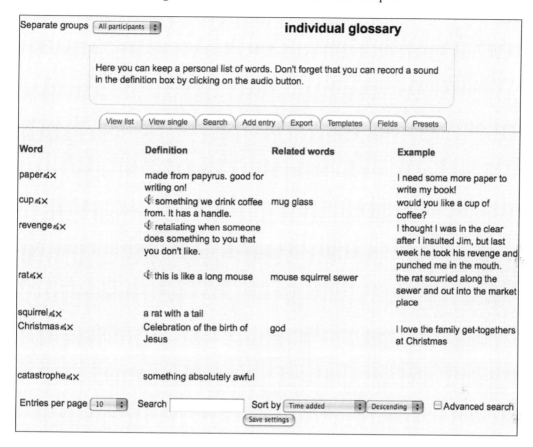

Here's how to do it

1. Set up a database. To do that, click on **Turn editing on,** which is on the course page.

2. Click on **Add an activity...** and add **Database** from the drop-down menu.

3. Make sure we include the following settings. Other settings are optional.

Settings	Details
Common module settings	Check **Visible groups**. That will mean that individual groups can only edit their own databases, but all groups can see each other's databases.

Groups

Don't set groups to **Separate groups**. If you do that, students won't be able to add entries.

4. Click on **Save and display**.

5. Next, we'll set up the fields for our database.

Fields

"Fields" is the database term for each category of information that we enter into our database.

We'll need to create separate fields for every part of each record.

Sensible fields for this particular database would be:

- ○ Word
- ○ Definition
- ○ Related words
- ○ Example

Let's do that.

6. Click on the **Fields** tab and so that we can create our first field:

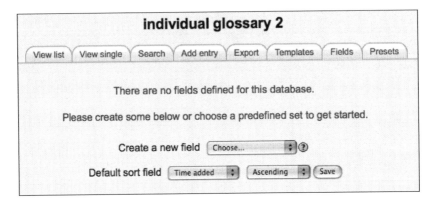

Now click on **Create a new field**, and choose **Text**.

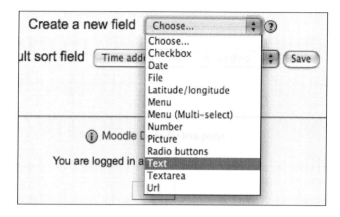

In the **Field name** let's write the name of the category we want in our first column—**word**.

In the **Field description**, let's put **write your new word here**. That's what teachers and students will read when they add words to the database later on.

Let's not check **Allow autolink,** because we don't want individuals' words to be linked to all the texts in Moodle.

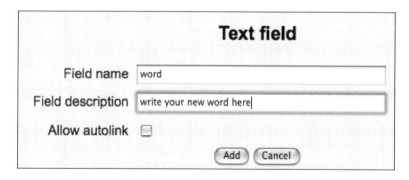

7. Now create a new field for the definition.

   Again, click on **create a new field**, and choose **text area.**

   In the **Field name**, let's write **definition.**

   In the **Field description**, put **write the definition here.**

   Don't check **Allow autolink.**

8. Now let's follow the same process (Steps 6 and 7) for two more fields, which we'll call **related words** and **example**. I suggest we make **related words** a **text field** and **example** a **text area**.

Formatting the data view

What we've done so far is set up the spaces for storing our data—the words. We next need to find a way of presenting the words in an orderly way. We do that by creating views. Our next step is to format these views. Let's start with the list view. That is where we format the list of the database entries. You may find that the default views for the other views are okay as they are.

1. Click on **Templates | List template**.

2. First of all, let's create the **Header**. That's the header row of our list of words.

   Create a table by clicking on the table icon 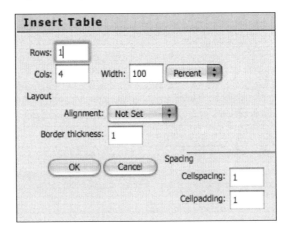. Choose **1** row, **4** columns.

   We need to decide whether to show table cell borders or not. The default border thickness is 1 (pixel), which is a very thin line. Let's go for that.

3. Click on **OK** to save the settings.

   Now let's write in the words we chose as our headers.

   This is what the final version of the header will look like:

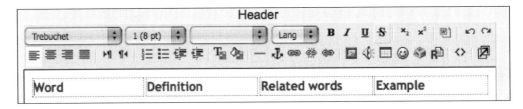

4. Now let's fill the **Repeated entry** box.

   Create a table by clicking on the table icon. Choose **1** row, **4** columns.

   Again, decide whether you want to show table cell borders or not.

5. Now click inside the first cell.

   Click on **[[word]]** in the **Available tags** column. It will be transferred to your first cell.

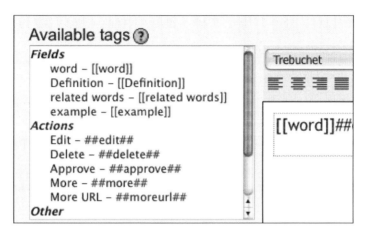

   In the same cell, also click on **##edit##** and **##delete##**. This will provide your students with useful edit and delete icons for their words.

6. Click inside the second cell, and click on **[[definition]]** in the **Available tags** column.

7. Do the same thing for **[[related words]]** in the third cell and **[[example]]** in the fourth cell.

   We can also change the font face and font color or background color if we want to make the database look a bit nicer. Click on the icons in the editor menu to do that—top left-hand button for font faces and for font colors.

   This is what the final version of the **Repeated entry** box will look like:

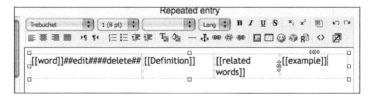

8. Now we've finished, let's click on **Save template** at the bottom of the page.

Well done! It's a bit fiddly getting the view right, but it's worth it. The database is now ready for students to add entries. If you have set up groups (see Chapter 2, *Getting Started with Moodle* for help with this), then each student will only be able to see his/her own vocabulary database, in addition to the teachers, who can view all databases.

Database not visible?

Don't forget … students will have to start inputting their own vocabularies before they can see anything. Also, if we as course teachers have added some words to try out the system, we'll need to delete them unless we want all students to see them.

9. To add words, students click on the database activity on their course page. They add the four bits of information:

- Word
- Definition
- Related words
- Example

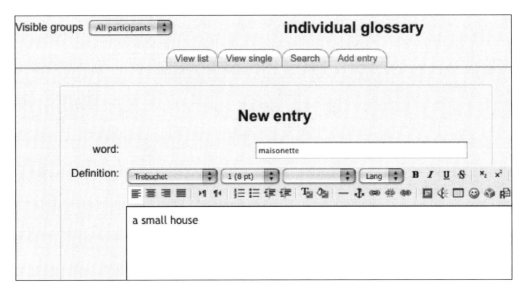

Then they click on **Save and view** or **Save and add another**.

Activity 11: Creating a gap-fill using the Quiz module

Aim: Help students predict and practice vocabulary based on a given context.

Moodle modules: Quiz

Extra programs: Audacity needed for *Variation 2*

Ease of setup: ***

We're more than likely to want to test our students' memory and knowledge of vocabulary at some point. And testing is one of the things Moodle does best, which is why the whole of Chapter 9, *Assessment* is devoted to it. Moodle has a Quiz module with many different task types: short answers, multiple choice, true/false, matching, and several more. The Quiz module may seem a bit daunting at first, but if we work steadily through an example and see how quizzes are organized in Moodle, it shouldn't take too long to feel comfortable with it. Once you've learned how to use it, you can use it to test listening, writing, reading, speaking, and grammar, too.

Hot Potatoes

If you want a simpler option, use Hot Potatoes. This is an easy-to-use external program which lets you make a variety of quizzes, and is quite intuitive to use. We can import Hot Potatoes quizzes directly into Moodle by adding a Hot Potatoes activity to your course. The disadvantages are that we will not have so much statistical information on our students' attempts afterwards, and we'll have less choice in setting up question types. See Chapter 2, *Getting Started with Moodle* for more information about Hot Potatoes, and see *Activity 9* for an example.

If you're still reading, then you've decided to take the plunge. You won't regret it, as the results will look good.

We'll look at just three variations of the Quiz module in this activity. *Variation 1* uses text as the stimulus for students to complete gaps. That's a great way to use the context to work out what the best word is. *Variation 2* has students doing a gap-fill, but this time they listen to a recording first. This can be a fun way to learn vocabulary. There's help on using the recording program Audacity in Chapter 2, *Getting Started with Moodle*. The two examples in *Variation 3* show how we can use pictures as part of a gap-fill activity. Pictures often provide an attractive stimulus that makes it easier and more interesting for students to complete gaps.

As we'll see, one of the other helpful features in Moodle is that we can organize it so that students get quick feedback on their efforts. That way they should feel motivated to go on. And we will have some gratification for the hard work of producing this activity in the first place.

Variation 1: Using a text as a stimulus for a gap-fill

What we're aiming to do here is reproduce a gap-fill that we could easily use in class. The big advantage of Moodle is that students can take their time, do it when it suits them, and get quick feedback on their efforts.

We start with a text like this:
Everyday John got up early to check the post. Why was it taking so long to reply? He urgently wanted to get the all-important letter. What would he do if he didn't get the job?

As an example, we'll remove the words **post** and **get** from the text so that the gap-fill (called **cloze** test in Moodle) looks like this:
Everyday John got up early to check the _____. Why was it taking so long to reply? He urgently wanted to get the all-important letter. What would he do if he didn't ____ the job?

Here's how to do it

1. On your course page, click on **Turn editing on**. Then click on **Add an activity....**

Adding to existing quizzes

If you already have a quiz that you want to add a matching question to, just open the quiz instead and go to Step 4.

2. We're going to make a quiz question, so choose **Quiz** from the drop-down menu.

3. Complete the set-up page. See Chapter 2, *Getting Started with Moodle* if you need help with this. Remember that a quiz activity is a collection of quiz questions, not just this particular question. So a good name will be something like **Week 1 test**.

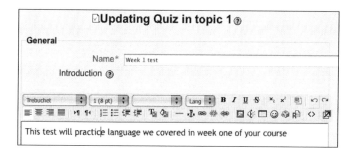

When we have finished, click on **Save and display**. Don't worry if **Save and return to course** gets clicked on by mistake. Simply find the activity we have just created on the course page, and click on the hand icon to edit it.

4. Lots of people get puzzled here. Where's the quiz gone? Well, in fact we've just produced the quiz wrapper. The next steps will produce the actual questions for our quiz.

    From the **Question bank**, go to **Create a new question**, and choose **Embedded Answers (Cloze)** from the drop-down menu.

5. This takes us to the introduction page for our new quiz question, as opposed to the quiz activity. And just to recap, since this is often confusing to teachers, the front page (Step 2) gives general information about the quiz (availability, etc.), and this introduction page provides specific information about this quiz question, **Embedded Answers**, only.

Adding embedded answers (cloze)

Settings	Details
Category	Decide which category of quizzes you want your quiz to belong to.
Question name	Let's give our question a name. How about **cloze 1**?
Question text	Now enter the text. To make the gaps work, you have to supply some extra information in brackets for each gap. The brackets look like this: { }.
	It should look like this:
|  | ```
Everyday John got up early to check
the {:SHORTANSWER:~=post}. Why was it
taking so long to reply? He urgently
wanted to get the all-important letter.
What would he do if he didn't ¬¬¬¬¬¬{:
SHORTANSWER:~=get} the job?
``` |
```

Don't forget to:

- Put the correct answer in braces: { }
- Put a colon after the type of answer: SHORTANSWER:
- Put ~= before the correct answer

This is what the edited set-up page will look like:

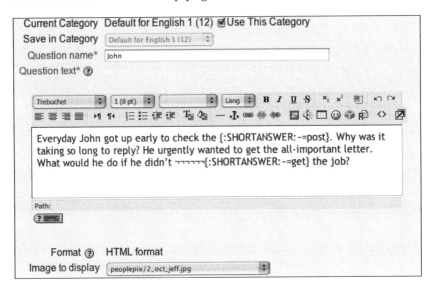

Enhancing your gaps

We can also provide feedback by putting a # after the answer. For example, {:SHORTANSWER:~=post#well done!}.

We can also reward partially-correct answers. To do this, we need to add the following: {:SHORTANSWER:~=post#well done! ~%50%mail#nearly right!}.

In that example, the ~ precedes the next set of feedback, and the %50% indicates what percentage of the mark the user will get.

We can also add an image to the text. See Chapter 2, *Getting Started with Moodle* for help with uploading images to Moodle.

Remember that the gap-fill is not case sensitive.

6. Once we've written the text, click **decode and verify the question text** to make sure we've included the text, answer type, and feedback that we want. We can go back and edit it if necessary.

7. We've nearly completed the activity, but not quite. The quiz activity we've just created now appears in the **Question bank**, but it's not in the course yet. As a final action, we need to click on the left-pointing arrow ❮❮ against our new activity to move it into our quiz. If you can't see the arrows, you might need to click on the **Quiz** tab:

But note that we can't add or edit questions when students are already in the middle of attempts on one of the quiz questions.

Adding more questions

You could now add other quiz questions if you so wished. Just go back to Step 4.

Our activity question is now ready to use—finally! We can check what it looks like by going to the course page, clicking on the activity, and then switching to **Student** view.

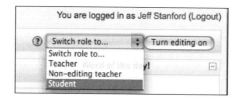

Then if we click on the quiz we've just created, we can see what the quiz looks like for students. Students can try it out by clicking on the quiz link on the course page. This is what they'll see:

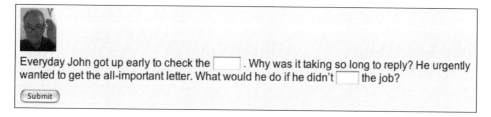

We can check how well they're doing by clicking on the activity in our normal view and then clicking on results. This takes us to the gradebook. You'll find lots of information on the gradebook in Chapter 9, *Assessment*.

Variation 2: Completing the lyrics of a song from an audio file using Audacity

One of the great things about Moodle is that it allows us to combine lots of different media in our quest for learning. So, as a particularly enjoyable way of practicing vocabulary is to listen out for words in a song, this variation does just that. First of all, we need to choose a song we'd like our class to listen to. Obviously, we want it to be fun and useful at the same time. If we choose a good song, our students will be singing it to themselves a lot, and will learn that vocabulary in no time at all. If for any reason you don't want other people to have access to your song, don't forget that a course enrolment key will stop non-authorized people from entering it. See Chapter 2, *Getting Started with Moodle* for more information on that.

If you can't find a good, copyright-free song, you could consider singing it yourself or getting a colleague or friend with a good voice to sing it.

Here's how to do it

Edit Step 5 in *Variation 1* so that the introduction includes an audio of the song you want to use. Don't forget that you'll need the lyrics to create the gap-fill script. See Chapter 2, *Getting Started with Moodle* if you need help for uploading audio files.

Making audio files work

Make sure the media filter is set to on.

Learn how to create a mini player in Chapter 2, *Getting started with Moodle*.

This is what the song gap-fill based on *Old MacDonald had a farm* will look like when it's finished:

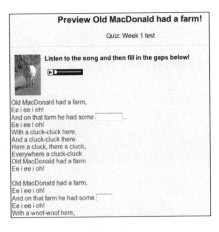

Variation 3: Completing texts based on charts and other images

Images make a lasting impact on students. They often make it much easier to understand language, and they are an important part of our daily lives. So another engaging way of building gap-fill exercises is to include images as part of the information that students need to understand.

Let's try this out with a few examples. We'll need to prepare an image that we want students to transfer information from. For example:

- A family tree
- A picture of an activity

Next, we need to write a task that uses the image. Let's try out the following examples.

Example 1: Family tree diagram

In this example, students look at a diagram of a family tree and deduce information from it, which helps them complete a text. We need to produce an image like this one and import it into the introduction to our question.

Here's how to do it

1. We'll need to edit Step 5 in *Variation 1* to import the picture. Otherwise, the steps are the same. We can produce a simple diagram like this in a simple drawing program.

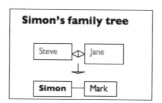

There are links to many drawing programs at `http://www.drawingcoach.com/free-drawing-programs.html`.

2. Once we've produced the drawing, we click on the import image button ▨ in the HTML editing menu to upload it and import it into our instruction page.

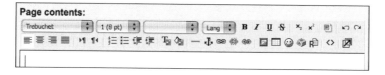

See Chapter 2, *Getting Started with Moodle* if you need more help with uploading images.

3. Once we've uploaded the image, we'll need to change the text to something like this:

This is Simon's family tree! Simon is 24 years old. He is Mark's { : SHORTANSWER:~=brother}**. They look like twins but Mark is one year older. He's Jane's** {:SHORTANSWER:~=son}.

Here's what the set-up page looks like:

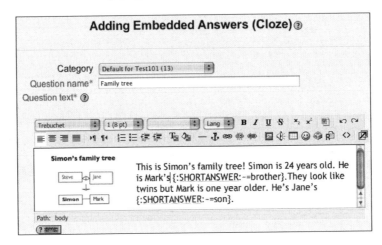

And here's what the final version will look like:

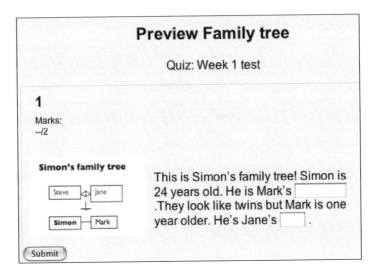

Example 2: Picture of an activity

The last example shows how we can take an interesting photo and encourage students to think about it via a gap-fill. The following picture taken in 2008, for example, shows all sorts of contrasts and is interesting to look at in its own right. What's that building at the back? Why's a man holding up a Soviet flag?

Here's how to do it

As in the last example, we need to edit Step 5 in *Variation 1* to import the picture and change the text. Otherwise the steps are the same as in the first variation. The text below gives an example of varied feedback depending on the correctness of the answer.

Example Text:

This is what the Bolshoi Theatre, Moscow, looked like in October 2008. What a lot of contrasts! There is a man holding a {:SHORTANSWER:~=flag#well done! ~%50%banner#nearly right!} **wishing things were back the way they were in the Soviet** {:SHORTANSWER:~=Union#well done! ~=period#well done!~%50%time#nearly right!}. **There are two children running around. Pink for** {:SHORTANSWER:~=girls#well done! ~%50%girl#nearly right!} **and blue for boys. Things haven't changed. You can spot the two policemen because of their wide** {:SHORTANSWER:~=caps#well done! ~%50%hats#nearly right!}. **What's all that** {:SHORTANSWER:~=scaffolding#well done! ~%50%building#nearly right!} **in front of the Bolshoi? Well, workers are busy** {:SHORTANSWER:~= restoring#well done! ~%50%changing#nearly right!} **it to its former pre-revolutionary glory.**

Notice that the gap after **Soviet** has two correct answers. Here's what one student's attempt looks like:

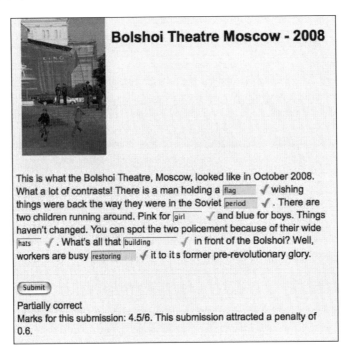

It's really worth reviewing students' progress on these tests once they start using them. We can do that by clicking the quiz activity on the course page, then on the **Results** tab.

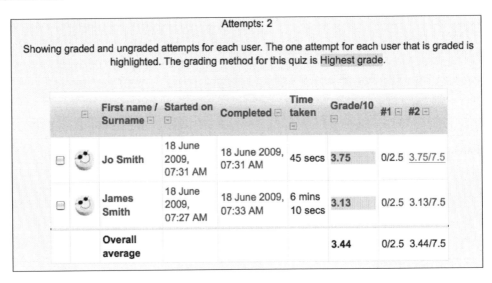

The **#1** and **#2** refer to the quiz questions we have set up. By clicking on them, we can see the students' actual responses. Maybe they thought of something we didn't. We can use that information to edit the gap-fill text. A useful thing to do, for example, is to partially reward more partially correct answers. One student wrote "Soviet Country" instead of "Soviet Union". We could amend the gap like this:

```
{:SHORTANSWER:~=Union#well done! ~=period#well done!~%50%time#nearly
right! ~%20%country#you're on the right track, but think of the
official name of the country!}
```

Gradebook/Importing files

See Chapter 10, *Extended Activities* for much more information on how to access, interpret, and export quiz scores in the Moodle gradebook.

Questions can be imported into the Moodle quiz module in a large number of other formats, such as Hot Potatoes and XML. See Chapter 2, *Getting Started with Moodle* for more information on Hot Potatoes.

Activity 12: Creating a text/text matching activity using the Quiz module

Aim: Help students create associations between words and other words/images/audio

Moodle modules: Quiz

Extra programs: Audacity needed for *Variation 2*

Ease of setup: ***

It's well known that making associations between words and other objects, thoughts or sounds, is a good way to learn them. These other things can be images, sounds, other words, movements, emotions. Buzan's website `http://www.buzanworld.com/` is a good source of information on this.

There is Quiz question type in Moodle that lets us set up a matching question, which helps students make associations. The way this works is that pairs of items are arranged in two separate columns. The student matches them by choosing an item from a drop-down menu in the right-hand column.

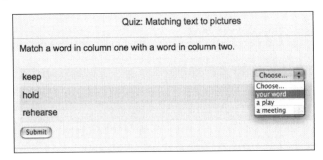

Lots of teachers get put off setting up Quiz module questions, because they are a little more complex than most of the other activities in Moodle. The pay-off is that once we've got them working, they can be a powerful tool for assessing our students and helping them learn in an enjoyable way. We can edit questions and feedback on our questions easily. We can access a wide range of statistics, and we can build up a versatile question bank. But … if these things aren't important, an easier suggestion would be to create our matching question in Hot Potatoes and then import it into Moodle, as suggested in *Activity 9*.

So, what things can we match? Well, the items in each column can only be text, but the introduction to the exercise can include images, video, or audio. When students do the matching activity, they are presented with a drop-down menu of all the possible matching items.

Let's look at three variations. The first one matches words as in the screenshot above. The second one matches pictures with text, and the last variation matches audio recordings with text. The last two take a bit more time to prepare, of course, but feedback from students is often positive when pictures and audio are included.

Variation 1: Matching words

There are all sorts of things we could match. The following are a few examples:

Collocations	Words that frequently go with other words, such as "hold" + "a meeting" or "as a" + "result"
Antonyms	"black" + "white"
Common replies	"how are you?" + "I'm fine, thanks."

In this variation we'll set up a collocations-matching exercise.

Here's how to do it

1. Click on **Turn editing on** on our course page. Then click on **Add an activity....** We're going to make a quiz question, so choose **Quiz**.

2. Complete the set-up page. We can give an introduction and details about the sort of general feedback we want to give. See Chapter 2, *Getting Started with Moodle* for help with this. Remember that a quiz activity is a collection of quiz questions, not just this particular question. So a good name will be something like **Week 1 test**.

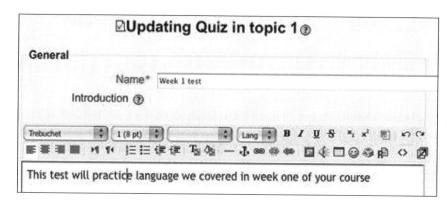

Now we have finished. Click on **Save**.

Alternatively
Open an existing quiz where we want to add a matching question. To open an existing quiz, click on the activity link in the course. Then click on the **Edit** tab. We can now go straight to creating another question.

3. We are now inside the quiz environment. From the **Question bank**, go to **Create a new question**, and choose **Matching** from the drop-down menu.

Adding a matching question

4. We now come to the introduction page for our new quiz question. Don't forget that whereas the front page gives general information about the quiz activity (availability, etc.), this question introduction page provides specific information about the quiz question. It's easy to mix them up.

Settings	Details
Category	Decide which category of quizzes we want our question to belong to. (See Chapter 9, *Assessment* for information on categories.)
Question name	Give our question a name. Let's call this one **Collocations 1**.
General box	Write the instructions for the activity. This is where we would include audio, video, or images if we want them.
Question text	Let's write **Match a word in column one with a word in column two**.

5. Now enter the words for column one, one at a time in the **Question** box, giving the **Answer** below.

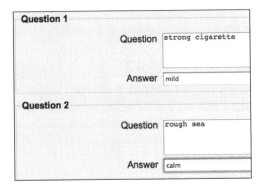

6. Click on **Save**. The quiz activity question we've just created now appears in the **Question bank**. It's not in the course yet. Just one more thing to do: click on the left pointing arrow « against the new activity to move it into the quiz. Sometimes, teachers end up with a question bank but no arrows. If that happens, click on the **Quiz** tab and the arrows will appear.

 Expanding the quiz
We could now add other quiz activities if we want.

7. Our activity question is now ready to use. Not such a big deal after all!

We can check what it looks like by going to the course page, clicking on the activity, and then switching to **Student** view.

Then if we click on the quiz we've just created, we can see what the quiz looks like for students. Students can try it out by clicking on the quiz link on the course page.

We can check how well they're doing by clicking on the activity in our normal view and then clicking on results. This takes us to the gradebook. There is lots of information on the gradebook in Chapter 9, *Assessment*.

Variation 2: Creating a picture/text matching activity using the Quiz module

The only difference between *Variation 1* and *Variation 2* is that we're adding labeled pictures. Our quiz question will get students to match the labels with their definitions.

Here's how to do it

Stages 1-3 are the same as in *Variation 1*. We will cover the next steps here.

4. In the introduction box, import the pictures we want to include in our matching task. Don't forget to number them. The numbers will go in column one below.

Our **General** box would look something like this:

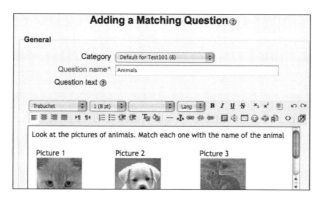

 Uploading images: Go to Chapter 2, *Getting Started with Moodle* for help with uploading images.

5. For the questions below the **General** box, write.

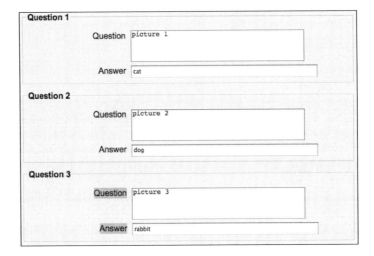

To finish off, just follow Steps 6 and 7 from *Variation 1*. And voilà! We have a matching question with pictures.

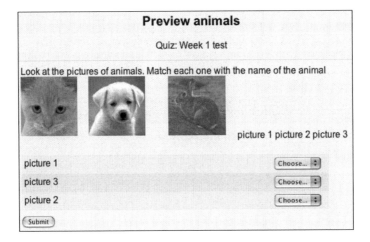

Variation 3: Creating an audio/text matching activity using the Quiz module

In this variation we'll have a question introduction text which includes sound recordings. See Chapter 2, *Getting Started with Moodle* for help with creating recordings. Each recording will be labeled, and the students will match the labels with their definitions. This is what it will look like:

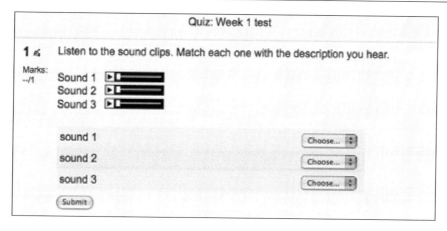

This is a great way to help students listen for the meaning of a word. So sound clip 1 could be a description like "this is the first thing I do in the morning". And the matching word could be "yawn". Of course, the other verbs shouldn't be possible answers.

Sound clip 2 could be a description like "this is what I do to my clothes after I wash them", which would match with "rinse". And the third clip could be something like "this is what I do to the food in my mouth", which would match the word "chew".

Here's how to do it

Steps 1–3 are the same as in *Variation 1*. We will cover the next steps here.

4. In the **Question text** box, import the sound clips we want to include in our matching task. Don't forget to number them. The numbers will go in column one below.

    Our **General box** would look something like this:

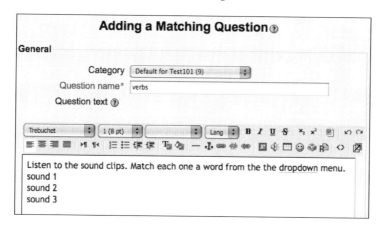

There's a section on importing audio files and creating flash players in Chapter 2, *Getting Started with Moodle*.

Mini-Flash players on your web page

Don't forget that the Mini-Flash players only appear after you save the page.

5. For the questions below the **Question text** box, write:

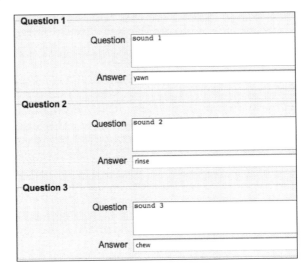

Keeping the same order of questions

Don't forget to uncheck **shuffle questions** on the quiz set-up page so that the sound clips remain in the same order as we write them.

To finish off, just follow Steps 6 and 7 from *Variation 1*. And now we have a matching question with sounds!

4
Speaking Activities

Speaking and listening are at the heart of most people's foreign language learning. Moodle makes it easy to practice speaking by helping students at various stages in the development of their speaking skills. For example, they can practice identifying sounds they need to use. They can also do lots of helpful repetition practice—think how that can save your voice. They can prepare vocabulary and other language material for class activities, and they can actually practice speaking on Moodle. With those ideas in mind, this chapter's Moodle speaking activities are divided into four areas:

- Pronunciation—identifying sounds
- Listening and repeating activities
- Preparing for speaking in class
- Online speaking activities

Pronunciation exercises: Activities 1 and 2

Exercises like these on Moodle can help low-level students practice basic pronunciation by identifying correct sounds and matching sounds. To prepare these exercises, we'll use core Moodle modules together with NanoGong or Audacity (or your preferred recording software) to produce the recordings. Audacity is a free recording program. There's more information about it in Chapter 2, *Getting Started with Moodle* and a discussion of the pros and cons of using it in Activity 5.

Listening and repeating activities: Activities 3 and 4

Being able to repeat new or difficult sounds ad infinitum is a helpful feature of Moodle. Students can practice saying things such as individual sounds, word stress, intonation, as well as longer utterances. Students' recordings can be uploaded for teachers to check, or students can compare them to original versions themselves.

Preparing for speaking in class: Activities 5 to 7

The flexibility with time that an online system like Moodle gives allows students to do some useful preparation for speaking activities before they come to class. They can prepare their roles in role-plays, debates, or other activities. They can also think about and practice vocabulary and grammar or idiomatic language that they want to use in advance of an activity that will need it. For example, they could use a wiki to build up ideas on pros and cons for a debate before they actually have the debate in class or in an online forum.

Online speaking activities: Activities 8 and 9

Students can submit their NanoGong recordings to the teacher or just play them to make their own assessment of themselves or each other.

The activities within each of these four sections are ordered according to the ease of setup.

NanoGong

Unfortunately, Moodle doesn't currently have an in-built recording device, but fear not. There is an excellent add-on module, called **NanoGong,** which allows us to record directly onto Moodle web pages via an extra audio button. I'd also recommend installing the add-on modules OUblog and OUwiki, which will allow you to use NanoGong in blogs and wikis on Moodle.

Installing add-on modules

You'll need to get your Moodle administrator to install these three add-on modules. There are instructions in Chapter 2, *Getting Started with Moodle* on this.

Once you have NanoGong, you and your students can record, play back, and save your audio recordings as WAV files through a simple audio player. WAV is one of the many formats available for saving recordings. You're probably familiar with the popular MP3 format used in MP3 players.

This is what the Moodle web page editing menu will look like with the extra NanoGong button:

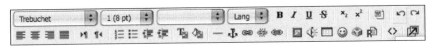

Notice that there's a new audio button . To use NanoGong, simply click on the button and a NanoGong recorder will appear.

Click on the red button to record, the square button to stop, the play button to play back the recording. The **x1.0** button allows us to speed up or slow down the recording during playback, which is a handy feature for students who are struggling to understand a recording and need to play it more slowly.

We can record about 5 minutes of sound. The quality's fairly good, and it's a convenient way of recording. We have the option to write a **Caption** here that will appear on the web page. Once you're happy with our recording, click on **OK** and an audio icon will appear in our web page.

Now all our students have to do is click on the audio button and the NanoGong player will appear. Here's an example of what we could write on a Moodle web page with a NanoGong recording:

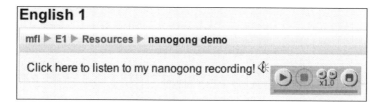

The Save button on the right of the panel allows students and teachers to save the file to their computers. The audio file format choices are WAV, FLV, and SPEEDEX. The default WAV files are readable in most audio players. So it's probably best to stick with that. But, note that the Moodle Flash player does not play WAV files. You can convert a WAV file to an MP3 file in Audacity. To do that, open the WAV file in Audacity. Then export it as an MP3 file. See Chapter 2, *Getting Started with Moodle* for help with this.

Possible delays: If you record a long NanoGong file, it can take well over 20 seconds to load, depending on the speed of your connection. A 5-minute WAV file will be at least 6 MB in size—that's quite large. If you make short recordings of up to a minute, NanoGong works quickly and efficiently.

NanoGong not working?

If for some reason you can't install NanoGong on your Moodle, don't worry. Seven of the nine activities in this chapter don't need it. A slightly time-consuming workaround for you, the teacher, is to get your students to make recordings on their computers and email them to you. You can then create Flash audio players as described in Chapter 2, *Getting Started with Moodle*. Flash audio players look like the following and are built into Moodle: ▶▮━━━━━.

Here's an overview showing which activities require NanoGong:

Activity	Module	NanoGong
1	Forum	✘
2	Quiz	✘/✔
3	Database	✔
4	Mediacenter	✘
5	OUwiki	✔
6	Wiki	✘
7	Chat	✘
8	Blog	✘/✔
9	Assignment	✘/✔

Web conferencing: Another way of practicing speaking is through web conferencing. This is an online activity that allows us to interact with other people in real time. For example, it allows us to chat, see each other via our webcams, share views of our Desktop, share presentations, etc. There are now open source web conferencing programs, such as Dimdim and WiZiQ Live Class, which aren't covered in this book, even though they can be used with Moodle. As they become more reliable, they could be well worth using in your online classes to practice synchronous speaking activities. See `http://www.dimdim.com/products/what_is_dimdim.html for more information`:

Activity 1: Helping students improve pronunciation using the Forum module

Aim: Provide oral feedback on students' pronunciation

Moodle modules: Forum

Extra programs: None

Ease of setup: **

How often have you listened to students' pronunciation errors, and thought "I wish there was an easy way for them to listen to correct versions and repeat them"? Well, one way Moodle can help out is providing a recording of the correct versions for students to listen to in their own time and as many times as they want. We can collect examples of errors we hear and then record a short commentary with examples of more natural versions.

Here are some examples of the sorts of pronunciation errors students might make that we could correct.

- Individual sounds.
- Elision (where a sound should be left out). For example, the "t" in "football".
- Assimilation (where the first of two adjacent sounds changes to match the second one). For example, "Great Britain" sounds like "Grape Britain".

- Intonation. This is used to express a grammar or attitudinal function. Students may benefit from:
    - Making their initial pitch higher to show more interest
    - Having a clear rise or fall on the last content word of the sentence
    - Practicing marked stress where a word gets extra emphasis

In the example below, we'll use a forum to store the recorded commentary. The advantage of a forum is that we can also include written commentaries, and students can easily respond with questions or spoken examples of pronunciation. Moodle forums don't allow us to use NanoGong. So we'll create a Flash audio player. That has the advantage of allowing us to make a recording longer than 5 minutes, if we need to. This is what our forum introduction will look like when it's finished:

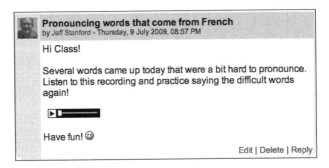

Using other modules for storing recordings

If you don't want to use a forum, create a web page instead. Then you can use NanoGong to record your commentary. See Chapter 3, *Vocabulary Activities*, *Activity 3* for help with setting up a web page. The introduction to this chapter will guide you through recording with NanoGong.

You could also consider using a database if you plan to build up a bank of recordings and want students to be able to see categorized errors. Or, if you simply want students to hear your commentary, you could consider making a podcast using the add-on Mediacenter block. See *Activity 3* for an example database and *Activity 5* for an example podcast.

Here's how to do it

Preparation

First we need to make a recording for our students to listen to.

Here's an example. Imagine that your students have been having problems with the pronunciation of words that come from French and you want to provide them with a few guidelines and examples. This is the sort of instruction you might include:

There are lots of French words used in English every day. Some of them are so common we don't even realize they're French. Occasionally, we need to make them sound a bit more French. Here are some words that came up last week. One word was 'debut'. Don't forget:

You shouldn't pronounce the 't' at the end. Try saying it: 'debut'... 'debut'. Another word that came up was 'chauffeur'. That's not a 'ch' sound as in 'church' but a 'sh' sound as in 'shower'. Try saying it: 'chauffeur'. Notice that the stress is on the second syllable 'eur' 'chauffeur'. Etc.

1. Make a recording of this instruction using your preferred recording program. If you don't have one already, I'd recommend Audacity. See Chapter 2, *Getting Started with Moodle* for download details.

Practice makes perfect

If you're new to this, you might find that you need to record your commentary a few times to get the hang of it.

Leave a pause after key words to give students time to repeat.

Write down the keywords in the forum text so that students can read them, too.

Don't speak too fast.

If the students' level of understanding is low, make your recording of the introduction to the activity in their first language.

2. Save your recording as an MP3 file, by clicking on **Save As** in the **File** menu in Audacity, as in this screenshot. See Chapter 2, *Getting Started with Moodle* if you need help saving MP3 files in Audacity.

Activity

Now we'll set up the Moodle forum that will use this recording.

3. Click on **Turn editing on** on your course page. Then click on **Add an activity...**.

4. Choose **Forum**.

5. Complete the introductory page. See Chapter 2, *Getting Started with Moodle* if you need help with grades, outcomes, and common module settings. If you're uncertain, just leave them, but do pay attention to the following:

Settings	Details
Forum name	Let's call it **Pronunciation clinic**.
Forum type	Decide what type of forum you want. I suggest you choose either a single simple discussion (this may be the most appropriate if you only want one discussion on pronunciation) or a standard forum (that's useful if you want students to be able to start new threads on the forum). A thread is a new discussion within the same forum. The following screenshot shows us three threads: one on **adverbs**, one on a **pronunciation question**, and one on **like to go**.

As you can see, students start new threads to change the topic.

Forum introduction	Explain what the purpose of the forum is. In this case, it is to help students review their pronunciation, so you could write something like this:

Varying the introduction to the activity

You could also include a spoken introduction, images, or even video. Images could make the page more attractive, or focus students' attention on the activity. See Chapter 2, *Getting Started with Moodle* for help with uploading images and videos.

6. Click on **Save and display**. Your forum should look like this:

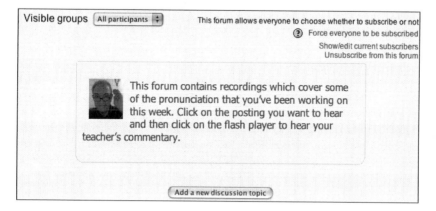

7. Next, click on **Add a new discussion topic**. Then start a new post. In the post, write an introduction to the recording. Upload the recording we made for this activity, following the instructions in Chapter 2, *Getting Started with Moodle* if you need help.

8. Now click on **Post to forum** at the bottom of the page. We can now see our forum posting with the mini Flash player. If students want to reply to our message with queries, they just click on **Reply**.

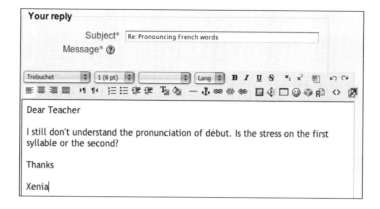

And after that, they click on **Post to forum**.

Activity 2: Creating a word stress matching activity using the Quiz module

Aim: Help students identify sounds

Moodle modules: Quiz

Extra programs: NanoGong

Ease of setup: ***

When students are at early stages of learning, matching exercises can be an effective way of helping them identify sounds. In this activity we'll use the Quiz module to create two variations of a matching exercise. In Variation 1, students will group sound patterns without hearing them, so no recording equipment is needed. In Variation 2, they will listen to sound recordings.

If you cut your teeth on the Quiz module in Chapter 3, *Vocabulary Activities*, *Activity 12*, you might enjoy having another go here. You can also use Hot Potatoes to prepare a quiz, but you can't record directly into Hot Potatoes. So Moodle is possibly easier to use for matching activities which include sound.

In a matching exercise, pairs of items are arranged in two separate columns. The items in each column can only be text, but the introduction to the exercise can include images, video, or audio.

Example 1: Word stress

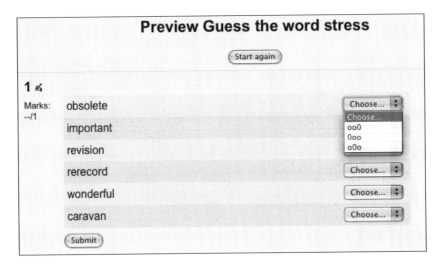

Here students have to decide whether the stress of a column 1 word like **wonderful** is on the first (**Ooo**), second (**oOo**), or third (**ooO**) syllable and match the word accordingly, choosing a stress pattern from the drop-down menu on the right.

Column 1	Column 2
wonderful	Ooo
caravan	Ooo
important	oOo
revision	oOo

Example 2: Sounds with audio

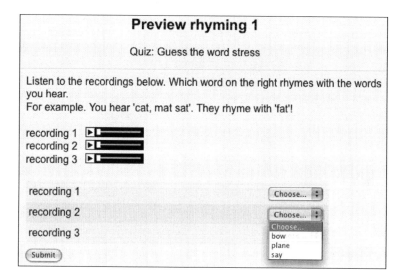

Here students hear an audio introduction, which includes a group of rhyming words. They have to match what they hear to another word with the same sound. In the following example, *pane, drain,* and *vein* in *recording 1/Column 1* rhyme with *stain* in *Column 2*.

This is the text that you would record:

recording 1: pane, drain, vein rhyme with…

recording 2: go, snow, throw rhyme with…

recording 3: ray, play, weigh rhyme with…

These are the matching columns you'd produce:

Column 1	Column 2
recording 1	stain
recording 2	blow
recording 3	eBay

Example 3: Intonation patterns

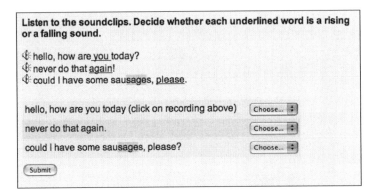

In this example students see a text with an underlined word. They click on the audio button and hear the utterance. They then decide whether the intonation is falling or rising and choose the corresponding intonation in column 2.

Other ideas

This activity type is useful for practicing:

- Word stress (as in Example 1)
- Individual sounds (matching words with different spellings but the same sound, like "sea" and "see", "sieve" and "give")
- Intonation (see Variation 2)

Variation 1: Getting students to identify word stress

Let's look in detail at how we can create the word stress matching question activity illustrated in *Example 1*.

Here's how to do it

1. We can either open an existing quiz and add a matching question to it or we can create a new quiz activity. To do that, we click on **Turn on editing** on the course home page. Then click on **Add an activity**. We're going to make a quiz question, so choose **Quiz.**

2. Complete the introduction page for the quiz activity (see Chapter 2, *Getting Started with Moodle* if you need help with this). When we have finished, click on **Save and Display**. Don't worry if you clicked on **Save and return to course** by mistake. Simply find the activity we have just created and click on the hand icon 🖎 to edit it.

3. We are now inside the quiz environment. From the **Question bank**, go to **Create a new question**, and choose **Matching** from the drop-down menu.

Adding a matching question

4. Now we come to the introduction page for our new quiz question. Whereas the front page gives general information about the quiz activity (availability, etc.), the question introduction page provides specific information about the quiz question.

Settings	Details
Category	Decide which category of quizzes we want our question to belong to (see Chapter 9 for information on categories). We can leave it as it is for now and change it later if necessary.
Question name	Now we give our question a name. Let's call it **Guess the word stress**.
General box	Write the instructions for the activity. This is where we would include audio, video, or images if we want them (see Variation 2 in a bit).
Question text	Let's write this: **Match a word in column one with the right stress pattern in column two.**

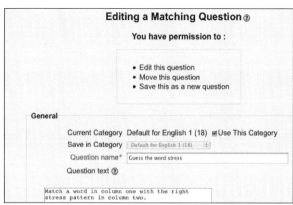

5. Now we enter the words in the first column, one at a time in each question box. In the answer box, we indicate the word stress using the **o** and **0** letters, where **0** represents the stressed syllable in each case. Here are the first three words. We can create more question boxes by clicking on the **3 more sets of blanks** button at the bottom of the page.

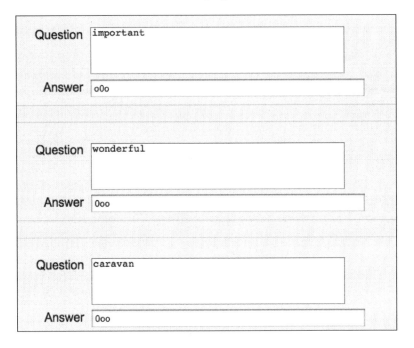

6. Click on **Save as new question**. The quiz activity question we've just created now appears in the **Question bank**. It's not in the course yet. Just one more thing to do: click on the left pointing arrow ❮❮ against the new activity to move it into the quiz.

7. Our activity question is now ready to use. We can check what it looks like by going to the course page, clicking on the activity, and then switching to **Student** view.

    Then if we click on the quiz we've just created, we can see what the quiz looks like for students. Students can try it out by clicking on the quiz link on the course page.

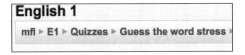

We can check how well they're doing by clicking on the activity in our normal view and then clicking on results. This takes us to the gradebook, which is covered in some detail in Chapter 9, *Assessment*.

There is a screenshot of the finished question in the introduction to this activity.

Variation 2: Getting students to identify intonation

In this variation the introduction text to our question includes sound recordings. The sound recordings can be individual sounds, examples of word stress, intonation, or any other aspect of pronunciation (see examples given in this activity). Each recording will be labeled, and the students will match the labels with their definitions. This is what we want to achieve:

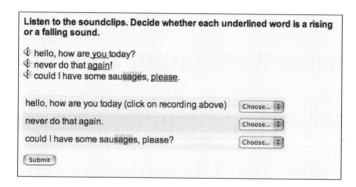

First you need to make sure that NanoGong is installed on your Moodle so that you can record directly into the instructions box. A slightly more fiddly alternative is to make recordings separately and import them into Moodle. See Chapter 2, *Getting Started with Moodle* for details on how to do this.

Here's how to do it

Stages 1-4 are the same as in Variation 1. We will cover the next steps here.

5. In the introduction box, write the instructions as seen in the last screenshot. The audio buttons are NanoGong recordings. Go back to the introduction to this chapter if you need to be reminded how to use them.

This is the text we read out for each recording:

Recording 1: hello, how are you today? (falling intonation on "you")

Recording 2: never do that again (falling intonation on "again")

Recording 3: could I have some sausages, please (rising intonation on "please")

The introduction text will look like this:

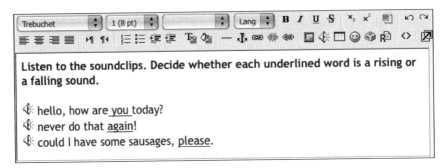

These are the matching columns we'll produce:

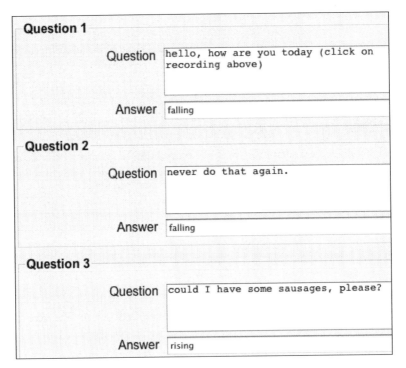

6. Click on **Save changes**. Our activity question is now ready to use.

Other ideas

Gradebook: See Chapter 9, *Assessment* for information on how to access, interpret, and export quiz scores in the Moodle gradebook.

Importing files: Questions can be imported into the Moodle quiz module in a large number of other formats such as WebCT, Hot Potatoes, and XML. See Chapter 2, *Getting Started with Moodle* for more information.

Activity 3: Adding a sound extension to vocabulary lists

Aim: Help students practice the pronunciation of words in their vocabulary lists

Moodle modules: Database

Extra programs: NanoGong

Ease of setup: *

It's often useful to be able to add sound to a student activity. This activity provides an extension to *Activity 10, Using a database to set up categorized vocabulary lists* in Chapter 3, *Vocabulary Activities*. The addition will mean that students can read a word, see its definition, look at related words, and hear how it's pronounced.

This is a fairly simple operation, and is a matter of adding a recording to your existing definition. Your enhanced database would now look something like this:

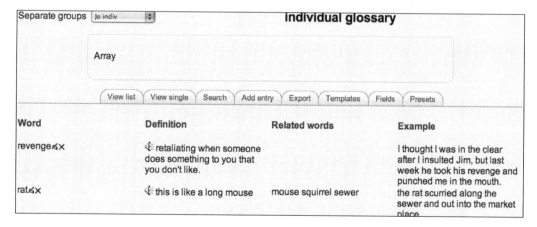

Here's how to do it

1. Click on the database you created in Chapter 3, *Vocabulary Activities*, *Activity 10*.

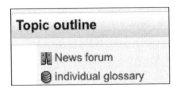

2. Now click on the editing icon next to the first word, **paper**.

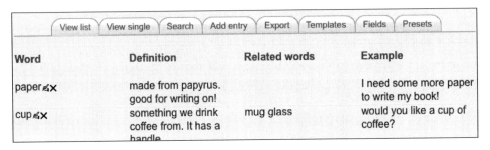

3. Click on the cursor to the left of the first word, **made**.

4. Now we click on the audio button in the editing menu and record the word **paper**, which is the word being defined here. See the introduction to this chapter if you need help with using the NanoGong audio button

5. Abracadabra! We now have a definition with a recording.

6. Click on **Save and view**. The recordings are now ready to be used. See the screenshot in the introduction.

Problems with NanoGong in database

If, by any chance, you have problems making your NanoGong recording appear in the Database module, don't forget that you can save the NanoGong recording to your computer and create a mini Flash player instead. Instructions for this are in Chapter 2, *Getting Started with Moodle*. It will then look like this instead:

Word	Definition	Related words	Example
paper ✍ ✗	▶ ▭▭▭▭	made from papyrus. good for writing on!	I need some more paper to write my book!

Other possibilities

*   Change the instructions so that students add their own pronunciation of words to their lists.

*   Use the group tool in Moodle to divide your class up.

*   Make each group consist of just one person so that individuals only contribute to their own lists or to group lists.

*   Set a rule that whoever provides the word and definition also makes the recording for the word.

Activity 4: Using OUwiki to help students learn by repeating

Aim: Help students practice speaking by listening and repeating

Moodle modules: OUwiki

Extra programs: NanoGong

Ease of setup: **

There is much value in helping students listen repeatedly to the targeted language. It helps them get used to the sounds and the meaning. This activity goes one step further as it allows students to listen to a model text and then to record their own version of the same text. The easiest way to organize this on Moodle is by using NanoGong to record and OUwiki to write the scripts and embed the sounds. Don't forget that NanoGong doesn't work in the normal Moodle Wiki.

In this example we're going to record a poem line by line. Poems often work well, because there is a strong rhythm, and they can be interesting and enjoyable as well as useful.

What it will look like

Each mini-recording will go in a table on a wiki. Students click on the audio button to hear the model. Then they record their own version next to it. Here's what the final version will look like:

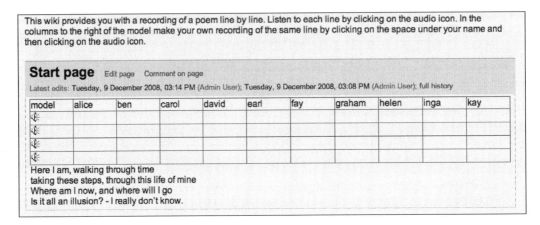

Here's how to do it

1. Click on **Turn editing on** in the top right-hand corner of the course home page.

2. Now click on **Add an activity...** and choose **OU wiki**.

3. Complete the introductory page. Pay particular attention to the following:

Settings	Details
Name	Now we give our question a name. Let's call it **Poem practice**.
Summary	This is what students will see when they open the OUwiki. Let's write this:
	This wiki provides you with a recording of a poem line by line. Listen to each line by clicking on the audio icon. In the columns to the right of the model make your own recording of the same line by clicking on the space under of your name and then clicking on the audio icon.

Settings	Details
Sub-wikis	There is a choice between:
	Single wiki for course: This means that everyone on the course sees the same wiki. That's what we'll choose for this activity. If you have a lot of students, it's worth creating groups and going for the next option. See Chapter 2, *Getting Started with Moodle* for information on creating groups.
	One wiki per group: This means that each group sees a totally different wiki according to what the group members contribute. Our introduction will still be the same.
	Separate wiki for every user: This could be useful if you don't want students to hear and see each other's contributions.
Time allowed for edit	Choose **No timeout**, as we want students to have as much time as they need when making their recordings.

See Chapter 2, *Getting Started with Moodle* for information on common module settings and outcomes.

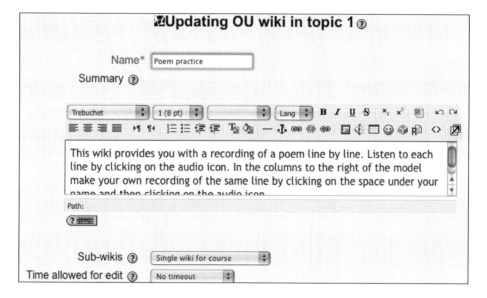

4. Click on **Save and display**.

5. Now click on **create a page**. This is where we set up the table with the model recording and the space for students to make their own recordings.

6. Imagine there are ten students who are going to use this wiki. Create a table with **11** columns and **5** rows by clicking on the table icon 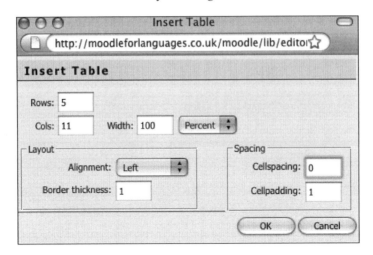.

We click on **OK** once we've entered the details.

The first column is for your recording. The other columns are for students to record their voices. So, label the first column **model**. Then label the other columns with the students' names. The rows are for you to record your 4-line poem, line by line.

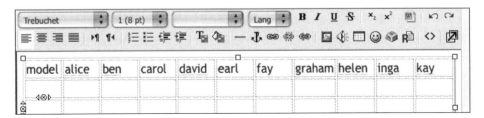

7. Click in the cell immediately under **model**. We need to do that because that's where we want to position the first recording.

8. Now we click on the audio icon in the editing menu.

9. Make a recording of the first line of the poem. There are full instructions on recording with NanoGong in the introduction to this chapter if you need them.

10. Next, click in the third row and record the next line. Do the same for every line of the poem. We can also write the full text at the bottom, too, to help students. The finished wiki will look like this:

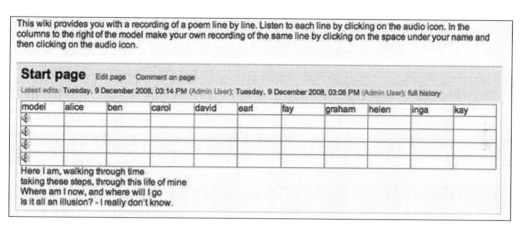

When students use the wiki, they will click on the model audio to hear it, then click in a cell in their own column, click on the audio icon in the editing menu, and record their own version. They do the same thing for each line just as we did.

Now your OUwiki is ready to use.

Assessing instead

If you want to assess students' attempts at pronouncing, you could adapt *Activity 9*.

Activity 5: Dialog Minus One—helping students build dialogs using a podcast

Aim: Help students participate in a dialog

Moodle modules: Mediacenter (Inwicast)

Extra programs: Audacity

Ease of setup: **

How can we use Moodle to help students prepare themselves for dialog work? Well, one way is to set up a recording where they hear just half the dialog and they have to provide the other half, using prompts that they can listen to independently. Let's call it **Dialog Minus One**. This sort of activity can help students listen carefully and get used to new words or expressions and practice new language functions such as interrupting, inviting, asking questions, and refusing. The big advantage of Moodle is that they can listen in their own time as often as they want.

Other ideas

You could also consider producing a video podcast, sometimes called a vodcast. The only disadvantage might be that they're bigger in size and so take up more of your and your students' storage space. The advantage would be that you could act out the scenes and illustrate body language as well. You'd need a video recording program, such as Movie Maker or iMovie. See Chapter 2, *Getting Started with Moodle* for more information on this.

Which recording program?

What's the best recording program to use? Maybe you have a preferred recording program on your computer already. If not, I'd suggest Audacity. Why use Audacity rather than NanoGong, you might be asking? NanoGong is excellent for making short recordings within HTML blocks, blogs, and wikis (though NanoGong only works within the OU versions of blogs and wikis: OUblog and OUwiki), but the media module offers several advantages:

- **Higher quality recordings**—that is particularly important if the recording is longer, or includes several sound sources
- **Longer recordings**—the maximum recording length for NanoGong is 5 minutes
- **More manageable recordings**—playback features allow you to pause and start recordings anywhere in the recording

Which Moodle module?

And what's the best Moodle module to use? Well, there's no built-in module for collecting recordings. So we're going to use the add-on media module, Inwicast, which appears under the name Mediacenter on Moodle. It provides a clean interface and allows us to create a directory of different media. They can be:

- Audio recordings
- Video recordings
- Embedded videos (that is, links to videos hosted on other sites, such as YouTube)

It has a few other attractive features, too:

- **Choice of recording format** — converts AVI, MP3, and WAV to Flash files.
- **Choice of media** — video, audio, slidecasts, and screencasts.
- **Organization** — all podcasts are available within one Moodle podcast directory.
- **RSS** — recordings available as an RSS feed. Once you have made your podcast, students can download it onto their iPods, iTunes, or cell phones to listen to and use

Mediacenter/large files

You'll need to get your Moodle administrator to install the Inwicast Mediacenter module for you. There are instructions for installing add-ons in Chapter 2, *Getting Started with Moodle*.

You'll also need to check that the server settings allow you to upload large files. Alternatively, you can FTP the files to your server. Chapter 2, *Getting Started with Moodle* provides more information on these topics.

In the following example we're going to set up a dialog in which two people discuss their plans for the evening.

Here's how to do it

Recording

1. First you'll need to open your recording program. Since Audacity is free and works extremely well, we'll use that in this example.

   Before we make a recording, we need to think carefully about what we plan to say. Let's imagine we want our students to practice a simple dialog in which they greet and exchange personal information. They will hear one part of the dialog and then get a prompt from us so that they can respond with the other part of the dialog. Our prompts can either be in the language students are learning or in their first language, depending on their level. Ideally, we'll have a partner to record with us. It works best when there is a woman's and man's voice, as the contrast in pitch is greater. However, Audacity also allows you to change the pitch of recordings so that one voice is higher or lower than the other. (See the *Sound* section in Chapter 11, *Formatting and Enhancing Your Moodle Materials* for more information on how to do this.)

   Write out the dialog instructions in advance. They could look something like this:

   Jane: Hi. How are you?

   Sam: In a half whisper, say you're OK. Ask Jane how she is.

   3 seconds pause. Then say:

   I'm OK. How are you?

   Jane: I'm good. Are you doing anything this evening?

   Sam: In a half whisper, say you're not doing anything. Ask her what she has in mind.

   5 seconds pause. Then say:

   No, I'm not doing anything. Why? What do you have in mind?

   Jane: Well there's an interesting exhibition on at the Met, and I don't fancy going alone. I was wondering if you fancied coming with me.

   Sam: In a half whisper, say you'd be delighted. Ask her what time she wants to go.

   5 seconds pause. Then say:

   I'd be delighted! What time do you want to go?

   Jane: How about quarter after six?

   Sam: In a half whisper, say you can't manage that as you have a meeting till 6.30, and ask her if 7 would be OK.

   5 seconds pause. Then say:

   I can't manage that, as I have a meeting till 6.30. Would 7 be OK?

Jane: 7 would be fine. That's great!

Sam: in a half whisper, tell Jane you're looking forward to it and that you'll see her later.

5 seconds pause. Then say:

I'm looking forward to it. See you later.

When you're ready, record the dialog and save it as an MP3 file.

Making the podcast

2. Now we need to open up a media block. To do that, click on **Turn editing on**.

3. Go to the **Blocks** menu, and choose **Mediacenter**.

4. Now a new Mediacenter block will appear on our page. Click on **course videos** in the block to access the Mediacenter.

5. Next, click on **Upload media**.

6. Browse to the audio or video file that you have saved, and fill in the rest of the details carefully. The description that we give is what students will read when they open the Mediacenter, so provide useful, focused information here, as in the next screenshot:

7. Once the details are in place, click on **Upload**. The dialog recording will now be added to the files available in the center.

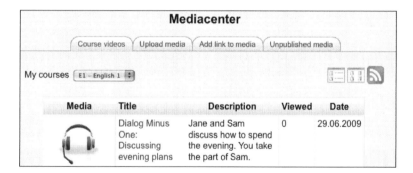

8. Students can access the file through the Mediacenter block on the course home page.

RSS feeds

Students can also download the media file to their computers or other electronic devices by clicking on the orange RSS button on the Mediacenter page.

See Chapter 2, *Getting Started with Moodle* for more information on collecting RSS feeds.

Activity 6: Preparing for class speaking practice using a Wiki

Aim: Help students prepare contents for later class speaking activities

Moodle modules: Wiki (or optional, OUwiki)

Extra programs: None

Ease of setup: **

Sometimes useful preparation can be done for speaking without actually doing any speaking. In this kind of activity, students prepare content for a speaking activity that they will later do in class. The class activity could be a role-play, an interview, or a debate, for example.

The following examples show how we can set up dialog practice (*Variation 1*) and a debate (*Variation 2*). In each case, students will have time to think about what they would say in advance, and to look up words, if necessary. Also, in the dialog in *Variation 1*, it is only by reading the subsequent part of the dialog that the student can work out what to say. So the student will also have valuable reading practice.

We can adjust the number of students responding to the wiki by making groups with one or two students per group, or we can allow a whole class to edit the wiki. (See Chapter 2, *Getting Started with Moodle* for setting up groups, if necessary.)

Variation 1: Building a dialog

This first variation will help students prepare for a dialog.

Here's how to do it

1. First, click on **Turn editing on** on the course page.

2. Choose **wiki** or **OUwiki**. We don't need OUwiki for this activity unless we want to add sound or make the wiki available for editing between fixed dates. So let's stick with the Moodle wiki for now.

    Don't forget that if you do want to use OUwiki, you'll need to get your Moodle administrator to install it for you. See Chapter 2, *Getting Started with Moodle* for help with this.

3. Fill in the settings page. Pay attention to the following:

Settings	Details
Name	Enter an appropriate name. Let's write **Dialog: negotiating a solution!**
Summary	This will tell the students what to do. Let's write this: **This wiki gives you practice at building a dialog in advance of our class on 2nd May. Read part A of the dialog and try to write in part B. You will be working in groups of 4 so together produce the best version you can. You can always go back and edit your text if necessary.**
Type	Let's choose **Student**, so that each student has his/her own wiki.
Common module settings	Let's choose **Visible groups**. That way only the student and the teacher can edit the student's wiki, but all students can see each other's wikis, which could be useful. If we don't want students to choose each other's wikis, we can choose **Separate groups** here.
Student admin options	Don't check any of these.

Timebound

If you're using the OUwiki, consider making the wiki editable between certain dates and telling students the dates so that they can organize their time.

4. Click on **Save and display**.

5. We now have a ready-to-use wiki in front of us. Let's create a table in the wiki with two columns. To do that, we click on the table icon ▦ in the edit menu. We're going to organize the page that students will read from and write onto. This dialog is ten lines long, so let's create a simple table with one column and eleven rows. That includes one extra row for the heading. See *Activity 4* if you need more help with setting up tables.

Our wiki will now look like this:

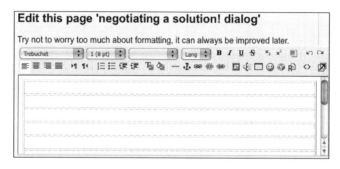

6. Now we can input our dialog.

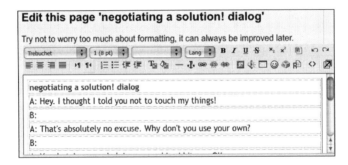

7. Once we've finished, we click on **Save**. The wiki is now ready for students to try to complete. Here's what they'll see:

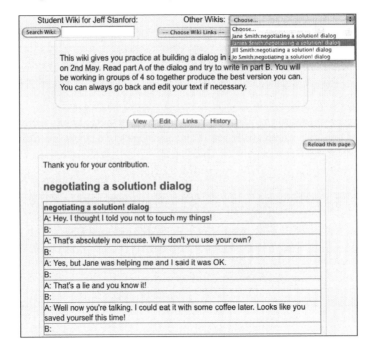

Notice that we can choose which student wiki to use from the drop-down menu in the top-left corner.

Discuss how to use wikis with the class in advance.
- Set a strict timetable for using the wiki
- Agree on a wiki etiquette; for example, being polite and friendly

Variation 2: Preparing for a debate

The setup for the debate wiki is similar to the dialog one, except that we're going to create two groups and allocate half the class to one group and half to the other. See Chapter 2, *Getting Started with Moodle* if you're not sure about setting up groups.

Before setting up the wiki, make sure you have divided your students into two groups. When they prepare for the debate, each group will only see the ideas generated by its own group.

Here's how to do it

1. First, click on **Turn editing on** on the course page.

2. Choose **wiki**.

3. Fill in the settings page. Pay attention to the following:

Settings	Details
Name	Enter an appropriate name. Let's write **negotiating a solution! dialog**.
Summary	This will tell the students what to do. Let's write this:
	This wiki gives you practice at preparing ideas for a debate. In class on 4th September you will debate the pros and cons of the following topic:
	### Should the voting age be lowered?
	Angela, Benjamin, Chrissy, David, Earl and Fay should write down pros in this wiki. Graham, Helen, Inga, John, Kay and Lorna should write down the cons. Write your ideas below. Put your name by your idea. Remember the wiki will close on 2nd September.
Type	Let's choose **Groups**, so that the different groups in our class have their own wiki.
Common module settings	Let's choose **Separate groups**. Then groups can only see their own wiki.
Student admin options	Don't check any of these.

4. Click on **Save and display**.

5. Now the wiki is ready for the students to pool their ideas. This is what they'll see when they click on the activity from the course page:

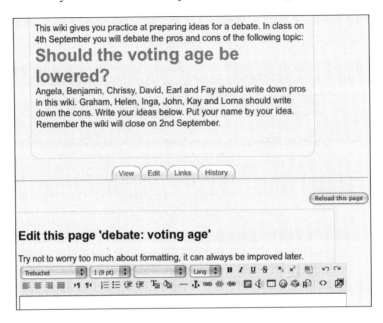

Activity 7: Preparing a class discussion using Chat

Aim: Help students prepare vocabulary and points of view for a face-to-face discussion

Moodle modules: Chat

Extra programs: None

Ease of setup: *

One way of preparing students for a chat in class is to write your chat in the Moodle Chat module first. This gives students more time to think of the vocabulary they need and allows you to feed in new vocabulary or expressions. Since it's hard to have a Moodle chat with more than about six participants, try breaking the class into two or more groups and inviting them to separate chat sessions. Each one could last about ten minutes. This separation allows you to prepare different aspects of the same topic. So if, for example, you're going to have a discussion about the pros and cons of watching videos on cell phones, you could chat with one group about the pros and with another group about the cons.

You could just nominate groups in your f2f (face-to-face) class to attend Moodle chat sessions at certain times, but if you create Moodle groups within your course, you can publish the times of the chat and ensure that only specified group members enter the chat room at the published time.

Here's how to do it

1. Set up a chat session. To do that, click on **Turn editing on**.
2. Add a **Chat** activity.
3. Fill in the settings page. Pay attention to the following in particular:

Settings	Details
Name of this chat room	Enter an appropriate name. Let's put **pros and cons of video on cellphones**.
Introduction text	This will tell the students what they'll be chatting about. We can include pictures by clicking on the image icon in the edit menu. Let's write **Preparation chat on the pros and cons of using cellphones to watch videos**.
Next chat time	Choose the date and time of the chat session. Students will see this scheduled time when they click on the activity. Remember, you'll need to update these details for the second chat session.
Save past sessions	Let's choose **Never delete messages**. That way we always have access to the chat transcript.
Group mode	Make sure this is set to **Separate groups**. That way we can ensure that the groups we've set up don't come to the chat room at the same time. See Chapter 2 for help with setting up groups.

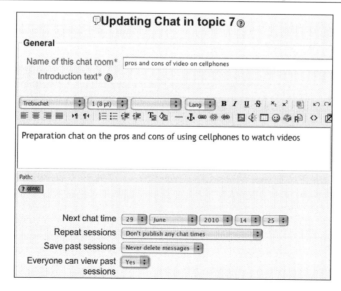

4. Click on **Save and Display**. The chat session is now ready to use. When students click on the chat activity on the course page, they'll see this:

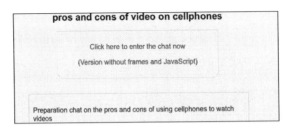

5. They click on **Click here to enter the chat now**. Then they can take part in the chat as in Chapter 3, *Vocabulary Activities, Activity 7*.

Preparing for your chat session

Before you start the chat session, make a note of the points you want to include. So for the session on the "pros of using cellphones for watching videos" you could write something like this:

Pros of using cellphones for watching videos:
*   You can watch videos whenever you want to
*   You can download directly from the Internet
*   You can listen privately with earphones
*   You can learn on the go
*   You can watch streamed video

Just in case you've never been in a chat session before, here's how your chat session might go:

You: Hello everyone! As you know tomorrow we're going to have a discussion about using cellphones to watch videos. You're going to think of good reasons. The other group will think of reasons for not doing it.

Juan: OK

Pii: OK

You: What good reasons can you think of?

Pii: Well, you can see it all places

You: Yes, you can watch it anywhere

Pii: You can watch it in the bus for example.

You: Exactly.

And so on…

As you can see, the chat room allows you to pick up on errors and reformulate them. Some students will pick up on their errors straight away. Others may not, but the activity will make you more aware of problem areas, and will provide useful practice.

Saving your chat session

You might find it useful to make the transcript available to yourself and the students after the chat session finishes. In that case, don't forget to 'save past sessions' on the chat update page.

Activity 8: Producing presentations using an OUblog

Aim: Get students to present monologs in their Moodle blogs

Moodle modules: OUblog

Extra programs: NanoGong

Ease of setup: *

There's nothing like having to give an oral presentation to focus students' minds and help them prepare and develop their speaking skills. This activity combines an OUblog and a sound recorder on Moodle to do that: students record their own presentations and publish them in their own blogs. Once again, we'll use NanoGong to record voices and the add-on OUblog to present the recordings.

Using a regular Moodle blog

If your administrator has not added the OUblog module, you can use a regular Moodle blog, but you won't be able to include the instructions in the blog, and you won't have a comment facility.

Once students have made their recordings, they can embellish their blogs with text and images. Here are some examples of presentations our students could do:

- Narratives
- Stories
- Diaries
- Descriptions
- News

In our example they're going to talk about their ideal days.

There are several advantages of recording a monolog online, rather than just presenting it in class. Students will be aware that their work will remain accessible and judgeable, and will often want it to be as good as possible. That means they will practice harder to create a good product.

We have a choice as to whether we help students prepare their monologs in class or via Moodle. It's likely that preparing in class will motivate students and help ensure that the various elements they will need to take into consideration are absolutely clear.

Even if we prepare students for the task in the classroom, we still need to ensure there is a clear statement of the task on Moodle.

Here's how to do it

Let's set up the OUblog.

1. On your course home page, click on **Turn editing on.** Then click on **Add a resource....**

2. Choose **OUblog** from the drop-down menu.

 No OUwiki? If you can't see OUwiki in the menu, it's because you haven't installed it, or it is hidden. See Chapter 2, *Getting Started with Moodle* for installing add-on modules like OUwiki, and for unhiding modules and blocks in the **Site Administration** menu.

3. Complete the settings page. Pay particular attention to the following. The other settings are optional.

Settings	Details
Blog name	Let's call it **My ideal day**.
Summary	Write something like this:
	Hello, Class 4b!
	Instructions for writing your OUblog
	The blog link is below this link.
	The topic is 'My ideal day'.
	Preparation
	Make some notes about 4 or 5 things that would make your ideal day. You can also add some pictures if you want to.
	When you're ready, click on the audio button and start recording your blog. If you're not happy the first time, you can delete it and start again.
	You can also add:
	• **weblinks to your blog for anything that relates to what you wrote.**
	• **tags or keywords which will help other people find your blog.**
Allow comments	Now we decide whether we want to allow comments or not. Allowing comments means that students can ask each other questions about their blogs. Students are likely to be used to doing this already.

4. When you're ready, click on **Save and display**. The OUblog is now ready for students to use. The instructions are on the right-hand side of the page, out of the way.

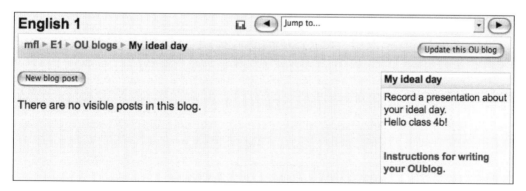

5. To use the OUblog, students click on the OUblog link on the main course page and then on **New blog post**. If they haven't produced a blog before, it's worth producing an example blog for them to see. For example:

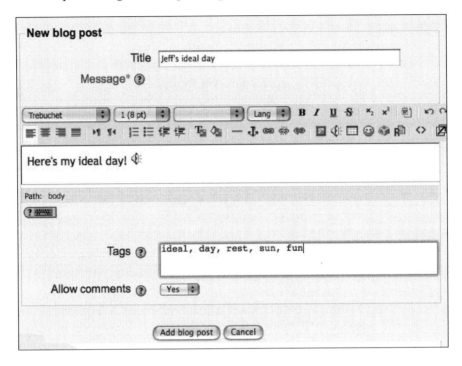

Don't forget to separate the tags with a comma. Once the blog post is saved, the tags will be visible in a tags block on your OUblog page. To save the blog post, simply click on **Add blog post**. Point this out to the students. It can be a good way of rousing interest.

You'll also notice that when you open a completed blog post, there is an option to add a related web link. Just click on **Add link**.

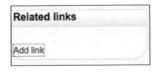

Then complete the details of the link. Afterwards, click on **Add link**. This is a good way to get the students to help each other and encourages them to point out sites that have a link. Don't forget to write in the **Full Web address** (sometimes called URL). For example:

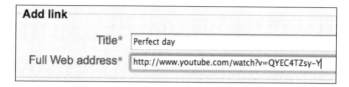

Students can also comment on each other's presentations by clicking on **Add your comment** under the blog post.

After another student has added a comment, the OUblog page will look something like this:

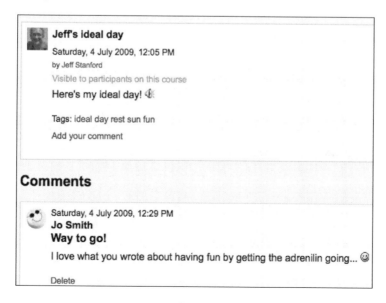

Giving feedback

Consider how you're going to give feedback, if at all. There are various options:

- Discreetly collect errors, which you could use anonymously in an error clinic later on

- Use the comments facility to respond to the content (not the language errors) in the blog

- Create an error analysis wiki (see Chapter 3, *Vocabulary Activities, Activity 7* for details)

Podcast alternative

An alternative to students' publishing their recordings in their own blogs is to get them to use NanoGong to save their recordings, which you can then upload into the Mediacenter directory. See *Activity 5* for an example.

Activity 9: Presenting a monolog using the Quiz module

Aim: Help students produce monologs for assessment

Moodle modules: Quiz

Extra programs: NanoGong (optional)

Ease of setup: ***

In Activity 8 we helped students create blogs for public viewing. Sometimes it is more appropriate to make the presentation private. The Quiz module helps us do that. Here are the main reasons for using a Quiz module, rather than a Blog or Forum, as a showcase for students' recordings:

- Quizzes are private.

- It's easy for teachers to record individual feedback.

- Teachers can grade student attempts: the grades are automatically incorporated into the Moodle gradebook.

- Students may be more motivated to produce the recording if they know that their peers won't hear it. Though for some students the chance to show off is the key motivator.

The easiest type of recording is a monolog, but it may well be feasible for students to get together and record a dialog. In fact, that could be a fun, useful process in itself. The list of possible dialogs is endless. Here are some obvious categories:

- Interviews
- Discussions
- Problem-solving
- Role-plays
- Simulated telephone calls

Monologs are likely to include the following:

- Describing a photo
- Planning
- Narrating or telling a story
- Presenting something (family, product, holiday)
- Giving directions

As always, it's important that students have clear instructions on how to complete the task. It might be useful to do some preparation in class beforehand. It's also generally good practice to include an example task and answer.

Here's how to do it

1. We can either open an existing quiz and add a matching question to it or we can create a new quiz activity. To do that, we click on **Turn on editing** on the course home page. Then click on **Add an activity...**. We're going to make a quiz question, so choose **Quiz**.

2. Complete the introduction page for the quiz activity (see Chapter 2, *Getting Started with Moodle* if you need help with this). When we have finished, click on **Save and display**. Don't worry if you clicked on **Save and return to course** by mistake. Simply find the activity we have just created, and click on the hand icon ✍ to edit it.

3. We are now inside the quiz environment. From the **Question bank**, go to **Create new question**, and choose **Essay** from the drop-down menu.

Adding an Essay

4. Now we come to the introduction page for our new quiz question. Whereas the front page gives general information about the quiz activity (availability, etc.), the question introduction page provides specific information about the quiz question.

Settings	Details
Save in Category	Decide which category of quizzes we want our question to belong to (see Chapter 9, *Assessment* for information on categories). Let's leave it on default for now. We can change it later, if necessary.
Question Name	Write the name of the activity. Let's call it **Presentation practice 1**.
Question text	Let's write something like the following:

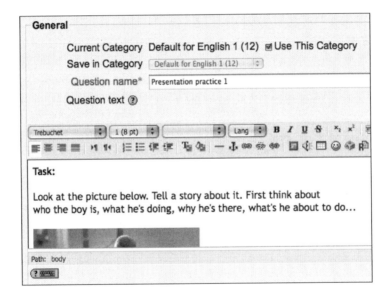

More help with images and settings

See Chapter 2, *Getting Started with Moodle* if you need help with uploading images or if you need help with Common module settings. See Chapter 11, *Formatting and Enhancing Your Moodle Materials* if you need help with image layout.

5. Click on **Save changes**.

6. Click on the arrows ⟪ next to the **Presentation practice** question we've just made to add it to our quiz.

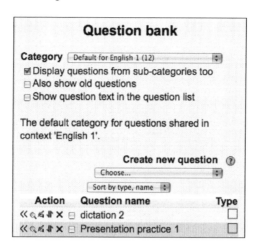

If you can't see the quiz, click on the quiz tab at the top of the page. This is what students will see when they click on the presentation quiz:

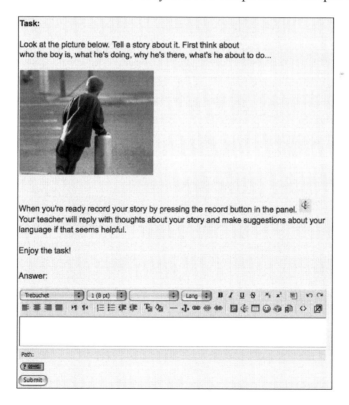

7. They record their answer in the **Answer** box. They then click on **Submit**. To see and listen to students' attempts, click on the quiz activity that we created on the course home page, called **Presentation practice**. Click on **Attempts** at the bottom of the page. Of course, if there are no attempts, we won't be able to see any. This is the overview we'll get:

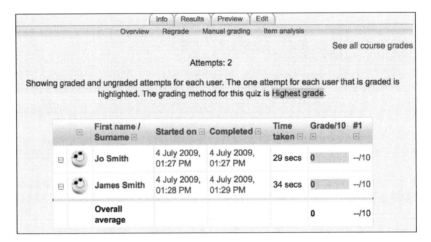

8. Next, we click on the **Grade**, highlighted in green. That takes us to a link where we can grade or comment on the student's submission.

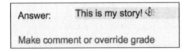

9. We can then add comments, include our own recording to help students practice anything they found difficult, and we can give a grade if we want.

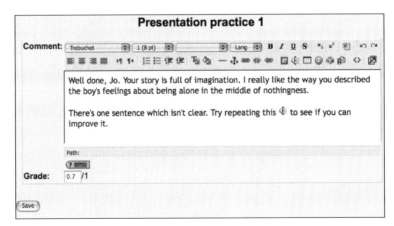

5
Grammar Activities

Most teachers like to teach grammar, but do all students like to learn it? Sometimes it may seem boring. Sometimes it seems too difficult. Using Moodle, we can try to spice up grammar a bit, by introducing images, sound, video, and a game element. We can incorporate helpful feedback, which individual students can process in their own time so that they begin to understand grammar points better. Also, students have the advantage of being able to repeat exercises to their hearts' content.

This chapter is organized in grammar sections that might be taught in a **communicative language teaching** classroom.

Section	Section contents
1	**Presentation and knowledge**—*Activity 1*
	Moodle is ideal for explaining and illustrating grammar with audio, video, image, and text support.
2	**Noticing activity**—*Activity 2*
	This activity helps students identify aspects of grammar within a spoken or written text. Authentic texts can be used here, as they are invariably more interesting and fun to use for students.
3	**Controlled practice**—*Activities 3–5*
	Moodle lends itself well to the more mechanical aspects of controlled grammar practice. For example, sorting language according to grammatical categories, testing grammatical knowledge. One key advantage is that students can review difficult grammar as often as they like.
4	**Production activities**—*Activities 6–8*
	Students can produce longer texts and receive feedback on the grammar they use in a variety of ways, either from the teacher or from peers.

The activities have been arranged according to ease of setup within each of the above sections.

Activity 1: Creating a Podcast lecture to present grammar in a lively way

Aim: Provide students with a recorded presentation, illustration of grammar and drills

Moodle modules: None

Extra programs: Mediacenter block, Audacity

Ease of setup: **

Listening to a grammar explanation is not everyone's cup of tea, but some students like it and find it useful. One way of making recordings like this available on Moodle is by creating a Podcast. Podcast is computer speak for an audio recording that is posted to a website and is made available for download so that people can listen to it on their personal computers or MP3 players. Making a Podcast requires quite a lot of preparation work for the teacher, but it can really pay off in terms of personalizing the information you give to your students, and can be used over and over again. What's more, you can try to make the presentation entertaining by choosing memorable examples of grammar so that students actually look forward to your grammar presentations.

Before you make the recording, you'll need to think carefully what you're going to say. Some useful questions to ask yourself are:

- What grammar point are you going to cover?
- What problems are students likely to have?
- How is it similar or different to the same grammar item in the students' first language?
- What examples can you give?
- Should I speak in the students' first language or in the target language?

There are several ways of preparing the recording. The longest, but easiest way is to write out the whole transcript and then record it. An alternative would be to make notes on the key areas you're going to talk about and base your recording on the notes. Of course, it's also possible that your Podcast is just going over some grammar problems that have recently come up in class, in which case you might be able to make a recording more spontaneously as if you were giving feedback in class. The recording could also usefully include gaps where you allow students to repeat a model.

If you haven't heard a language-teaching Podcast before, Praxis Language Ltd provides a few good examples. You could listen to the Spanish, Chinese, French, or Italian Podcasts, available at `http://spanishpod.com/`, `http://chinesepod.com/`, `http://frenchpod.com/`, and `http://italianpod.com/`. Click on **Sample a Lesson**, and then click on the **Lesson** player to hear the Podcast.

In this activity we're going to make a Podcast that illustrates how you talk about making plans in English. The Mediacenter with the final Podcast will look like this:

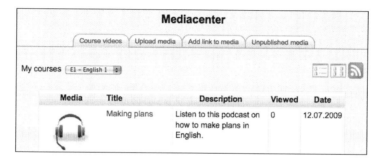

What students see when they click on **Making plans** will look like this:

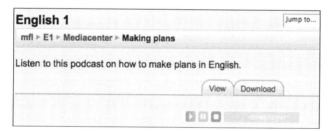

Before we begin, make sure your administrator has installed the Mediacenter block on your Moodle site. See Chapter 2, *Getting Started with Moodle* for more information on how to do that.

Here's how to do it

Making the recording

1. First you'll need to open your Audacity sound recording program. See Chapter 2, *Getting Started with Moodle* if you need help with this. You can use other recording programs if you prefer. Since Audacity is free and works well, we'll use it in this example.

We're making a recording for a low-level class. This one is in English, but you might consider recording it in the students' first language. Here's the beginning of our example transcript:

Hi class! We're going to practice making plans in English. One way to do that is to use the construction "-ing". Yes, I know that's also used for talking about what you are doing now, but it's a common way of talking about definite plans in the future, too. Listen to this dialog:

Jane: Hi, John. What are you doing tonight?

John: I'm going to the cinema. Do you want to come?

Jane: I'd love to, but I'm preparing for my presentation tomorrow.

John: Sounds good! I'm coming, by the way!

Jane: Really! You didn't tell me!

John: I wouldn't miss it for anything.

In the dialog Jane says "what are you doing tonight?", not "what will you do?" or "what are you going to do?". She wants to know what John's plans are, so she uses the "-ing" form: "what are you doing tonight?". The "-ing form" is used for telling other people about our definite plans. Now you try saying that: "What are you doing tonight? [3-second pause]". OK. And now try repeating the answer: "I'm going to the cinema [3-second pause]", etc.

When we're ready, we can record the dialog in the Audacity program and save it as an MP3 file. See Chapter 2, *Getting Started with Moodle* if you would like to know more about Audacity or need help with this.

Setting up the Podcast

2. Now we need to upload our recording into the Mediacenter so that students can listen to it. First we need to open up a Media block on our course page if we don't have one already. To do that, click on **Turn editing on** by clicking the button in the top right-hand corner of the page.

3. Scroll down to the drop-down block menu on the right, and select **Mediacenter**.

This is what we'll now see in the Blocks column.

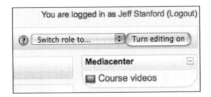

4. Click on the **Course videos** link in the **Mediacenter** block.

5. We want to upload our recording to the Mediacenter, so let's click on **Upload media**.

    Here we fill in the details of the recording. The description that you give is what students will read when they open the Mediacenter, so provide useful focused information here. Then we browse to the audio or video file that we have saved.

Once the file is uploaded, students will be able to access it through the Mediacenter block. They will also be able to download it to their computers or other electronic devices by clicking on the orange RSS button 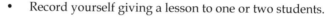 on the Mediacenter page. They can also add it to an RSS Aggregator—that's a website that collects multiple RSS feeds—so that we can refer to it easily. See Chapter 2, *Getting Started with Moodle* for more information.

Other ideas

*   Record yourself giving a lesson to one or two students.

*   Use Audacity to include an authentic interview or presentation which allows you to focus on a grammar point. For example, news broadcasts often start with the present perfect.

*   Use snippets of mood music to introduce your recordings. See Chapter 2, Getting *Started with Moodle* for help with editing your Audacity recordings.

Activity 2: Using the Lesson module to get students to notice grammar points

Aim: Help students identify grammar points

Moodle modules: Lesson

Extra programs: Audacity, YouTube

Ease of setup: ***

One useful process is to help students spot grammar points as they are actually used in real life; for example, in authentic texts. This authenticity makes it easier for students to see the meaning that the grammar has, and authentic texts are often interesting and therefore motivating for students, if chosen with care. Of course, this requires a bit more work on the teacher's part in terms of selecting and preparing texts, but the payback is good.

The texts could be written, audio, or video. The written texts can usefully be illustrated with images. Videos and audios from websites that provide embeddable code (such as Google, TeacherTube, and YouTube) can very conveniently be included in your lessons. See Chapter 2, *Getting Started with Moodle* for help with embedding videos. Here are some ideas for texts:

Written texts

- Personal letters or emails (made anonymous where appropriate)
- Stories
- Reviews
- Reports
- Blogs
- News
- Poetry

Audio and video texts

- Stories
- News
- Clips from interesting radio programs
- Interviews
- Presentations
- Songs
- Poetry
- Documentaries

The Lesson module allows students to progress through a lesson one step at a time. Students read or hear a text, then read the question that goes with that text. Depending whether they get the answer right or not, they either do it again or go on to the next question. They can also go back over the questions if necessary, providing we ensure that multiple attempts are allowed on the settings page.

In this activity students will listen to a story taken from YouTube, called *There's an alligator under my bed*, and will notice the grammar that they hear. I found the story by doing a search for "story time" on the YouTube website. Here's what the first question will look like:

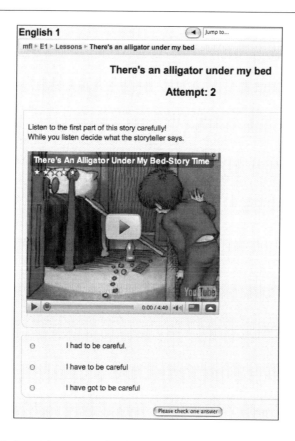

Note that the YouTube video is not broken up into chunks, so students will be presented with the whole video lasting 4 minutes 49 seconds each time. There are three solutions to this:

- Students get the whole video and use the player controls to listen to the part they want.

- Students listen to the whole story for each question. Younger students in particular enjoy that.

- Edit the video into smaller chunks. See Chapter 2, *Getting Started with Moodle* for help with this.

To keep things simple, we're going to embed the whole video each time in this activity. The complete lesson consists of 3 pages plus. Since the process for each new page is the same, we'll just look at how we produce one page. Then you're free to add as many question pages as you want.

Here's how to do it

Preparation

1. First we need to go to the YouTube website and find the video. In this case, it's `http://uk.youtube.com/watch?v=sNE8p0E4NVU`.

2. We want to embed our chosen YouTube video in the lesson content. To do that, we click on the **Embed** box on the right-hand side of the YouTube page:

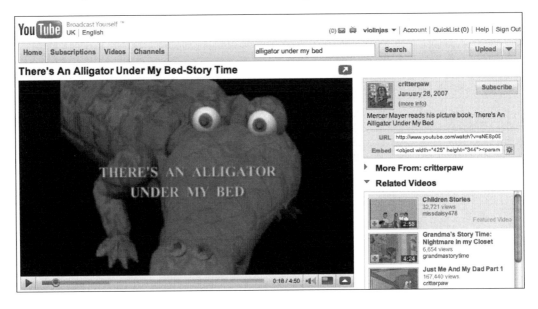

Click in the **Embed** box and copy it onto your computer memory (clipboard) by clicking on *Cmd + C* (on a Mac) or *Ctrl + C* (on a Windows computer).

Setting up the Lesson

3. Next we need to set up the Lesson introduction page. To do that, go to the course page and click on **Turn editing on**. Go to the **Add an activity...** drop-down menu, and select **Lesson**.

4. Complete the introductory page as follows. Pay particular attention to the following items. The other settings are optional.

Settings	Details
Time limit	This is not a test, so don't put a time limit.
Maximum number of branches	This is the number of possible answers students will have. The default is **4**. Let's leave it at that. It doesn't matter if we just include **2** or **3** answers to some of the questions.
Practice lesson	If we check this, the results will not show up in the gradebook. Since we want the exercise to be used for fun, don't check it.
Maximum grade	Leave this at **0**, as the grade won't appear in the gradebook.
Student can re-take	Check this. We want students to do the practice as often as they want.
Handling of re-takes	Ignore this, as we won't be grading students' work.

Settings	Details
Display ongoing score	Don't check this. Scores are not relevant to this activity.
Allow student review	Check this so that students can change their answers.
Display review button	Don't check this. If you do, it won't be possible for students to follow the path we have set up for them.
Maximum number of attempts	How many times will we allow students to try to answer any of the questions? Let's put **10** so that students can try out the activity up to ten times.
Action after correct answer	The default is **Normal – follow lesson path**. Leave it at that. Once we have written all the situation (question) pages, we will edit the path.
Lesson formatting	Don't check **Slide Show**.

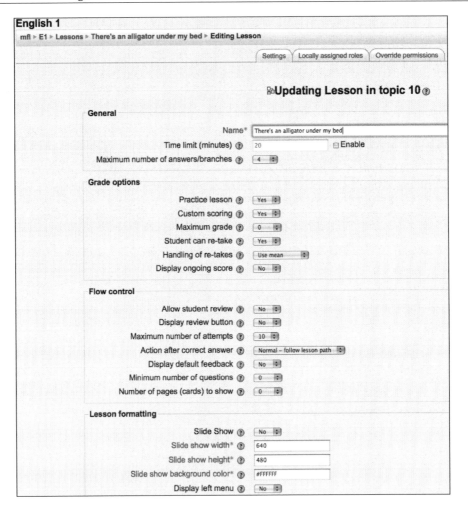

5. Click on **Save and display** at the bottom of the page.

6. Now we have a choice. Let's keep things simple and just add a series of **Question Pages**. Click on **Add a Question Page**.

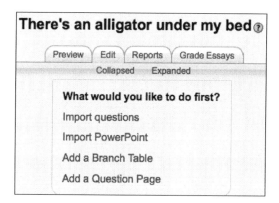

This is where we can start building our questions.

7. We have a choice of question types. Let's choose **Multiple Choice**.

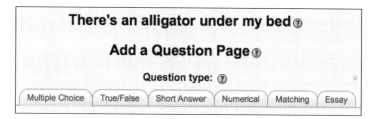

8. Now fill in the details for the first question:

Settings	Details
Multianswer	Leave this unchecked, as we want only one correct answer for each question.
Page title	The text is a linear sequence. So let's write 1. We can write 2, 3, etc., for subsequent pages.
Page contents	Let's write the first chunk of text here. For example:

Listen to the first part of the story carefully. While you listen decide what the storyteller says.

Next, we're going to embed the YouTube video. To do that, click on the HTML toggle tag ⟨⟩.

If you're just recording a sound using NanoGong, or writing a text, you won't need to click on the HTML tag. You can go straight ahead and write and go to Step 10 in these instructions. But we're going to embed code, so we need the HTML code page to do one simple copy and paste.

We now need to paste the embed code that we copied in Step 2. To do that, Press *Ctrl+V* on a Windows machine or *Cmd+V* on a Mac. Alternatively, you can right-click the mouse and choose **Paste**.

This is what the **Page contents** will look like now:

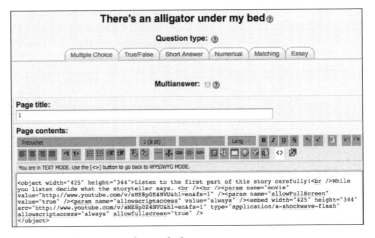

Now complete the answer boxes below.

Answer 1	**I had to be careful.**
Response 1	**well done! He is telling us what happened when he was a boy. So he says "I had to..."**
Jump 1	Set this to **Next page**. Students can then go on to the next question.
	Write **1** for **Score**.
Answer 2	**I have to be careful.**
Response 2	**No. This happened in the past. Try again.**

Settings	Details
Jump 2	Change this to **This page**. That means that students will have a chance to try the question again.
	Write **0** for **Score**.
Answer 3	**I have got to be careful.**
Response 3	**No. This happened in the past. Try again.**
Jump 3	Leave this at **This page**.
	Write **0** for Score.

9. We've now completed our first page. Click on **Add a Question Page**, to add this page to the lesson.

10. Next we're going to add a new question page. To do that, we navigate to the bottom of the screen and click on **Add a question page here**. Don't click on **Add a question page here** at the top of the page by mistake. If you do, you'll be inserting a question *before* the one we just wrote. We want the next question to come *afterwards*.

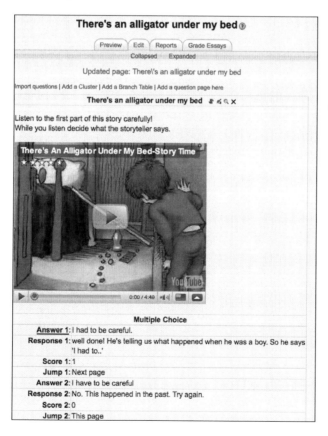

If you see the following screenshot instead, don't worry. Just click on **Expanded** to get the full version.

Later on, if we discover that the question pages are in the wrong order, we can change the order. To do that, click on the move icon ⊕ at the top of a page you want to move. And then click on the position you want to move it to.

Now we can write a second question. For the second question and all other questions, we need to embed the video again so that students can listen to it while they notice the grammar. If the video is chunked (edited into smaller sections), then we can embed the second part plus some appropriate noticing questions, and then the third part and so on until all the parts have been included.

11. We now repeat the process of adding questions and responses for the rest of the text. That's going to be just three question pages in total. When we reach the end of the third question page, we must make sure that our jump link choice for the correct answer is **End of lesson**. You can see an example at the bottom of the following screenshot. Otherwise, the activity will not close itself when students reach the end.

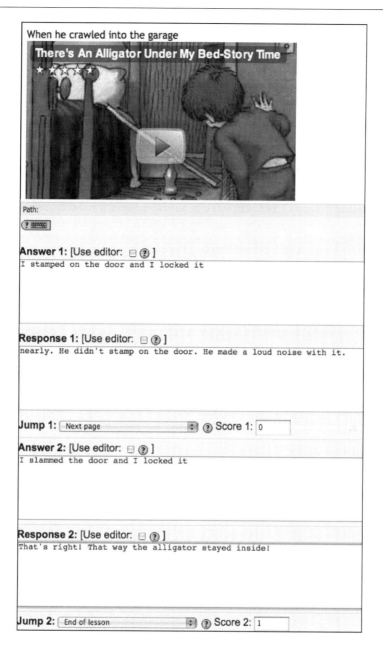

When he crawled into the garage

There's An Alligator Under My Bed-Story Time

Path:

Answer 1: [Use editor: ☐ ⑦]

I stamped on the door and I locked it

Response 1: [Use editor: ☐ ⑦]

nearly. He didn't stamp on the door. He made a loud noise with it.

Jump 1: Next page ⑦ **Score 1:** 0

Answer 2: [Use editor: ☐ ⑦]

I slammed the door and I locked it

Response 2: [Use editor: ☐ ⑦]

That's right! That way the alligator stayed inside!

Jump 2: End of lesson ⑦ **Score 2:** 1

12. We can test out our lesson at any time—even before it's finished—by clicking on the **Preview** tab. And we can edit any pages by clicking on the edit icon ✍.

Students access the lesson by clicking on the link from the course page. When they click on the correct answer, they'll see this:

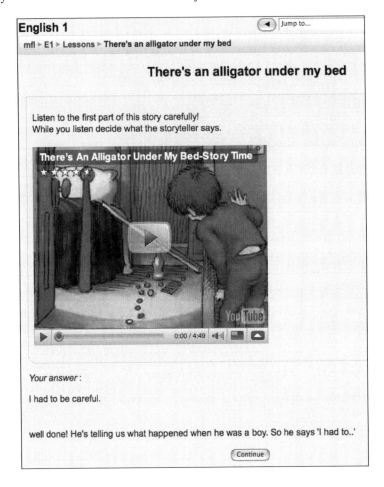

* You can change the question type by choosing true/false, short answer, essay, numerical, matching, etc.
* You can use the next page to provide feedback in the form of images, video, or audio to provide extra support for the students.
* Click on **Update** (top right-hand corner) if you need to change the basic settings for this lesson. You can convert the lesson into a test by changing the lesson settings, where you can set time limits, the number of attempts, the grading, etc.

Activity 3: Using polls to get students to vote on the correctness of grammar items

Aim: Get students to focus on a grammar point in a fun way

Moodle modules: Choice

Extra programs: NanoGong (optional)

Ease of setup: *

Another way of bringing a fun element into grammar is to turn it into a game. In this activity, students vote on whether some grammar is correct or not. The activity is similar to Chapter 3, *Vocabulary Activities*, *Activity 6* in which students vote on the meaning of a word. Here are some ideas for questions that we could set up:

- Agreement (subject + verb)
- Tenses
- Word order
- Spelling
- Punctuation
- Modal verbs

In this example students have to vote on whether a sentence is acceptable in a given register. This is what students will see:

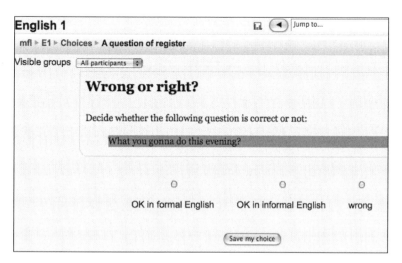

Here's how to do it

1. On the course page, click on **Turn editing on**. Go to the **Add an activity...** drop-down menu, and select **Choice**.

2. Fill in the settings page as follows.

Settings	Details
Choice name	Write an appropriate title for the activity. Let's call this **A question of register**.
Choice text	Write a simple question for students to answer. I've written: **Wrong or right?** **Decide whether the following question is correct or not:** **What you gonna do this evening?**
Choice 1	Next to **Choice**, write **OK in formal English**.
Choice 2	Next to **Choice**, write **OK in informal English**.
Choice 3	Next to **Choice**, write **wrong**.
Display mode	If we have a lot of students, we can go for **horizontal**. If we have few, then **vertical** would be appropriate. Let's put **horizontal** for now.

Listening instead

Instead of writing a **Choice text** in the settings above, we could click on the NanoGong audio button ◈ and record an utterance.

3. Click on **Save and display**. The poll is ready to use. Students click on the activity and then choose the answer.

The results could lead to an interesting discussion in class (or a forum discussion on Moodle) on what is acceptable and what isn't in different registers of English. For example, students could learn to distinguish between:

- Careful style
- Neutral style
- Casual style

...and learn when informal grammar is acceptable.

Identifying register is a fairly high-level activity. Here's what a choice activity that gets students to decide on a relatively simple choice of tenses could look like:

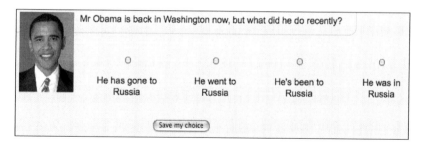

Activity 4: Practicing grammar through dictation

Aim: Get students to listen out for grammar and transcribe it accurately

Moodle modules: Lesson or Wiki

Extra programs: NanoGong

Ease of setup: **

Dictations are an excellent way to get students to home in on grammar. There isn't a Dictation module in Moodle, but there are several alternatives which can be used effectively. We'll look at two variations. The first uses Lesson and helps us lead students through the dictation. The second uses a Wiki and encourages collaboration.

If you don't have the audio recorder, NanoGong, installed, you can follow the procedure for creating an audio player in Chapter 2, *Getting Started with Moodle*. Using NanoGong is a quicker way of setting up the activity.

Preparing for a dictation

First we need to choose a text that illustrates some grammar points that we want to practice with our students. Make sure it's an appropriate length. If possible, choose a text that will motivate the students because of its content, too. For both variations, it's worth remembering the conventions for producing dictations.

- Read the text three times. First time round, read the whole text. Second time round, read individual phrases. Third time round, read the whole text.
- Read in a natural manner.
- Divide up the text into natural chunks and leave pauses between phrases.

In our example we'll provide a recording of the whole text first. This should help students get a general understanding of the passage. We'll then provide chunked recordings which students listen to and transcribe. On Moodle they can listen as many times as they like before submitting their version.

Variation 1: Creating a dictation using Lesson

In this variation we'll use the Lesson module to dictate a text phrase by phrase. This time we'll use the short answer question type to check students' answers. We can set up Lesson to allow individuals to spend as much time as they want on each segment of the recorded text. Each segment appears on a lesson page. So to set up the activity, we will create a suite of question pages. We can provide feedback in the form of hints, which will help students get the answers right. This is what students will see when they click on the dictation lesson:

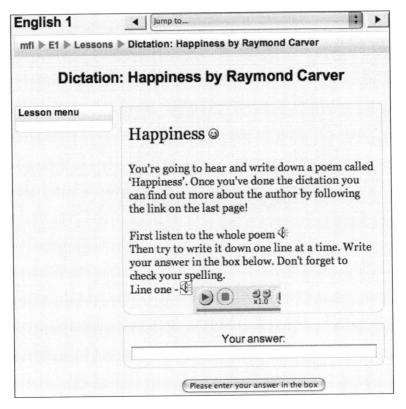

Here's how to do it

1. First we need to set up the lesson introduction page. To do that, go to the course page, and click on **Turn editing on**. Go to the **Add an activity...** drop-down menu, and select **Lesson**.

2. Complete the introductory page as follows. Pay particular attention to the following items. The other settings are optional.

Settings	Details
Time limit	This is not a test, so don't put a time limit.
Maximum number of branches	This is the number of possible answers students will have. Let's set this to the maximum, which is **10**. That way we can provide feedback on up to ten variants of the answer. We can increase this later if need be.
Practice lesson	If we check this, the results will not show up in the gradebook. Since we want the exercise to be used for fun, don't check it.
Maximum grade	Leave this at **0**, as the grade won't appear in the gradebook.
Student can re-take	Check this. We want students to do the practice as often as they want.
Handling of re-takes	Ignore this, as we won't be grading students' work.
Display ongoing score	Don't check this. Scores are not relevant to this activity.
Allow student review	Check this so that students can change their answers.
Display review button	Don't check this. If you do, it won't be possible for students to follow the path we have set up for them.
Maximum number of attempts	How many times will we allow students to try to answer any of the questions? Let's put **10** so that students can try out the activity up to ten times—the maximum.
Action after correct answer	The default is **Normal – follow lesson path**. Leave it at that. Once we have written all the situation (question) pages, we will edit the path.
Lesson formatting	Don't check **Slide Show**.

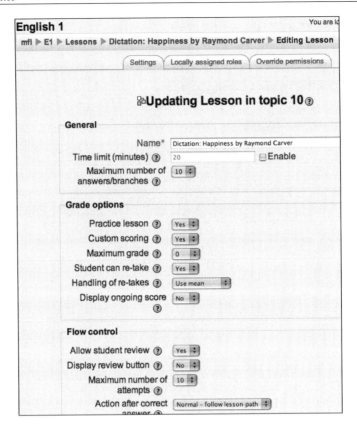

3. Click on **Save and display**.

4. Now click on **Add a Question Page**.

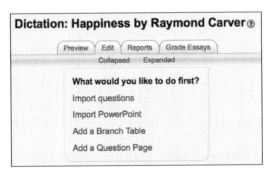

This is where we can start building our questions.

5. We have a choice of question types. Let's choose **Short Answer**. This will allow students to write down the short phrase that they hear.

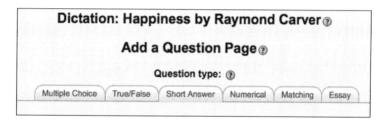

6. Now we are ready to produce the contents of the first step of the dictation. We need to try to predict the mistakes our students will make and write down slightly wrong answers in the **Answer** boxes, giving hints as to what students should change.

Settings	Details
Page title	Write **1**. This is the first step of the dictation. Future steps can be labeled **2**, **3**, etc.
Page contents	We could write something like this:
	You're going to hear and write down a poem called 'Happiness'. Once you've done the dictation you can find out more about the author by following the link on the last page!
	First listen to the whole poem ◈
	Next you should record the whole poem using NanoGong. To do that click on the NanoGong audio button in the HTML editing menu ◈. See the introduction to Chapter 4, *Speaking Activities* if you need more help with using NanoGong. See Chapter 2, *Getting Started with Moodle* if you need to install NanoGong.
	Then write in the contents box on the same page:
	Then try to write it down one line at a time. Write your answer in the box below. Don't forget to check your spelling.
	Now record the first line again, separately. Then complete the sections below
Answer 1	**So early it's still almost dark out.**
Response 1	**well done!**
Jump 1	Set this to **Next page**. Students can then go on to the next question.
	Write **1** for **Score**.
Answer 2	**so early it's still almost dark out.**
Response 2	**Nearly. Don't forget to begin with a capital letter and finish with a period.**

Settings	Details
Jump 2	Change this to **This page**. That means that students will have a chance to try the question again.
	Write **0** for **Score**.
Answer 3	**So early, it's still almost dark out.**
Response 3	**Almost right, but there's no need for a comma.**
Jump 3	Change this to **This page**. That means that students will have a chance to try the question again.
	Write **0** for **Score**.
Answer 4	**So early its still almost dark out.**
Response 4	**Nearly right. Check the apostrophe.**
Jump 4	Leave this at **This page**.
	Write **0** for **Score**.

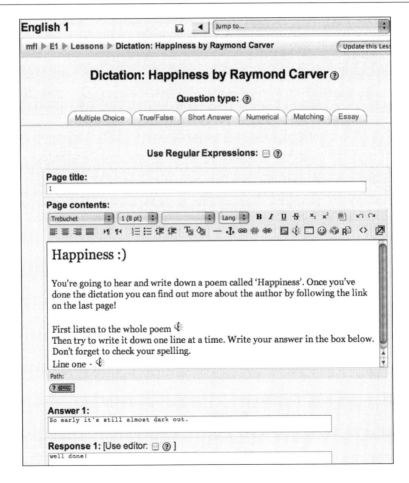

It's a good idea to check what sorts of responses are given by clicking on the **Reports** tab (see Step 4). That information will help us add more possible answers and feedback.

7. Now click on **Add a question page** to save your new page.

8. Now navigate to the bottom of the new screen and click on **Add a question page here**, because we're going to add a new page for the next segment of the poem. Don't click on the **Add a question page here** at the top of the page by mistake. If you do, you'll be inserting a question *before* the one we just wrote. We want the next question to come *afterwards*.

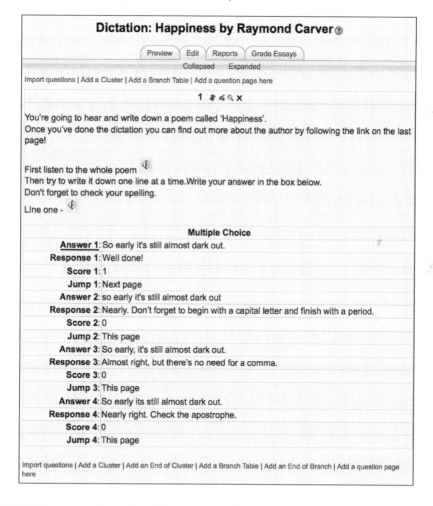

N.B. If you can't see the above screenshot, you're probably seeing the **Collapsed** view. Click on the **Expanded** tab at the top and you will see the full page.

Now we can record the second line of the poem/dictation. The procedure is the same as in Step 6. Before we insert the recording, write down the line of the poem (or dictation) that students have just heard, in case students couldn't get it or need to be reminded of it. Then write a little introduction like:

Now listen to the next line and write it down.

Click your cursor at the beginning of the next line. Then click on the audio button in the HTML menu ◉ to make a recording. Make your recording of the next line here. Page 2 would look something like this once you've saved it:

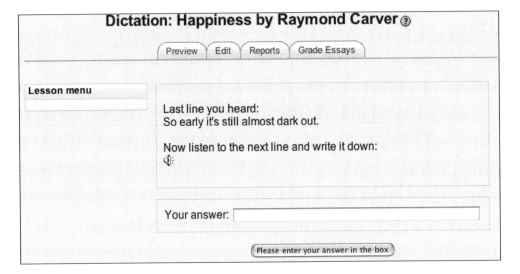

9. Now repeat Steps 6 to 8 to add more questions to your lesson until we have dictated every line of the poem. When we reach the end of the last question page, we must make sure that our jump link choice for the correct answer is **End of lesson.** See *Activity 2* for an example.

Also, when you get to the final "question", in other words the final line of the poem, you could include a link to a relevant page on the Web or on your website. In this case we could include a hyperlink to the Wikipedia page about Raymond Carver; for example, http://en.wikipedia.org/wiki/ Raymond_Carver.

Here's what the report mentioned in Step 6 might look like:

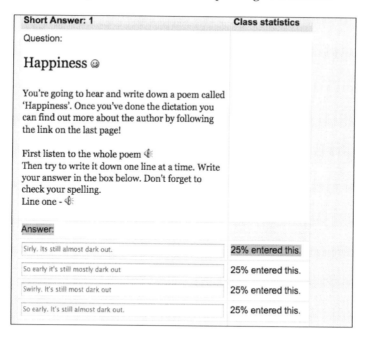

To get to that page, we click on the **Reports** tab that we saw in Step 8. We can now use that information to write more answers and accompanying feedback to try to help our students. For example, a new **Answer 5** in Step 6 could now be:

Answer 5	Sirly Its still almost dark out.
Response 5	Nearly right. 'Sirly' is two words, though.
Jump 5	Leave this at **This page**.
	Write **0** for **Score**.

Don't forget

- You can preview your lesson at any time by clicking on the **Preview** tab.
- You can use the next page to provide feedback in the form of images, video, or audio to provide extra support for the students.
- Click on **Update** (top right-hand corner) if you need to change the basic settings for this lesson.
- You can convert the lesson into a test by changing the lesson settings. For example, you can set time limits, the number of attempts, the grading, etc.

Variation 2: Creating a collaborative dictation using a Wiki

Wikis are web pages which can be edited by all users. They are a good way of getting students to work collaboratively and to allow us to set up a group dictation in which small groups of students help each other to write down what they hear.

It's probably best to divide the class into small groups of say 4 people per group. That way students benefit from each other's input without the pages getting too full of comments. You'll need to have set up groups beforehand. That's a fairly straightforward activity. See Chapter 2, *Getting Started with Moodle* if you need help. Once you've set up groups, you can use them for most other activities, too, if you wish.

This is what we're aiming to produce. Students read the introduction. They listen to the poem line by line. Then they click on the **Edit** tab and write in a transcription of what they hear. Students in the same group can check and re-edit any line.

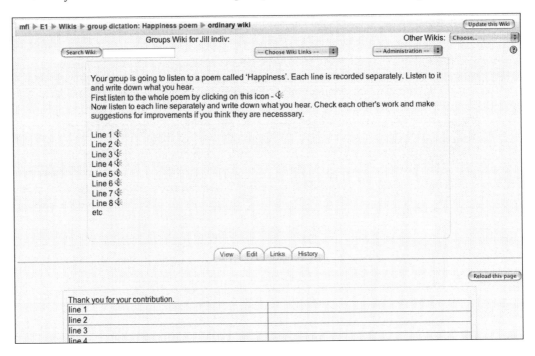

If you don't have NanoGong installed, you can follow the slightly longer procedure for embedding an audio player in the normal wiki. (See Chapter 2, *Getting Started with Moodle* for information on this).

Here's how to do it

1. First we need to set up the wiki introduction page. To do that, go to the course page, and click on **Turn editing on**. Go to the **Add an activity...** drop-down menu, and select **Wiki**.

2. Fill in the settings page. Pay attention to the following:

Settings	Details
Name	Enter an appropriate name. Let's write something like **group dictation: Happiness poem**.
Summary	This will tell the students what to do. Let's write the same as in the earlier screenshot: **Your group is going to listen to a poem called 'Happiness'. Each line is recorded separately. Listen to it and write down what you hear.** **First listen to the whole poem by clicking on this icon -** ✿**. Now listen to each line separately and write down what you hear. Check each other's work and make suggestions for improvements if you think they are necessary.**
	We now record the text for the whole poem and for each line separately as in *Variation 1*. To record, we click on the audio button ✿ in the HTML editing menu.
	Don't forget, you can use the enlarge icon ⊠ in the editing menu to increase the size of the HTML editing box if you need to be able to see more of the page. As this is a wiki, you can always go back and edit your text if necessary.
	Now finish writing the summary.
Common module settings	Let's choose **Visible groups**. That way only the student and the teacher can edit the student's wiki, but all students can see each other's wikis, which could be useful. If we don't want students to choose each other's wikis, we can choose **Separate groups** here.
Student admin options	Don't check any of these.

3. Click on **Save and display**.

4. We now have a ready-to-use wiki in front of us.

5. Now we need to set up the table. To do that, we click on the **Edit** tab.

6. First let's create a table in our wiki with 2 columns and 24 rows (the number of lines in the poem). To do that, we click on the table icon ▦ in the edit menu. See Chapter 4, *Speaking Activities, Activity 4* if you need more help with setting up tables. In each row of the left-hand column, write the line number: **line 1, line 2**, etc.

7. Click on **Save** to save the table we've just created.

   Our wiki will now look like the screenshot in the introduction.

8. Finally, we need to show students how to access the wiki.

Every group will be able to see the instructions and hear the recordings you included in the summary box, but they will only see their own group's version.

We (the teachers) can click on **Other Wikis** to see how each group is progressing. We can also add our own comments to the wiki if appropriate.

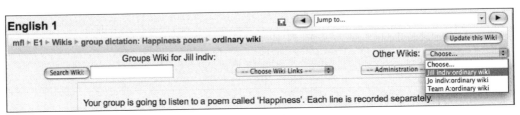

Notice that we can choose which student wiki to use from the drop-down menu in the top-left corner.

Discuss how to use wikis with the class in advance.

- Set a strict timetable for using the wiki
- Agree on a wiki etiquette; for example, being polite and friendly

It's often good to get different group members to agree on and use different colors for each other. For example, John = red, Latifa = green. That way you can easily distinguish users.

Give students time limits for completing the activity.

Agree on how students are going to contribute in advance: do they all write their own version? Do they delete each other's versions before writing their own version?

Activity 5: Using the Quiz module to practice grammar

Aim: Help students to identify correct grammar

Moodle modules: Quiz

Extra programs: None

Ease of setup: ***

Some students enjoy learning grammar in a controlled environment where grammar is set out methodically and they receive useful feedback on their attempts to use it. The Quiz module is well suited to this. There is a range of question types which can be used to practice or test grammar, such as multiple choice, true/false, gap-fill. See Chapter 9, *Assessment* for a full discussion of question types.

Quiz is flexible. If we change the settings in quiz to allow multiple attempts, students can keep practicing and improving. We can also enhance their learning more by providing informative feedback. All students' marks appear in the Moodle gradebook, which allows both students and teachers to get a good overview of students' progress. There's more information on the gradebook in Chapter 9, *Assessment*. Another nice feature of Moodle is that teachers can get a report on the responses students give. With that information we can improve the feedback we provide—making our students happier—and, if necessary, change the questions we ask. Chapter 9, *Assessment* also has more information on how we can exploit gradebook statistics.

We can test many aspects of grammar using Quiz. Here are a few of the many possibilities:

- Grammar focus
- Word order
- Verb agreement
- Structures
- Tense
- Spelling
- Punctuation
- Verb + ing
- Focus on false friends

As mentioned elsewhere, we could create a multiple-choice quiz using Hot Potatoes, but we would not get such detailed feedback on students' answers. To make sure that you can practice both Moodle Quiz activities and Hot Potatoes Quizzes, we'll practice three variations in Moodle Quiz this time.

Variation 1

Here we'll create a multiple choice quiz which asks students questions based on a text that they hear or read. They have to choose grammatically correct answers.

Variation 2

This variation is a gap-fill exercise which practices grammar points. This is similar to *Variation 1*, but focuses on small chunks of text.

Variation 3

This is a true/false test that gets students to decide whether a sentence is grammatically correct or not.

The complete procedure for setting up a quiz is described in *Variation 1*. Any differences for *Variations 2* and *3* are noted in the appropriate section.

Variation 1: Multiple-choice grammar quiz

Before we set up the Moodle Quiz, we need to work out what students are going to practice. In this example we're going to practice word order in phrasal verbs. Here are some example questions and answers:

Question 1: Where's Ahmed staying when he comes?

Answer 1: I'm putting up him here

Answer 2: I'm putting him up here

Answer 3: I'm putting him here up

Question 2: Really! I didn't know you had enough space. What are you doing with all those boxes?

Answer 1: I'm getting them rid

Answer 2: I'm getting rid them

Answer 3: I'm getting rid of them

Here's how to do it

1. On your course page, click on **Turn editing on**. Then click on **Add an activity....**

> **Adding to existing quizzes**
> If you already have a quiz that you want to add a matching question to, just open the quiz instead and go to Step 4.

2. We're going to make a quiz question, so choose **Quiz**.

3. Complete the set-up page. Most of the settings are optional, but pay attention to a few important ones. Note that your screen will either show **Adding Quiz in topic X** or **Updating Quiz in topic X**, depending on whether you're filling in the details for the first time or editing them, as in the screenshot below.

Settings	Details
Name	Let's call it **Phrasal verbs**.
Introduction	Let's write something attention-grabbing like: **Take off, take on, take up, take over...** **How well do you know your phrasal verbs?** **This quiz will practice some of the verbs we learned this week.**

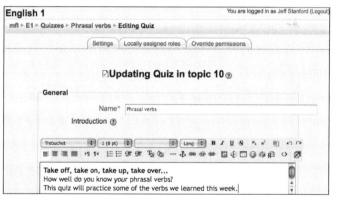

Attempts allowed	It's important to select unlimited attempts if we want students to be able to practice this as often as they want.
Adaptive mode	Let's select **Yes**. Students will then be able to benefit from our feedback and try the item again.
Grading method	Let's select **Highest grade**. That means that the highest score of each student's attempts will be entered in the gradebook. This could be a strong motivator for students to redo the quiz if they get a poor mark the first time.

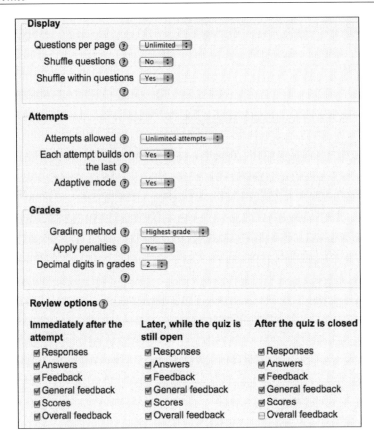

When we have finished, click on **Save and display**. Don't worry if **Save and return to course** gets clicked on by mistake. Simply find the activity we have just created on the course page and click on the hand icon ◄ to edit it.

4. Now we need to choose a question type for our quiz. From the **Question bank**, go to **Create a new question**, and choose **Multiple Choice** from the drop-down menu.

    If you can't see the **Question bank**, click on the **Edit** tab and then the **Questions** tab.

5. This takes us to the introduction page for our new quiz question, **Multiple Choice**.

Adding a multiple-choice question

Settings	Details
Category	Here we decide which category of quizzes we want our question to belong to. It's a good idea to create categories if we have a lot of questions and need to organize them. See Chapter 2, *Getting Started with Moodle* for more information on this. Let's leave it on default for now.
Question name	Let's give our question a name. How about **Phrasal verbs 1**?
Question text	Now enter the example text I gave earlier. Let's write question 1 in the **Question text** box: **Where's Ahmed staying when he comes?**
One or multiple answers	There's only one right answer, so select **One answer only**.
Choice 1	This is where we write in the distracters for question 1. For **Choice 1**, write **I'm putting up him here**.
Grade	**0.**
Feedback	**That's not right. The object goes straight after the verb.**
Choice 2	**I'm putting him up here.**
Grade	**100.**
Feedback	**well done!**
Choice 3	**I'm putting him here up.**
Grade	**0.**
Feedback	**That's nearly right. 'here' needs to go at the end though.**
Overall feedback	Here we can opt to provide standardized feedback for correct, partially correct, and incorrect answers. Note that the feedback boxes are all HTML boxes, so if we want we can include audio recordings and/or images to help explain. In this case we could remind students of the word order rules for phrasal verbs.
for any correct response	**well done!**
for any partially correct response	We're not accepting partially correct responses. So leave this.
for any incorrect response	**Remember for separable phrasal verbs the word order is Subject + Verb + object + adverb. For example:** **Paul took Maria out.** **Ahmed ate his chicken up.**

6. When you're ready, click on **Save changes**.

This quiz is going to consist of two questions. So now we need to repeat Steps 4 and 5 to create another multiple choice question, which we will call **Phrasal verbs 2**. The key things to change in our new questions are:

- ° Choice 1, 2, etc.
- ° Grade
- ° Feedback

Once both multiple choice questions are completed, our question bank will show both of them:

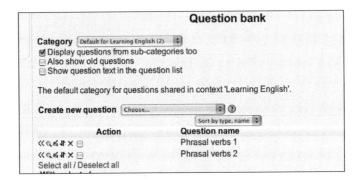

7. To insert them in our quiz we click on the chevrons (<<) to the left of the phrasal verbs questions and they will move into the quiz on the left-hand side of the page.

8. Then we click on **Save changes** and our quiz is ready to be used.

When students click on the quiz link on the quiz page, they'll see something like this:

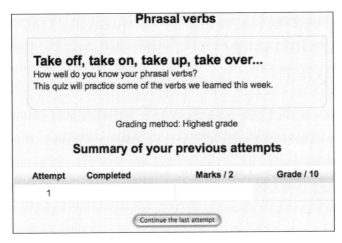

If they click on **Attempt quiz now** or **Continue the last attempt**, they'll see something like this:

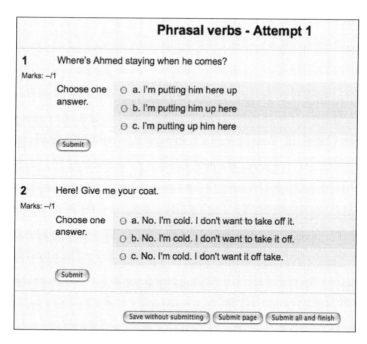

There are three choices for saving the question:

Save without submitting	The attempt will be saved and can be resumed later. The score will not go into the gradebook.
Submit page	Just this page of questions will be submitted and the marks entered in the gradebook
Submit all and finish	All the questions in the quiz will be submitted and the marks entered in the gradebook. If the student clicks on this, a dialog box saying "**You are about to close this attempt. Once you close the attempt you will no longer be able to change your answers**" will appear. But if we allowed **Unlimited attempts** on the set-up page for this button, students will in fact be able to try out the quiz again and again.

Variation 2a: Gap-fill focusing on grammar using Quiz

This variation is similar to *Variation1*, but focuses on small chunks of text within a whole text. In this example we'll focus on articles. For each gap, students will have to choose between a zero, indefinite, or definite article. As always, prepare your text in advance.

Hot Potatoes instead?

In Moodle there's currently no graphic interface for preparing your gap-fill text. So you'll have to write in the answers in a simple code. This is straightforward, but if you're at all daunted by it, don't forget that you can create a Hot Potatoes quiz and import it into Moodle instead. There's an example of a Hot Potatoes gap-fill question in *Variation 2b*. If you have time, it's a good idea to try both out and see which you prefer.

This is what we're aiming for using Moodle Quiz:

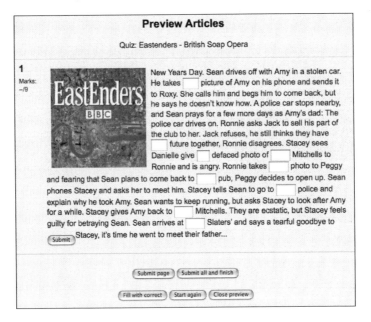

Note that one of the students' options here is **Fill with correct**. They could see all the correct answers and then click on **Start again** to see if they can remember a second time round.

Why choose the Moodle gap-fill?

Why would anyone want to choose the Moodle version of the gap-fill question (called Cloze in Moodle)? Well, as you can see below, there is more control over the marking scheme. If we're planning on editing the acceptable answers and marks, it'll also be much quicker to do that. It's also possible to mix gaps and drop-down multiple choice in the same quiz. There's an example of a multiple choice variant at the end of this variation. And the Moodle variant allows you to include penalty marks if you set up the quiz in adaptive mode. See Chapter 9, *Assessment* for more information on the adaptive mode.

Here's how to do it

The setup is identical to the gap-fill in Chapter 3, *Vocabulary Activities, Activity 11, Variation 1*. We will need to change the **Question text** in Step 5.

Here is a sample text we could use. In each case, students have to choose between -, *a*, *an*, or *the*.

Your gap-filled text could look like this (taken from the `http://bbc.co.uk` website):

Eastenders — British Soap Opera

New Years Day. Sean drives off with Amy in a stolen car. He takes _____ picture of Amy on his phone and sends it to Roxy. She calls him and begs him to come back, but he says he doesn't know how. A police car stops nearby, and Sean prays for a few more days as Amy's dad: The police car drives on. Ronnie asks Jack to sell his part of the club to her. Jack refuses, he still thinks they have _____ future together, Ronnie disagrees. Stacey sees Danielle give _____ defaced photo of _____ Mitchells to Ronnie and is angry. Ronnie takes _____ photo to Peggy and fearing that Sean plans to come back to _____ pub, Peggy decides to open up. Sean phones Stacey and asks her to meet him. Stacey tells Sean to go to _____ police and explain why he took Amy. Sean wants to keep running, but asks Stacey to look after Amy for a while. Stacey gives Amy back to _____ Mitchells. They are ecstatic, but Stacey feels guilty for betraying Sean. Sean arrives at _____ Slaters' and says a tearful goodbye to Stacey, it's time he went to meet their father...

The **Question text** in Step 5 (of *Chapter 3, Activity 11, Variation 1*) would need the following bits of code to create the gaps.

New Years Day. Sean drives off with Amy in a stolen car. He takes { : SHORTANSWER:~=a#well done! ~%20%an#nearly right!} **picture of Amy on his phone and sends it to Roxy. She calls him and begs him to come back, but he says he doesn't know how. A police car stops nearby, and Sean prays for a few more days as Amy's dad: The police car drives on. Ronnie asks Jack to sell his part of the club to her. Jack refuses, he still thinks they have** { : SHORTANSWER:~=a#well done! ~%20%an#nearly right!} **future together, Ronnie disagrees. Stacey sees Danielle give** { : SHORTANSWER:~=a#well done!} **defaced photo of** { : SHORTANSWER:~=the#well done!} **Mitchells to Ronnie and is angry. Ronnie takes** { : SHORTANSWER:~=the#well done! ~%50%a#it's possible, but we already know about the photo so 'the' is better here!} **photo to Peggy and fearing that Sean plans to come back to** { : SHORTANSWER:~=the#well done!} **pub, Peggy decides to open up. Sean phones Stacey and asks her to meet him. Stacey tells Sean to go to** { : SHORTANSWER:~=the#well done!} **police and explain why he took Amy. Sean wants to keep running, but asks Stacey to look after Amy for a while. Stacey gives Amy back to** { : SHORTANSWER:~=the#well done!} **Mitchells. They are ecstatic, but Stacey feels guilty for betraying Sean. Sean arrives at** { : SHORTANSWER:~=the#well done!} **Slaters' and says a tearful goodbye to Stacey, it's time he went to meet their father...**

Writing code the easy way

It's not as difficult as it looks at first glance. Copy the code for one gap. For example:

{ : SHORTANSWER:~=a#well done! ~%20%an#nearly right!}

Then paste it into the text wherever you want another gap. Afterwards, you just need to edit the answer, which comes before the first #, and the feedback, which comes after the last #. The key things to note in that example are:

- All answers must come between braces: {...}
- Each answer begins with a tilde: ~
- If you want to give a mark for a partially correct answer, it must be placed between percentage marks (%) and come straight after the tilde

---

Other gap-fill question types

In addition to the short answer question that we used above, there is also the possibility of creating multiple-choice gaps with drop-down menus.

Here's an example question text with a multiple-choice question:

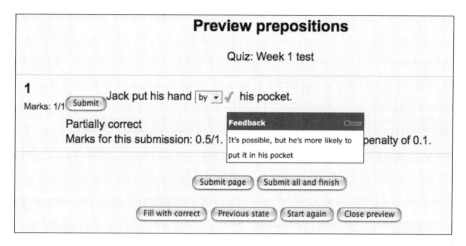

This is the question text we'd write to achieve that:

Choose the correct preposition

Jack put his hand `{1:MULTICHOICE:=in#OK~on#Wrong, try again!~at#Wrong, try again!~ %50%by#It's possible, but he's more likely to put it in his pocket}` **his pocket.**

The syntax for the answers is the same as for short answers.

See `http://docs.moodle.org/en/Embedded_Answers_%28Cloze%29_question_type` for more information on these gap-fill (Cloze) questions.

> **Other grammar items in gap-fills**
>
> Here are some other grammar items that we could test though gap-fill questions:
>
> - Articles
> - Prepositions
> - Punctuation marks
> - Tense
> - Adverb forms
> - Agreement between noun and verb
>
> Whenever possible, it's worthwhile trying to use real (authentic) texts, where the text is itself interesting and relevant to the readers. This increases motivation.

Variation 2b: Gap-fill focusing on grammar using Hot Potatoes

Most teachers I ask say they find Hot Potatoes easier to use than Moodle Quiz gap-fill. I suspect this is largely due to the attractive graphical interface that Hot Potatoes offers. So now let's create exactly the same activity as *Variation 2a*, using Hot Potatoes instead.

Here's how to do it

1. Make sure the Hot Potatoes program is on your computer. See Chapter 2, *Getting Started with Moodle* for more information on this.

2. Open the Hot Potatoes program, and choose **JCloze**.

3. We are now presented with page for entering the text. Save the file straightaway and regularly to avoid losing data. Also, we can't add an image unless we have saved our file first. To save it, click on the **File** menu and then **Save Data file**. As in other Hot Potatoes exercises, don't forget to keep all your images and files in the same folder. If you don't, any images that we insert won't be visible when we import the quiz into Moodle.

   Let's paste or write our text in:

4. Next, we highlight the words we want to gap, one at a time. That's the articles for this text. Let's start with **a** on line one. After we've highlighted it, we click on **Make Gap**. This is where we write in clues and alternative correct words.

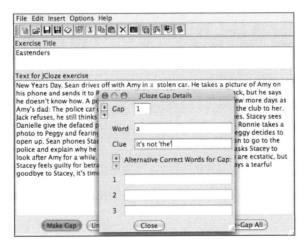

5. To finish off, we're going to add the image. To do that, place the cursor in the top left-hand corner of the text, before the word **New**. Then click on the **Insert Image** icon in the **Insert** menu. Then we browse to the image we want to use on our computer. Remember, it needs to be in the same folder that we saved this quiz in. So if it isn't, move it there first. Click on **OK** to insert the photo and we'll get this:

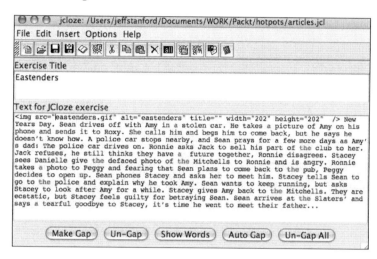

The image will show when we view the web page version. For now we have the file reference for the image. Even in Hot Potatoes we can't totally escape code.

6. Next, if we are using a Mac, we click on **Export** and **Create Standard V6 page**.

On a Windows machine, we would click on **Create a web page**.

Once we've saved our Hot Potatoes quiz, we can choose to view it straightaway by clicking on **View in Browser**. This is what we'll see:

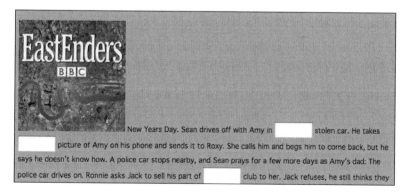

If you clicked on **Done**, you can preview the task by clicking on the saved file wherever you've saved it on your computer. That will open up the quiz in a browser.

7. Now we're going to import the matching quiz into Moodle. The procedure is exactly the same as in Chapter 3, *Vocabulary Activities*, *Activity 9*, Step 6 onwards.

   There's just one important thing to look out for. When you add the Hot Potatoes quiz to Moodle, make sure you upload the Hot Potatoes web page and the associated images to the same folder in Moodle. It's a good idea to create a folder in the Files section of your course page before you start uploading the Hot Potatoes files. See Chapter 2, *Getting Started with Moodle* if you need help with uploading images.

Variation 3: True or false? Decide if a sentence is grammatically correct or not

This is quite an effective way of reviewing students' errors or focusing on an error which is often problematical.

Here's how to do it

To create this True or False quiz, we need to follow Steps 1 to 4 of *Variation 1*, but this time we call the quiz **True or false**. These steps set up the quiz framework. Our set-up page will look something like this:

When we've finished the introduction page and reach the question bank, we need to choose **True/False** as our new question.

5   This takes us to the introduction page for our new Quiz question, **True/False**. Fill the details paying attention to the following.

Adding a True/False question

Settings	Details
Question name	Let's call it **T/F Question 1**. That way we can distinguish it from other Question 1s that might be in our Question bank.
Question text	Write the true or false sentence here. For example: **I have been here three times yesterday**
Feedback for the response 'True'	Write **Think again!**
Feedback for the response 'False'	Write **That sentence is not correct. Well done!**

Note that the **True** in the first feedback doesn't mean it's correct. It means that that's the feedback we'll give if the student thinks the sentence is true (correct).

When the page is finished, we click on **Save changes**. Now we can add more "true or false" questions to our quiz by repeating Steps 4 and 5, or we can transfer our question to our "true or false" quiz by clicking on the chevrons (<<) and pressing **Save changes** again as in Steps 7 and 8 of *Variation 1*.

The quiz is now ready to use. This is what a preview of our first question looks like:

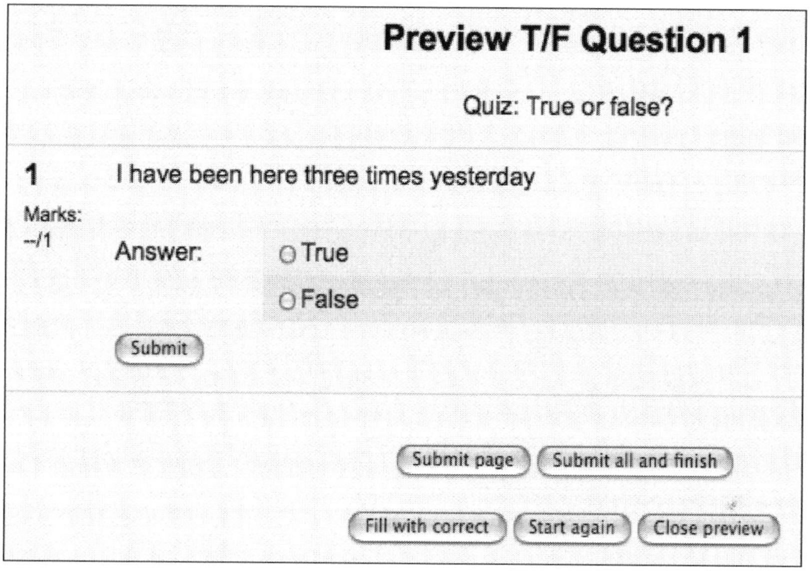

Activity 6: Using a chat session transcript to analyze grammar errors

Aim: Help students analyze language errors generated by an online chat

Moodle modules: Chat plus optional use of Wiki and Forum

Extra programs: Optional use of word processor or Audacity

Ease of setup: *

This activity is similar to Chapter 3, *Vocabulary Activities*, *Activity 7*. The key difference is that we are reviewing grammar errors rather than vocabulary errors. For the final analysis you might find it useful to add a middle column which uses symbols to indicate what the grammar mistake relates to. For example:

T	tense
WO	word order
Prep	preposition
Sp	spelling
Punc	punctuation

This is what Step 1b of Chapter 3, *Vocabulary Activities*, *Activity 7* might look like when we're analyzing it for grammar errors.

Online chat—correcting your errors		
INSTRUCTIONS		
1. Cover the corrections in the left hand column 2. Look at the words in bold in the dialog 3. Try to correct them 4. Then compare your answer to the corrected version		
Error	**Type of error**	**Correction**
Juanita: Hi Jaime. How are you? <u>Are you do</u> anything nice yesterday?	T	Did you do
Jaime: Hi Juanitaaaaa. Yes, I went with some <u>freinds</u> to a baseball game. How about you?	Sp	friends
Juanita: Ah, you know I like <u>very much</u> to go to the salsateca. I went there with Liliana last night. Great music! Hey, do you like salsa?	WO	I like to go to the salsateca very much
Jaime: Ah you know. It depends <u>of</u> the band. Some bands are cool, like Salsa Neuva. They're fantastic.	Prep	It depends on

Key: **T** = tense **WO** = word order **Prep** = preposition **sp** = spelling **punc** = punctuation

Other ideas

- You could make a Podcast based on students' errors, like the one in *Activity 1*.
- You could prepare an online version of this using an HTML page and use the mouse hover feature described in the introduction to Chapter 8, *Listening Activities*. Students could then see the correct answer when they hover over the pink square.

And here's what students would see when they hover over the pink square:

What's the error?	
First try to work it out yourself. Then hover your mouse over the pink square to hear the version.	
Your dialog - errors are underlined	
Juanita: Hi Jaime. How are you? <u>Are you do</u> anything nice yesterday?	Did you do anything nice yesterday?
Jaime: Hi Juanitaaaaa. Yes, I went with some <u>freinds</u> to a baseball game. How about you?	
Juanita: Ah, you know <u>I like very much to go to the salsateca.</u> I went there with Liliana last night. Great music! Hey, do you like salsa?	
Jaime: Ah you know. It <u>depends of the band.</u> Some bands are cool, like Salsa Neuva. They're fantastic.	

Activity 7: Peer grammar review using the Forum module

Aim: Get students to review grammar in each other's writing

Moodle modules: Forum

Extra programs: None

Ease of setup: *

Getting students to review each other's writing for grammar mistakes can be motivating and informative for both the writer and the corrector. In this activity we use the Forum module to get students to post texts. Other students then post replies which query any grammar they're not sure about, and which offer suggestions as well. At an agreed time, the tutor then reviews the forums and comments on any points that students have got wrong and commends students for points they got right. The activity helps all students get an opportunity to construct their knowledge through analysis, reflection, and discussion. It probably helps to set up groups of 4 or 5 students to restrict the amount of work students have to do.

This is what a finished forum exchange might look like:

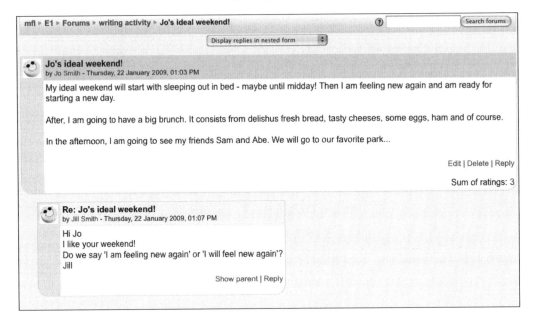

Here's how to do it

1. Set up a Forum activity. To do that, click on **Turn editing on**, which you'll find on the course page.

2. Go to **Add an activity...**, and then click on the **Forum** activity in the drop-down menu.

3. Complete the introductory page. This is what we're aiming for. Note that you will see **Adding Forum...** at the top of the page if you are adding the set-up page for the first time or **Updating Forum...** if you are editing the set-up page later.

Pay attention to the following in particular:

Settings	Details
Forum name	Let's call it **Writing review – my ideal weekend**.
Forum type	Decide what type of forum you want. I suggest we select **each person posts one discussion**. This will prevent students from starting additional posts.
Forum introduction	Explain what the purpose of the forum is. In this case it is to help students practice writing and to review grammar mistakes, so we could write something like this: **WRITING TASK** **Your task is to write a short essay called 'my ideal weekend'. You can add pictures if you want to. Pay particular attention to accuracy. Afterwards your group will read each other's writing and post replies about any grammar they think is wrong, or any grammar they think is really good. Remember you have up to 30 minutes to edit your posting once you have submitted it.** **Reviewing each other's work** **After you have written your piece, read each other's work and write a reply about any grammar mistakes. Look out for:** **Spelling, punctuation, tenses, agreement, prepositions in particular!** **At the end of the week I will review all the posts and let you know how you did.** **Teacher Jeff** You could also include a spoken introduction, images, or even video. Images could make the page more attractive, or focus students' attention on the activity. See Chapter 2, *Getting Started with Moodle* if you need help with this.
Aggregate type	There is a choice between: • **No ratings** • **Average of ratings** • **Count of ratings** – the number of times the student is rated • **Maximum ratings** – the highest of all the ratings • **Minimum ratings** – the lowest of all the ratings • **Sum of ratings** – all the ratings added together Let's choose **Maximum ratings** to motivate our students. N.B. We must choose a type other than **No ratings** for the **Grade** system to work (next section).

Settings	Details
Grade	Here you have the possibility of rating each contribution to the forum. Let's set a scale of 1-6 (see Chapter 9, *Assessment* for information on setting scales), which we will use to assess each posting. We can add our scales if we wish. See Chapter 2, *Getting Started with Moodle* for more information on that.
Common module settings	Set group mode to **Separate groups**. That means that students will work in separate groups and won't be able to see each other's work. See Chapter 2, *Getting Started with Moodle* for help with setting up groups if necessary.
	To help you visualize this, the introduction to the activity that we write will be seen by all groups, but each group member will only see postings from his or her own group.
	Helping your students:
	If your students belong to more than one group, make sure they select the appropriate group before submitting their first posting. For example, student Jo might be in an individual group, called 'Jo's individual group', which he uses for his individual glossaries. He might also be in a small group of 4 students, called 'Team A', which he uses for collaborative work. If Jo selects Team A, then all other members of Team A will see his writing and he will be able to see theirs.

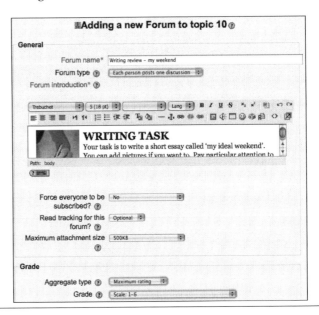

4. Save the settings by clicking on **Save and display**.

The forum is now ready to be used. Students should click on the forum activity **Writing review – my weekend** on the course page. They can then click on **Add a new discussion topic** to submit their short essay or click on **reply** to post their comments about each other's work.

Advising students

It's worth giving students some advice on how they are going to help each other. They won't be able to edit the original, but they will be able to comment on it. It often works if they write full sentences as in the introductory screenshot to this activity. Alternatively, you may like to develop a system where they write something like this in their forum replies:

Query: I am feeling well again

Suggestion: I feel well again

The **Query** is the bit of language the second student is not sure about. The **Suggestion** is what they think it should be. Such a system tends to be easier for students to cope with.

We teachers can choose to see different groups by selecting them from the drop-down menu in the top left-hand corner.

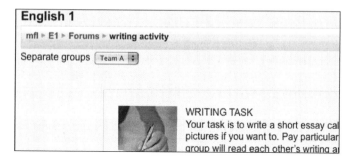

If you need a few reminders on how to continue with your forum after starting a new discussion, see Chapter 4, *Speaking Activities, Activity 1*.

As with forums in general, it's important to moderate the discussions. Be available regularly, to explain and help; also, to redirect the discussion if it's going off course.

Activity 8: Providing feedback on grammar using the Assignment module

Aim: Practice grammar in extended pieces of writing or speaking

Moodle modules: Assignment

Extra programs: None

Ease of setup: **

One way we can help students improve the grammar in their writing and speaking is by providing detailed feedback on a draft version of a text they are preparing, and then getting them to submit an improved version of that draft. The students' text can be written or spoken. To submit recordings, students can either use the add-on NanoGong audio recorder or they can record a file on their computer and submit it as an attachment. See Chapter 2, *Getting Started with Moodle* for more help with NanoGong and audio recording.

We can use the Assignment module in Moodle to give feedback on writing and speaking in two ways:

- We can use the Outcomes feature to set up a rating scale which provides a general comment on the student's grammar.
- We can provide detailed feedback in the form of hints, which get the students to try to correct their own errors. Later they can submit an improved version. Our feedback can be written or spoken. The easiest way to provide oral feedback is to make a recording by clicking on the NanoGong audio button ⊕ in the HTML editor. Don't forget, NanoGong needs to be installed first. See Chapter 2, *Getting Started with Moodle* if you need help with that.

The advantage of the second point is that students can try to process their mistakes and learn from them. The disadvantage for teachers is that we have to mark the students' work twice.

Process overview

Here's a quick overview of the whole process:

1. Teacher sets assignment task with online marking.
2. Student submits assignment task.
3. Teacher clicks on grading panel, gives mark for grammar and content, and hints on grammar mistakes.
4. Student reviews task, improves it, and resubmits it.
5. Teacher gives final mark.

This is the grading panel that teachers see in Step 3 after a student called Jane Smith has submitted a letter of complaint to a certain Mr Smith:

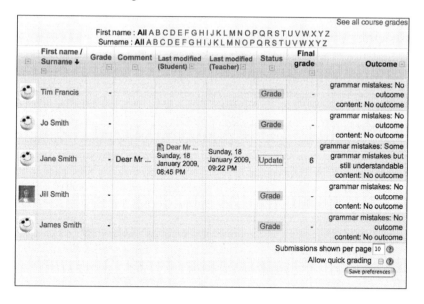

We click on **Grade** or **Update** in the **Status** column and that allows us to enter a mark for grammar mistakes and to provide hints on the grammar mistakes: Step 4.

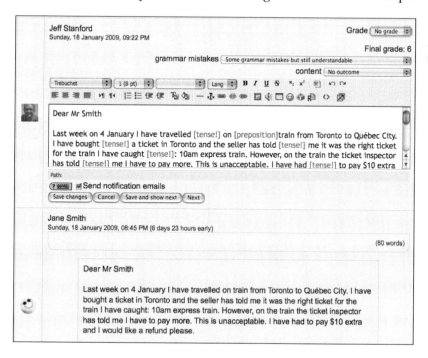

At the bottom of the screenshot, we can see a submission made by **Jane Smith** on **18 January, 2009**. In the middle panel, the teacher has added hints in red brackets, like [tense], which point students towards the corrections they should be making. So in the above example where Jane Smith wrote **I have travelled**, she should change it to **I travelled**.

In the top right-hand corner, there are three grading menus.

Type of feedback	Details
Grade	This is a drop-down menu in the top right-hand corner which allows us to give a grade based on the scale we chose in Step 3.
Grammar mistakes	This is an outcome in the form of a drop-down menu. It allows us to assess grammar in particular. This is the Moodle outcome that we set up before building this activity. We can also add other outcomes such as style, vocabulary, organization, responding to the task.
Inline comments	We enabled this on the set-up page. The top text box allows us to add comments on the students' texts. It's a good idea to change the color we use to distinguish our text from the students'. If the text is longer than a few lines, you may find it easier to click on the enlarge icon . The full-screen editor also gives us more editing options, such as strikethrough and table editing icons.

See Chapter 9, *Assessment* for a fuller explanation of outcomes.

> The student's final grade can be modified after the second submission.
>
> We could cut down on our work by correcting the mistakes straightaway, but then there's the danger that students won't learn from them. A common and popular teacher strategy is a hybrid solution where some mistakes are corrected and some receive hints.

Which texts?

The text submitted by students could be written or spoken. Teachers can provide grammar feedback on both. Here are a few ideas for the sorts of written and spoken texts students could work on:

Written	Spoken
story	story
letter	presentation
essay	role-play dialog
postcard	joke
email	review
translation	translation

We're going to set up a letter for the writing assignment in *Variation 1* and a review of a TV program for the speaking assignment in *Variation 2*.

Variation 1: Providing grammar feedback on a written text

In this variation students are going to submit a letter for us to mark. So we can assume that they have already had help with preparing a letter and have a good idea of the style, organization, and length that would be appropriate.

Here's how to do it

1. First we need to set up the Assignment introduction page. To do that, go to the course page and click on **Turn editing on**.

2. Go to the **Add an activity...** drop-down menu, and select **Assignments | Online text**.

3. Complete the introductory page as follows. Pay particular attention to the following items. The other settings are optional.

Settings	Details
Assignment name	Let's call it **letter of complaint**.
Description	We should try to include as much useful information as possible in the **Description** box so that students know exactly what is expected of them. Let's write this:
	## Writing a letter of complaint
	Have you ever had to pay too much on a train or a bus? Were you angry? In this task you can practice writing a letter of complaint to a train or bus company. **First make notes about the problem. Write down as many details as you can.** **Then write your letter and submit it.** **Happy writing!**
Grade	Here we can choose the scale we want to use for marking these assignments. Let's choose the **Scale: 1-6** from the dropdown menu. That means students will get a total mark out of 6. We can add our own scales if we want. See Chapter 2, *Getting Started with Moodle* for help with this.
Available from	Pay attention to the dates you want the assignment to be available.
Due date	Having strict dates helps students organize their time, in theory.
Allow resubmitting	Here we must select **Yes**. We want our students to be able to respond to our feedback and submit improved versions.
Email alerts to teachers	Let's click on **Yes** for this, too. It's very useful to receive an email alert as soon as students submit their work. Only teachers who have permission to grade the particular submission are notified. So, for example, if the course uses separate groups, then teachers restricted to particular groups won't receive any notices about students in other groups.
Comment inline	We need to click on **Yes** for this, too. It will enable us to comment inline on our students' work and provide them hints in a different color to their text.

Settings	Details
Outcomes	Here we check the outcomes we want to include.

If you can't see any outcomes, it's for one of two reasons: you haven't created any for your Moodle site and/or you have created them, but you haven't selected them for your course. See Chapter 2, *Getting Started with Moodle* for information about creating outcomes. Go to the **Outcomes** button on your course page to use the outcomes on your course.

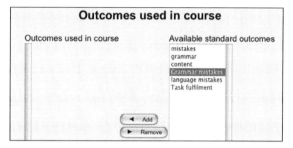

For this activity, let's create an outcome called **Grammar mistakes** and use the default called **content**. To use them in this assignment, we check both of them. Adding a content outcome, and maybe other outcomes, too, is often a good way of balancing out low marks for grammar when the student's content is still good.

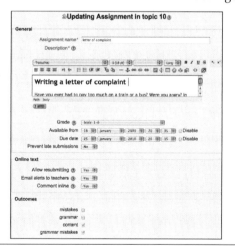

Outcomes

N.B. Once outcomes have been checked and we have started using them, we can't uncheck them.

4. Click on **Save and display**. The assignment is now ready for students to do.

5. To see the letters submitted by the students, we need to click on the assignment link on the course page. Then we click on the **View N submitted assignments** link in the top right-hand corner.

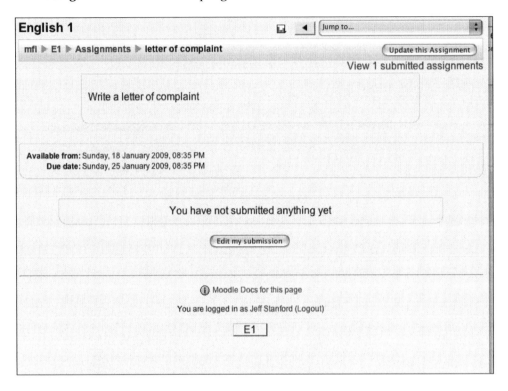

If no assignments have been submitted, we'll get a message saying just that: **No attempts have been made on this assignment.**

We are then presented with three ways of giving feedback on the grammar, as described in the introduction to this activity.

After we mark the first draft, students can check what we have written by clicking on the assignment link on the course page. They can click on **Edit my submission** and use the notes or hints that we have provided to try to correct their grammar mistakes. When they're happy with their new version, they click on **Save changes**.

When we click on **View assignments**, as shown in the introduction to this activity, Jane's entry now shows the message **Grade**, because it needs to be regraded. If Jane hadn't resubmitted her letter, the **Status** would still be **Update**, which is what shows when we have graded some work but the student hasn't submitted a second draft. When we regrade, we can change any or all of the grades mentioned in the introduction: the final grade and outcomes for grammar mistakes and content.

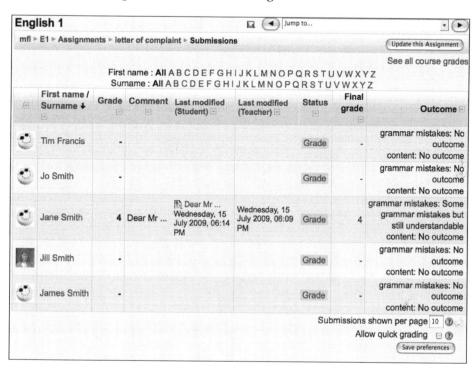

Variation 2: Providing grammar feedback on a spoken text

This variation is more or less the same as *Variation 1*. The main differences are:

We need to change the task description to a suitable spoken task.

We need to prepare students to upload a recording. They can either make a recording on their computer, save it, and then and upload it as a file, or they can record straight into NanoGong if you have it installed.

Here's what a submission with a NanoGong recording could look like:

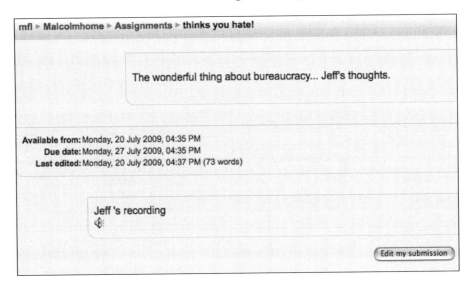

File size

On the assignment set-up page, increase the file upload to the maximum size as audio files, and make sure students know what the maximum size is. It's useful if you can show students how to save their audio file as a compressed MP3 file, as it takes up less space than a WAV file, which is uncompressed.

6
Reading Activities

Why would you want to use Moodle for teaching reading? There are the advantages that all **Virtual Learning Environments (VLEs)** like Moodle have. For example, you can use Moodle to store and organize large numbers of texts. They can be long or short and in different languages. You can also set up a variety of interactive activities based on reading texts. It's particularly useful that students can work in their own time. So if they're having problems with reading, they can take their time, go over texts and exercises several times, or go back to half-finished activities when it suits them.

There is a pleasing variety of activities that we can set up in Moodle, as we'll see in this chapter. As always, don't be daunted by the amount of time it takes to set up a reading activity. Start with a simple project. For example, produce one reading text and write some questions for it. Get colleagues or students to try it out. Then, as your confidence grows, try another activity. You'll be surprised how quickly you can build up a body of texts and exercises. You'll be pleased to know that you can copy all of these texts and exercises into other Moodle courses if you need to.

This chapter

Moodle provides many useful tools for helping students practice reading. This chapter will focus in particular on:

- Motivating students to read through reading authentic texts, discussion, polls, reviews, and questionnaires (*Activities 1, 2, 3*)
- Interacting with texts through anticipation and comprehension exercises (*Activities 4, 5, 6, 7*)

What's not covered

- Reading aloud — but it is covered in Chapter 4, *Speaking Activities*.
- Timed reading is not included, as there is no module available yet. It is, however, possible to change the period during which students can see the questions.
- Extended reading — but it is covered in Chapter 10, *Extended Activities*.

Sourcing texts

Where can you get your texts from? There are several possibilities. One option is for you or your students to write them yourselves, but this can be time-consuming. There are also many copyright-free texts on the Internet. For example, around 30,000 copyright-free texts are available at the Gutenberg project site: `http://www.gutenberg.org/`. Alternatively, check out the electronic texts archive on Google: `http://www.google.com/Top/Arts/Literature/Electronic_Text_Archives/`. Note that once the texts are included in your Moodle, only your Moodle site users will have access to them if you use an enrollment key for your course. See Chapter 2, *Getting Started with Moodle* for more information on this.

Word or scan?

On the whole, it's a good idea not to use scanned (picture) versions, because you can't edit the text contained in an image easily. If you copy and paste a Word text and end up with extra formatting code from Word, try highlighting the text on your web page in Moodle and then clicking on the Word cleaning icon 📝 in the top right-hand corner of the editing menu.

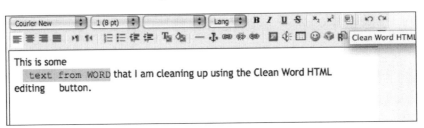

Autolinking

Once you have inputted your text into Moodle, you can make the most of built-in features like **autolinking**, which lets users look up difficult words in the Moodle Glossary. You'll need to set up the Glossary module for it to work.

To save inputting time, you could also think about importing wordlists from other sources into your glossary. See Chapter 2, *Getting Started with Moodle* for information on how to do that.

> **Attractive text**
>
> You can also tidy up your text by formatting it to look more attractive. See Chapter 11, *Formatting and Enhancing Your Moodle Materials* for some help with this.

Storing texts

Should you store texts within the Moodle system or outside it, on your computer hard disk for example? Keeping texts within Moodle means you have more opportunities to use them interactively. For example, students could use the search function in the glossary to look up keywords in texts stored there. Clearly, copyright issues and excessive length of texts will sometimes prohibit storing of texts on Moodle.

Any of the following modules will allow you to use Moodle as a text repository:

- Glossary.
- Book—this allows you to break down text into smaller segments. You can also use it for reading and listening activities.
- Moodle Web pages.
- RSS feed (see Chapter 2, *Getting Started with Moodle* for help with this).

Eye fatigue

Some students (and teachers) suffer from eye fatigue from spending a long time in front of the screen. It's worth taking advice on screen readability and physical support, if you think these areas might be problematical. For example, Chapter 11, *Formatting and Enhancing Your Moodle Materials* offers some advice on improving layout and readability. This website is one of many that offer advice on making the activity physically more comfortable: `http://www.computervisionreadingeyeglasses.com/eye_fatigue_symptoms.htm`.

Activity 1: Using Forum for a book discussion

Aim: Help motivate students by discussing what books to read

Moodle modules: Forum

Extra programs: None

Ease of setup: *

A key element in any activity is motivating our students. This is particularly so with reading, which requires stamina, concentration, and time for many students.

We can use the Forum module to personalize the choice of reading and build up excitement and anticipation.

In this activity we're going to focus on setting up a simple discussion in which students discuss what books to read. Before we do that, we need to think of some good questions to start a discussion. One could be an open question like:

This month our class is going to read and discuss some books in English. What books would you like to read? Post your thoughts and say why you chose your book!

If it's difficult for your students to suggest books themselves, or you would like them to consider a specific set of books, you could suggest some titles, describe them briefly, and get students to say which ones they'd prefer and why. For example:

This month our class is going to read and discuss some books in English. Take a look at the following list of books. Choose one or two you'd like to read and say why.

- **The Enchanted Castle by E. Nesbit**
- **Hammerfall by C.J. Cherryh**
- **Nothing to be frightened of by Julian Barnes**

Book covers

You can also brighten up the forum by including images of the book cover, which you can easily copy from Amazon.com—this is likely to be seen as "fair use" under your country's copyright law. Check if you're in doubt.

Here's how to do it

1. Set up a forum activity. To do that, click on **Turn editing on**, which you'll find on the course page.

2. Go to **Add an activity...**, and then click on the **Forum** activity in the drop-down menu.

3. Complete the introductory page. This is what we're aiming for. Note that you will see **Adding Forum...** if you are adding the set-up page for the first time or **Updating Forum...** if you are editing the setup page later.

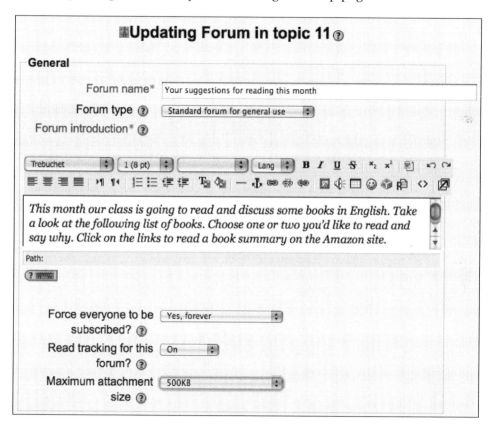

Pay attention to the following in particular:

Settings	Details
Forum name	Let's call it **Your suggestions for reading this month**.
Forum type	Decide what type of forum you want. Let's choose **Standard forum for general use**. That's useful if we want students to be able to start new discussion threads on the forum.
Forum introduction	Here we explain what the purpose of the forum is. It might be helpful if we put links to summaries of books on sites like Amazon.com. To do that, highlight the word you want to link, click on the hyperlink icon in the editor menu ⊕ , and add the URL (that's the web address) of the target site. If you're copying and pasting the URL, note that the http:// part is already filled in for you. It's easy to add a full URL yourself and end up with something like http://http:// which won't work.

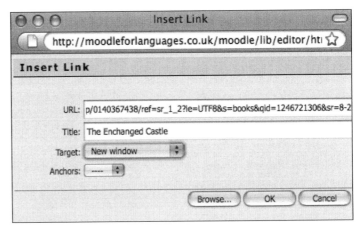

Don't forget to change **Target** to **New window** so that when students click on the link, it opens in a new browser window and doesn't hide the Moodle site. Click **OK** when you've finished adding the details.

4. Save the settings by clicking on **Save and display**.

The forum is now ready to be used. Here's what the forum introduction will look like:

5. As well as writing the forum introduction, it's sometimes a good idea for the teacher to write the first post to get the ball rolling. To do that, click on **Add a new discussion topic** and write away. Don't forget to save your post afterwards. If you need a few reminders on how to continue with your forum after starting a new discussion, see Chapter 4, *Speaking Activities*, *Activity 1*.

 As with forums in general, it's important to moderate the discussions. Be available regularly, to explain and help; also, to redirect the discussion if it's going off course.

Other Forum ideas

Book club forum:

If book reading is a regular part of your group's work, why not consider making your forum into a book club. A few guidelines to help you:

- Provide sufficient time for students to read the book in advance
- Give clear discussion questions
- Limit to the group size so that all students can participate
- Make it clear when the forum discussion will be available
- Moderate the group to help motivate and steer the students
- The BBC notes on setting up a book club might be helpful, too: http://www.bbc.co.uk/radio4/arts/bookclub/running1.shtml

Listen and comment forum:

You could also consider including an audio recording of people discussing the text. That could be a link to a recording on the Internet, or a recording you have made. See Chapter 4, *Speaking Activities* for more information on making recordings.

Read and compare forum:

Students read two texts on similar topics. They then compare and contrast them.

Activity 2: Using Web pages to read and listen

Aim: Help students follow text by allowing them to read and listen simultaneously

Moodle modules: Moodle Web page or Book

Extra programs: NanoGong or Audacity

Ease of setup: *

How can we help students when they find it difficult to understand what they hear? One simple solution is to let them read a transcript while they listen to the text. This is straightforward to set up. We can use a Moodle Web page for a one-page text, or we can use another module called Book if you want to divide up a text into several parts. The Book module is a helpful way of organizing web pages. It's like an independent website. Here's what a Book module with a selection of stories might look like. The **Table of Contents** is on the left and the text is on the right.

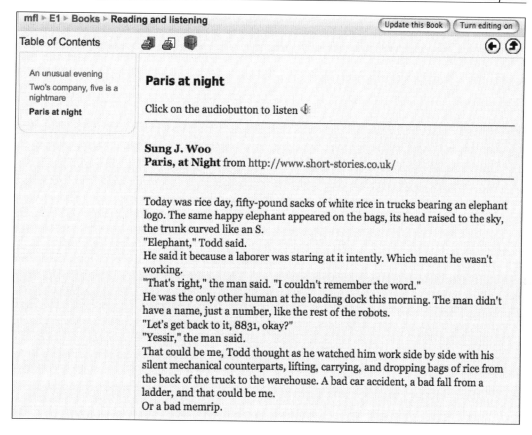

If the text is short, you can record it on NanoGong (the add-on recording facility), as in the screenshot above. That's the easy option. See the introduction to Chapter 4, *Speaking Activities* if you need help with using NanoGong. If you want to record a longer text or import a text recorded by someone else, it's probably better to use the Moodle audio player, which looks like this: ▶■▬▬▬. Other advantages of the latter option are that:

- You can create a better quality recording
- You can easily create fast and slower-speed versions of the same text
- Students can stop/start the recording more easily

Since we have a longer text in this example, we'll create a recording using Audacity, the free recording program. Then we'll embed it in a Moodle Web page module and add text. *Embed,* here, is computer speak for insert.

Here's how to do it

Preparing a recording

1. First we need to create a recording in Audacity. See Chapter 2, *Getting Started with Moodle* if you need help with this. At this stage you could also edit your recording to produce a slowed-down version if you think your students will benefit from it. You could even make slower and normal speed recordings available. Don't forget to export your recording(s) as MP3 files.

Creating a web page

2. Now we're going to create the web page where we'll put the recording and the text. First we need to go to our course home page and click on **Turn editing on**. Then we click on **Add a new resource...** and select **Compose a web page** from the drop-down menu.

3. Complete the introductory page. Pay attention to the following in particular:

Settings	Details
Name	Let's call it **Read and listen – Middlemarch**, because this example text extract is taken from the book of that name.
Summary	Write a brief statement about the page so that students know what to expect when they are browsing activities. Let's write: **This activity allows you to read and listen at the same time. The text is the beginning of the story, Middlemarch, by George Eliot.**
Compose a web page	This is where we provide a link to the recording and input the text. To upload the recording, follow the instructions in Chapter 2, *Getting Started with Moodle*. Then write or paste in the text.

4. Click on **Save and display**.

This is what it will look like when it's finished:

The player is simple, but it is easy to move backwards and forwards in the recording by dragging the play icon backwards and forwards.

Activity 3: Using Choice for voting on texts

Aim: Using polls to vote on a text

Moodle modules: Choice

Extra programs: None

Ease of setup: *

Yes, it's good to promote a serious attitude to learning, but whenever we bring in some fun, motivation levels always seem to go up. One way of doing this in Moodle, as we saw in Chapter 3, *Vocabulary Activities*, is to get students to vote on texts that they have read. Which one was better?

The texts could be simple, like motivational quotes, or longer like extracts from websites, or reviews. You could also get students to read the information on a story from a book cover or a website and then vote on it. The Choice module allows students to select just one response. In the example below they'll decide which of two books they'd rather read. The back cover information and images in each case are taken from Amazon.com. You can copy and paste the text and right-click on the images in Amazon to save them.

Here's how to do it

1. On the course page, click on **Turn editing on**. Go to the **Add an activity...** drop-down menu, and select **Choice**.
2. Fill in the settings page. If a setting isn't mentioned below, then it's optional.

Settings	Details
Choice name	Write an appropriate title for the activity. Let's call this **choose a book**. To include images, click on the image icon 🖼 . Then browse and upload your saved images. There's help on this in Chapter 2, *Getting Started with Moodle*, if you need it. Make sure that the size of the image does not exceed the Moodle maximum. Ask your administrator if you need help with this. Don't worry if you don't have picture now, you can come back to this page later, by clicking on the activity link on the course page and then clicking on **Update this page**.

Settings	Details
Choice text	Write a simple task for students to follow. I've written: 'Which of the following 2 books would you like to read? Read the blurb and vote below.'
Choice 1	Under **Choice 1**, write **Crows**.
Choice 2	Under **Choice 2**, write **Crows and Ravens**.
Display mode	If we have a lot of students, we can go for **horizontal**. If we have few, then **vertical** would be appropriate. Let's go for a **vertical**.
Publish results	Show results to students after they answer. They will probably want to see the results straightaway.

3. Press **Save and display**. The finished choice activity looks like this:

4. The poll is ready to use. Students click on the activity link on the course page, read the blurb, and vote by clicking on **Save my choice** at the bottom of the page.

Students will see a results page like this once they have voted:

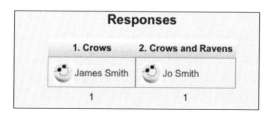

Activity 4: Using Blog to explore texts

Aim: Investigate the meaning of interesting words through their context

Moodle modules: Blog and Blog Tags block

Extra programs: Optional—HTML block with link to online dictionary

Ease of setup: **

One of the appealing features of Moodle is that parts of it can be personalized by students. We can see this in Chapter 3, *Vocabulary Activities* with the My Moodle Personal Glossary, in Chapter 7, *Writing Activities* with personal profiles and journals, and in most of the other chapters with blogs and wikis. In this activity we are going to apply the personal factor to blogs. We can help students choose their own texts, investigate them using an online dictionary, and highlight interesting words in Moodle Tags. Tags are keywords that we associate with a text. We can display a collection of tags in a tag block like this.

In the following screenshot, **music** is the most popular tagged word.

> **Tags - from Personal**
> **Profile interests and**
> **your BLOG tags** ⊟
>
> academic earth Activism Animal
> Rights architecture Art Athletics
> badminton bikes **books** bowling
> cinema cooking cooking and
> breathing. **dancing design** dog
> training Dogs - particularly flatcoated
> retrievers drama earth Eating ELT
> English Language exercising food
> food (!!!) football fresh air and
> sunshine funny things Gender Studies
> German Language GLBTT Rights
> hanging out hills. History ICT image
> International Relations iTunes kites
> languages **Literature** Making Music
> moodle movies **music** Online
> and Distance Learning peace
> philosophy **photography** playing
> guitar playing the bass guitar playing
> the guitar playing the instruments
> podcast pretty much everything
> psychobilly psychology reading
> Reading (mostly biographies) salsa
> shopping. **singing skiing** snorkeling
> soft things sport surf music swimming
> table tennis technology theatre
> Theology travel travelling travelling
> singing dancing cooking shopping
> fitnes violin vodcast voicethread
> walking watching and playing
> American football.

If we click on one of the tags, we can see the blog that they come from.

In this activity, students (or the teacher) select short texts which they copy and paste into their blogs. The texts could be anything that is interesting, relevant, and appropriate. They could come from:

- Students' own writing
- News articles
- Short stories
- Poems
- Songs
- Letters
- Reviews

The list is endless. The advantage of students choosing the texts is that they're texts that they want to read. If students need a helping hand, a halfway house would be for teachers to provide a selection of texts which students choose from.

Once the texts are in the students' blogs, students then select words they want to tag. These can be interesting, difficult, or important words, but, as with the texts, the important thing is that they are words that the student chooses. The teacher sets up a blog tag block on the course page; students can then click on one of the tags, and it will take them to the text where they can try to make sense of the interesting word in its context.

You might consider including a link to an online dictionary in an HTML block on the course page, so that students can look up difficult words. For English, for example, there is a downloadable search box available at `http://www.merriam-webster.com/downloads/index.htm`, as illustrated here. Look up "online dictionary widget" on Google to find dictionary search boxes for other languages.

See Chapter 2, *Getting Started with Moodle* if you need help with setting up an HTML block.

Other forum ideas

Most of the instructions below refer to what students need to do. Probably, the most effective way of preparing them for this activity is face to face in class. If not, consider writing clear instructions on a separate web page for students to follow. There are more ideas for preparing students to use Moodle in Chapter 12, *Preparing Your Students to Use Moodle*.

Here's how to do it

1. First, go to the course home page, and click on **Turn editing on**. Scroll down to the drop-down block menu on the right, and select **Blog Tags**.

    Later, when students have added tags to their blogs, this block will fill up with their tagged words as in this screenshot. The more often a word is tagged, the bigger the word in the blog tag becomes.

2. Now tell students to go to their blogs. They do that by clicking on their names in the top right-hand corner of the screen and then clicking on **Blog**.

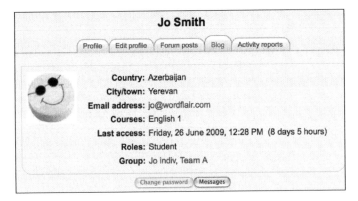

3. Students now click on **Add a new entry** from the **Blog** menu or from the link at the top of the text box.

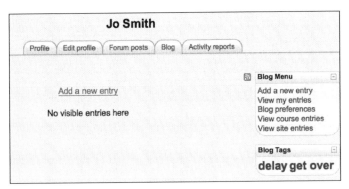

4. They can now paste their text into the **Blog entry body**. Here's an example from http://thejokes.co.uk/british-humour.php, with a bit of British humor:

    Postman: Is this letter for you? The name is smudged.
    Man: No, it can't be for me, my name is Smith.

5. Students should now identify any keywords. I'll choose the word **smudged** and write it in the **User defined tags** section at the bottom of the page.

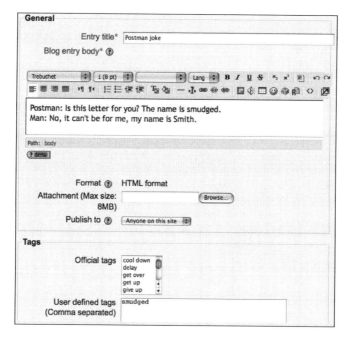

6. They should now click on **Save changes** to save their blog.

7. Once all students have done Steps 2 to 6, tell them to go to the course home page and choose some of the blog tags to investigate.

    It gets much more interesting and fun for students once there are lots of tags, as a sizeable blog tag cloud will grow.

Students can click on any word to see where the words were used. For example, if students click on the word **delay** in the blog tag cloud in Step 1, they'll see these two entries:

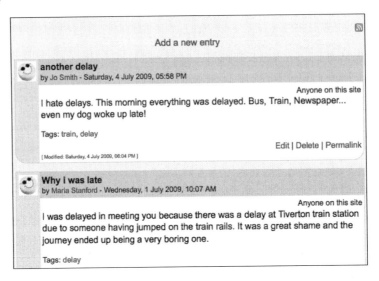

Activity 5: Using Questionnaire to explore texts

Aim: Get students to think about texts through a questionnaire

Moodle modules: Questionnaire add-on

Extra programs: None

Ease of setup: ***

Why would we want to use questionnaires to explore texts? They help us to get students to think about texts in some detail. Students can benefit from an overview of other students' opinions. Our questions can be as general or detailed as we want them to be. We could also get students to contribute questions beforehand, which may motivate them further. And finally, Moodle will calculate grades for the answers automatically.

Questionnaire is similar to Quiz in those respects with a few crucial differences:

- In Questionnaire, students can view their own and each other's responses easily (a bit like an elaborate poll).

- It allows students to print out or download the questionnaire easily.

- The range of question types is bigger and includes grid questions (also known as Osgood variations), which don't appear in Quiz. These are excellent for questioning connotation, attitude, and degrees of perception. Here's an example that we might use:

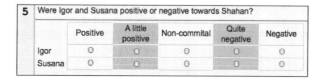

More information on question types

See `http://en.wikipedia.org/wiki/Semantic_differential` for more information on these grid questions, which check something known as semantic differential.

See `http://www.teachers.ash.org.au/researchskills/Dalton.htm` for a reminder of Bloom's Taxonomy, which analyzes the cognitive complexity of questions.

Alternative questionnaires

There is another add-on module called Feedback, which is simpler than Questionnaire and may become a core module in Moodle 2.0, but it does not include Osgood variations.

This activity

In the following example, students read a web-based news story that we have selected. We insert the link to the web page in the introduction to the questionnaire. Then we ask a set of questions related to the text. In this case, they include a range of question types from Bloom's Taxonomy. It's usually a good idea to start with easier questions and move on to more complex ones. This is what we're aiming for:

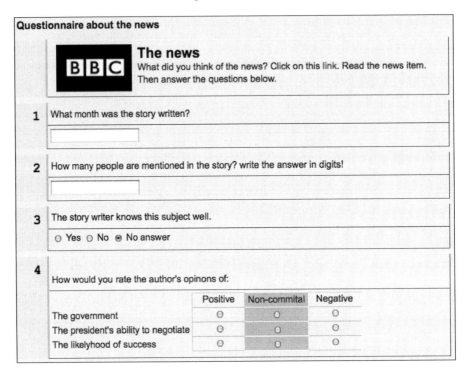

Here's how to do it

Preparation

1. Select a text for students to read. In this case, it'll be a news story on the Internet, so we'll need the URL of the story. For example: `http://thenews.com/newsitem1.htm`. Obviously, we want this story to be as interesting as possible for our students and at the right language level.

Activity

2. On the course page, click on **Turn editing on**. Go to the **Add an activity...** drop-down menu, and select **Questionnaire**.

No Questionnaire module?

If you can't see Questionnaire in the menu, it's because you haven't installed it, or it is hidden. See Chapter 2, *Getting Started with Moodle* for installing add-on modules like Questionnaire, and for unhiding modules and blocks in the **Site Administration** menu.

3. Fill in the settings page. The **Name** and **Summary** sections could look something like this:

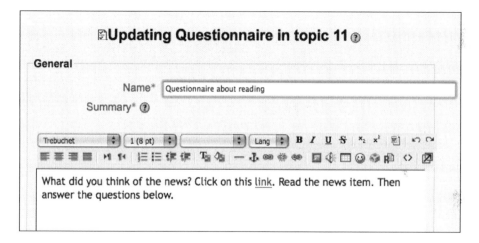

Pay attention to the following settings:

Settings	Details
Response options	Let's use **respond once** so that students don't submit more than one answer.
Students can view ALL responses	I'll set this to **After answering the questionnaire**.
Save/Resume answers	Let's choose **Yes**, so that students can go back to the questionnaire if they didn't finish it the first time they tried.
Submission grade	Let's leave this at **100** for now. That will give students a score out of 100. There is more information on grading possibilities in Chapter 9, *Assessment*.

See Chapter 2, *Getting Started with Moodle* if you need help filling in the **Common module settings**.

4. Now click on **Save and display**. You will see on the screen **No content currently displayed**. Don't worry. It's what you should see, because we haven't added any questions yet.

5. Now we have to make sure that students and teachers can actually see the questionnaire. The procedure is slightly different to other modules. First click on **Update this questionnaire** in the top right-hand corner of the screen. That takes us back to the settings page, but this time there are two additional tabs at the top of the page.

6. Now click on the **Override permissions** tab at the top of the page.

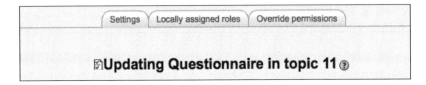

Next click on **Student,** so that we can allow students to see the questionnaire. Complete the grid by checking **Allow** for the permissions we want students to have, mainly the **Read** and **View** ones. Here are the key ones:

- **Download responses in a CSV file** (that's a Comma Separated Values file that we could read on a spreadsheet program)
- **Read all responses any time**
- **Read own responses**
- **Complete and submit a questionnaire**
- **View a questionnaire**
- **View complete individual responses**

The finished grid will look something like this:

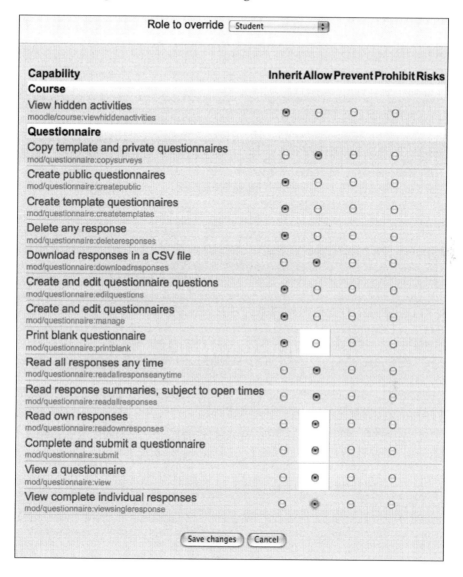

7. Click on **Save changes**.

8. Now we want to start adding questions to the questionnaire. To get to the right page, first click on the breadcrumb **Questionnaire about reading** near the top of the page.

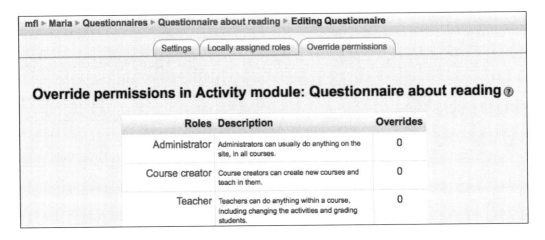

9. Now click on the **Questions** tab:

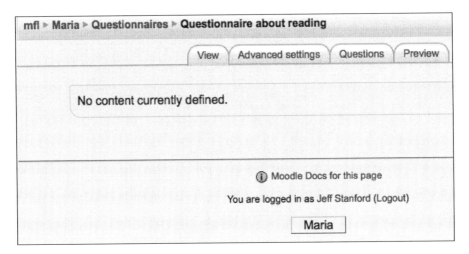

10. Now we can start adding questions by choosing question types from the drop-down menu.

Question types

We have a choice of the following question types:

- **Checkbox** — allows multiple answers to one question
- **Date** — requires students to supply an exact date in answer to a question
- **Dropdown Box** — requires students to choose one answer from a drop-down box
- **Essay Box** — allows students to write a long response to your question
- **Label** — allows you to insert labels into the questionnaire
- **Numeric** — requires students to supply a number in answer to a question
- **Radio Buttons** — require students to select one button in answer to a question
- **Rate (scale 1..5)** — allows students to evaluate something on a scale from 1 to 5
- **Text Box** — allows students to provide a short response to a question
- **Yes/No** — allows students to answer "yes" or "no" to a question

11. Here are a few example questions. Don't forget to click on **Save changes** after entering each question.

Question type	Question content
Text Box	In the **Question Text** box, write **What month was the news story written?** N.B. We can't choose a date question unless the text gives an exact date: day, month, and year. 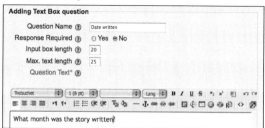 Note, also, that we can require students to answer, or make it optional. We can also stipulate the number of characters they can use: **25** in the above example.

Question type	Question content
Numeric	**How many people are mentioned in the story?**

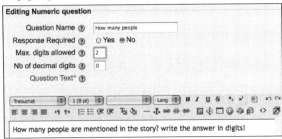

Let's set **Max.digits allowed** to **2**.

Yes or no	Let's write **The story writer is negative about the situation**.
Rate (scale 1..5)	This is a slightly more complex question to set up, but it allows for graded scales and a great variety of grids and categories. We want a three by three table. So we need to write in the following in the **Possible Answers** box:

1=Positive

2=Non-committal

3=Negative

The government

The president's ability to negotiate

The likelihood of success

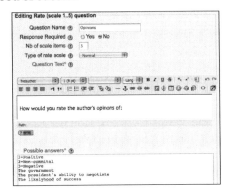

That will give us the following display:

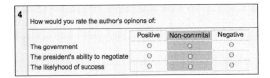

Make sure that **Type of rate scale** is set to **Normal**.

When you've finished adding questions, you can then preview them by clicking on the **Preview** tab at the top of the page. If you need to amend questions, you can click on the questions tab again and then click on the edit icon  to return to the question.

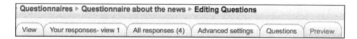

12. The questionnaire is now ready to use. Students can access it by clicking on the questionnaire link on the course home page. Then they should click on **Questionnaire about the news** in the **Name** column.

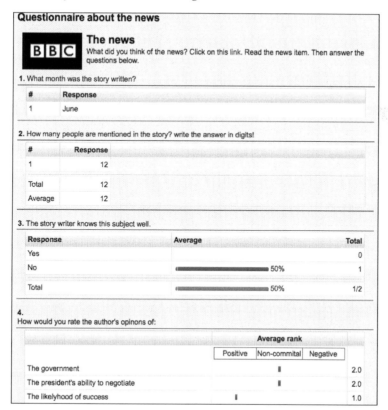

If students click on **View All Responses** after they've submitted their answers, they'll now see something like this:

They can also choose to see responses for all students one by one, or with totaled scores.

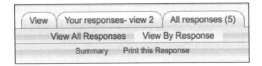

- Don't include too many questions as that could be demotivating
- Test out your questions first on a colleague if possible, so you can make changes if need be

Activity 6: Using Hot Potatoes to investigate texts

Aim: Help students understand texts better

Moodle modules: Hot Potatoes

Extra programs: None

Ease of setup: **

In Activity 5 we looked at using Questionnaire to ask questions which get students to think about texts and include question types for measuring degrees of perception and attitude.

Sometimes we may want more straightforward quizzes using matching or multiple-choice questions. We can either do these in Quiz, or we can use Hot Potatoes. The big advantages of Hot Potatoes are that it is much simpler to set up and you can easily embed images, sound, and video in the questions. The main disadvantages are that it is easier for students to cheat with Hot Potatoes by clicking on the back button and clicking on hint to see each letter of a word. Also, it is not a central part of the Moodle gradebook. So, if you want to set up an activity that could be used as a test, you may be better off using Quiz. However, as we already made a matching activity using quiz in Chapter 3, *Vocabulary Activities*, *Activity 12*, let's try out Hot Potatoes here. If you want to hone your Quiz skills, you could take the ideas from this chapter and follow the instructions in Chapter 3, *Vocabulary Activities*.

Let's try out two variations of reading questions:

Variation	Contents
Variation 1	Matching pictures to a text. This is an attractive, motivating way of checking general understanding of a text.

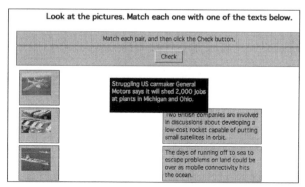

Variation	Contents
Variation 2	Multiple choice. We'll test understanding of vocabulary in context. Students read a text to decide which possible meaning of a word is being used.

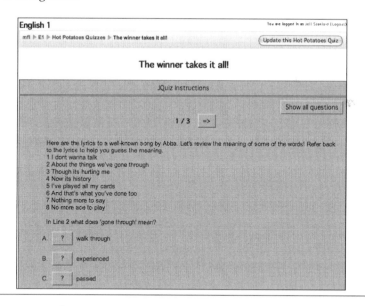

By the way, if you want to see how to set up Quiz multiple-choice question, there's an example in Chapter 5, *Grammar Activities*. The Quiz module would be a good way to set up scanning and skimming tasks, too. See http://42explore.com/skim.htm for a reminder of what they are.

Variation 1: Matching pictures to a text

We're aiming for a drag-and-drop matching exercise as in the Variation 1 screenshot above. Students use their mouse to drag the text on the right-hand side over to the correct picture on the left-hand side. We'll need three snippets of text and three images that match the three snippets.

Here's how to do it

Preparation

1. Create a folder on your computer for the Hot Potatoes activity and the associated images. Load the images into that folder. It's important to keep all files associated with the activity in one folder or the images may not appear in the quiz.

2. Upload all the images you want to use to your Moodle course files folder. See Chapter 2, *Getting Started with Moodle* for help with this. Again, make sure that all the images are in the same Moodle folder.

3. Make sure the Hot Potatoes program is on your computer. See Chapter 2, *Getting Started with Moodle* for more information on this.

4. Open the **Hot Potatoes** program, and choose **JMatch**.

5. We are immediately presented with a page for entering the matching pairs. The first thing to do is to save the file. Click on **File | Save data file** to do that. If we don't do that, Hot Potatoes won't let us insert images.

Now let's fill in the page like this:

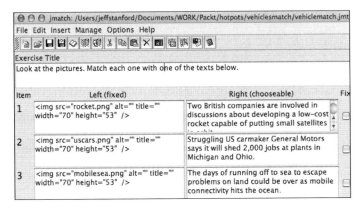

The **Right** column is the text that we're matching. The **Left** column is the image location for the matching pictures.

Inserting an image

To insert the images, click the mouse in the **Left** column next to **Item 1**. Now click on the image icon to insert an image. On your computer, **Browse** to the image that corresponds with the text in the **Right** column. When you click on **OK**, the location of the image file will appear as in the screenshot above. Don't fill in the **Alternative text for image**. If you do, students will see the name of the picture when they hover their mouse over it in the finished activity. That might give the game away.

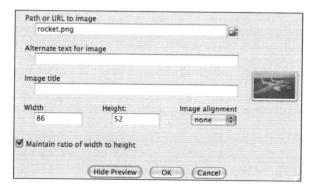

6. Do the same for the other images.

7. In the **Right** column, we enter the texts we want students to match with the images.

8. Next, if we are using a Mac, we go to **File | Export** and then select **Create Standard V6 page**.

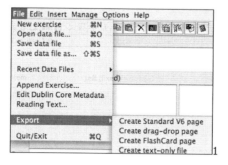

On a Windows machine, we would click on **Create a web page**. Then choose one of the following:

- **Standard Format**—this creates a drop-down menu for students to choose from

- **Drag/Drop Format**—here students drag the object on the right to match the word on the left

○ **Flashcard Format**—this presents the pairs in the form of flashcards, one pair at a time

Once you've saved your Hot Potatoes quiz, you can choose to view it straightaway by clicking on **View in Browser**.

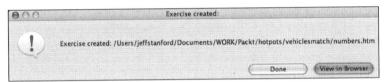

If you clicked on **Done**, you can preview the task by clicking on the saved file wherever you've saved it on your computer. That will open up the quiz in a browser.

9. Now we're going to import the matching quiz into Moodle. The procedure is exactly the same as in Chapter 3, *Vocabulary Activities, Activity 9*, Step 6 onwards.

There's just one important thing to look out for. When you add the Hot Potatoes quiz to Moodle, make sure you upload it to the same folder as the images. See Steps 1 and 2.

Other ideas for matching questions that practice reading
- Match news stories with their headlines
- Match texts with connotations (positive, negative etc.)
- Match images with text: which body language in an image goes with which text
- Match questions with answers

Variation 2: Identifying meaning of individual words using multiple-choice questions

Students often find whole texts interesting to explore. Such texts may contain new ideas and interesting perspectives. They're also a good way of exploring the meaning of words in context.

Imagine that students understand most of the words in a text, but aren't quite sure about a few of them. In this activity we'll give them multiple choice-answers, which will steer them in the right direction. The same activity could be used for general comprehension questions.

In this example we'll take the lyrics to a song by Abba. Students often know lyrics well, but don't always understand what they mean. There's a screenshot of the finished quiz in the introduction to this activity.

Here's how to do it

1. Make sure the Hot Potatoes program is on your computer. See Chapter 2, *Getting Started with Moodle* for more information on this.

2. Open the **Hot Potatoes** program, and choose **JQuiz**.

3. We are immediately presented with a page for entering the matching pairs. Let's fill it in like this:

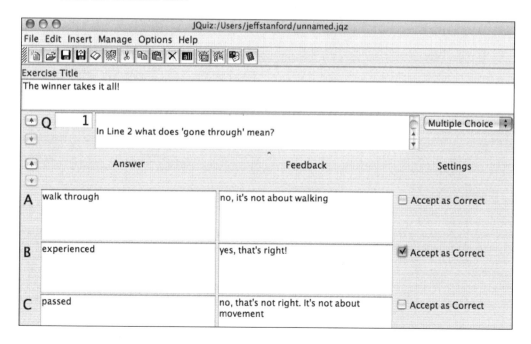

Here's a bit more detail. Next to **Q1**, we insert the whole text we want to use. You can't see it in the screenshot above, but this is the whole text:

Here are the lyrics to a well-known song by Abba. Let's review the meaning of some of the words. Refer back to the lyrics to help you guess the meaning.

1 I don't wanna talk

2 About the things we've gone through

3 Though it's hurting me

4 Now it's history

5 I've played all my cards

6 And that's what you've done too

7 Nothing more to say

8 No more ace to play

In Line 2 what does 'gone through' mean?

4. Now let's create question 2. It uses the same lyrics, but this time it's based on Line 5 and the word **cards**. To create a blank question page, we click on the arrow to the left of the **Q**.

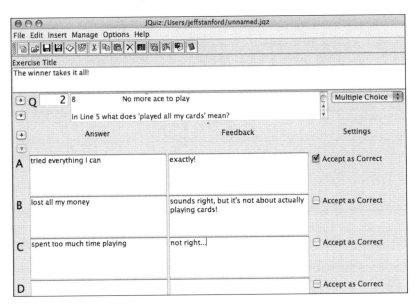

5. We can continue with any other words students might find difficult. For example, **No more ace to play** in line **8**.

A nice extra touch to this activity is to embed a YouTube video of the actual song. There's full information on that in Chapter 2, *Getting Started with Moodle*. Let's put the embed code under the title and before the instructions in **Q1**.

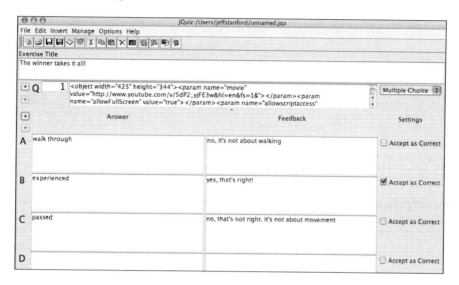

Now the finished activity will look like this:

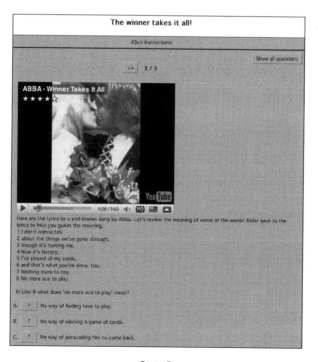

Activity 7: Using Lesson for text prediction

Aim: Help students predict text

Moodle modules: Lesson

Extra programs: None

Ease of setup: ***

Anything that involves games and guessing is likely to make learning more fun and effective. One way of making reading fun is to set up an anticipation exercise. The way it works is that we present some text—for example, a news item, a story, a poem—and then give students three or four options for the next line of the text. This gets students to think about the context and the language. The main thing is to make sure you've chosen a suitable text in the first place. There is not necessarily a wrong answer, but using the Moodle Lesson module, we can make different answers lead in different directions.

Let's take an example of a poem. Maybe you have a poem with different versions that the author contemplated, or that you made up. The different versions could become options for students to select. You could even get students to write their own texts and optional answers.

This is an activity that can be used with all sorts of texts: poems, newspaper reports, stories, songs. We're going to try it out with a cautionary tale by Hilaire Belloc, *Matilda told such dreadful lies*.

Matilda told such Dreadful Lies,
It made one Gasp and Stretch one's Eyes;
Her Aunt, who, from her Earliest Youth,
Had kept a Strict Regard for Truth,
Attempted to believe Matilda:

After reading that, students have to guess the next line. Is it a, b, or c?

a) **But the lies only aggrieved her**

b) **Couldn't believe it happened to her**

c) **The effort very nearly killed her**

In case you're wondering, you'll find out at the end of the activity.

We're going to use the Lesson module for this activity. It's a little complicated to set up, but it does let us create branched questions. It's essentially a set of quiz questions, but with the big difference that each student answer leads them to a different question, depending on how they answered. This is what the opening page will look like:

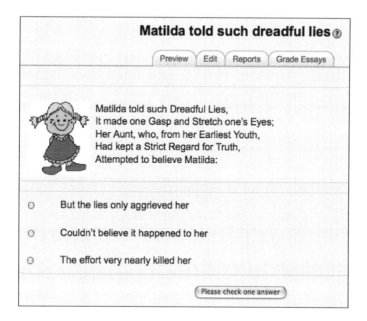

The clip art came from the free clip art site:
http://www.free-clipart-pictures.net.

Here's how to do it

1. On the course page, click on **Turn editing on**. Go to the **Add an activity...** drop-down menu, and select **Lesson**.

2. Complete the introductory page as follows. Pay particular attention to the following items. The other settings are optional.

Settings	Details
Time limit	This is not a test, so don't put a time limit.
Maximum number of branches	This is the number of possible answers students will have. The default is **4**. Let's leave it at that.
Practice lesson	If we check this, the results will not show up in the gradebook. Since we want the exercise to be used for fun, don't check it.

Settings	Details
Maximum grade	Leave this at **0**, as the grade won't appear in the gradebook
Student can re-take	Check this. We want students to do the practice as often as they want.
Handling of re-takes	Ignore this, as we won't be grading students' work.
Display ongoing score	Don't check this. Scores are not relevant to this activity.
Allow student review	Check this so that students can change their answers.
Display review button	Don't check this. If you do, it won't be possible for students to follow the path we have set up for them.
Maximum number of attempts	How many times will we allow students to try to answer any of the questions? Let's put **10** so that students can try out the activity up to ten times.
Action after correct answer	The default is **Normal – follow lesson path**. Leave it at that. Once we have written all the situation (question) pages, we will edit the path.
Lesson formatting	Don't check **Slide Show**.

3. Click on **Save and display**.

4. Now we have a choice. Let's keep things simple and just add a series of question pages. Click on **Add a Question Page**.

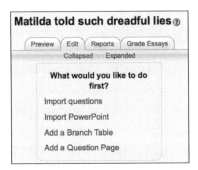

This is where we can start building our questions.

5   We have a choice of question types. Let's choose **Multiple choice**.

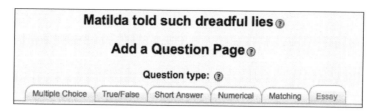

6.   Now fill in the details for the first question:

Settings	Details
Multianswer	Don't' check this, as we only want one correct answer for each question.
Page title	The text is a linear sequence. So let's write **1, 2, 3**, etc.
Page contents	Let's write the first chunk of text here. For example:
	Matilda told such Dreadful Lies, **It made one Gasp and Stretch one's Eyes;** **Her Aunt, who, from her Earliest Youth,** **Had kept a Strict Regard for Truth,** **Attempted to believe Matilda:**
Answer 1	Write **But the lies only aggrieved her.**
Response 1	Here we can right a commentary. For example, **It fits, but it's not what Belloc wrote. Try again.**
Jump 1	Choose **This page**. That means that the student will jump back to this page – in other words do it again.
Score 1	Write **0**. The student gets 0 points.
Answer 2	Write **Couldn't believe it happened to her.**
Response 2	Write **This is the right idea, but not what Belloc wrote.**
Jump2	Choose **This page**.
Score 2	Write **0**. The student gets 0 points, because the answer is wrong.
Answer 3	Write **The effort very nearly killed her.**
Response 3	Write **Well done. That's what Belloc wrote. Now read a bit more.**
Jump 3	Choose **Next page**. That means that if the student chooses Answer 1, he/she will be taken to the next page, because they got Answer 1 right.
Score 3	Write **1**.

Add an image

We can also add an image, recording, or video here to brighten up the page. See Chapter 2, *Getting Started with Moodle* if you need help with uploading images.

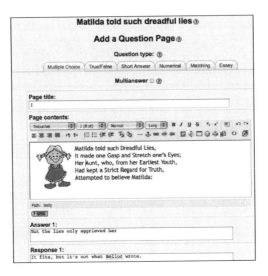

7. Now navigate to the bottom of the screen and click on **Add a question page here**. Don't click on the **Add a question page here** at the top of the page by mistake. If you do, you'll be inserting a question *before* the one we just wrote. We want the next question to come *afterwards*.

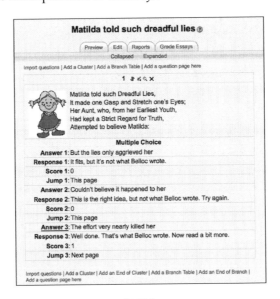

If you see this instead, don't worry. Just click on **Expanded** to get the full version.

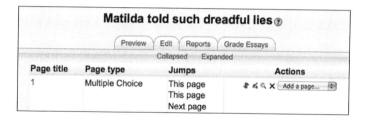

Later on, if we discover that the question pages are in the wrong order, we can change the order. To do that, click on the move icon ⬍ at the top of a page you want to move. And then click on the position you want to move it to:

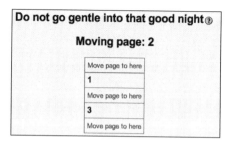

8. We now repeat the process of adding questions and responses for the rest of the text. That's going to be just three question pages in total. When we reach the end of the third question page, we must make sure that our jump link choice for the correct answer is **End of lesson**. Otherwise, the activity will not close itself when students reach the end.

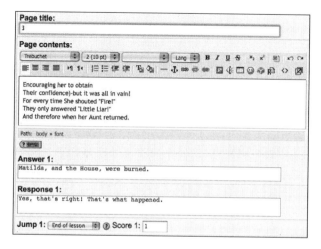

9. We can test out our lesson at any time—even before it's finished—by clicking on the **Preview** tab. And we can edit any pages by clicking on the edit icon ✐.

Students access the lesson by clicking on the link from the course page. When they click on the correct answer, they'll see this:

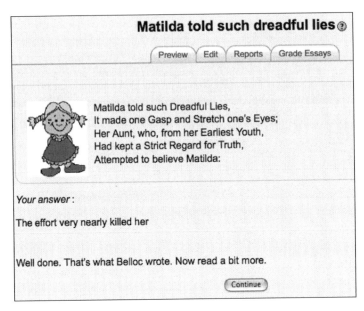

Now you know that answer, too.

7
Writing Activities

I often get feedback from language teachers that their students really enjoy doing writing activities on the computer. Why is that? It's a medium they're comfortable with. They can easily add pictures and sound. They can change the color and size of the fonts and the font faces themselves. Younger students particularly like to be able to do that.

What writing activities do we have in mind exactly? Producing texts at *word* level or *sentence* level is a writing activity, but it is covered better in the chapters on vocabulary and grammar in this book. For example, the gap-fill in Chapter 3, *Vocabulary Activities*, *Activity 11* gets students to fit words into sentences. This chapter focuses more on helping students produce *paragraphs* and *whole texts*.

The chapter is divided into five sections which relate to the way writing is taught in **communicative language teaching**. Within each section, activities are ordered according to the ease of setup. That level of complexity is indicated in the table below.

Activity	Focus	Module	Description
1 ***	Awareness-raising	Quiz	Making students aware of text structure can help them construct their own texts in a more appropriate way.
2 ***	Guided writing	Lesson	Guiding students to use appropriate language in a text will build confidence and help them write more independently.
3 *	Brainstorming	Mindmap	Students share ideas on keywords and themes before writing their assignment.

Activity	Focus	Module	Description
4 *	Production	Personal profile	This kills two birds with one stone: students can make sure they have a Moodle profile and make sure it's as well written as possible.
5 *		Journal	Students use a private space to write a diary.
6 *		Blog	Students use the Moodle Blog for creative writing. Other students and teachers then comment on it.
7 *		Glossary	Students create their own encyclopedia entries.
8 *		Chat	This helps students to practice writing fluently—paying attention more to the message than to accuracy.
9 **		Assignment	Students use the Assignment module to post a text and get detailed feedback on it from the teacher.
10 **		Forum	Students choose a selection of images and write a commentary for them.
11 **		RSS and Forum	Students read or listen to a news item and then summarize it in a forum posting where other students can read and comment.
12 **	Collaborative writing	Wiki	Students use a wiki to write a joint project.

Approach to writing

There's a mixture of a *genre approach* and *process approach* to writing in this chapter. A *genre approach* provides students with a model based on a particular genre of writing, such as a letter, a story, or an email. Focusing on genre also means that tasks take into consideration the reason for writing and the person students are writing to, thus making it a more realistic experience. A *process approach* to writing emphasizes the process of gathering and sharing ideas, then planning, drafting and editing texts. Writing can be done individually (Activities 3 to 10) or in collaboration with other students (Activity 12). Feedback on writing can be immediate (as in Activities 1 and 2) or delayed (as in Activities 4 to 12).

Attractiveness/authenticity

One of the attractive features of Moodle is that it enables writing to be enhanced by images and attractive layouts. There's more help with this in Chapter 11, *Formatting and Enhancing Your Moodle Materials*.

Activity 1: Raising awareness of text structure using Quiz

Aim: Raise students' awareness of how certain texts are ordered

Moodle modules: Quiz with add-on Ordering question

Extra programs: None

Ease of setup: ***

One element of writing that's sometimes tricky for learners in any language is getting the parts of their text in the right order. That could be because they're not used to the type of text (genre) that they're writing, or because the order in the language they're learning is different to that in their own language. For example, in German you would write *Liebe Grüße*, which means "greetings" at the *end* of a letter and not at the beginning as you would in English. German writers in English need to know that.

We can practice ordering parts of texts with a variety of genres: they could be simple ones such as postcards, invitations, reminders, or memos, or more complicated ones such as essays, reviews, or reports.

This activity starts by getting students to recognize the order of key elements of a letter and then gets them to write a text themselves following the same order. You can use any sort of text. The key thing is to be able to break it down into significant parts. Let's take a formal letter to a company as an example. One common order would be:

1. Writer's address
2. Recipient's address
3. Date
4. Greeting
5. State purpose of letter
6. Give details
7. Sum up
8. Close letter

To help students practice the order, we'll set up a Quiz module, present students with a text, and get them to order the parts of the text according to what they read. After that, they'll write a letter as an essay question. The instructions will remind students of the text order, and will get them to write their own letter following that order. In theory, an increased awareness of the order will help students control their own writing better. It will certainly reinforce the framework for organizing their texts.

N.B. This is one of the more complex activities in this chapter. It will take time to set up, especially if it's your first quiz activity. But this time is well worth it in the end, as the activity can be stimulating and useful for students and the material can be used over and over again.

If you're still relatively new to Moodle, the production activities (3–12) are much simpler to set up. So you might find it easier to start there.

Getting things in order

You won't be able to set up this activity unless you've installed the add-on question type Ordering. See Chapter 2, *Getting Started with Moodle* for more details. You will need your site administrator's help to install the question type called Ordering.

Here's how to do it

Part 1: Analyzing the order of text elements

Before we set up the activity on Moodle, we need to choose a text, analyze the component parts, and label them as above. Here's a standard text about ordering some windows:

Hawthorns, 4 Station Road, Middleton

Mr. P Spencer
Shiny Building Company
44 Heyworth Avenue
Birmingham

2 February 2010

Dear Mr. Spencer

Thank you for your invoice of 19 January. I enclose a check in payment.

I see from your letter that while you undertook the repairs to my roof, you found that several of the upstairs window frames had rotted and need replacing. I would be grateful if you could send me an estimate for the work that you feel needs to be done and let me know when you would be able to start.

I would also like to know how much a UPVC replacement for the kitchen window would be likely to cost.

I look forward to hearing from you at your earliest convenience.

Yours sincerely

Jimmy Hill

It's not the most exciting of letters, but it could be useful for students to know how to write a letter like this.

1. On your course page, click on **Turn editing on**. Then click on **Add an activity...**.

2. We're going to make a quiz question, so select **Quiz** from the drop-down menu.

3. Complete the set-up page. Most of the settings are optional, but pay attention to a few important ones. Note that your screen will either show **Adding Quiz in topic X** or **Updating Quiz in topic X,** depending whether you're filling in the details for the first time or editing them, as in the screenshot below. If this is the first time you've set up a quiz activity, you'll find details on Security, Common module settings, and Overall feedback in Chapter 2, *Getting Started with Moodle.*

Settings	Details
Name	Lets' write **Ordering a window – text order activity**.
Introduction	Let's spell out what the students have to do. The quiz consists of two questions: an ordering question and then an essay. Write the following: ### Writing a letter to order something **In this activity you're going to learn how to write a short letter to request a service. There are two parts to the activity:** **1 - Read the letter and identify the order it's written in.** **2 - Write your own letter following the same order.** We can add an image to make the instructions more attractive, as in the screenshot later.

Settings	Details
Shuffle questions	This must be set to **No**. Otherwise, students could be asked to do the essay before they've done the ordering activity.
Attempts allowed	It's important to select **Unlimited attempts** if we want students to be able to practice this as often as they want.
Adaptive mode	Let's select **Yes**. Students will then be able to benefit from our feedback and try the item again.
Grading method	Let's select **Highest grade**. That means that only the highest score from each student's attempts will be entered. This could be a strong motivator for students to redo the quiz. We want them to do the quiz until they get it right so that they are familiar with the model for writing.

When the page is completed, click on **Save and display**. Don't worry if **Save and return to course** gets clicked on by mistake. Simply find the activity we have just created on the course page and click on the hand icon ✍ to edit it.

4. Now we need to choose a question type for our quiz. From the **Question bank**, go to **Create a new question**, and choose **Ordering** from the drop-down menu. If you can't see the **Question bank**, click on the **Edit** tab and then the **Questions** tab.

No Ordering question available?

Don't forget, the Ordering question is an add-on. Get your administrator to add this question type if it is not yet available.

5. This takes us to the introduction page for our new quiz question, **Ordering**. Complete the page paying attention to the information below:

Settings	Details
Category	Here we decide which category of quiz we want our question to belong to. It's a good idea to create categories if we have a lot of questions and need to organize them. See Chapter 2, *Getting Started with Moodle* for more information on this. Let's leave it on default for now.
Question name	Let's give our question a name. How about **Window letter**?

Settings	Details
Question text	Let's write Question 1 in the **Question text** box:
	Jimmy is about to spend lots of money on a new window. Sometimes it's useful to write letters like this! Take a look at the letter and then put the different parts of the letter in the right order by dragging them into position using the mouse.
	After that introduction, copy the letter we wrote in the introduction, which began:
	Mr. P Spencer *Shiny Building Company* *44 Heyworth Avenue* *Birmingham*
	2 February 2010
Display items horizontally	Don't select this. It's more appropriate for ordering separate words that don't take up too much space.

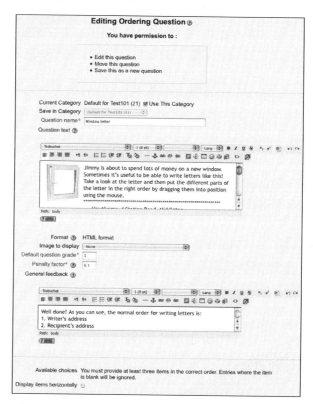

Since we have more than three items, we will need to click on **Add more items** at the bottom of the page.

Item 1	Write **Writer's address**.

Settings	Details
Item 2	Write **Recipient's address**.
Item 3	Write **Date**.
Item 4	Write **Greeting**.
Item 5	Write **State purpose of letter**.
Item 6	Write **Give details**.
Item 7	Write **Sum up**.
Item 8	Write **Close letter**.

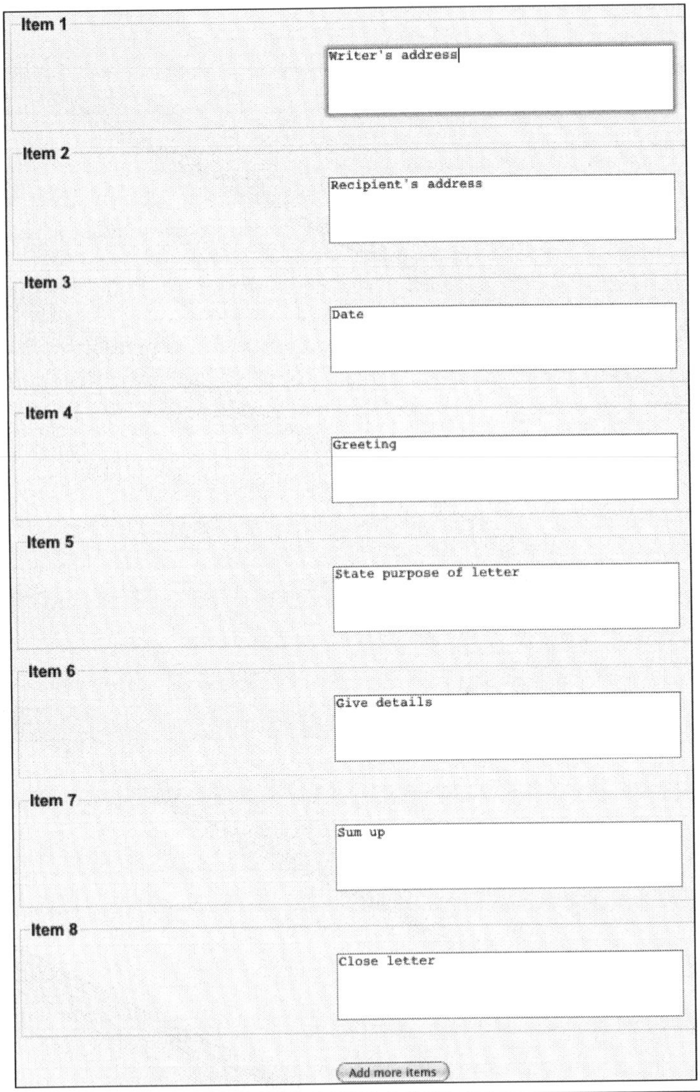

Item 1

Writer's address

Item 2

Recipient's address

Item 3

Date

Item 4

Greeting

Item 5

State purpose of letter

Item 6

Give details

Item 7

Sum up

Item 8

Close letter

(Add more items)

Students' first language

Since some of that metalanguage might be more difficult than the language of the letter itself, you might consider writing these labels—"greeting", etc.—in the students' first language.

6. When you're ready, click on **Save changes**. That should bring you back to the quiz overview page. If it doesn't, click on the **Edit** tab and then the **Quiz** tab.

Part 2: Adding an essay question

7. This quiz is going to consist of two questions. We have just produced the ordering question. Now we need to add our essay question. From the **Question bank**, go to **Create a new question**, and choose **Essay** from the drop-down menu.

Let's complete the settings page for the essay question.

Settings	Details
Category	Here we decide which category of quiz we want our question to belong to. It's a good idea to create categories if we have a lot of questions and need to organize them. See Chapter 2, *Getting Started with Moodle* for more information on this. Let's leave it on default for now.
Question name	Let's give our question a name. In the letter, students are going to order some iPod speakers. So let's call the letter **Writing a letter: ordering some speakers'**.
Question text	Now let's enter some instructions, something like this: **Your turn!** **Now you have a chance to write a letter yourself!** **Imagine you took your iPod for repair to Rick Davies at Rick's Rapid Repairs. He told you that he needed to order some parts in order to complete the repair. You want to know how much the repair will cost and how long it will take.** **Here's the order again:** **1. Writer's address** **2. Recipient's address** **3. Date** **4. Greeting** **5. State purpose of letter** **6. Give details** **7. Sum up** **8. Close letter**

Settings	Details
General feedback	As before, we can write something useful that all students will read. Let's write this for now:
	Well done! **I'll get some comments back to you by next Monday.**
	Teacher Jeff ☺

8. When you're ready, click on **Save changes**. That should once again bring you back to the quiz overview page. Both questions—the ordering one and the essay one—are now available to add to our quiz.

9. To insert them in our quiz, we click on the chevrons (**<<**) to the left of the questions we want. First, the **Window letter**. Then **Writing a letter: ordering some speakers**. They will move into the quiz on the left-hand side of the page.

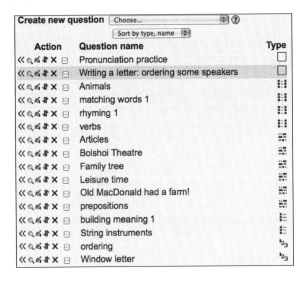

10. The quiz will now look like this:

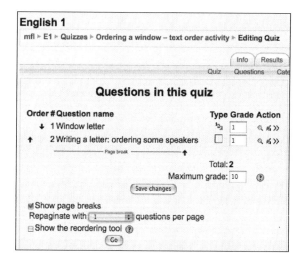

Notice that we can click on the arrows to the left of the questions to change the order if it's wrong. We want the ordering task to be first and the essay to be second. If you need to change the order, don't forget to click on **Save changes** to save the new order.

Before we leave the page we should check **Show page breaks**. We want Question 1 to appear first and Question 2 to appear when Question 1 is completed. So select **Repaginate with 1 question per page**.

11. Now click on **Go**, which is slightly odd Moodle-speak here for **Save changes**.

Part 3: Student attempts at the quiz

12. When students click on the quiz link on the quiz page, they'll see something like this:

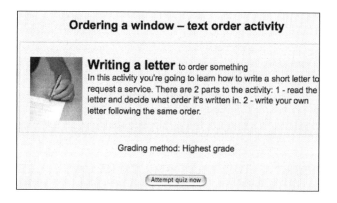

13. They should click on **Attempt quiz now**. Here is a preview of the screen they will see:

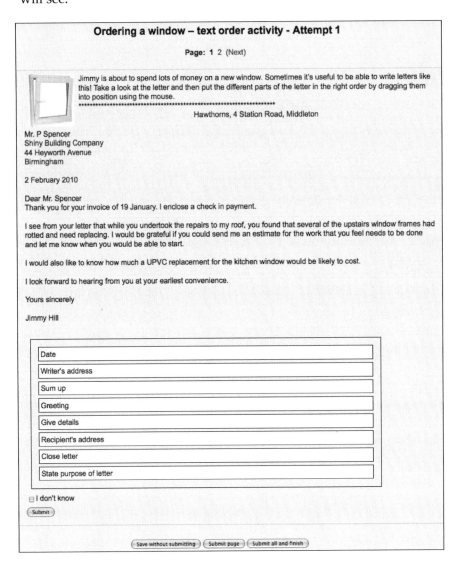

14. To do the task, they drag the parts up and down using the mouse.

Afterwards, they can **Save without submitting**, **Submit page**, or **Submit all and finish**.

- ° **Save without submitting** is useful if the attempt is only partially completed and students want to resume their attempt later on

- ° **Submit page** is useful if students want to submit just this question

- ° **Submit all and finish** is the best choice when students have finished their attempts on all questions

Once students have clicked on one of the **Submit** buttons, they'll get feedback on their attempt, and they'll see the instructions which we wrote in Step 5 to go on to the next page where they write their essay.

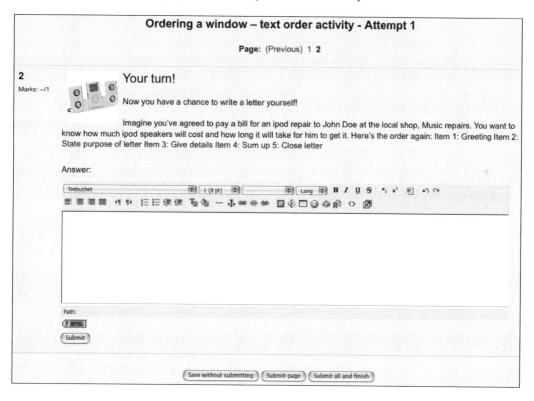

15. Again, they can **Save without submitting**, **Submit page**, or **Submit all and finish**.

    When they are satisfied with their letter, they should click the **Submit all and finish** button, so that we can assess it.

16. To access the students' attempts, click on the activity on the course page. Then click on the **Results** tab.

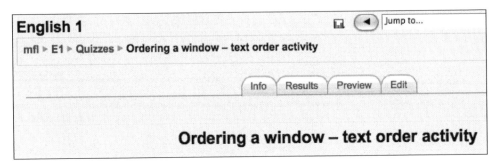

17. Then we need to click on the slot below **#2** so that we can grade the essay.

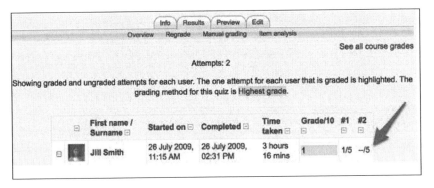

18. Now we can read the response. To write a comment, we should click on **Make comment or override grade.**

2 🔊
Marks: --/1

Your turn!

Now you have a chance to write a letter yourself!

Your turn! Now you have a chance to write a letter yourself! Imagine you took your iPod for repair to Rick Davies at Rick's Rapid Repairs. He told you that he needed to order some parts in order to complete the repair. You want to know how much the repair will cost and how long it will take. Here's the order again:

1. Writer's address
2. Recipient's address
3. Date
4. Greeting
5. State purpose of letter
6. Give details
7. Sum up
8. Close letter

Answer:

The Cottage, Manor Town, Maine

Rick Davies
Rick's Rapid Repairs
48 Jefferson Avenue
04001 Moonyville

6 January 2010

Dear Rick

As you know, I need my iPod repaired. The one which I brought to you on Monday this week. Please tell me how much the repair will cost and when it will be ready.

I look forward to hearing from you.

Yours sincerely

Jill Smith

Make comment or override grade

19. We can then see the student's attempts in one window and the comments box in another window. We could write something like this:

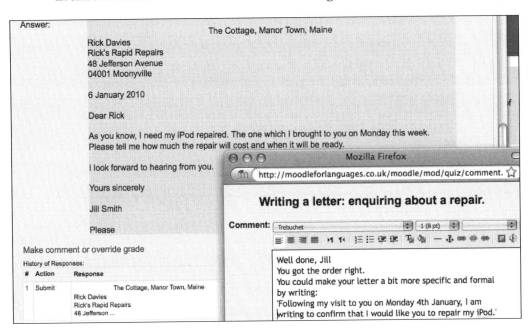

An alternative way of giving feedback would be to make a NanoGong audio recording by clicking on the audio button. See Chapter 4, *Speaking Activities* if you need more help with using NanoGong.

20. Click on **Save** to save our comments and marks.

21. When the student comes back to the activity, she will be able to read our comments.

Activity 2: Practicing register using Lesson

Aim: Raise students' awareness of register and develop their ability to manipulate it in their writing.

Moodle modules: Lesson

Extra programs: None

Ease of setup: ***

Before we help students to use register appropriately in their writing, we first need to make them aware of it. We can then set up a task which gets them to use what they've learned. In this activity, students will be asked to distinguish between formal and informal styles of writing.

Formal writing is characterized by more attention to accuracy, clarity of meaning, spelling, grammar, punctuation, and choice of more neutral vocabulary. By contrast, an *informal* style is often chosen where writers don't feel it is necessary to be so clear, because the situation is not formal or because writers know each other well and don't need things to be spelled out. Clearly, there are some situations where it is important to get the register right.

Let's have a look at a letter of invitation to a party. It's a fairly friendly one, celebrating a fortieth birthday. Here is a possible text with options for informal and formal language. The informal language would be more appropriate. Which option would you choose from the following?

Dear John

As you know, Mandy

> *a)* *'s going to be 40 on 3rd Jan.*
>
> *b)* *will be celebrating her 40th birthday on 3rd January.*

We are writing to invite you to her party.

> *a)* *It won't be a posh do,*
>
> *b)* *It will not be a formal affair,*

but we hope it'll be full of fun and will be a memorable day!

> *a)* *We're starting off*
>
> *b)* *We will commence the day*

with games on the lawn.

In each case version a) is more informal. It's not that version b) is wrong grammatically. It's that it doesn't feel so natural.

The Lesson module will allow us to give feedback pointing out features of the language that make it more or less formal. Once students have been through the lesson pages which relate to register, they can move on to the last page where they write their own invitation using an essay question.

Here's how to do it

1. On the course page, click on **Turn editing on**, Go to the **Add an activity...** drop-down menu, and select **Lesson**.

2. Complete the introductory page as follows. Settings which aren't mentioned below are optional. If in doubt, click on the help icon ② for more information.

Settings	Details
Time limit	This is not a test, so don't put a time limit.
Maximum number of branches	This is the number of possible answers students can choose from. There will be a choice of two for each question. So let's write **2**.
Practice lesson	Let's select **Yes**. Otherwise, we will not be able to grade the essay, which is our last question.
Custom scoring	Select **Yes**. We want to be able to assign different points for the multiple-choice and the essay questions. We'll give 1 point for each of the multiple-choice questions and 7 points for the essay.
Maximum grade	Let's put **10**. That way, students will get a mark out of 10.
Student can re-take	Select **Yes**. We want students to do the activity as often as they want.
Handling of re-takes	Let's write **Use mean**. That means that students' final score will be an average of all of their attempts.
Display ongoing score	Let's choose **No** so that it doesn't distract students.
Allow student review	Select **Yes** so that students can change their answers.
Display review button	Choose **No**. If you choose **Yes**, it won't be possible for students to follow the path we have set up for them.
Maximum number of attempts	How many times will we allow students to try to answer any of the questions? Let's put **10** so that students can try out the activity up to ten times.
Action after correct answer	The default is **Normal – follow lesson path**. Leave it at that.
Lesson formatting	Choose **No**.
Slide Show	

3. Click on **Save and display**.

4. Now we have a choice. Let's keep things simple and just add a series of question pages. Click on **Add a Question Page**.

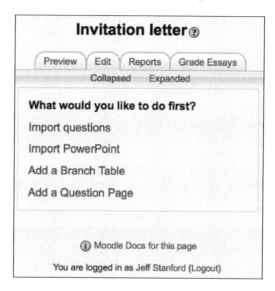

This is where we can start building our questions.

5. We have a choice of question types. Let's choose **Multiple choice**.

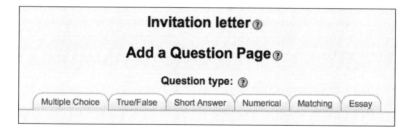

6. Now fill in the details for the first question.

Setting	Details
Multianswer	Don't check this, as we only want one correct answer for each question.
Page title	The text is a linear sequence. So let's write **1** for the first question, **2** for the second, etc. In this example, this would go up to **4**, because we have four questions in total.
Page contents	Let's write the first chunk of text here, ending with the first sentence of the letter. For example:

Invitation letter

This lesson will help you write an invitation letter in an appropriate style. There are two parts to the lesson:

1 – Read the letter below and whenever you have a choice, choose the best way of continuing the letter. The feedback should help you if you are in doubt.

2 – Then follow the link to the Assignment page and write your own invitation letter based on what you've learned.

Here is the letter

Dear John

As you know, Mandy

Answer 1	Write **'s going to be 40 on 3rd Jan.**
Response 1	Here we can write a commentary. For example: **Yes, that's the right sort of conversational style that we would use in an invitation like this.**
Jump 1	Choose **Next page**. That means that if the student chooses Answer 1, he/she will be taken to the next page, because he/she got Answer 1 right.
Score 1	Let's give 1 point. Write **1**.
Answer 2	Write **will be celebrating her 40th birthday on 3rd January.**
Response 2	Write **The grammar is fine, but it's a bit too formal for this invitation.**
Jump 2	Choose **This page**. That means that the student will jump back to this page—in other words, do it again.
Score 2	The answer's wrong. So let's write **0**.

Add an image

We can also add an image, recording, or video here to brighten up the page. See Chapter 2, *Getting Started with Moodle* if you need help with uploading images.

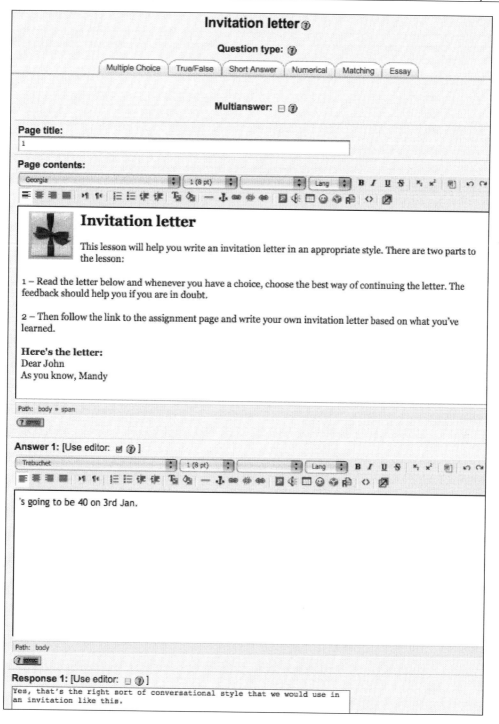

7. Now navigate to the bottom of the screen and click on **Add a question page**. That will bring us to an overview of the question we have written.

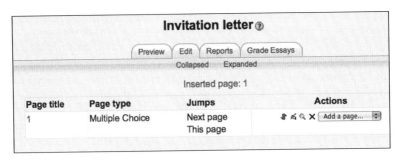

If we click on the **Expanded** link, we'll see the whole question.

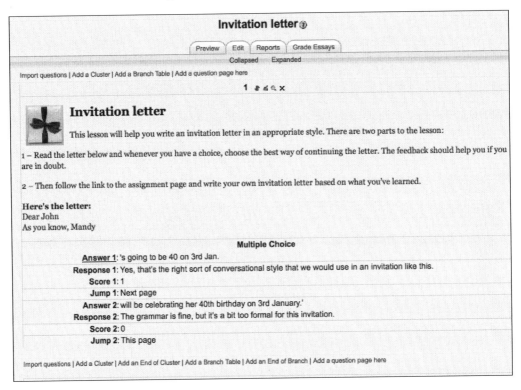

8. Next we click on **Add a question page here** at the bottom of the page. Don't click on the **Add a question page here** at the top of the page by mistake. If you do, you'll be inserting a question *before* the one we just wrote. We want the next question to come *afterwards*.

Later on, if we discover that the question pages are in the wrong order, we can change the order. To do that, click on the move icon 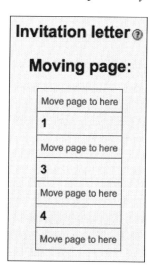at the top of a page you want to move. And click on the position you want to move it to:

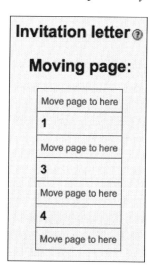

9. We now repeat Steps 6–8 to add questions and responses for the rest of the letter. There are three question pages with multiple-choice questions and then there will be one question page with an essay question. That's going to be four question pages in total. When we reach the end of the fourth question page, we must make sure that our jump link choice for the correct answer is **End of lesson**. Otherwise, the activity will not close itself when students reach the end.

The text for pages 2 and 3 will be based on these answers. The answer a) is correct in each case.

Settings	Details
Page 2 contents	Here's the next line of the letter:
	We are writing to invite you to her party.
Answer 1	**It won't be a posh do,**
Response 1	correct
Jump 1	Next page
Score 1	1
Answer 2	**It will not be a formal affair,**
Response 2	too formal
Jump 2	This page
Score 2	0

Settings	Details
Page 3 contents	Here's the last line of the letter:
	but we hope it'll be full of fun and will be a memorable day!
Answer 1	**We're starting off**
Response 1	**correct**
Jump 1	**Next page**
Score 1	**1**
Answer 2	**We will commence the day**
Response 2	**too formal**
Jump 2	**This page**
Score 2	**0**

10. Question page 4 is a different question type. So after saving the changes to page 3, remember to click on the **Essay** tab at the top of the page. Now complete it as follows. Remember to select **End of lesson** for the **Jump** choice this time. Otherwise, students won't be able to finish the activity. Also, the score is 7 for this question as it's much harder than the multiple-choice questions.

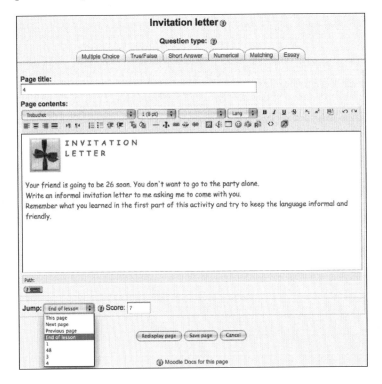

11. We can try out our lesson at any time—even before it's finished—by clicking on the **Preview** tab. And we can edit any pages by clicking on the edit icon ✍ on the overview page, which we saw in Step 7.

12. Students access the lesson by clicking on the link from the course page. When they click on the correct answer, they'll see this:

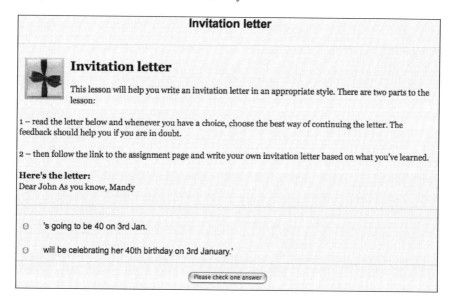

13. Once students have written their essays, we can click on the lesson activity to mark them. The first screen you'll get will be the task:

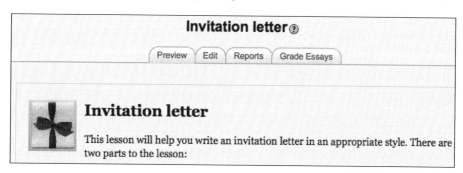

You need to click on the **Grade Essays** tab to be able to grade it.

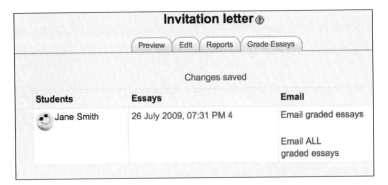

Click on the submission, labeled **26 July 2009**, to open a comment box for Jane Smith's essay. You'll notice that the essay question doesn't allow students to include layout, unfortunately.

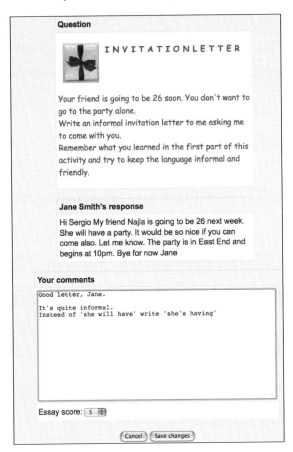

14. Give some feedback in the **Your comments** box, add an **Essay score**, then click on **Save changes**.

15. Now we can click on the **Email graded essays** link that we saw in Step 13 to alert students that their essay has been marked – a nice feature.

Activity 3: Using Mindmap to brainstorm writing assignments

Aim: Help students explore and organize a range of ideas which they can use for writing

Moodle modules: None

Extra programs: Mindmap

Ease of setup: *

Before students begin their writing projects, they may find it useful to share ideas and vocabulary that they can use. One way of doing this is to use the add-on module, Mindmap. It's a simple program, and doesn't have the sophistication of other Mindmap programs that allow you to embed audio, video, and hyperlinks. However, it's useful for setting out a multi-level Mindmap on a topic that students are going to write about. It can be used in conjunction with Activities 5, 9 and 12, which focus on creative writing. It can also be treated as a vocabulary activity. We can modify the settings (Step 3) to make this an individual activity, a small group activity or a whole class activity. To achieve the first two groupings, you'll need to set up groupings. There's help with that in Chapter 2, *Getting Started with Moodle*.

In the example below we'll build a Mindmap based on reasons for and against speed dating. Students can later use this to write a text. This is what a Mindmap could look like:

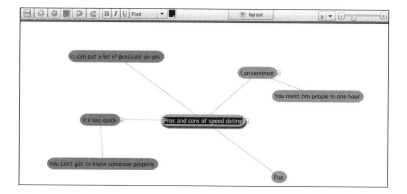

Here's how to do it

1. On the course page, click on **Turn editing on**.

2. Scroll down to the drop-down block menu on the right, and select **Mindmap**.

3. Now let's complete the set-up page. There are just a few settings:

Settings	Details
Mindmap Name	Let's call it **Speed dating**.
Editable	Check this so that teachers and students can view, edit, and save the Mindmap.
Group mode	Let's leave this on **No groups** for now. If you have a large class and want to divide it into smaller groups, it may be a good idea to choose **Separate groups** here. That means that groups designated by you can only see their own group's work. See Chapter 2, *Getting Started with Moodle* for help with setting up groups.

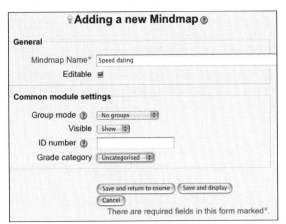

4. Click on **Save and display** at the bottom of the page.

   The Mindmap is now ready for students to use. The screenshot below shows the key functions available.

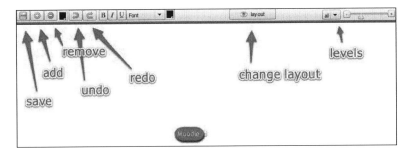

5. First let's click on the Moodle cloud and change the text from **Moodle** to **Pros and cons of Speed dating**.

6. Now click on "add" to create our first link. A blue ball will appear. Grab it and move it where you want it. Click in the middle of the ball and write **Convenience**. Do the same again for the word **Fun**. You should now have two new words in your Mindmap. If you write a word you don't want or create a ball where you don't want one, you can click on the "undo" icon to remove it.

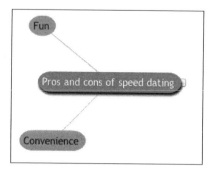

It's worth saving your Mindmap regularly just in case you lose your connection.

Click on the color palette to change colors. This is a good way of showing:

- Different users
- Different parts of speech (if it's a grammar Mindmap)
- Ideas which are more important or less important

7. To create a second level, click on *Insert* on your keyboard. If you don't have an *Insert* key, click on the "add" icon. Then drag the icon on top of an existing ball. For example, we may want to add **you meet ten people in one hour** under the word **convenience**.

8. You can't export your Mindmap, but you can use screen capture software mentioned in Chapter 2, *Getting Started with Moodle* to take a photo of it, or you can print it by right-clicking on the image and choosing **Print**.

Simultaneous use?

Students can use the Mindmap simultaneously, but you need to take two things into consideration:

- They need to save their Mindmap regularly so that all users can see the words they've added
- They need to refresh the page (*F5*) to see what other students have added

Activity 4: Producing effective personal profiles

Aim: Help students write engaging personal profiles

Moodle modules: Personal profile

Extra programs: None

Ease of setup: *

One of the first things that many Moodle users do is look up the personal profiles of other users. This should motivate users to make sure that their own profiles are written as accurately and engagingly as possible. It's therefore a good place to start this section on production activities. It's worth agreeing with your class what they think useful ingredients are. It could include some or all of the following:

- Some background information
- Something about your interests
- Why you are a user
- Links to your favorite websites

This is what we're aiming for:

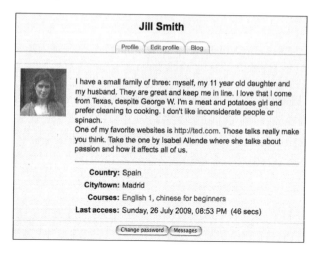

Here's how to do it

1. Show students examples of different personal profiles. Get them to comment on which ones they like or don't like. You could do this face to face in class, or you could post texts on a Moodle web page. See Chapter 3, *Vocabulary Activities*, *Activity 3* if you need help with setting up a web page.

2. Agree on a list of elements that students would like to include, like the ones in our introduction.

Writing profiles

3. Students write their profiles by clicking on their name in the top right-hand corner of the Moodle screen and then clicking on **edit profile**.

If you're doing this face to face in class, you can help individuals by correcting any of their writing. If you're doing the activity remotely, you could send students messages using email or the message block on the course page, for example.

Brightening up profiles

Remind students that they can brighten up their profiles by embedding video, audio, and images. See Chapter 2, *Getting Started with Moodle* for instructions on how to embed video.

Students can also change the font face, font size, and layout to make a more pleasing page. There are more ideas on formatting text and images in Chapter 11, *Formatting and Enhancing Your Moodle Materials*.

Activity 5: Using Journal for reflective or private writing

Aim: Help students keep a diary

Moodle modules: Journal

Extra programs: None

Ease of setup: *

It is useful to provide a place where students can keep a private journal. This could be a diary of events in their lives, a reflective diary based on their learning, or a way of asking questions about the course they're studying. The text that students write in journal can only be seen by them and the teachers on their course. That text can be graded using percentage marks or a separate marking scheme (called a scale) created by the teacher. The teacher can also simply respond to the student's text by writing a comment or recording one using the NanoGong recorder. See Chapter 2, *Getting Started with Moodle* for help with creating scales and using the NanoGong recorder.

The module lends itself well to the following sorts of writing:

- Project diary
- Reflections on the course
- Students' questions and teachers' answers
- Drafts of writing assignments
- Plans

You might find articles like the following useful for ideas on how to use reflective journals:

http://iteslj.org/Techniques/Arciniegas-LearnersJournals.html

Many people, young and old, enjoy talking and writing about what they did last night. Let's set up a journal in which students do that. In this case we won't be grading their work. The journal is more an opportunity to practice and enjoy writing in another language about something interesting to the student. Ideally, students will write the journal every day, but if you have a large number of students, and they write a lot in their journal, that's a huge marking burden on you. So set a realistic amount of writing.

This is what a student's finished journal might look like.

Jill Smith Last edited: Monday, 3 August 2009, 10:34 AM

Last night I watched an amazing show on TV. It was about butterflies.

I learned some interesting things. For example, butterflies taste food by standing on it because they don't have a mouth. Also they have six legs and feet. They weigh almost nothing and you can see through their wings. The next time I see a butterfly, I will look at it in a new way.

More on Journals

As on many other Moodle pages, the help pages in the module indicated by a ⓘ icon provide additional help for students to think about writing and reading carefully what they have written.

Journal module is a core module in Moodle Version 1.9, but will become an add-on from Version 2.0.

You could also use the Assignment module. Selecting **Advanced upload** will allow a "to and fro" between student writing and teacher comments. The Journal module is more straightforward to use, however.

Here's how to do it

1. On the course page, click on **Turn editing on** by clicking the button in the top right-hand corner of the page.

2. Scroll down to the drop-down block menu on the right, and select **Journal**.

3. Now let's complete the set-up page. Pay particular attention to the following. Common module settings and grade categories are optional, and are covered in Chapter 2, *Getting Started with Moodle*.

Settings	Details
Journal name	Let's call it **What I did last night**.
Journal question	Make this as explicit as possible, giving clear instructions and examples of the sort of writing students should produce. Remind students that they should choose **HTML format** in the **Formatting** option (see Step 6 below) so that they can change the layout and fonts, add images, etc. Let's write the following: ## What I did last night... **What this is?** **This is your private space for writing a diary. Only you and your teacher can see it. It's a good place to remember the nice things in your life.** **What to write about** **So... what did you do last night? Maybe you went to the cinema, played a game, met some friends, read a good book. Write about it here. Maybe you took a photo or a video that you'd like to keep as a memory.** **Adding pictures** **You can add images by clicking on the image icon above.** **Asking questions** **You can also ask me questions and I'll write a little note to you about your diary. Have fun!**
Format	The only setting available here is **HTML format**. Students, however, will have the choice of using other text formats, which are described in Chapter 11, *Formatting and Enhancing Your Moodle Materials*.
Grade	Decide whether you want to grade the students' writing. If the emphasis is on fluency and getting ideas, it's probably better to leave this on **No grade** so that students feel less under pressure. If you want to assign a scale, choose an appropriate one from the drop-down menu. See Chapter 2, *Getting Started with Moodle* for help with setting up scales.
Days available	Let's leave this on **always open**. You can also limit it to a specific number of days or weeks.

4. Click on **Save and display** at the bottom of the page.

   The Journal is now ready for students to use.

Helping students use Journal

5. When students click on the journal link on the course page, they'll see this.:

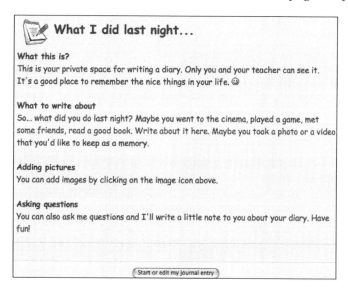

6. They then click on **Start or edit my journal entry** and can start writing down their memories.

   Notice that students have the option to change the text format at the bottom of their screen. If they want to include images, they should keep to the **HTML format**, as in the screenshot below.

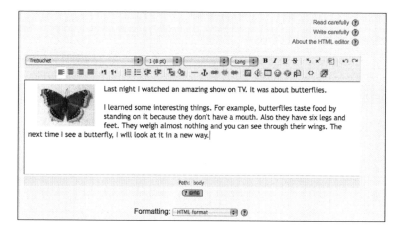

7. When we teachers click on the journal link on the course home page, we will see:

Click on **View journal entries**. We can now give some feedback.

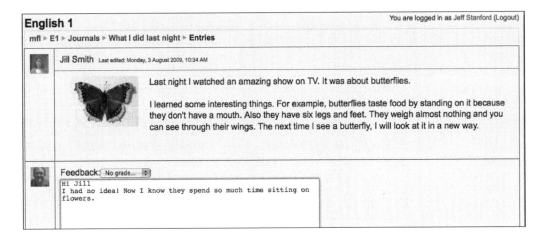

8. Afterwards, click on **Save all my feedback** at the bottom of the page.

Activity 6: Using a Blog or Web page for creative writing

Aim: Help students write creatively

Moodle modules: Blog, OUblog

Extra programs: Kompozer

Ease of setup: *

The previous activity created an opportunity for private writing. You might also want to create a showcase for students' work which other students on the course can view. This can be fun, motivating for writers, and may even be useful to readers. Here are just a few examples of the sort of free writing students could do on Moodle:

- Diaries
- Recipes
- Reviews
- Jokes
- Funny stories
- Writing about niche interests
- How-to articles

There are various ways of setting up a showcase of students' writing on Moodle. The simplest is to get students to create a Moodle blog. In case you're unfamiliar with blogs, they stand for web logs, and are a sort of public diary. If you've installed the add-on OUblog, you could also allow other students to comment on the blogs. A third variation would be to use the Book module. The disadvantage of this is that students cannot edit pages. So students would have to create separate web pages using an external program like Kompozer (mentioned in Chapter 2, *Getting Started with Moodle*). They would then have to send them to the teachers by email, or teachers could access them on a school network, for example. The teacher would then put them in one directory and import the whole directory into Book. That involves more teacher time, but does have the advantage that teachers can check the students' work before it goes live. A fourth alternative is to use a portfolio. There's an example of that in Chapter 10, *Extended Activities*.

In this chapter we'll look at three variations:

Variation	Details
Variation 1	Blog for students to tell stories
Variation 2	OUblog for students to comment on the news and comment on each other's comments
Variation 3	Book with student web pages in which they introduce their houses

Variation 1: Blog stories

Often the secret to making a blog work is finding the right topic. It's well worth asking students what they would like to write about. In this variation, students have decided that they'd like to share their thoughts about a trip they went on. They can include pictures to liven up their pages. Here's what a story blog might look like when a student views it:

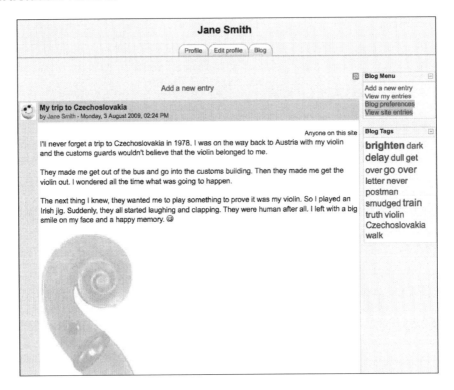

Note that teachers see three more tabs: **Forum posts**, **Notes**, and **Activity reports**.

There are two ways students can add images. The easiest way is to add one as an attachment, as in the screenshot above. The image then appears below the text. Alternatively, we can click on the Insert Image icon which brings up the dialog box in the screenshot opposite. The advantage of the doing that is that students can place the image to the left or right of the text. (See Chapter 11, *Formatting and Enhancing Your Moodle Materials* for help with that). The disadvantage with this method is that students cannot browse to images on their own computer. They need to upload them to an online image program like Picasa or Flickr, then copy the URL into the Image URL box. In the following example, the URL for a photo of a violin is `http://picasaweb.google.com/violinjeff/Miscellaneous#5365746327541002050`. You can find it in the address bar of your browser when you display the photo you've uploaded to Picasa or whatever program you're using. See Chapter 11, *Formatting and Enhancing Your Moodle Materials* if you need more help on using Picasa.

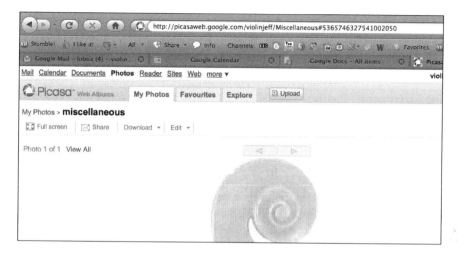

Below is a screenshot of the **Insert Image** dialog box where you would add the **Image URL**. You can also see the **Attachment** option at the bottom of the set-up page.

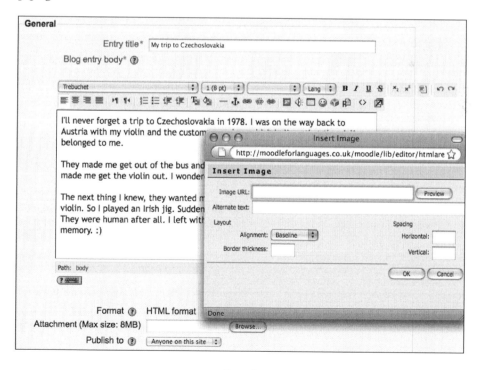

Here's how to do it

Follow the procedure in Chapter 6, *Reading Activities*, Activity 4, Steps 1–7.

- Students could enhance their pages with images or interesting layouts
- You could add a blog tag block to the course page, then get students to add tags (keywords) at the bottom of their blogs. Those keywords then show up in the blog tag blocks. See Chapter 6, *Reading Activities* for an example of this.

Variation 2: Blog stories

The main reason for choosing OUblog instead of the normal Moodle Blog is to allow students to comment on each other's work. So the main challenge for us is to find a topic that students want to comment on. Some students are quite keen on finding out interesting facts. So we'll take that as our example. In general, it's good to find something provocative, maybe controversial to get students interested. Here's what an OUblog based on interesting facts could look like:

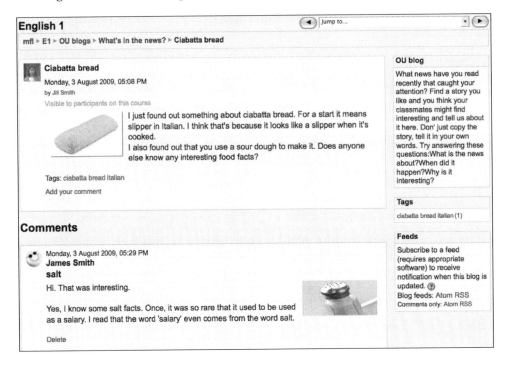

Here's how to do it

Follow the procedure in Chapter 4 Activity 8, Steps 1–5. Remember to allow Captions on the Set-up page.

On the set-up page you could write an introduction like this:

What's in the news?

What news have you read recently that caught your attention? Find a story you like and you think your classmates might find interesting and tell us about it here. Don' just copy the story, tell it in your own words.

Try answering these questions:
What is the news about?
When did it happen?
Why is it interesting?

Variation 3: Using Book to display student descriptions of their houses

Book makes a good showcase for organizing students' writing. As suggested in the introduction to this activity, students can make web pages using a free web page maker. They send them to us. We put all the web pages in one directory. Then we upload the entire directory into Book in just one action.

Here's what a display of students' houses could look like:

Here's how to do it

Follow the example of how to create a book using student web pages in Chapter 6, *Reading Activities*, *Activity 2*, Steps 1–4.

Activity 7: Writing encyclopedia entries using Glossary

Aim: Help students improve their ability to write clear descriptions

Moodle modules: Glossary

Extra programs: None

Ease of setup: *

If you tell students they're going to write an encyclopedia, they'll probably look bemused. It sounds like a daunting task. But if you know that the students live in a pretty town with lots of tourists, and you tell them they're going to do a project in which each student takes photos and describes various parts of the town, they might well get interested. So the key challenge is to find a topic that is appropriate to your class and present it in an enticing way. If we use Glossary to present the bits of information, the end result will be a mini encyclopedia.

Here is a quick brainstorm of topics that might work, but the topic for the encyclopedia depends very much on the age, interests, and language level of the students:

- Towns in your area/country/the world
- Historical events
- Musicians
- Famous people
- Tourist sights in your town
- Favorite poems/songs and why you like them
- FAQs (Frequently Asked Questions)

This is a similar idea to Chapter 3, *Vocabulary Activities*, *Activity 4*. In that activity the focus was on providing definitions for vocabulary. In this activity the focus is more on elaborating definitions and helping students make them as clear as possible. Students are likely to be motivated to be clear, informative, and helpful if they know that other students are going to read what they write.

In this example, we're going to set up a mini encyclopedia about capitals of the world. The end result will look something like this:

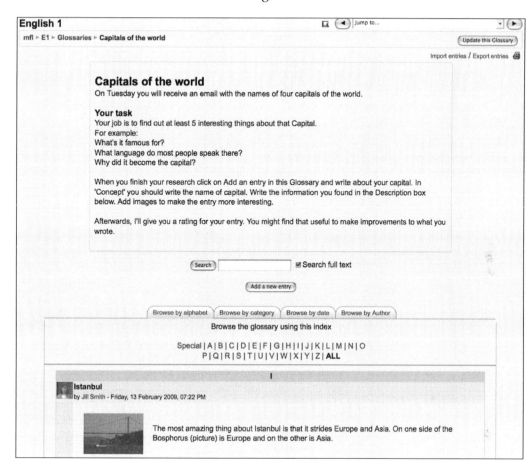

Here's how to do it

Follow the instructions in Chapter 3, *Vocabulary Activities*, *Activity 4*, Steps 1–8 for setting up a glossary. We will cover the next step here.

While you're doing that, there are various variables that it's worth taking into consideration. You should read these notes in conjunction with Chapter 3, *Vocabulary Activities*, *Activity 4*.

9. Here are the key changes on the set-up page. Don't worry about the other choices, as they are optional and won't affect the glossary in any fundamental way.

Settings	Details
Name	Let's call it **Capitals of the world**.
Description	Write something like:
	Capitals of the world **On Tuesday you will receive an email with the names of four capitals of the world.**
	Your task **Your job is to find out at least 5 interesting things about each capital.** **For example:** **What's it famous for?** **What language do most people speak there?** **How many people live there?** **What's the ethnic mix like?**
	When you finish your research click on Add an entry in this Glossary and write about your capital. In 'Concept' you should write the name of capital. Write the information you found in the Definition box below. We can add images to make the entry more interesting.
	Afterwards, I'll give you a rating for your entry. You might find that useful to make improvements to what you wrote.
Display format	Choose **Encyclopedia**. That will give author information for each entry. Attached images are shown inline, but with no space between images and text.
Allow entries to be reated?	Let's keep the same system as in Chapter 3, *Vocabulary Activities*, *Activity 4*. It could be useful to provide feedback on students' writing and allow them to re-edit their entries. See later for more information on the rating system.

This is what a student entry could look like:

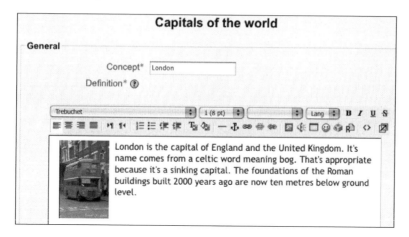

A few more things to think about

Which rating system?

On the set-up page, we can choose whether just the teacher can rate entries or students too. We can also choose the rating system we want to use. Your administrator can set up an appropriate rating system by going to the main site page, then to **Site Administration | Grades | Scales | Add a new scale**. See Chapter 2, *Getting Started with Moodle* for more information on this.

This is what the setup for a new scale for clarity could look like.

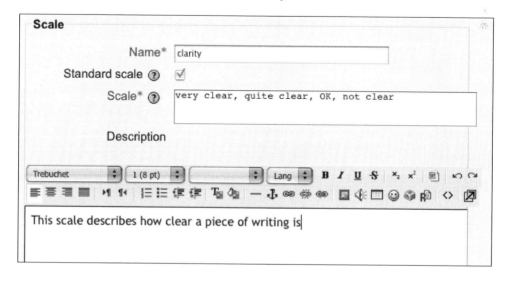

If you set up your own scale, don't forget you can click on the help icon ⑦ next to **Grade** (in the screenshot below) to get more information.

Now, when we go to the set-up page for the **Capitals of the world** glossary, this new scale appears as an option.

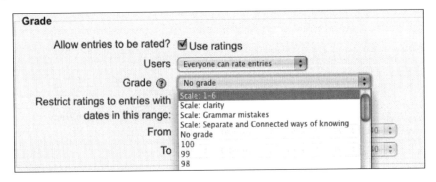

If we select **Everyone can rate entries** and save the changes, students can now rate the clarity of each other's writing. Students who get poor ratings will then be prompted to try to improve their entries.

N.B. Students can't rate their own writing. There is an option to do that in the Workshop module. See Chapter 10, *Extended Activities* for an example.

Once entries have ratings, all users can now click on the average rating (**very clear** in the screenshot below) and details of the rating will appear in a pop-up window.

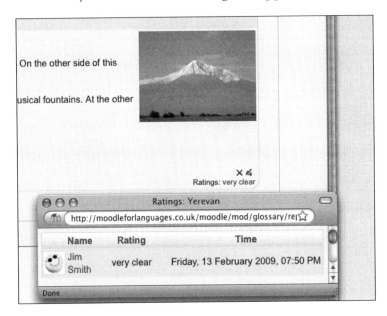

Images

It's probably better to tell students to avoid using attachments. There are several reasons for this:

- You can't delete them once they are part of your entry. So if you don't like your attachment, you're stuck with it. The solution would be to delete the whole entry by clicking on the ✖ and starting a new entry.

- There's no choice over the position of the attached image. It automatically goes in the top right-hand corner against the text.

If students use the **Insert Image** icon in the editing menu, they have more choice over where they place the image. They can also delete the image. See Chapter 11, *Formatting and Enhancing Your Moodle Materials* for more information on inserting images.

> **What next?**
> Once you have a glossary up and running, you could link it to other Moodle modules. For example, you could create a quiz based on entries. You could create a forum to discuss an interesting aspect of some of the entries.

Activity 8: Promoting fluency writing using Chat

Aim: Help students improve their ability to get their meaning across quickly through writing

Moodle modules: Chat

Extra programs: none

Ease of setup: *

Most of the activities in this chapter have been about providing frameworks for students to improve the accuracy of their writing in one way or another. There is something to be said for just letting students write without being corrected with the aim of getting their meaning across as efficiently as possible. The Chat module is perfect for this. It encourages students to use strategies such as back-channeling (showing the other speaker that you're following what they're saying), paraphrasing, reformulation, and asking for clarification so that they can write a meaningful conversation with others.

As in Chapter 4, *Speaking Activities*, *Activity 7* and Chapter 3, *Vocabulary Activities*, *Activity 7*, be careful not to include too many people in your chat session. If you have more than six people, for example, it will be increasingly difficult for all students to feel that they are participating.

The essential thing is to decide what to chat about. Find something you think the students will enjoy and have something to say about. Imposing a potentially boring topic just won't work. You could ask students what they'd like to chat about or suggest things you think they might be interested in. It could be simple conversation about leisure plans, opinions about controversial subjects, the news, issues, or problem solving. Flag up the activity in advance so that students can prepare their thoughts and language, if necessary.

You can see what a chat session in progress looks like in Chapter 3, *Vocabulary Activities*, *Activity 7*.

Here's how to do it

Follow the instructions in Chapter 4, *Speaking Activities*, *Activity 7* for setting up a chat.

Other things to consider

Save the transcript to analyze errors anonymously in a later error clinic. See Chapter 3, *Vocabulary Activities*, *Activity 7* for an example of an error clinic.

Activity 9: Using Assignment to submit and evaluate semi-authentic writing

Aim: Provide students with feedback on written assignments

Moodle modules: Assignment

Extra programs: None

Ease of setup: **

We usually write a text in response to some sort of stimulus. If we receive a letter, we reply to it. If we see a job ad, we send a letter of application and a resume. In fact, it's quite unnatural when a teacher tells students to write for the sake of it. So to help motivate students and to provide a more realistic, semi-authentic situation, we can use the Assignment module to provide a stimulus and set up a writing task. Here are just a few of the stimuli we could consider using together with suggestions for appropriate responses:

Stimulus	Response
Letter	Reply
Job ad	CV and letter of application
Invitation	Reply
New music track	Review
Film	Review
Agony aunt letter	Reply

Once we've decided on a stimulus, we need to find a good way to present it on Moodle. Here are some options for presenting the stimulus using the examples above:

Stimulus	Options for presenting the stimulus
Letter	Type in a letter.
	Scan a real letter. Upload the image.
Job ad	Type in a letter.
	Scan an ad. Upload the image.
	Provide the URL of a live ad.
Invitation	Type in an invitation.
	Scan an invitation. Upload the invitation.
New music track	Embed an audio in the instructions box.
	Provide the URL of a web page with the audio file.
Film	Embed a video in the instructions box.
	Provide the URL of a web page with the film file.

Feedback

The **online text** Assignment module lets us engage in so-called *process* writing in that it allows students to submit a draft, get feedback, submit further drafts and get more feedback. Teachers can provide feedback in a variety of ways. This can be:

Quantitative (a mark on a number scale)

- Grades (a mark out of a given number)
- Outcomes (a mark for a particular area of language competence, such as accuracy)
- Stars or smileys (rewards in the form of collectable smileys or stars)

Qualitative (comments)

- Written feedback on drafts
- Analytic or holistic feedback

Check out Chapter 2, *Getting Started with Moodle* for ways of setting up **grades** and **outcomes,** which you can then apply to students' writing. You can add smileys by writing **colon + closing parenthesis** in a comments box. They will automatically be converted into a ☺.

Outcomes are a good way of providing qualitative feedback on students' writing. They allow us to provide a range of comments for a given area of language competence, such as grammar, fluency, or text organization. Consider whether you want holistic or analytic feedback. Holistic feedback gives an overview of the writing. We could create an **outcome** called "writing" to do this. Analytic feedback breaks writing down into component skills and therefore provides more feedback to students. For writing, we could consider the following as component skills:

- Task fulfillment
- Organization
- Vocabulary
- Content

If we choose these skills, we would need to create a separate outcome for each area and then select them on the assignment settings page. Chapter 5, *Grammar Activities, Activity 8* gives several examples of outcomes being used to provide feedback.

It's worth consulting a book on assessing writing for more help with this. For example, *Assessing Writing* by Sara Cushing Weigle, published by Cambridge University Press.

Let's set up an assignment using job ads as a stimulus. Students read the ads, then write a reply to the one they like the most.

Here's how to do it

1. Follow the instructions in Chapter 5, *Grammar Activities*, *Activity 8*, *Variation 1* to set up outcomes for content, task fulfillment, and grammar.

2. Set up an assignment following the instructions in Chapter 5, *Grammar Activities*, *Activity 8*, *Variation 1*.

   The main differences are in the description area of the set-up page. We want to include job ads. Students tend to respond better to this activity when they have a selection of job ads to choose from. Let's give students a link to a job website: `http://jobs.guardian.co.uk/?setHome=GB`. This one's from the UK, but there are hundreds of similar sites. Local newspaper websites are often a good source of local jobs. If you don't know the web address of the jobs page, doing a Google search (`http://google.com`) for "local jobs" should give you a choice.

   Here's the job page for the UK's Guardian newspaper:

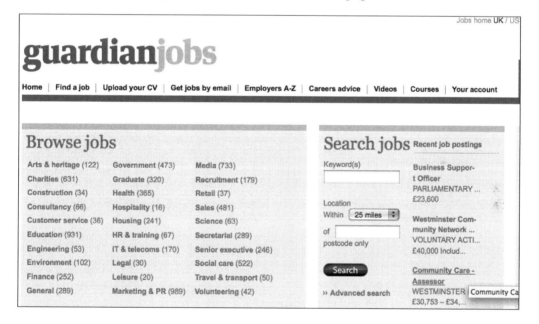

Our instructions could be:

Finding a job
Follow this link to the Guardian Jobs web site.
http://jobs.guardian.co.uk/job/
Do a search for a job you are interested in. When you find the job ad, copy and paste it into your reply. Then write your letter of application.

Here is what one student's reply might look like. The task instructions are at the top. The job description is in the middle. The beginning of the student's reply is at the bottom.

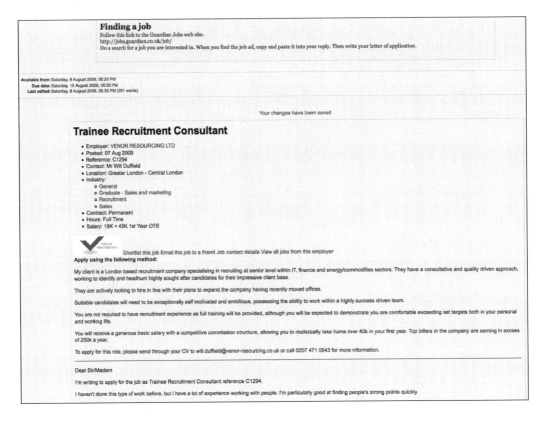

We can now mark it using outcomes and/or grades, as in Chapter 5, *Grammar Activities, Activity 8, Variation 1*.

Activity 10: Writing a slideshow commentary using Forum

Aim: Get students writing about a set of images

Moodle modules: Forum

Extra programs: None

Ease of setup: *

Images often motivate us and provoke a response. If we see a set of photos of an event we were involved in, we often feel like commenting on it. If we see a picture of a news item, the story comes to life. If we see a work of art, we may be moved to talk or write about it. The simple idea behind this activity is to choose an image or a set of images and encourage our users to write a commentary.

There are many sources. We can look for copyright-free images on the Web, or even better, use students' own photos or photos we've taken in class.

We're going to use the Forum module to create the slideshow. It allows us to keep all students' slideshows in one place. Here's what a forum slideshow might look like.

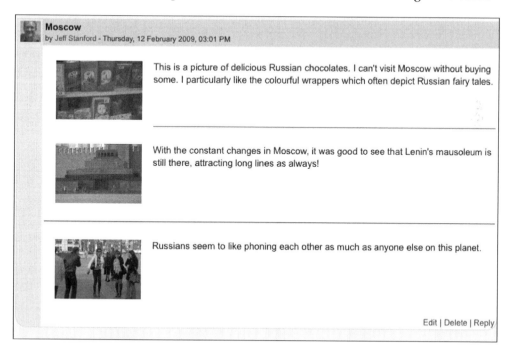

The forum also allows other users to comment on narratives.

Let's create a slideshow based on a recent trip to Moscow.

Here's how to do it

1. First select the image or images you want to use. If they are large photos, use free photo-editing software like Picasa, available free from `http://picasa.google.com`, to compress them and reduce the dimensions. See Chapter 11, *Formatting and Enhancing Your Moodle Materials* if you need help with processing images. The slideshow will look more professional if all the images are the same size. In the earlier screenshot, they are 150 px wide and 100 px high.

Setting up a forum

2. Click on **Turn editing on** on your course page. Then click on **Add an activity...**. Select **Forum** from the drop-down menu.

3. Complete the introductory page. See Chapter 2, *Getting Started with Moodle* if you need help with grades, outcomes, and Common module settings. If you're uncertain, just leave them, but do pay attention to the following:

Setting	Details
Forum name	Let's call it **Our trips**.
Forum type	Let's choose **Each person posts one discussion**. That means the finished forum directory will display a list of each student destination.
Forum introduction	Explain what the purpose of the Forum is. Let's write something like this: **Our trips** **Where did you go in the summer holidays?** **Choose some of your favorite photos and post them in a forum. You can each start one Discussion by clicking on 'Add a new discussion topic'. Then upload images by clicking on the Insert Image icon in the editing bar -** **Next to the image write a commentary. Tell us what's going on and what you thought about it.** **Have fun.** **If you don't have any images or have problems, send me an email.**

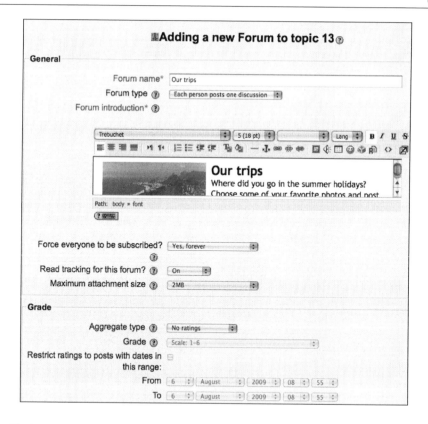

4. Click on **Save and display** at the bottom of the page.

    The forum is now ready to use. When students click on the **Our trips** forum link on the course page, they will see this:

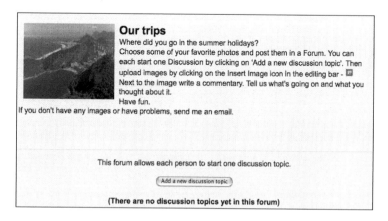

They should click on the **Add a new discussion topic** button. They can then add their slideshow by uploading photos and captions.

Aligning photos

As we saw in the forum instructions, students should insert images by clicking on the **Insert image** icon 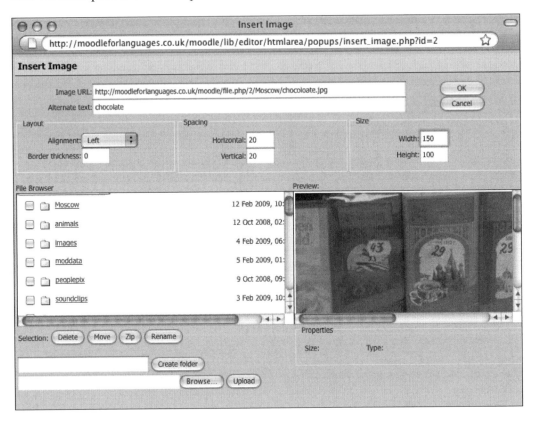. When students are editing postings with images and commentary, remind them to align the photo left or right and create a horizontal and vertical space around the picture.

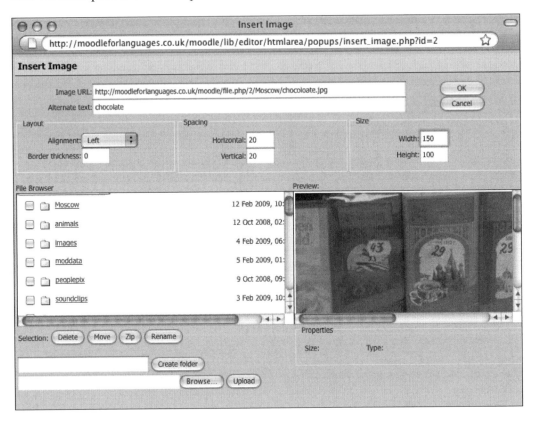

In this case, we click on the Moscow directory and choose the chocolate photo. Then we write the **Alternative text**: **chocolate**. That's the text that you see when you hover the mouse Insert cursor over the image on the web page. The key specifications are in the **Layout**, **Spacing**, and **Size** areas.

The final image has **Left** alignment, a **Vertical** space of **20** pixels (that's the space above and below the picture) and a **Horizontal** space of **20** pixels (that's the space to the right of the image). The image size is **Width** = **150** px and **Height** = **100** px. You can reduce the size of the image manually here, but you'll save resources if you process the image to the size you want before you upload it.

BEFORE

This is what an image without alignment looks like.

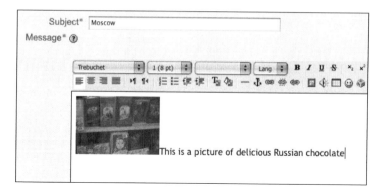

AFTER 1

This is what an image with alignment, but without spacing, looks like.

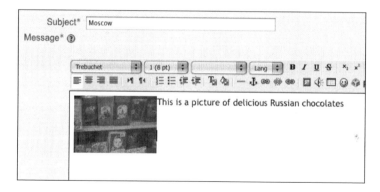

AFTER 2

And finally, you'll get an image with alignment and spacing as shown in Step 4.

N.B. You could also use tables to position elements. See Chapter 11, *Formatting and Enhancing Your Moodle Materials* for more information on editing and using images.

Helping students

It's probably best to demonstrate to students how they can edit their photos and improve layout in a training session. Alternatively, you could create a how-to movie, using one of the methods suggested in Chapter 2, *Getting Started with Moodle*.

When all students have added their slideshows, the forum directory will look something like this:

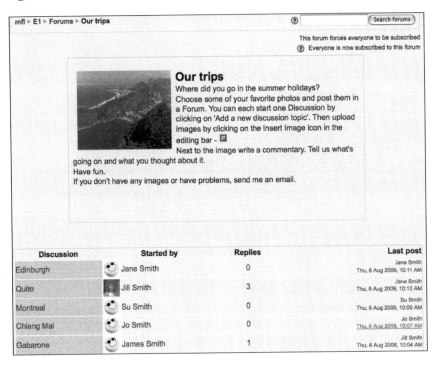

Students can click on the **Discussion** topic to read and comment on other students' slideshows.

Word images

An alternative to a slideshow which is popular with younger students is to use a Paint program to create a shape and fill it with text relating to that image. For example, they could paint a house and write text about it inside the picture. They could then save the image and insert it into the forum. Here's an example of a house.

Activity 11: Summarizing RSS news items

Aim: Help students improve each other's writing

Moodle modules: RSS block and forum

Extra programs: None

Ease of setup: **

Summarizing text can be a good way to practice reading and writing. It focuses students on key bits of information and encourages them to organize and express that information in concise ways.

The idea behind this activity is that students select a story from the Internet. They then write a summary of it in a forum. To make it more interesting, you could get students to include why they chose that particular item. That might provoke comment and discussion from other forum members.

To make it easier for students to select a story, we will provide news feeds to stories. News feeds contain just the headlines and first few words of the news stories. They make it easy for students to skim over several stories. Here's an example of a news feed for IMDb news:

News feeds are also called RSS feeds. **RSS** stands for **Really Simple Syndication**. It's a method websites use to send out alerts about updated content—a very handy way of getting quick notice about changes on your favorite websites.

To get regular feeds, you just need to copy the RSS feed link from the site you're interested in. You may have seen the RSS icon 🔊 on the websites you've visited. Usually, if you click on that icon, you'll get the feed link. Another way of finding RSS links is to do an Internet search for the "website name + rss". For example, if we want the RSS feed for the movie database site, `http://imdb.com`, we search for "imdb + rss". We then right-click on the RSS icon and copy the link provided. It will look something like this: `http://rss.imdb.com/news/`.

You can use so-called aggregator programs, like `http://bloglines.com`, to display the RSS items, or you can use Moodle's RSS block, which is what we're going to do.

Once your feed is on display, users can click on any of the items to go to the news story. We can also set how many headlines are shown in the feed.

Here are some of the sites offering RSS feeds that you might consider:

- News sites
- Movie sites
- Blogs
- Cartoons like Dilbert
- Recipe sites
- Sports sites
- Joke of the day sites
- Property sites
- Journals
- Stocks
- E-book catalogs like Gutenberg: `http://www.gutenberg.org`
- RSS mountain — provides a handy, categorized list of feeds in several languages: `http://www.rssmountain.com/directory_category.php`

Make an RSS feed for your forum

Once the Forum is set up, you can even turn it into an RSS feed. To do that, the administrator needs to go to **Site Administration | Server | RSS** and then check **enable RSS feeds**. After that a clickable 🔊 will appear at the top of your forum.

Here's how to do it

1. Click on **Turn editing on** on your course page. You'll find the **Add Blocks** menu at the bottom of the right-hand column.

2. Select **Remote RSS feeds**. That will create a block shell for you to add RSS details to. It looks like this:

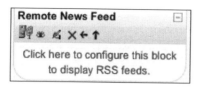

3. At the moment the block is just an empty shell. We need to provide an RSS feed link. To do that, click on **Click here to configure this block to display RSS feeds**.

4. Now click on the **Manage all my feeds** tab.

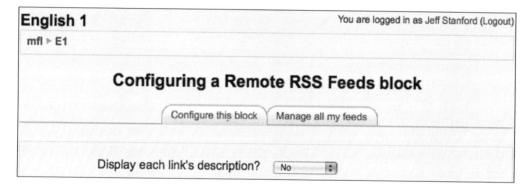

5. Copy the RSS feed link from the site you want to track into the box **Add a news feed URL**. Let's imagine we want an RSS feed from the website Technology Slice. The website gives us this URL `http://www.technologyslice.com.au/feed`.

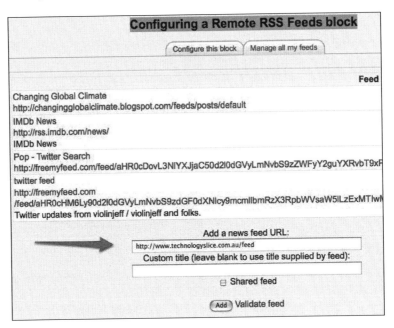

6. Click on **Validate feed** to make sure the feed is working. If you get a **Congratulations!** message, click on the **Add** button. If you don't, there's something wrong with the feed. Try copying it again, or choose another feed.

7. Now click on the **Configure this block** tab. This page allows you to choose which feeds you want and how many entries per feed you want to show at a time. Beware that showing the link to the original site might be attractive, but helps clutter up the Moodle blocks. So it's set to **No** in the following setup. If you have a large number of students in your class, it might be helpful to make the **Max number entries to show per block** a higher number than the default **5**. For example, **10** would provide a wider choice of stories, though it will take up double the space, too. You could also set up several RSS blocks for different websites. That would cater for different tastes in your class and give students a wider choice of stories to read and write summaries on.

Configuring a Remote RSS Feeds block

Configure this block | Manage all my feeds

Display each link's description? `No`

Max number entries to show per block. `5`

Choose the feeds which you would like to make available in this block:
- ☐ Changing Global Climate
- ☐ IMDb News
- ☑ Technology Slice
- ☐ twitter feed
- ☐ Pop - Twitter Search

Title:

Should a link to the original site (channel link) be displayed? (Note that if no feed link is supplied in the news feed then no link will be shown) : `No`

Show channel image if available : `No`

(Save changes)

8. Click on **Save changes**. The block will now show the RSS feed on the course page and will look similar to the example screenshot in the introduction.

9. Now you can set up a forum as in Activity 9. Don't forget to include clear instructions which take students through the process of choosing a feed, reading the entry, posting a summary to the forum, and responding to other students' postings. You could write something like this in the forum introduction:

Summarizing the news

Look at the RSS News feed block on the course page. Choose a story that looks interesting. Then click on **Add a discussion in this Forum**. Write a short summary of the story you read. Get the main points across in just a few words. Remember to write full sentences, though.

Once you've posted your own summary take a look at the other summaries in the Forum. Write a comment or two on the stories that interest you most.

Imagine a student had chosen the Jetstar story from the RSS feeds block. This is a glimpse of what they would then read:

10. In the forum, they could then **Add a discussion** with a summary, which might look something like this:

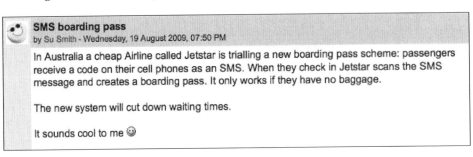

An alternative to using a forum is to set up an assignment as in Activity 8 in this chapter. You can then provide detailed feedback on the students' language. The advantage of the forum is that it's potentially more motivating for students to write for each other. Some options for sending feedback on summaries are to reply to the forum postings, use the Moodle Message facility, or email comments.

Activity 12: Collaborative writing using Wiki

Aim: Help students write different parts of a writing project

Moodle modules: Wiki

Extra programs: None

Ease of setup: **

Getting students to cooperate on a writing project can be beneficial in several ways. They can motivate each other, help each other to write and contribute one part of a bigger project. They can also compare and contrast their writing with other students' writing.

In this activity, students use a wiki to make different and separate contributions to the same project. A wiki is an editable web page or set of web pages. Any course member can edit any page on a wiki. You can also use the Moodle Group feature with wikis. Then only group members can see their own wiki. There's another example of a wiki in Chapter 3, *Vocabulary Activities, Activity 7*.

We're going to use a wiki to help students contribute to different parts of a School Guide. They'll need preparation first. This could either be face to face in class, or you could set up a discussion forum, depending on the age and independence of the students.

Here's how to do it

1. First we need to set up the wiki introduction page. To do that, go to the course page, and click on **Turn editing on**. Go to the **Add an activity...** drop-down menu, and select **Wiki**.

2. Fill in the settings page. Pay attention to the following:

Settings	Details
Name	Enter an appropriate name. Let's write **Our School Guide**.
Summary	This will tell the students what to do. Here are some possible instructions:

A guide to our school

Dear class

For this activity, you're going to work on one big project. Your job is to describe our school to the group from France that is visiting us next month.

Each person will write about a different aspect of the school. Check below to see what you job is!

Student	Subject
John	**Library**
Sarah	**Sports facilities**
Maria	**Our classroom**
Stacey	**Our timetable**
Ben	**The teachers**
Dan	**What we wear to school**

Click on the link below to go to your Wiki page. Don't forget to take and include pictures! Write your piece in the section below.

Don't forget, you can use the enlarge icon ▣ in the editing menu to increase the size of the HTML editing box if you need to be able to see more of the page. As this is a wiki, you can always go back and edit your text if necessary.

Type	Select **Groups**. This will allow groups of students to work on one project.
HTML mode	Select **HTML only** so that students have more options for formatting text.
Allow binary files	Select **Yes** so that students can include graphics. In fact, this is only necessary if you didn't select **HTML Mode**.

Settings	Details
Common module settings	Let's choose **No groups**. That way students can all see each other's contributions.
Wiki auto-linking options	Do not select **Disable CamelCase linking**. CamelCase gives us hyperlinks, which we want.
Student admin options	Don't check any of these options.

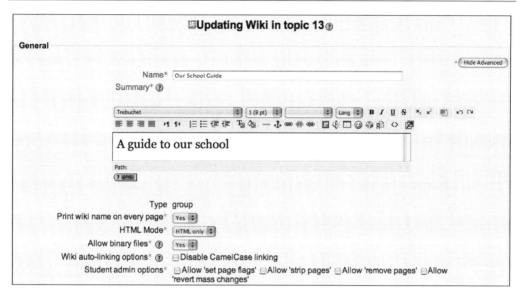

3. Click on **Save and display** at the bottom of the page.

4. We now have a ready-to-use wiki in front of us. To make it easier for students to use, let's set up the initial menu.

   Make sure you're in edit mode by clicking on the **Edit** tab. We then write the names of the pages we want to create between square brackets. For example:

   [Library]

   [Sports facilities]

   [Our classroom]

   [Our timetable]

   [The teachers]

   [What we wear to school]

   This is the CamelCase referred to in Step 2.

5. Now press **Save**.

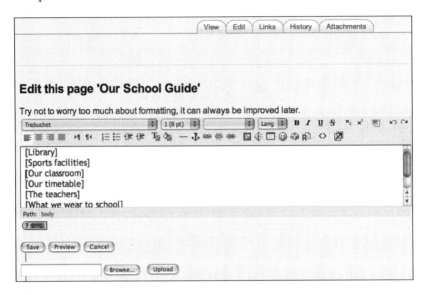

6. These items will now appear as a menu on the first page.

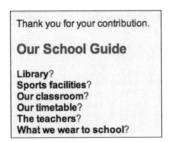

7. The wiki is now ready for students to start using. When they select the wiki, they will be able to choose from the following four tabs to create text, review, or amend their work.

To edit their page, students should click on the **Edit** tab, then they should click on the question mark (**?**) that comes at the end of their menu item; for example, at the end of **Library**. Once text is entered on the new **Library** page, the question mark will disappear from the main menu.

If at any time you or the students get "lost", you can click on the **Choose wiki links** drop down menu, select site map, and you'll get a list of the pages you've created so far.

If you want to create a new page, you simply place the new page title in square brackets; for example, **[new page]**.

It's worth checking students' progress quite frequently at first to make sure they're able to use the activity OK. Once they're comfortable inputting basic texts and setting up links, you can work on improving layout and incorporating images.

Encourage students to read each other's pages so that they can harmonize their style.

Other ideas

Wordles

Students give their interpretations on Wordles. Wordles are word pictures which highlight the most common words in a given text. See if you can guess where the following one comes from:

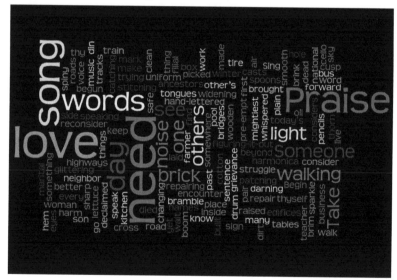

It's from Elizabeth Graham's poem that she read at Barrack Obama's inaugural speech in January 2009.

You can create a Wordle by entering any text in any language on the website: `http://wordle.net`. You can then save it anonymously on the website. That gives you the embed code which you can use to embed the Wordle in your wiki. See Chapter 2, *Getting Started with Moodle* if you need help with embedding code on your Moodle web pages. As you'll see, once you start experimenting, short texts work better. Poems are particularly good because of the in-built repetition that many of them have.

Students look at the Wordle which you embed in the introduction to the wiki. They then make their own attempt at creating a text from it. Afterwards they compare each other's texts. Finally, they get to see the original text. The embedded Wordle may be quite small. If that happens, click on it in Moodle and it will take you back to the Wordle website where you'll see a bigger version.

Reviews

Students write reviews of books, films, or music that they are familiar with or learn about. Students could take responsibility for writing about different aspects of the product. If it's a film, for example, there could be writing on background music, photography, the acting, and the storyline.

Lecture notes

Students write up notes from a lecture or a programme that the class watched.

Silent video viewing

Upload two versions of a video: the first without sound which students see at the beginning of the activity, the second with sound which students see at the end of the activity. After seeing the first version, students collaborate writing the transcript for the video. See Chapter 2, *Getting Started with Moodle* for help with using video in Moodle.

8
Listening Activities

Listening is often a challenging activity for language learners. This could be because they have to deal with a range of accents and speeds or because the content may be difficult to follow. Sometimes background noise on the recording makes it more difficult to understand. In natural speech it is normal to interrupt, use ellipsis, or leave sentences unfinished. So recordings based on natural speech are also likely to be difficult.

Using Moodle, students can listen repeatedly to recordings until they feel more comfortable with them. We can also help students understand by using a recording program like Audacity to manipulate recordings, providing slower and faster versions of the same text. Certain Moodle modules, like Quiz and Lesson, can be used effectively to help students notice important features of texts, after which they are likely to understand the whole recording better.

The communicative language teaching classroom often focuses on activities that take place *before*, *during*, and *after* listening. This chapter follows the same pattern.

Before activities aim at motivating students to listen and getting them to anticipate texts and focus on key vocabulary in advance. Forum and Mindmap are two modules which enable us to do this.

During activities focus on the detail of the text and include listening and matching, gap-fill, ordering tasks, identifying attitude, and summarizing tasks. Quiz and Lesson modules are well suited to this.

After activities get students to review and evaluate texts they have listened to. Forum and Questionnaire are good for this purpose.

The chapter is organized as follows:

Activity and ease of setup	Focus	Module	Description
1 *	Before listening	Forum and Mediacenter	Students discuss recordings they would like to hear.
2 *		Mindmap	Students brainstorm ideas or vocabulary.
3 ***	During listening	Quiz	Students answer gist and detailed questions about recordings.
4 ***		Lesson	Students predict text in recordings.
5 *	After listening	Choice	Students vote on recordings.
6 ***		Questionnaire	Students review and evaluate the content of recordings
7 *		Forum	Students discuss recordings.

You'll notice that there are fewer activities in this chapter than in most others. However, listening is included in at least twelve activities elsewhere in this book, as shown in the following table:

Reference	Module	Details
Chapter 3, *Vocabulary Activities, Activity 11*	Quiz	Students complete a gap-fill while listening to the lyrics of a song.
Chapter 4, *Speaking Activities, Activity 1*	Forum	Students listen to model pronunciation of language they are learning.
Chapter 4, *Speaking Activities, Activity 4*	Mediacenter	Students listen and repeat at normal or slower speeds.
Chapter 4, *Speaking Activities, Activity 5*	OUwiki	In this Dialog minus one activity, students listen to one speaker in a conversation and play the part of the other speaker.
Chapter 5, *Grammar Activities, Activity 2*	Lesson	Students listen to a recording and notice grammar.
Chapter 5, *Grammar Activities, Activity 4*	Lesson or Wiki	In this dictation activity, students listen and transcribe what they hear.
Chapter 6, *Reading Activities, Activity 2*	Web page or Book	Students listen and read at the same time.
Chapter 6, *Reading Activities, Activity 6*	Hot Potatoes JQuiz	Students investigate the meaning of song lyrics, then listen to the song.

Reference	Module	Details
Chapter 7, *Writing Activities, Activity 11*	RSS and Forum	Students read texts and summarize them. Substitute listening texts for reading texts and this becomes a useful listening activity.
Chapter 7, *Writing Activities, Activity 12, Variation 2*	Wiki	Students watch a silent video, predict the text, and then listen carefully to compare their versions with the original. More emphasis can be put on listening to make this a useful listening activity.
Chapter 10, *Extended Activities, Activity 1*	Webquest	Parts of students' Webquest research can include listening to texts on the Internet.
Chapter 5, *Grammar Activities, Activity 4*	Reader	We can adapt the reader activity in Chapter 10, *Extended Activities* by using recordings instead of books. This would help students follow an extended listening program.

Since there are various ways we can use Moodle to help students, the introduction to this chapter looks in detail at the types of players we can use. There is also some guidance on the range of sources of listening material available on the Internet. The final section in the introduction demonstrates how we can show and hide text on Moodle pages while students listen.

Players

This book offers four main ways of presenting listening material. The introduction to Chapter 4, *Speaking Activities* offers additional information on the pros and cons of these ways. Chapter 2, *Getting Started with Moodle* provides more information about all the players and programs mentioned below.

- **Built-in Flash player**: Recordings have to be made on an external recording program, such as Audacity. You need to do some simple editing of the HTML code on your pages, but it doesn't require any add-on modules and the player fits neatly into the page:

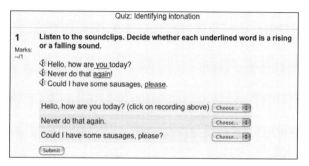

The player usefully includes a pause facility.

- **Mediacenter**: This podcast player requires the add-on Inwicast module. It allows you to include high-quality recordings whose length is limited only by the maximum upload settings as set in the administration panel. The player is again simple and attractive:

There is a full example of it in Chapter 4, *Speaking Activities, Activity 5*. Mediacenter helps you organize recordings in one place. Recordings can be used in a variety of formats, such as Flash-FLV, MP4 and MOV, WMV and MP3. If your recording equipment records in another format, such as WAV, for example, you can use tools like Audacity to convert the audio format if necessary. You might find it useful to convert from WAV to MP3 format, which works in Mediacenter. Mediacenter also allows you to link to remote files on other websites.

- **NanoGong player**: This requires the add-on NanoGong module. It's well worth including in your Moodle setup, as it allows simple recording and playback on most HTML pages within Moodle.

The major constraints as far as Moodle is concerned are the time limit of 2 minutes per recording and the lower recording quality. However, for ease of use and convenience, it's suitable for many of the activities.

- **Embedded flash video players**: You can embed Flash video players in Moodle HTML pages by pasting embed code from the source site on your page. Embed, here, means insert it into the page.

You must check that there are no copyright issues when you embed video. Some sites allow it, some don't. Some request that you seek permission first. Since the video is sourced from another website, you are using its bandwidth as well as its content. So it is doubly right that you seek permission.

Sources of listening material

It's worth considering the range of sources of listening materials available. The following are the typical sources:

- You
- Your students
- Your colleagues
- Local interviewees, such as friends and professionals. You could approach representatives of local services, such as the police or tourist services, and ask if you can make short interviews.
- Recordings of local announcements from railway stations or airports
- Internet recordings
- Websites, such as Woices (`http://woices.com`) and voicethread (`http://voicethread.com/`), which combine audio with maps and images

Activity 1 has an extended list of listening sources.

Recording speed

One of the many useful features of Audacity is that it allows us to reproduce recordings at different speeds without the pitch changing. It's well worth including slower recordings if you think your students will benefit from it. Presentations could include two recordings: the first one at a slower speed; the second at a faster, more natural speed. Alternatively, you could start with a recording at a natural speed and make slower speed versions available for students who need remedial help.

You can use Audacity to record from the Internet (also known as grabbing). See Chapter 2, *Getting Started with Moodle* for more information on Audacity.

Showing the text before listening

In many of the activities below and in other chapters, you might want to create a facility for allowing students to see text before and/or after they hear it. Here is a simple way of doing that using ALT tags (Computer-speak for Alternative text).

First, prepare a small GIF image that students will hover their mouse cursor over to see the text.

 In case you don't know, GIF is one of the formats you can save an image in. Other formats you may have heard of are JPG and PNG.

You can do that using a simple graphic program like Paint. Alternatively, you can copy this pink square image from `http://moodleforlanguages.co.uk/images/pinksquare.gif`. To do that, right-click (or *Ctrl*+click on a Mac) on the image and select **Save Image As...**. Then, in the HTML area on your Moodle activity, upload the image, and write the text you want to show in the ALT area.

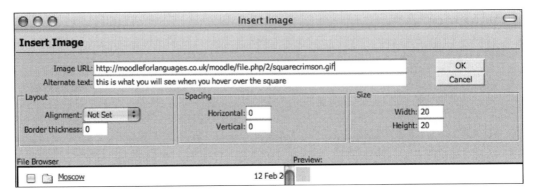

The HTML page will now look like this. The text you write in the **Alternate text** box will appear in a separate box on the screen when you hover the mouse cursor over the pink square.

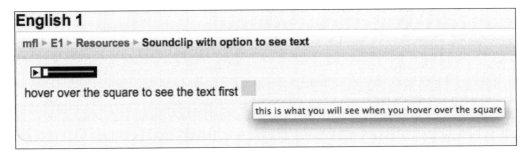

Web conferencing

If you have the add-on module Dimdim, mentioned in the introduction to Chapter 4, *Speaking Activities*, you could also create live listening sessions.

Activity 1: Using Forum to motivate students

Aim: Help motivate students by discussing what recordings to listen to

Moodle modules: Forum

Extra programs: Mediacenter (optional)

Ease of setup: *

As with many language-learning activities, it's important to try to motivate students at the outset. In this activity, students discuss what recordings to listen to. The choice of recordings will depend on the age, interests, and language level of the students. There are thousands of sources on the Internet, many of which you can find through good search engines. Here are some examples:

Source	Ideas
News sites	You could also consider getting students to listen to and compare news from different countries. The open directory project is a good place to look: `http://www.dmoz.org/News/`.
Media repositories	Sites like YouTube and Google Video are good sources of songs, presentations, TV clips, stories, and many other recordings. Sound archives are also good places to look. Some useful sources are: • `http://sounds.bl.uk/` • `http://www.bbc.co.uk/archive/collections.shtml`
Poetry sites	Many of these include recordings: • `http://poems.com/` • `http://www.dmoz.org/Arts/Literature/Poetry/Performance_and_Presentation/`
Story sites	More and more audio books are now available on the Internet often free, as with project Gutenberg: `http://www.gutenberg.org/wiki/Gutenberg:The_Audio_Books_Project`
Discussions	Public broadcast stations like DW, BBC, CBC and CNN are good sources: • `http://www.dw-world.de/` • `http://bbc.co.uk` • `http://www.cbc.ca/` • `http://www.cnn.com/services/podcasting/`
Film trailers	Several websites are devoted to film trailers. For example: `http://www.imdb.com/Sections/Trailers/`
Soap operas	A search for "podcast soap opera" should provide a good catch.

Source	Ideas
Documentaries	Again, public broadcast stations offer an increasingly wide range of documentaries, which you can link to via your Moodle Mediacenter: `http://tinyurl.com/publicbroadcast`.
Lectures	These can be made by you, your students, or sourced from websites such as `http://www.ted.com/`.
	A search for "online lectures" will yield many more sites.
Advertisements	Try `http://www.google.com/Top/Arts/Television/Commercials/` for a directory of advertisements.

There is also a database of sites with recordings at `http://teachereducation.org.uk/moodle/mod/glossary/view.php`. Search for "listening".

Do remember to check copyright if you plan on copying audio content. Direct links to audio material require no special permission, though YouTube users have the ability to block access to videos that they uploaded. So before you set students work on a YouTube activity, check that the video link is still working.

Also, schools may censor some of the above sites. If necessary, you can download recordings. There is help with this in Chapter 2, *Getting Started with Moodle*.

You could also set up an RSS feed to regular broadcasts. See Chapter 7, *Writing Activities* for an example of how you can do this on Moodle.

In our example, we'll set up links to the TED website: `http://www.ted.com/`. All the recordings we want students to consider and research are on the same website. There's a wide range of topics for students to browse. We will ask them to choose a recording they want their classmates to listen to. They will then start forum discussions saying why they think their choice is a good one. N.B. We can also use the Mediacenter as a central directory of recordings. See Chapter 4, *Speaking Activities*, *Activity 5* if you need help with setting up the Mediacenter.

After a given period, students go on to *Activity 2* of this chapter and vote for the recording they want the class to listen to and discuss. They come back to the forum to discuss the recording.

Here's how to do it

Set up a forum activity. See Chapter 4, *Speaking Activities, Activity 1*, Steps 3 and 4, for an example. We will cover the next steps here.

3.   Complete the introductory page. Pay attention to the following in particular:

Settings	Details
Forum name	Let's call it **Your suggestions for listening this month**.
Forum type	Decide what type of forum you want. Let's choose **Standard forum for general use**. That's useful if we want students to be able to start new discussion threads on the forum.
Forum introduction	Here we explain what the purpose of the forum is. To create a link to the TED website, highlight the word you want to link, click on the hyperlink icon in the editor menu ⊜, and add the URL (that's the web address) of the target site.

We could write something like the following:

Listening choice

This month we're going to explore the TED website: http://ted.com.
Here's what you need to do:

1 Browse the website looking for recordings you think would be interesting for the class to listen to and discuss.

2 Choose your top choice and write a Forum posting saying what it is and why you chose it.

3 Read each other's posts, ask questions and give opinions.

4 On Friday I will set up a poll and you will vote on which recording you want to listen to. N.B. You can't vote for the one you recommended.

5 Once we have the result, I'll post the winner on this Forum.

6 Listen to the recording and answer the following questions which I'll post in the forum: What new words did you learn? Do you think they're useful? What do you agree/disagree with? Why? Name at least one point.

Write your answers in the Forum.

* If you have problems understanding the recording, post a message on the Forum so that everyone can benefit from the answer.

4. Save the settings by clicking on **Save and display**.

The forum is now ready to be used. This is what the instruction page will look like:

Listening choice

This month we're going to explore the TED website: http://ted.com.
Here's what you need to do:

1 Browse the website looking for recordings you think would be interesting for the class to listen to and discuss.

2 Choose your top choice and write a Forum posting saying what it is and why you chose it.

3 Read each other's posts, ask questions and give opinions.

4 On Friday I will set up a poll and you will vote on which recording you want to listen to. N.B. You can't vote for the one you recommended.

5 Once we have the result, I'll post the winner on this Forum.

6 Listen to the recording and answer the following questions which I'll post in the forum: What new words did you learn? Do you think they're useful? What do you agree/disagree with? Why? Name at least one point.

Write your answers in the Forum.

* If you have problems understanding the recording, post a message on the Forum so that everyone can benefit from the answer.

It's also possible to embed the TED website in the forum introduction so that students can access the forum and the website from the same screen. See Chapter 2, *Getting Started with Moodle* for instructions on how to do this.

If you have a class of more than ten students, consider creating two or more groups so that it is easier for students to participate. There is information on creating groups in Chapter 2, *Getting Started with Moodle*.

Activity 2: Using Mindmap to anticipate content of a recording

Aim: Help students think of likely content of a recording they are about to hear

Moodle modules: None

Extra programs: Mindmap

Ease of setup: *

It's helpful to focus students on the content of a listening text and get them to anticipate ideas and vocabulary. Mindmap is a good way of doing this. As in the Mindmap activity in Chapter 7, *Writing Activities*, students can do this individually (groups of one), in small groups, or as a whole class. The following screenshot shows the sort of Mindmap that students might produce if you tell them they're going to listen to a recording about The Olympic Games and ask them to predict what themes and vocabulary might be mentioned.

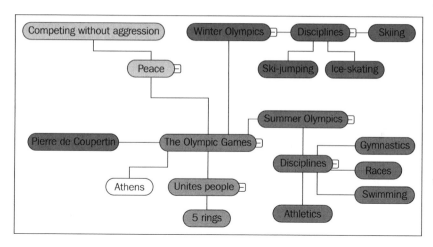

Here's how to do it

Follow the instructions in Chapter 7, *Writing Activities*, *Activity 3*.

Activity 3: Investigating texts using Quiz

Aim: Using quiz to investigate texts

Moodle modules: Quiz

Extra programs: None

Ease of setup: ***

As noted elsewhere, Quiz can be a useful module for practicing different language skills. This is primarily because we can build in helpful feedback and because we can allow students to spend as much time as they want practicing.

There are various ways that Quiz can help students listen. Here are some examples:

- Listening and matching: students listen for gist information and match answers to general questions about the text.

- Ordering task for arranging events in a sequence.

- Multiple-choice for information transfer, identifying speakers' attitudes, and identifying numbers.

- Gap-fill tasks:

  Students listen to a song, poem, or other text, and fill in the missing words. It's worth thinking carefully about what sorts of words you want to blank out. Do you want to focus on grammar words (prepositions, pronouns, and conjunctions, etc.), words that are difficult to spell, or keywords (words that convey the main meaning of the text)?

To exemplify each of these examples, we'll make one quiz with four different question types. You could choose to have quizzes with any number of different question types. We'll take as our listening text a story which we recorded ourselves. We could record it in a recording program like Audacity. The story is about a rather special trip to the zoo.

Here is a possible transcript abridged from `http://www.onlyfunnystories.com/ZooJob.asp`:

One day an out of work mime artist is visiting the zoo and attempts to earn some money as a street performer monkey. As soon as he starts to draw a crowd, a zoo keeper grabs him and drags him into his office. The zoo keeper explains to the mime artist that the zoo's most popular attraction, a gorilla, has died suddenly and the keeper fears that attendance at the zoo will fall off.

He offers the mime artist a job to dress up as the gorilla until they can get another one. The mime artist accepts.

So the next morning the mime artist puts on the gorilla suit and enters the cage before the crowd comes. He discovers that it's a great job. He can sleep all he wants, play and make fun of people and he draws bigger crowds than he ever did as a mime. However, eventually the crowds tire of him and he tires of just swinging on trees. He begins to notice that the people are paying more attention to the lion in the cage next to his. Not wanting to lose the attention of his audience, he climbs to the top of his cage, crawls across a partition, and dangles from the top to the lion's cage. Of course, this makes the lion furious, but the crowd loves it.

At the end of the day the zoo keeper comes and gives the mime artist a raise for being such a good attraction. Well, this goes on for some time, the mime keeps taunting the lion, the crowds grow larger, and his salary keeps going up. Then one terrible day when he is dangling over the furious lion he slips and falls. The mime artist is terrified.

The lion gathers itself and prepares to pounce. The mime artist is so scared that he begins to run round and round the cage with the lion close behind. Finally, the mime artist starts screaming and yelling, "Help me, help me!", but the lion is quick and pounces. The mime artist soon finds himself flat on his back looking up at the angry lion and the lion says, "Shut up you idiot! Do you want to get us both fired?"

The questions start with general gist questions (matching). Then comes an ordering question, which requires slightly more attention to detail. The last two are multiple-choice and gap-fill questions, which get students to focus on detailed aspects of the listening text.

Here's how to do it

All the setups have been detailed elsewhere in the book. The following sections refer you to those activities and point out any major differences.

Setting up the quiz

The setup for quiz is the same as for Chapter 3, *Vocabulary Activities*, *Activity 11*. We could call the quiz **Pleasing the crowd**.

Listening and matching question

See Chapter 3, *Vocabulary Activities*, *Activity 12* for instructions on how to create matching tasks. Use NanoGong to create sound clips which replace pictures and texts in the Chapter 3, *Vocabulary Activities* examples.

Here are some examples of the matching questions you could set up. These are general questions which help students get the gist of the story.

Question	Answer
How many animals are there in the story?	Three
Where does this take place?	The zoo
Where does the zoo keeper find the mime artist?	On the street
How many animals are there in the cages?	Two

This is what your matching question might look like:

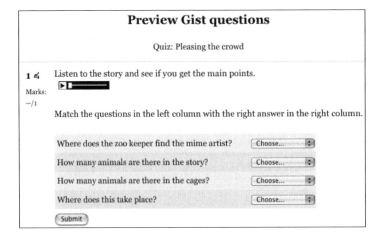

Here are a few more matching questions you could consider:

- Match recordings to pictures. Students could hear a description of an image (painting, photo) and identify the description.

  The easiest way to do this would be to take some photos of similar scenes.

- Match individual words to sounds. Students hear the recording and decide which words they are hearing.

Recording	Choice
A. "I hear you're coming"	hear/here
B. "It's over here"	hear/here

Ordering question

In this variation students listen to a story and then order events in sequence.

See Chapter 7, *Writing Activities*, *Activity 1* for instructions on how to create the ordering question.

We need to make sure that the sequence is not guessable without hearing the story. Here are the stages from our story that you could include in the question:

1. The zookeeper grabs the mime artist.
2. The zookeeper offers the mime artist a job.
3. The gorilla lies on top of the neighboring cage.
4. The lion tries to attack the gorilla.
5. The lion tells the gorilla off.

This is what the ordering question would look like:

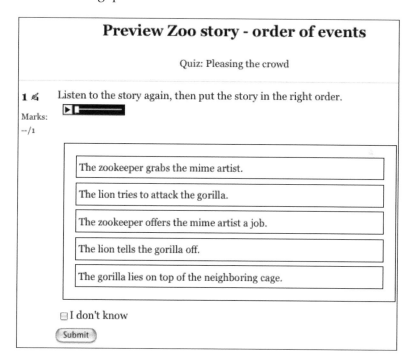

Multiple-choice question

Multiple-choice questions are a good way of getting students to investigate texts in more detail.

See Chapter 5, *Grammar Activities, Activity 5, Variation 1* for instructions on setting up a quiz multiple-choice question.

Here are some possible questions we could include in this activity.

Question 1	According to the story, why does the mime artist accept a job as a gorilla?
Answer 1	His work on the street isn't going well.
Answer 2	The zookeeper has an urgent need for a gorilla.
Answer 3	He always wanted to work as a gorilla in a zoo.
Answer 4	The last gorilla quit the job.

Question 2	Why did the gorilla climb on top of his cage?
Answer 1	He was tired of staying at the bottom of the cage.
Answer 2	He wanted to lose the attention of his audience.
Answer 3	He wanted to watch the lion.
Answer 4	He wanted to entertain the audience.

Question 3	Why was the lion angry?
Answer 1	He thought the gorilla was going to stop pretending to be a gorilla.
Answer 2	He wanted to attack the gorilla.
Answer 3	He had run round and round the cage too much.
Answer 4	He didn't like having the gorilla in his cage.

Here's a preview of the first question:

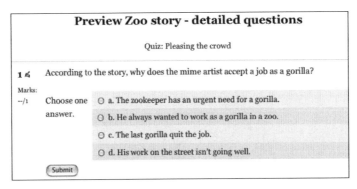

Other ideas

- Students identify the attitude of the speaker by his/her intonation: sarcastic, happy, worried, etc.
- Students listen to different accents and decide which country the speaker comes from.
- Students evaluate the story or think of ideas related to it. For example, what other things could the lion and gorilla do to please the crowd?

Gap-fill question

In this question we can gap particularly useful words and provide helpful hints for students who have problems getting them right. The following screenshot gaps verbs, for example.

See Chapter 3, *Vocabulary Activities*, *Activity 11* for instructions on gap-fill tasks. Insert the audio recording in the HTML instruction box using the Moodle Flash player or the NanoGong player.

Here's what the verb **gap-fill** would look like for the **Pleasing the crowd** story.

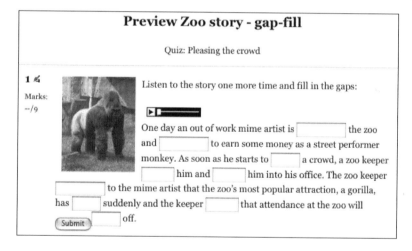

Activity 4: Prediction activity using Lesson

Aim: Help students predict a recorded text

Moodle modules: Lesson

Extra programs: None

Ease of setup: ***

It's often challenging for students to follow conversations between native speakers. One way of helping them attune themselves to natural conversation is to get them to predict what people will say. The Lesson module allows us to set up such a prediction activity in much the same way as we did in *Chapter 6, Reading Activities, Activity 7*, where students anticipate text that they read.

For this activity, record a conversation. Write out a transcript. Use the Lesson module to provide multiple-choice questions on what comes next.

Here's how to do it

See Chapter 6, *Reading Activities, Activity 7* for instructions on setting up the Lesson module. In the **Page contents** box, replace text with recordings using the Moodle player or NanoGong. Moodle player is more appropriate if you are using pre-existing recordings. NanoGong might be more convenient if you are making the recordings yourself.

Settings	Details
Page contents	Record the following text here, using NanoGong or the Moodle Flash player.
	Jane: Hey Roger. How are things going?
	Roger: Not so bad. I got it working.
	Jane: What did you get working? Oh, you mean the car. Great stuff. Can we go for a drive?
	Roger: I'm tied up, but how about tomorrow?
	Then write the following: **Listen to the recording then try to guess what Jane says next. In each case one sentence is more probable than the others.**
Answer 1	Write **That would be brilliant.**
Response 1	Here we can right a commentary. For example, **Yes, she's already shown that she's enthusiastic.**

Settings	Details
Jump 1	Choose **Next page**. That means that if the student chooses Answer 1, he/she will be taken to the next page, because he/she got Answer 1 right.
Score 1	Write **1**. The student gets 1 point.
Answer 2	Write **Shall I untie you?**
Response 2	Write **She might say this as a joke, but it's unlikely. Try again.**
Jump 2	Choose **This page**.
Score 2	Write **0**. The student gets 0 points, because the answer is wrong.
Answer 3	Write **I'm leaving the country tomorrow.**
Response 3	Write **I'm leaving the country tomorrow.**
Jump 3	Choose **This page**. That means that the student will jump back to this page—in other words, do it again.
Score 3	Write **0**.

When you write the responses, don't forget to click on **Use Editor**, so that you can insert a recording into the answer.

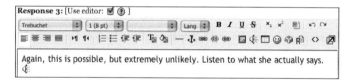

You'll need to complete the dialog yourself and add several more pages for students.

This is what page 1 of the lesson could look like:

Activity 5: Reviewing recordings using Choice

Aim: Using polls to vote on a recording

Moodle modules: Choice

Extra programs: None

Ease of setup: *

Students may find it fun and motivating to vote on recordings that they have listened to. Voting is also a natural outcome of *Activity 1* in which students discuss which recording to listen to and then vote on their favorite one.

If possible, make the recording available on the same page as the poll. There are various ways of doing this:

- If it's a website, embed the website in the instructions
- Use the Moodle audio player
- Use the add-on audio recorder NanoGong
- Embed video from YouTube or other similar sites

There's help with all the above in Chapter 2, *Getting Started with Moodle*.

Here are some ideas for presenting recordings that students can vote on. There's a longer list of possible sources in the introduction to *Activity 1*.

- Students listen to a selection of adverts and decide which one they think is best
- Students listen to two versions of a song and vote on the best one
- Students hear several versions of a sentence and decide which one is the clearest

Let's set up a choice based on two adverts which students will listen to. They will vote on which one is the funniest. In each case, the adverts will be embedded in the introduction to make it easier for students to watch them. We could alternatively provide a link to the website or direct students to the Mediacenter.

Here's how to do it

Follow the instructions in Chapter 5, *Grammar Activities*, *Activity 3*.

Step 2 needs to be modified as in the following table. If a setting isn't mentioned below, then it's optional.

Settings	Details
Choice name	Write an appropriate title for the activity. Let's call this **Choose an ad**.
Choice text	Write a simple task for students to follow. I've written **Which of the following two adverts is the funniest? Watch the adverts and then vote below.** After the text, embed the two videos. The ones in the screenshot below are from YouTube.
Choice 1	Under **Choice 1**, write **Advert 1**.
Choice 2	Under **Choice 2**, write **Advert 2**.
	If you need to add more choices, click on **Add more choices** at the bottom of the page.
Display mode	If we have a lot of students, we can go for **horizontal**. If we have few, then **vertical** would be appropriate. Let's go for a **vertical**.
Publish results	Show results to students after they answer. They will probably want to see the results straightaway.

This is what the final choice activity could look like:

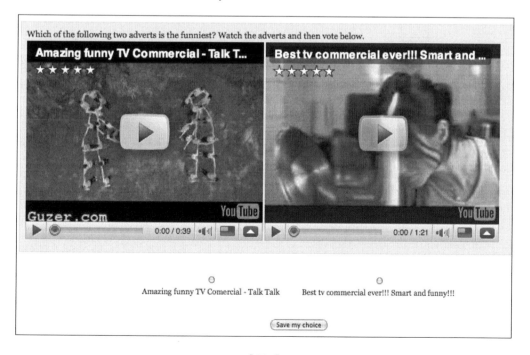

Activity 6: Reviewing recordings using Questionnaire

Aim: Get students to think about recordings through an evaluation questionnaire

Moodle modules: Questionnaire add-on

Extra programs: None

Ease of setup: ***

Questionnaires can be used to get students to evaluate recordings in the same way as written texts. Consider the list of sources in *Activity 1* as a starting point. You could also use questionnaires to find out what sorts of recordings or movies your class would like to watch. Imagine we've selected the news from bbc.co.uk for a given date. We can place the URL for the news item in the question text.

Here's how to do it

Follow the instructions in Chapter 6, *Reading Activities*, *Activity 5*.

Here's what the set-up page for the first question text could look like:

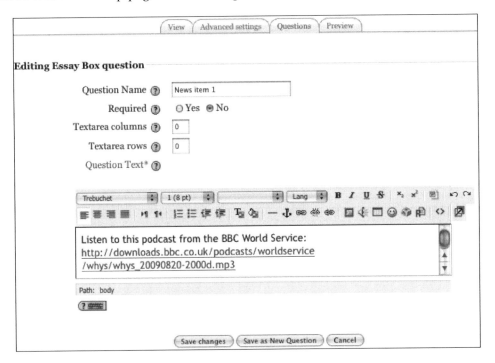

As before, we can choose from a wide range of questions. Each time we can make a recording available either by inserting a Moodle audio player, a NanoGong recording, or a URL to a recording on a website.

Here's what the finished above question would look like:

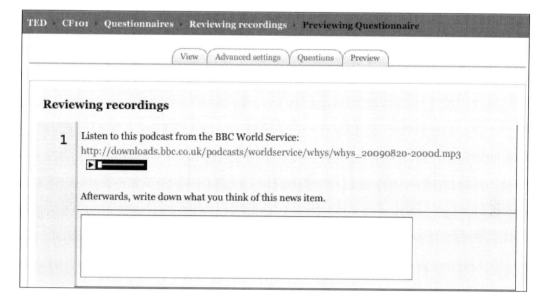

Activity 7: Developing students' critical faculties through online discussion about recordings they've listened to

Aim: Stimulate online discussion about recordings that students have listened to

Moodle modules: Forum

Extra programs: Mediacenter

Ease of setup: *

The Forum is an excellent module for discussions about recordings that students have listened to. You might find the list of texts in the introduction to this chapter useful as a starting point for choosing texts. You could also consider including texts in the Mediacenter. One helpful feature of that module is that you can create direct links to the copyright recordings on other websites from the Mediacenter directory. Ideas you might like to consider:

- Students listen to the same text and compare ideas.
- Students listen to different texts on the same subjects and compare ideas on the content. This works well with news websites.
- Students listen to an online talk/lecture and discuss what the key ideas are.

Here's how to do it

Follow the instructions in Chapter 6, *Reading Activities*, *Activity 4*.

9
Assessment

If you mention the word "assessment" to a lot of teachers, they'll run a mile. It sounds boring, stressful, and formal, and it's not what a lot of teachers want to do. But, assessment, in one form or another, is what most teachers do a lot of the time. Much of it tends to be less formal and comes in the form of comments, feedback, and encouragement, but it still measures the ability of our students, which is what assessment is all about.

Why use Moodle for assessment?

Many teachers still produce tests on their word processor. That's easy to do, easy to organize, and easy to administer. So why change? Moodle offers a range of assessment tools known as **CAT (Computer Assisted Testing)** tools, and there are many good reasons they can make assessment easier and more satisfying in the long term.

Assessment can be enjoyable

Moodle offers ways of providing both informal and formal assessment. Several of the utilities for making informal assessments can even be quite fun. While students are playing games and quizzes, they may not even realize that there is some quiet measuring going on in the background. They can collect colorful tokens as a reward for achievement, using the add-on Stamp collection. They can participate in competitions to see which student got the right answer to a quiz grammar question. In both cases, the game element softens the sense of being assessed and increases motivation.

Moodle Assessment can save you time

Teachers are busy people. So it's good to know that Moodle can mark your homework for you, or instead of having to write loads of comments, you can easily add comments from a drop-down menu. Yes, this takes a while to set up, but once it's there, you can really whiz through your marking. Also, you can store your questions into something called an Item Bank. It's then easy to access and modify old questions.

Moodle's instant feedback is popular with students

Students can benefit from instant feedback on many of the quizzes. This takes more time for us to set up, but in the long run, it automates the assessment process, thus freeing up our time and helping students to work out things for themselves. Another helpful feature in Moodle is the comments system. Several modules allow teachers and/or students to provide comments on students' work in a personal, non-threatening way.

More accurate

When we set up an assessment that generates a score, computers are much more accurate at scoring than we humans. So you'll have fewer students coming to you with "Teacher. This doesn't add up properly!"

Adaptive testing

Several Moodle modules can assist us to help students understand their mistakes by building on their attempts to answer. Let's say they get a question wrong the first time. The response won't be just "wrong". It can give a clue to help the student. When students try the question again, they see how they answered before and what feedback they got. That way they can make a more reasoned attempt the second time around.

Reporting results

Several Moodle modules provide scores, which are collected in the Moodle Gradebook. That in turn provides a useful and automatic overview of students' progress. The Gradebook also provides basic statistical information, which we can use to find out how well our questions are working and improve them, if necessary.

So what's the downside?

This all sounds great, but there is a drawback: you will need some time to understand how the system works and build up useful tests. You'll also need to think about the most appropriate way to assess your students and how you organize your Item Bank. There's help on this later in this chapter.

Add-ons

If the built-in tools aren't enough, there are a few add-ons which are worth considering, as they help enhance the process of assessing language skills. These include the self-assessment program called Lolipop, mobile quizzes (which allow teachers to send quiz questions to students' mobile phones), and the Stamp collection mentioned on the first page.

This chapter

To make it easier to see how you can use Moodle for assessment, it's worth working through one of the examples suggested in Section 1. The overview in Sections 2 and 3 should give you a good general feel for the range of assessment possibilities. Sections 4 and 5 go into much more detail about how you can manage the assessment tools. Several of the tools include *Here's how to do it* sections, but this chapter is a guide and not a set of activities. You might find it easier to come back to these later sections when you're about to set up a test. Section 6 considers some other interesting possibilities for assessing using add-ons such as mobile phone quiz and self-assessment portfolios.

Reading up on assessment

Examples of assessing are spread throughout this book, but a more detailed awareness of assessment possibilities covered in this chapter should help you choose the right tools from the start. The chapter assumes that you are familiar with key concepts in assessment. If you are not, it is well worth reading up on this rich area to review these key issues:

- The connection between communicative language teaching and testing

- Deciding what to test, how to test it, when to test it, and who should test it

- How an understanding of basic test statistics can help you improve your tests

See the end of Chapter 2, *Getting Started with Moodle* for a few suggestions for books on assessing language skills.

This chapter is divided into six sections:

Section	Topic
1	*Assessing language – working through an example*
2	*What is assessment: A brief overview of assessment and how Moodle supports it*
3	*Who is assessing whom?*
4	*Moodle assessment tools*
5	*Moodle Gradebook*
6	*Useful Moodle add-ons*

Assessing language—working through an example

It's often easier to learn by doing. It's a good idea to work through one of the several examples using Quiz in this book before you go on with the rest of the chapter. Here are some possibilities:

Chapter	Activity	Description
3	11	Gap-fill question which tests vocabulary in context
4	2	Matching question which gets students to identify word stress
4	9	Speaking assignment with feedback on performance from teacher
5	5	<ul><li>Multiple-choice question to practice grammar</li><li>Gap-fill question to practice grammar</li><li>True/False question to practice grammar</li></ul>

There are also several practice activities, like Chapter 5, *Grammar Activities*, *Activity 2*, which use the Lesson module and which could easily be converted into tests by selecting **No** in the **Practice lesson** option on the set-up page, which you can see in the screenshot that follows. You should also check the **Flow control** settings to make sure they are appropriate.

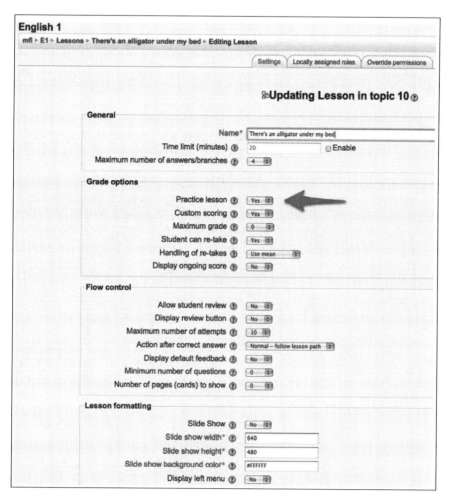

Once you've been through an example activity, the Moodle assessment features covered in the rest of this chapter should be easier to understand.

What is assessment: A brief overview of assessment and how Moodle supports it

You may be familiar with the concepts of qualitative and quantitative approaches to assessment. We can describe students' work in words, commenting on strengths and weaknesses. That's called *qualitative assessment*. Alternatively, we can assign a numerical score to their work. That's called *quantitative assessment*. They both have pros and cons:

Qualitative	Quantitative
Describes behavior and is often easier for students to understand	Easier to classify
Students can act on feedback more easily	Easier to count
Provides data in the form of words	Easier to do statistics
More subjective	More objective
Takes longer to set up	Harder for teachers and students to interpret
Takes longer to review	-

Choosing which type of assessment to use depends very much on what you want to achieve. If you want to encourage students to practice and work things out for themselves, qualitative assessment will be more helpful. If you need to grade students for more formal purposes, such as end-of-course tests, or placement tests, then quantitative assessment will be more helpful.

Since Moodle provides a variety of ways of doing both, let's take a look at how Moodle features cover these aspects of assessment. The features are explained below.

Qualitative assessment

Feature	Glossary	Database	OUblog	Quiz	Hot Potatoes	Lesson	Assignment	Journal	Workshop	Questionnaire	Lolipop	Forum
Outcomes							✓					
Public Comments	✓	✓	✓						✓	✓		✓
Private written feedback				✓		✓	✓	✓			✓	
Prompts				✓	✓	✓						

Moodle feature	Description
Outcomes	In Moodle speak, an outcome is an area of language competence that we want to measure. For example, grammar, text organization, and pronunciation. Moodle allows you to set your own marking scales to measure these outcomes. So, for the outcome "grammar", students could receive a description of their work with comments like "grammar mistakes make it difficult to understand" or "very few grammar errors".
Public comments	Many of the modules allow you to add comments to students' work. In the Forum, other users can make comments by replying to posts. The Questionnaire could be used to collect feedback on activities.
Private feedback	Teachers can write extended comments on essays submitted by users in the Lesson and Quiz modules. The advanced uploading of files and online text assessment options for the Assignment module allow teachers to provide feedback on drafts.
Prompts	In the Quiz module, it is possible to provide feedback prompts on incorrect answers in multiple-choice questions. In the Lesson module, you can provide feedback, which helps users with subsequent questions. Like Quiz, Hot Potatoes also allows us to provide hints when students have difficulties answering a question.

Quantitative assessment

Feature	Glossary	Database	OU Blog	Quiz	Hot Potatoes	Lesson	Assignment	Journal	Workshop	Questionnaire	Lolipop	Forum
Rating	✓	✓		✓	✓	✓	✓	✓	✓	✓	✓	✓
Penalty grades				✓					✓			
Adaptive grades				✓								
Outcomes							✓					

Moodle feature	Description
Rating	Moodle allows users to rate contributions from other users. Scales can be defined by the teacher. See later for more information on scales. In the journal, only the teacher can rate students.
Penalty grades	You can apply penalty marks (deductions) for items that students get wrong.
Adaptive grades	If you choose adaptive grading in the Quiz setup, Moodle will award a mark for the correct answer minus penalties for wrong answers which students chose while trying to get the right answer.
Outcomes	Outcomes define an area of language competence (as in the previous table). To use them in a quantitative way, we use a numerical marking scale. For example, 1 – 6, where 6 is the best and 1 the worst.

Who is assessing whom?

Many of Moodle's modules are organized so that the teacher gives feedback on students' performance, but other assessment relationships are also possible. Each can contribute in positive ways to language learning. Here are examples of how Moodle features or modules can be used to change the assessment relationship to other than the default—teacher assessing students. The rating and comments features are controlled on the module set-up pages.

Students assess students

Feature	Details	Examples in this book
Rating feature	Students can grade each other's work on a simple rating scale.	• Chapter 3, *Vocabulary Activities*, Activity 4 • Chapter 7, *Writing Activities*, Activity 7
Comments feature	In the Glossary, Database, OUblog, E-Portfolio, Workshop, and Forum modules, students can comment on each other's contributions. Students can comment on and grade draft and/or final versions of each other's work according to predetermined assessment criteria.	• Chapter 3, *Vocabulary Activities*, Activity 1 • Chapter 10, *Extended Activities*, Activity 3

Students assess themselves

Feature	Details	Examples in this book
Workshop module	Students can assess their own work based on agreed assessment criteria.	Chapter 10, *Extended Activities, Activity 3*
Lolipop module	Using the add-on module, Lolipop, students can assess their level and set up learning goals in different skills.	See the *Useful Moodle add-ons* section in this chapter
Journal module	This allows students to reflect on their own performance.	Chapter 7, *Writing Activities, Activity 5*

Students assess teachers

Feature	Details	Examples in this book
Choice module	This allows students to vote on teacher decisions and to comment on classes.	Chapter 8, *Listening Activities, Activity 5*
Questionnaire module	This module also allows students to provide detailed feedback on aspects of courses run by the teacher.	Chapter 6, *Reading Activities, Activity 5*

Moodle assessment tools

Let's take a closer look at the tools provided by Moodle for assessing students' work. The wide range of possibilities might seem overwhelming at first, but once you get the hang of the key features, it becomes quite intuitive to use.

Quiz module

The Quiz module is the main assessment engine in Moodle. It provides a wide range of question types, and enables us to control key assessment elements such as feedback comments, setting timing for tests, assessment criteria, scales, weighting student responses, and the organization of questions. In this module, the same question can be presented as a practice question that students can keep working at and learning from, or as a tightly-controlled test item with strict access rules.

The easiest way to understand the way the Quiz module works in Moodle is to think of it as an **Item Bank** — a place where you store all your questions — which you can dig into to create a quiz, a set of questions. When you first set up a Quiz, the set-up page will ask you to provide specifications for a particular quiz. Think of that setup as a framework which can include any questions that exist in the Item Bank — they don't have to be new questions.

There are three steps involved in making a quiz.

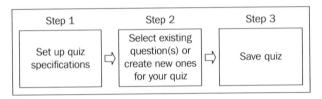

The beauty of this system is that you can recycle questions (also called items) for different purposes at different times according to your reason for assessing.

Practicing a quiz activity

If you're not familiar with the Quiz module set-up yet, you might find it useful to go through a quiz activity. For example, Chapter 3, *Vocabulary Activities*, *Activity 12*.

Quiz module: Categorizing questions in the Item Bank

Before you start building up questions in the Item Bank, it's worth thinking about how you're going to organize them. Imagine a list of hundreds of questions that you want to use and have to sift through each time you set a quiz. That could be frustrating. Even a list like the one in this screenshot could benefit from some organizing into writing, listening, and grammar categories, for example, though the drop-down menu with **Sort by name**; **Sort by type, name**; **Sort by age** will help you to order them if they aren't in categories.

Action	Question name
≪ ⚲ ✎ ⇕ ✗ ☐	Instructions for describe and draw
≪ ⚲ ✎ ⇕ ✗ ☐	dictation 2
≪ ⚲ ✎ ⇕ ✗ ☐	Essay 2
≪ ⚲ ✎ ⇕ ✗ ☐	Essay 3
≪ ⚲ ✎ ⇕ ✗ ☐	Presentation practice 1
≪ ⚲ ✎ ⇕ ✗ ☐	speech
≪ ⚲ ✎ ⇕ ✗ ☐	animals
≪ ⚲ ✎ ⇕ ✗ ☐	collocations 1
≪ ⚲ ✎ ⇕ ✗ ☐	conversation gambits
≪ ⚲ ✎ ⇕ ✗ ☐	intonation 1
≪ ⚲ ✎ ⇕ ✗ ☐	Match the word stress
≪ ⚲ ✎ ⇕ ✗ ☐	soundclips
≪ ⚲ ✎ ⇕ ✗ ☐	John
≪ ⚲ ✎ ⇕ ✗ ☐	adverb review
≪ ⚲ ✎ ⇕ ✗ ☐	ordering events
≪ ⚲ ✎ ⇕ ✗ ☐	Choose a topic
≪ ⚲ ✎ ⇕ ✗ ☐	definitions
≪ ⚲ ✎ ⇕ ✗ ☐	Question 1

You can avoid the nightmare of never-ending lists easily by subdividing your Item Bank into categories. This is useful for several reasons:

- You can organize items according to skill, level, or exam types
- They are easier to navigate and manipulate than long lists
- You can predetermine which category of questions are drawn on for random questions

Categories first

It's a good idea to create your categories before you start adding questions. Then you can assign questions to categories at the same time as you create the questions.

Here's how to do it

We're going to create categories for different levels.

1. First of all, here's a quick reminder of how you'd set up a Quiz.

   If you're creating a quiz for the first time, go to your course page, click on **Turn Editing on**, and then click on **Add an activity...**. After that, select **Quiz** from the drop-down menu. Complete and save the set-up page. If you have already created a **quiz**, click on **Quizzes** in the **Activities** block on your course page to access a quiz. If you don't have an **Activities** block, click on one of the quizzes on the course page.

2. Now click on the **Edit** tab and you will see the following menu:

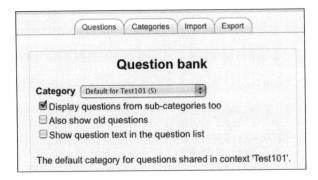

3. Click on the **Categories** tab.

   You'll now have a list of any existing categories.

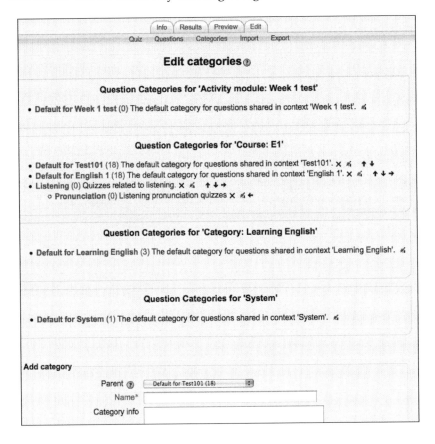

At the bottom of the page there's a box for you to create a new category.

4. Here you can choose whether to make your category a Parent category or a Child category. For example, to set up a parent category "listening" and a child category (or subcategory) "listening for pronunciation", we write the following:

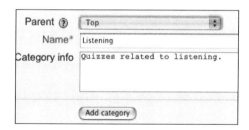

5. Now select **Top** in the **Parent** drop-down menu to make this a top-level category. Click on **Add category** to save the new category.

Now we can make a child category (subcategory) for **Listening**, called **Pronunciation**.

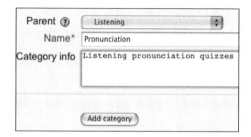

Later on, when you're selecting questions for a new quiz, you'll see an option to add random questions at the bottom of the Item Bank for the category you have selected. If you click on **Add n random questions** (n = any number), you can pick which categories and subcategories the questions are drawn from. To select a category, click on the **Category** drop-down menu.

In the example below, we're about to select the **Pronunciation** category from the **Category** drop-down menu. And we're going to add one random question from it.

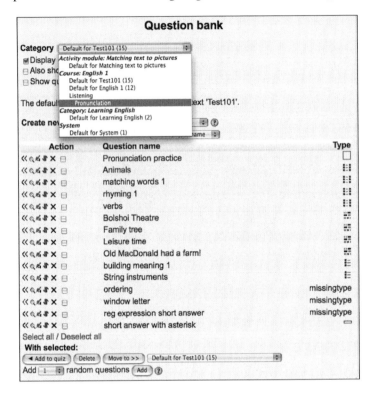

Random questions

You can't add random questions based on categories after students have started making attempts at the quiz.

By default, teachers only have access to questions in the course where they are a teacher. There are two ways round this:

- Your administrator can enable teachers to share questions from other courses by creating a new role with appropriate permission. They should add this information to the new role.

- The administrator can add a permission to the normal teacher role, which allows all teachers to access all questions. Administrators need to go to the Moodle home page, select **Users** | **Permissions** | **Define roles**, then click on **Teacher**.

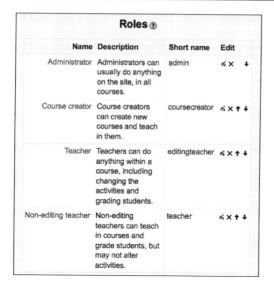

Next, click on **Edit**.

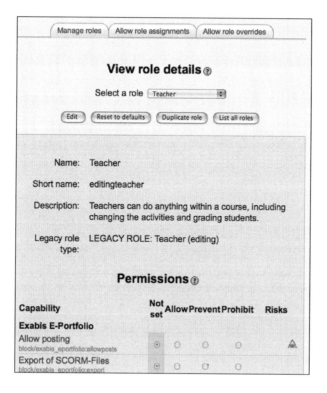

Scroll down to the **Course** section. Now you can click on the **Allow** column for the following:

- **Add new questions**
- **Edit all questions**
- **Move all questions**
- **View all questions**

Click on **Save changes**, when you've finished. See Chapter 2, *Getting Started with Moodle* for more information on adding and editing roles and permissions.

Quiz module: Question types

One of the attractive features of the Quiz module is the wide range of question types it offers. For example, you're not restricted to multiple-choice and essay questions. Below is a list of the question types that are available for students to practice language skills. The list includes the add-on Ordering, as it is particularly useful for language learners. You'll need to get your administrator to add this. See Chapter 2, *Getting Started with Moodle* for more information.

This is what you see when you create a new question after completing the Quiz set-up page:

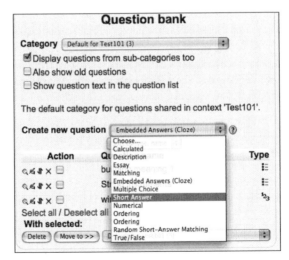

The **Create new question** drop-down menu also includes **Description**. This is not a task type, but allows you to provide some textual and/or graphical information to accompany a set of questions that you are using in one of your quizzes.

Question type	Details
Calculated	This is for testing mathematical formulae, so is unlikely to be useful on a language course. If you want to test simple sums, the short-answer question would be easier to use.
Essay	The student writes an answer in essay format in response to a question (that may include an image). Once students have made a final submission of their essay, teachers can provide comments in an HTML box. We can also add a voice recording using NanoGong, if it's been installed.
Matching	The student is presented with prompts or questions in Column A and must "match" the correct responses to that prompt in Column B.
	Examples of matching tasks for practicing language: • Matching images with descriptions • Matching audio recordings with text • Matching one text with another text
	N.B. The more similar the items for matching are, the more difficult the task is likely to be.
Embedded Answers (Cloze)	The task consists of a passage of text in which you can embed various questions, including multiple-choice, short answers, and numerical answers. It's suitable for practicing or testing listening, grammar, and vocabulary.
Multiple Choice	Students choose one or more correct answers from the options that you create. These options take some careful thinking to create well, but the options (also called distracters) can usefully focus on common misconceptions in grammar, vocabulary, knowledge, and pronunciation.

Question type	Details
Short Answer	Students write a short response to a question. To avoid the problem of small mistakes being penalized, teachers can include regular expressions in the acceptable answers. These are symbols like wildcards, which allow slight deviations from the correct answer. In the following example, if we use a wildcard, all answers, with or without correct punctuation and with full or short answers, can be deemed correct: *Q: Where was John sitting?* *A1: in the bar* *A2: he was sitting in the bar* *A3: He was sitting in the bar.* (See the *Moodle Gradebook* section for more information on regular expressions.)
Ordering	Students are presented with a list of words or texts that needs to be ordered. This can be used for checking or testing understanding of the order of words in a sentence, sentences in a paragraph, or sequences of events in a whole text. N.B. The program rewards only exactly the right answer. In other words, if just one element is out of place, but the others are all in the correct order, the student would still get no points.
Random Short-Answer Matching	From the student's point of view, this looks just like a matching question. The difference is that the sub-questions are drawn randomly from short-answer questions in the current category. See the categories section earlier for a screenshot showing this.
True/False	Students can choose whether a statement is true or not. This can be useful when you don't want to confuse students with too many choices, but want to test key points. For example, if you're asking students to distinguish between two different spellings, or match words with something they hear.

So which type should you choose? Let's review the language-testing question types in the previous table in terms of their pros and cons. Then it's up to you to decide. Many of the pros and cons relate to validity—making sure the test tests what we want it to test, or reliability—the degree of accuracy of the score.

Question type	Pros	Cons
Essay	• Allows more creativity in the student • Possibility of providing feedback on a variety of language skills, using outcomes or descriptive feedback • Task is easier to set up	• Subjective marking, therefore more difficult to mark consistently • Takes longer to mark
Matching	• More controlled than an open essay • Easier than multiple-choice for teachers to set up • Easier for students to do than multiple-choice	Can be fairly easy to guess the answers. If student gets 3 out of 4 items right, the 4th will automatically be right.
Embedded Answers (Cloze)	• Good for focusing on a particular aspect of language • Can be based on authentic texts • Can be simplified by including a bank of possible words in the rubric	Time-consuming to set up

Question type	Pros	Cons
Multiple Choice	• Good for focusing on a particular aspect of language. • Easy to mark. • Moodle can shuffle distracters to make it less easy to cheat.	• Time-consuming to set up. • Difficult to find plausible distracters which should look similar to the correct alternative. • Need to ensure correct answer is genuinely correct and has a context. • Need to make sure the correct answer fits the question. • The question should not be answerable through knowledge of the world. • There's a danger of the test not being valid, because we test things which are easy to test rather than things which are useful or important.
Short Answer	Only short text (few words) required. Therefore it's easier to answer than essay, but harder than multiple-choice or true/false.	Students may be marked incorrect when their answer only deviates slightly from the "correct" answer.
Ordering	Good for testing order of a set of elements; for example, words in a sentence or sentences in a paragraph.	• Doesn't reward partially correct answers. So if students get one element in the wrong place but the others in the correct order, they still get no points. • Can be difficult to find groups of text that only go in one order.
True/False	Good for quick check.	Easy to guess; 50-50 chance of students being right.

Bloom

Use Bloom's taxonomy as a guide for setting questions at different levels of cognitive complexity to make sure you are providing a suitable range of questions. See Chapter 6, *Reading Activities*, *Activity 5* for more information on Bloom's taxonomy.

Using the Quiz module for different test types

The Quiz module in Moodle can be used for unlimited practice, but it is also suitable for different sorts of language testing. The set-up page allows you to customize key options. To get to this page, go to your course page, and click on **Turn editing on**. Then click on **Add an activity...**.

Select **Quiz** from the drop-down menu.

Settings	Details
Open the quiz/ Close the quiz	You can set dates and times for when the test is available.
Time limit	This is set in minutes. A floating timer window is shown with a countdown. When the timer has run out, the quiz is submitted automatically with whatever answers have been filled in so far. If a student manages to cheat and spends more than 60 seconds over the allotted time, then the quiz is automatically graded zero. N.B. JavaScript needs to be enabled on your browser for this to work. Ask your administrator if in doubt.
Time delay between first and second attempts and between later attempts	The options are **None**, **30 minutes**, **60 minutes**, then hourly intervals.
Shuffle questions	Questions can be shuffled, making it harder to cheat.
Shuffle within questions	This means that distracters within a multiple-choice question can be shuffled, also making it less easy to cheat.
Attempts allowed	The number of attempts can be limited or set to unlimited. The fewer attempts we allow, the more test-like our quiz is.
Adaptive method	Each attempt can build on the last one. When students try to answer a second time, they see the first answer they gave as well as any feedback you provided. They can then try again, understanding their mistake a little better. See *Adaptive Items* in a bit, for more information on this.

Settings	Details
Grading method	When multiple attempts are allowed, you can set Moodle to treat any of the following as the grade: the highest mark, the average mark, the first mark, the final mark. Setting the highest mark as the grade may well be an incentive for students to keep trying till they improve their score.
Apply penalties	This setting only works in adaptive mode. When a student tries a question again after a wrong response, you can impose a penalty for each wrong response, which is subtracted from the final mark for the question. The amount of penalty is chosen individually for each question when setting up or editing the question.
Security	There are various ways of making access to the quiz dependent on security measures. See Chapter 2, *Getting Started with Moodle* for more information on this.

This customizability means you can adapt Quiz for different sorts of tests. Here are some ideas:

Test type	Ideas
Placement	If you're running a placement test, you may want to shuffle the options, limit the time available for the test, and limit the number of attempts each student is allowed to one or two.
Diagnostic	You will probably want to include questions with different degrees of difficulty and/or weight the questions according to their difficulty. Consider limiting the time available for the quiz.
Progress	You might consider allowing multiple attempts on recently learned material, and accepting the highest mark from those attempts.
Achievement	You'll probably want to limit the number of attempts students can make, and will want to set a time limit.

Adaptive items

Adaptive items respond to test-takers' responses by providing feedback to help them answer the questions. This type of assessment is known as formative assessment—in other words, assessment for learning. By contrast, we sometimes give students a mark without feedback; for example, for an end-of-course test. The score they receive then is an example of summative assessment, which is assessment of learning.

Let's look at adaptive items in a bit more detail.

Adaptive items in the Quiz module

In the quiz customization section previously, we have the option to turn on the **Adaptive mode** on the Quiz set-up page

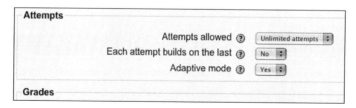

For the Adaptive mode to work, we have to set **Attempts allowed** to at least **2**.

Each new attempt builds on the last like this: students can save their last attempt, return to the quiz at a later date, then review their last attempt before trying again.

You can edit the quiz question to set a penalty if you wish.

Using Overall feedback to suggest higher or lower level tests

Moodle doesn't currently offer adaptive tests which provide easier or harder questions depending on students' responses, though if you wanted to, you could use the Lesson module to produce this sort of test. An easier way to ascertain students' level is to create a series of tests at different levels and set the feedback for the final score to include a recommendation for taking a higher level. For example, if a student takes a level-1 test and gets 90%, the feedback can include a text like:*You have done well on this test! Consider taking the level two test.* To do this, add details to the Overall **Feedback** box at the bottom of the Quiz set-up page.

The overview of the quiz attempts could look something like this:

		First name / Surname ⊟	Started on ⊟	Completed ⊟	Time taken ⊟	Grade/10 ⊟	#1 ⊟	#2 ⊟	Feedback ⊟
				Attempts: 3					
			Jo Smith	3 April 2009, 05:12 PM	3 April 2009, 05:13 PM	38 secs	10	5/5	5/5	Consider taking the level 2 test.
		Jane Smith	3 April 2009, 05:15 PM	3 April 2009, 05:15 PM	28 secs	5.83	0.83/5	5/5	Good. You're at the right level.
		Jill Smith	2 April 2009, 12:57 PM	2 April 2009, 12:58 PM	34 secs	5.33	0.33/5	5/5	Good. You're at the right level.

Showing graded and ungraded attempts for each user. The one attempt for each user that is graded is highlighted. The grading method for this quiz is Highest grade.

Feedback

The **Overall feedback** box in the previous section gave an example of how you can recommend levels to students who've taken a placement test. We could use the same box to motivate our students and guide them on their performance. For example:

Grade boundary: 100%

Feedback: Well done. You obviously studied hard this week!

Grade boundary: 80%

Feedback: Good job. You got most of the questions right. Check out the few that you got wrong.

Grade boundary: 60%

Feedback: Not too bad. Too many slips, though. Review your work and have another go at the test next week.

In this example, students getting between 81% and 100% would get the first comment, between 61% and 80% the second comment, and 60% or less the third comment.

Scales

Moodle comes with default scales for measuring students' performance.

The default numeric scales range from 1 to any number between 2 and 100. When you assess students' work in the Assignment module, you can then select a number on the chosen scale as their grade. The **Grade** drop-down menu appears in the top right-hand corner:

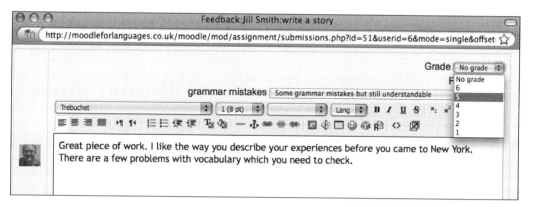

The other default scale in Moodle is non-numeric and is called "Separate and Connected ways of knowing". This has three elements: "Mostly Separate Knowing", "Separate and Connected", "Mostly Connected Knowing". These phrases relate to a theory about how people approach the world. There's more information about the Moodle default scale at `http://docs.moodle.org/en/Separate_and_Connected_ways_of_knowing`.

You may be able to fit this into your approach to teaching languages, but you might find it more useful to set up your own scales which match the work you're doing. For example, perhaps your school uses the Common European Framework and wants to use that as a scale:

Common European Framework

Level	Description
A1	*Can understand and use familiar everyday expressions and very basic phrases aimed at the satisfaction of needs of a concrete type. Can introduce him/herself and others and can ask and answer questions about personal details such as where he/she lives, people he/she knows and things he/she has. Can interact in a simple way provided the other person talks slowly and clearly and is prepared to help.*
A2	*Can understand sentences and frequently used expressions related to areas of most immediate relevance (e.g. very basic personal and family information, shopping, local geography, employment). Can communicate in simple and routine tasks requiring a simple and direct exchange of information on familiar and routine matters. Can describe in simple terms aspects of his/her background, immediate environment and matters in areas of immediate need.*
B1	*Can understand the main points of clear standard input on familiar matters regularly encountered in work, school, leisure, etc. Can deal with most situations likely to arise whilst traveling in an area where the language is spoken. Can produce simple connected text on topics which are familiar or of personal interest. Can describe experiences and events, dreams, hopes & ambitions and briefly give reasons and explanations for opinions and plans.*
B2	*Can understand the main ideas of complex text on both concrete and abstract topics, including technical discussions in his/her field of specialisation. Can interact with a degree of fluency and spontaneity that makes regular interaction with native speakers quite possible without strain for either party. Can produce clear, detailed text on a wide range of subjects and explain a viewpoint on a topical issue giving the advantages and disadvantages of various options.*
C1	*Can understand a wide range of demanding, longer texts, and recognise implicit meaning. Can express him/herself fluently and spontaneously without much obvious searching for expressions. Can use language flexibly and effectively for social, academic and professional purposes. Can produce clear, well-structured, detailed text on complex subjects, showing controlled use of organisational patterns, connectors and cohesive devices.*
C2	*Can understand with ease virtually everything heard or read. Can summarise information from different spoken and written sources, reconstructing arguments and accounts in a coherent presentation. Can express him/herself spontaneously, very fluently and precisely, differentiating finer shades of meaning even in more complex situations.*

Your new scale could include just the letter grades or all the description if that is appropriate.

The scale given in the previous table is for general language use. See http://www.coe.int/portfolio if you want to refer to detailed scales for different aspects of language, such as speaking, writing, listening, and reading.

Creating a new scale

New scales can be created by teachers with editing rights or by administrators or by any user with the manage scales role capability. Scales can be local to a course, or can be site-wide. If a scale is local, that means only users for a particular course have access to it. If it's a site-wide scale, it can be accessed by all courses on the site. Site-wide scales are created via the Site Administration block on the site home page. Course scales are produced via the Course Administration block on the course page. Let's go through the procedure for setting up a course scale.

Here's how to do it

1. Go to the **Administration** menu on your course page. Click on **Grades** to start the process.

2. Then click on **View** below the **Scales** heading.

3. On the next screen, click on **Add a new scale**, then follow the procedure in Chapter 2, *Getting Started with Moodle* for setting up a new scale.

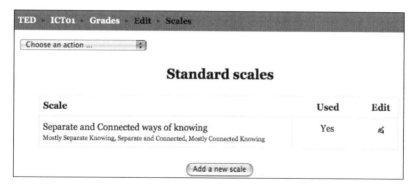

Outcomes

Scales can be used to measure a variety of language skills. We can use outcomes to apply those scales to specific language areas. You can create outcomes to grade different parts of one assignment separately; for example, grammar, vocabulary, pronunciation, cohesion, coherence, and task fulfillment. The same scale, if it is general enough, could be used for different outcomes. The procedure for creating an outcome is covered in Chapter 2, *Getting Started with Moodle*. Let's assume that we've created outcomes called **content** and **Grammar mistakes**.

Imagine we've set up an assignment activity, and we want to use those outcomes as part of the feedback that we can give students. We need to make those outcomes available on our course.

Here's how to do it

1. To make sure the outcomes are available on the course, click on **Outcomes** in the **Administration** menu on the course page.

2. On the Assignment set-up page, we select the outcomes that we want to include. You might find it useful to refer to Chapter 5, *Grammar Activities, Activity 8* for a full description of how to set up an Assignment.

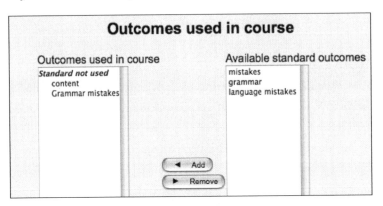

3. When we come to grade students' work, we will now see those outcomes. To grade students' assignments, we click on the assignment activity, and then on **View N submitted assignments** in the top right-hand corner.

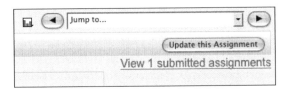

4. Then we click on the outcome we created so that we can provide some feedback.

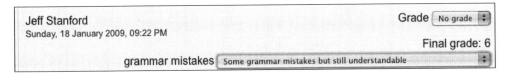

See Chapter 5, *Grammar Activities, Activity 8, Variation 1* for an example of outcomes applied to an assignment activity.

Lesson module

This module has some of the characteristics of the Quiz module. The main distinguishing feature is that the questions students are presented with depend on how they answered the previous question. This is excellent for providing constructive feedback. There are fewer question types than in Quiz—just the five that you can see in the following screenshot:

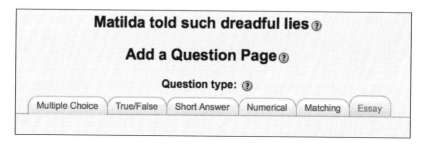

In case you've forgotten how to get to the page, go to the course page, and click on **Turn editing on**. Then go to the **Add an activity...** drop-down menu, and select **Lesson.**

Complete the set-up page. Click on **Save and display** and then you'll see the question types tabs in the first screenshot above.

Interesting variables

Lesson can be used for testing purposes. You must make sure that you select **No** for **Practice lesson** in the Lesson set-up page.

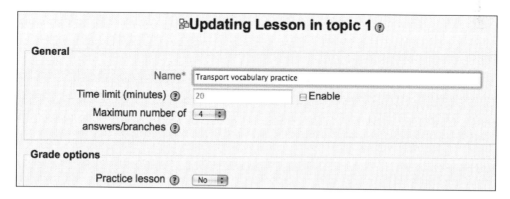

Once **Practice lesson** is set to **No**, students' grades will appear in the gradebook.

There is also a **Slide Show** setting. If we choose this, the lesson pages appear in a fixed format. A colored progress bar also appears at the bottom of the slide, so that students can see how far through the lesson they are.

There are examples of lesson activities in Chapter 6, *Reading Activities* and Chapter 2, *Getting Started with Moodle*. The Moodle site also offers a good overview of the possibilities: `http://docs.moodle.org/en/Lesson`.

Moodle Gradebook

The Moodle Gradebook provides a wealth of information about student grades. To access the Gradebook, click on **Grades** in the **Administration** menu on the course page.

The default view will be something like this, depending on how many quizzes and assignments you have in your course.

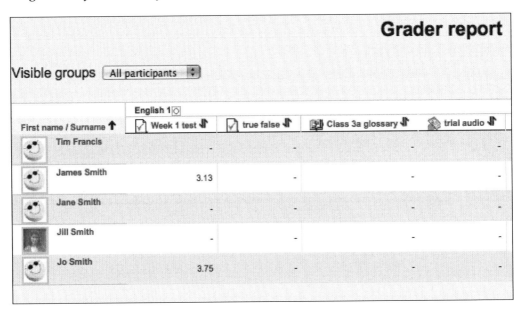

At a glance you can get an overview of individual grades with the option to see averages, group scores, ranges (the range of scores generated by students on a given scale), and Outcomes.

If you click on an activity (for example, **Week 1 test** in the graphic on the previous page), you can then get the following information:

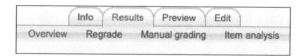

Gradebook item	Description
Info	Gives you the description of the item that you wrote.
Results	Gives you the chance to regrade or manually grade results.
Item analysis	Gives you statistics about questions you wrote. For example:

- Standard deviation
- Item difficulty
- Discrimination index

Here's what we get if we click on **Item analysis**:

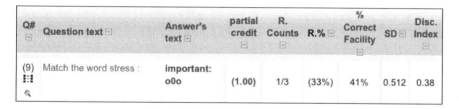

Q#	Question text	Answer's text	partial credit	R. Counts	R.%	% Correct Facility	SD	Disc. Index
(9)	Match the word stress :	important: o0o	(1.00)	1/3	(33%)	41%	0.512	0.38

Here's a reminder of what those terms stand for:

Statistic	Description
partial credit	Allows you to give a partial score for a partially correct answer.
R. Counts	Records the number of students who gave this answer.
Correct Facility	Gives the facility value for the item. In other words, how many students got it right. In the above case, only 41% got it right, making it a relatively difficult item.

Statistic	Description
SD	This is the standard deviation, which is a simple measure of the distribution of scores for the item. 1 SD above the mean represents about 34% of the test-takers. So 68% of test-takers are 1 SD below or above the mean.

Here's an example. If the total score for a test is 100, the mean is 50, the SD is 6, then 68% would have between 44 and 56 (6 points below and 6 points above the mean). That's a pretty low SD, and it means that most of the scores are clustered around the average.

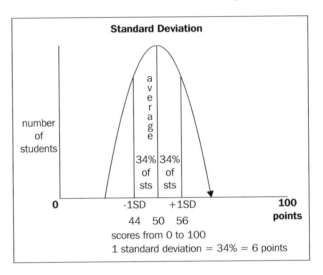

A high standard deviation indicates that the scores are more "spread out" over a large range of values.

There is no "correct" standard deviation. For example, if you set an achievement test in which you expect students to gain high scores, then you'd expect the standard deviation to be low (because all the scores would fall in a narrow range). If you have set up a placement test where you expect a wide range of scores, then you would expect the standard deviation to be higher.

In case you're wondering, the SD of 0.512 in the previous screenshot is fairly meaningless at the moment, because, as the **R. Counts** column shows us, only **3** people answered the question.

Statistic	Description
Disc. Index	Dis. Index (or DI) is the Discrimination Index. It shows whether the test successfully discriminates between strong and weak students. You would expect strong students to get difficult items correct and weak students to get them wrong. The nearer the discrimination index is to 1, the better the test item is discriminating. A DI of 1 means all the strong students got the item right and none of the weak ones did. A low DI, say between 0.3 and 0.0, means that the item didn't discriminate so strongly. When we want our test to show differences between students, we aim at a DI of 0.4 or above. A negative DI is always bad news. It means that generally weak students are getting an item right and generally strong ones are getting it wrong. When that happens, you must look at the item, because it usually means that you have either entered the wrong "key" (correct answer) or the wording is very confused. See if there are obvious corrections you can make. Alternatively, reject the item.

If you want to know more about these basic statistical functions and other aspects of assessment, there is suggested further reading in Chapter 2, *Getting Started with Moodle*.

Reviewing and improving your quiz tests

It's worth reviewing student responses to quiz questions regularly to make sure they are working well and that they are getting fair marks. Here are three examples of how you can review your questions:

Multiple-choice item distracters—are they working?

Imagine we've set up a stem, three distracters, and a right answer as follows:

What would you do if you won a million dollars?

a) If I win a million dollars, I go on a world trip.

b) If I won a million dollars, I'd go on a world trip.

c) If I'd won a million dollars, I'd go on a world trip.

d) If I'd win a million dollars, I'll go on a world trip.

For a multiple-choice question to work well, we want *all* the distracters to catch *some* of the students. The item analysis for that item will tell us exactly how many students are choosing each distracter.

Task: Take a look at the Item analysis table below and try to identify the problem distracter.

Question text ⊟	Answer's text ↓ ⊟	partial credit ⊟	R. Counts ⊟	R.% ⊟	% Correct Facility ⊟
1. If question : What would you do if you won a million dollars?	If I win a million dollars, I go on a world trip.	(0.00)	0/17	(0%)	59%
	If I won a million dollars, I'd go on a world trip.	(1.00)	10/17	(59%)	
	If I'd won a million dollars, I'd go on a world trip.	(0.00)	4/17	(24%)	
	If I'd win a million dollars, I'll go on a world trip.	(0.00)	2/17	(12%)	

As we'd expect, the **R. Counts** column shows us that the correct option, option b, has ten hits (see the previous table for definition of R. Counts). However, we see that none of the students chose option a. This provides us with an opportunity to revise the test to create a distracter that is closer to the sort of answer weaker students might produce themselves. For example, in future tests, we could change it to:

If I would win a million dollars, I'd go on a world trip.

This process is the sort of thing that happens in pilot tests to improve them.

Using wild cards with short-answer questions

When reviewing our students' answers to our short answer questions, we may see that they are being penalized unfairly for adding extra words. For example:

Question: What's the capital of England?

Student answer: Of course, it's London.

This would be marked wrong if the teacher declares "London" as the correct answer in the answer box. But if you write "*London", the answer would be considered correct. You would need to monitor the answers by checking the gradebook to make sure it doesn't allow gibberish, of course. The wild card allows grammatically correct and incorrect answers. So it's not very reliable. For example, you could place an "*" at the end of a word. "big*" would match "bigg", "bigger", "biggest", and "bigs".

Using regular expressions with short-answer questions

A more accurate way of allowing a variety of answers is the add-on regular expression Short Answer question type, which is explored below. Like the Ordering question type, this is straightforward for your administrator to add. See Chapter 2, *Getting Started with Moodle* for more information on installing add-ons.

There is a wide range of regular expressions that you can add to the answer to allow for different, but correct or partially correct answers. Regular expressions are symbols which allow variations in the text that are acceptable as an answer. For example, the regular expression ? means that the character immediately before it is optional.

Here are some of the key regular expressions. You can find out more by reading the help files on Moodle.org. N.B. In each case, the first answer that we write must be the correct answer and must not be a Regular Expression.

Allowing alternatives—using "|"

In the following example, **Answer 1** is correct—**He saw two people**. **Answer 2** is also correct—**He saw (2|two) people**. The bar means that either "2" or "two" is acceptable.

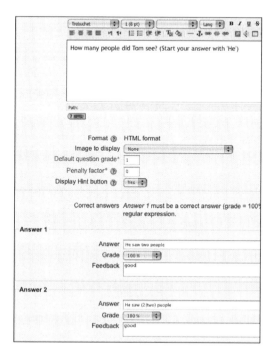

Allowing a character to be included or not—using "?"

Question: Red, green, and blue are all examples of …?

Answer 1: colors

Answer 2: colou?rs

The "?" in answer two means that students can answer with the US spelling "color" or the UK spelling "colour". The "?" must be placed immediately after the optional character.

Allowing a range of answers—using "[ ]"

Question: Write down the name of an animal that ends in "at". It's three letters long.

Answer 1: cat

Answer 2: [bcr]at

The [ ] will accept "bat", "cat", and "rat".

Removing case sensitivity—using "/i"

If you write "/i" in the answer box immediately after your answer, Moodle will not penalize the use of different cases; that is, lower case letters instead of upper case ones. For example:

Question: Why did the cat jump on the wall?

Answer 1: To escape from the dog/i

That answer would mean that all the following would be accepted:

- *To escape from the dog*
- *To Escape fRom the dog*
- *to escape from the Dog*

Don't include extra spaces between the symbols, as it may stop them from working properly.

If you already use a printed test, consider adapting it to the Moodle Quiz, so that you can check how well it is performing as a test—is it discriminating between strong and weak students?

Security

There are several things you can do to help avoid cheating. On the Quiz set-up page you will find the following options:

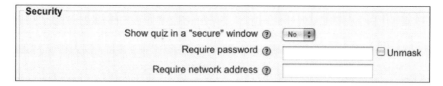

They are covered in detail in Chapter 2, *Getting Started with Moodle*.

Useful Moodle add-ons

Here are some of the add-ons that can enhance your assessment practice in Moodle. They can all be downloaded from the download modules page on the main Moodle site. See Chapter 2 for downloading add-on Modules.

Hot Potatoes

This popular quiz program is easy to set up and use. If you don't need Moodle's detailed results and feedback summaries, you might find it easier to use Hot Potatoes instead. There are instructions on how to download it in Chapter 2, *Getting Started with Moodle*, and there are some example activities that use it in Chapter 3, *Vocabulary Activities* and Chapter 6, *Reading Activities*.

Lolipop module

It looks like the British word for a Popsicle, but this isn't a way of bribing youngsters into doing tests. Lolipop stands for Language Online Portfolio Project. It uses the Common European Framework to help students evaluate their current and target language skills. Lolipop's main website is at `http://lolipop-portfolio.eu/about.html`.

It's a useful tool for getting students to review what's motivating them to learn languages. It gets them to think about how well they're doing in speaking, reading, writing, and listening skills, and helps them set language learning goals for themselves. They can upload evidence of their language performance in different skills, which teachers can then review. They can also set themselves reminders for doing tasks.

This is what the main Lolipop menu looks like once installed on Moodle:

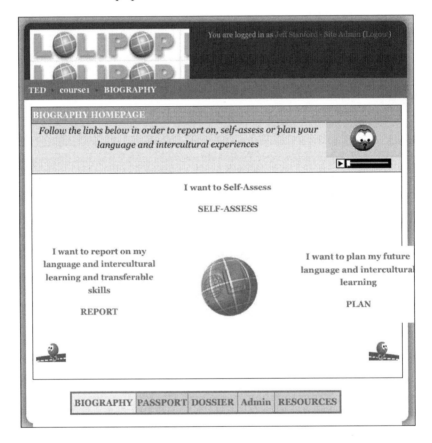

The Flash player provides spoken support for each page. Descriptions of language levels are based on the Common European Framework language descriptors. Here's an example of a description of listening skills at **A2** level. The student reads the description, then clicks on the appropriate icon.

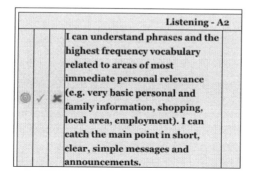

- Clicking on the two circles sets these skills as an objective
- Clicking on the green tick means the student can already do it
- Clicking on the red cross means the student can't do it

Once students have self-assessed their skills, they'll get a graphic overview like this:

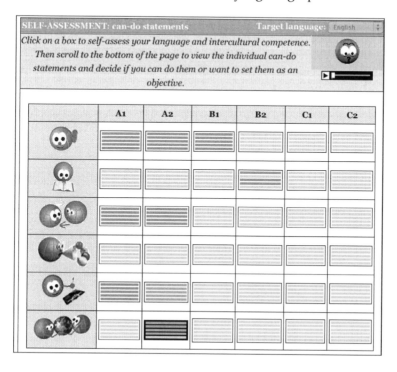

The green lines indicate skills students already have. The orange lines indicate language goals. Where students have indicated they can do something, they are invited to upload an example as evidence.

This is clearly a very useful tool for structuring courses, organizing learning, raising awareness of language learning, and, above all, motivating students to learn.

If you plan to use Lolipop, you'll need to think about how you want to integrate it into your whole course. Here are some useful questions to ask yourself:

- Is self-evaluation a key part of your course or do you want it to be?
- Do students know how to evaluate themselves?
- Do they understand the CEF evaluation criteria?
- Will they have evidence to upload in support of the level they claim to be?
- What kind of learner support or learner training will I need to provide? And how?

Mobile Quiz module

This add-on allows students to download quizzes onto their mobile phones, or looking at it the other way round, allows teachers to have even more access to students. Still, some students clearly like this use of mobile phones. It's quite likely to catch on.

What students get on their phones is a limited version of the Quiz. For example, it doesn't allow penalty points, responses can't be added to the gradebook, and it only works with true/false, multiple-choice and short-answer question types. Nevertheless, it's a great way of making quizzes more fun and fitting them into the lives of busy students. One of the settings allows teachers to include their own mobile phone number so that they can receive the results of their students' attempts.

Here are a few ideas for using Mobile Quiz:

- Quiz trailers: students get a foretaste of a quiz to come
- Reminder system: true/false quiz about an upcoming assignment they have to do
- Vocabulary review test, which students can play over and over again on their way to classes
- Use short-answer question type as a poll to get students to vote on what topic they'd like to study, or what film they'd like to see

Before we can make Mobile Quiz work, we need to have created a quiz.

Here's how to do it

1. On your course page, click on **Turn editing on**. Then click on **Add an activity....**
2. Select **Mobile Quiz**.
3. Complete the set-up page. To convert a regular quiz into a Mobile Quiz, select a quiz from the dropdown menu. Fill out the mobile phone number where you want to receive results. Then click on **Save changes**.

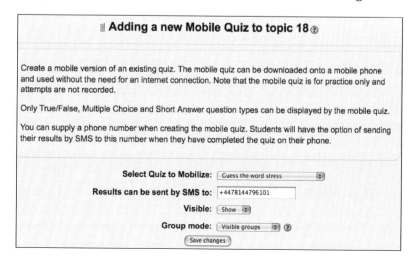

4. We're then presented with a lengthy page about what we can and can't do with the Mobile Quiz. The key link is half way down the page, where we can find the URL for downloading the quiz.

Install the mobile quiz via your phone's internet connection

If your phone has a Web Browser and a connection to the internet, then you can follow these steps to install the mobile quiz.

1. On your phone, navigate to the location that allows you to enter a URL (web address). On many Nokia phones, you would select the 'Menu' button then go to 'Web/Options/Navigation options/Go to web address'. See your phone's operating instructions for more information.
2. Enter this URL: http://www.mobilestudy.org/content/3310/m/
3. The browser should then display a download page for the mobile quiz. Simply select the download link and follow the prompts.

Brought to you by mobilestudy.org

---

5. We need to give this URL to our students, who should access it via their mobile phones. The easiest way to do this is to send students an SMS message which includes a hyperlink to the URL.

Bulk SMS

If you're planning on sending bulk text messages regularly, it's worth looking into an educational account that will provide them at a discount. If you do an Internet search engine search for "bulk sms education", you will find a list of suppliers.

Once students have visited the URL on their mobile phones, they will receive a message asking them to download and install Mobile Quiz. After they have installed it, they will find it in their mobile phone `Applications` folder. When they open it, they'll see an invitation to download the quiz.

They click on **Download** and they'll get the True/False quiz that we made available.

They click on their response, **True** in this case, and get the feedback that we prepared as part of the quiz.

Finally, they can opt to send the results to the teacher, if they want to. N.B. That action is not automatic.

NanoGong audio recorder

As featured in most chapters, the NanoGong audio recorder allows students to record onto Moodle and for you to then assess their performance, also using NanoGong. It's a bit like having a conversation using answer-phone messages.

Chapter 4, *Speaking Activities* has a full introduction to NanoGong. Chapter 5, *Grammar Activities* includes an activity which assesses speaking using NanoGong.

Ordering question type

This is a question type which you can add to your quiz question Item Bank. It allows you to set questions which test the order of letters, words, sentences, and sequences of events. It's covered in more detail earlier in this chapter, and there's an example activity using it in Chapter 7, *Writing Activities*. In this screenshot, students drag the words into the right position to make the sentence syntactically correct.

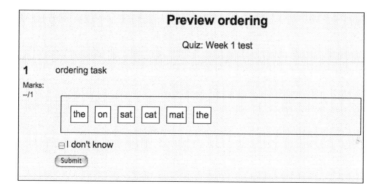

Regular Expression Short Answer question type

This add-on allows us to assess students' short answers more fairly, by letting us include variations of the correct answer. The *Moodle Gradebook* section of this chapter explores this area.

Questionnaire module

This add-on is similar to the Quiz module. In fact, a wider range of questions is possible with Questionnaire, but you cannot score questions in the way that Quiz allows you to, nor is it integrated into the Quiz module. It's a stand-alone module which is excellent for gathering feedback, getting students to think about nuances when trying to understand texts. It also has very useful reporting facilities.

Chapter 6, *Reading Activities* includes a complete activity using Questionnaire.

Stamp collection

This module allows you to reward students for a chosen behavior with colorful stamps, as illustrated in the coming table. This goes down well with children all ages and can help reinforce a sense of achievement.

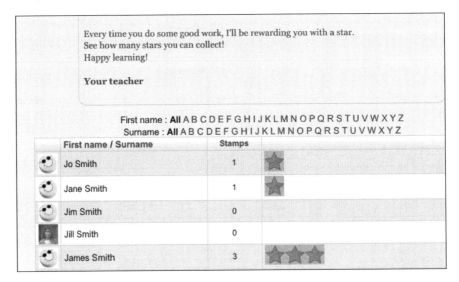

Here are some ideas for giving stamps:

- Achievement on a language test
- After students finish reading a book (see Chapter 10, *Extended Activities* for an example activity)
- Performance in a chat session
- Helpfulness
- Effort

You can choose any image as your "stamp".

Here's how to do it

1. On your course page click on **Turn editing on**. Then click on **Add an activity**.

2. Select **Stamp collection**.

3. Complete the set-up page. Pay particular attention to the following:

Settings	Details
Name	Give it a suitable name. Here we're calling it **your stamps**, but we could call it **pronunciation rewards** or **effort tokens**, for example.
Description	Write something like: **Every time you do some good work, I'll be rewarding you with a star.** **See how many stars you can collect!** **Happy learning!**
Stamp image	We can choose any image we want as the token. If we don't already have one, we can upload one. See Chapter 2, *Getting Started with Moodle* for more help with uploading images.
Display users with no stamps	Let's leave this on **Yes**, to encourage students with no stamps to earn some.

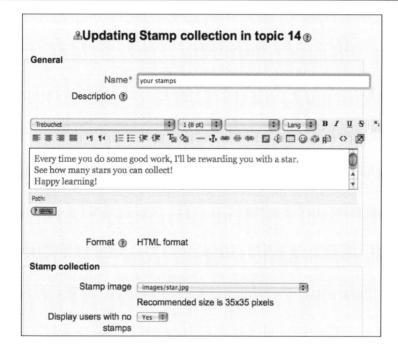

4. Then click on **Save and display**.

The add-on Reader activity in Chapter 10, *Extended Activities* is a good example of how you can combine a reading activity, quiz questions, and a stamp collection.

Stamps for all

By default, it is teachers who give stamps to students, but if we click on the **Override permissions** tab at the top of the Stamp collection set-up page, we can enable students to give stamps to other students or even to teachers. Here's an example of the buttons we should select to allow students to give stamps to each other:

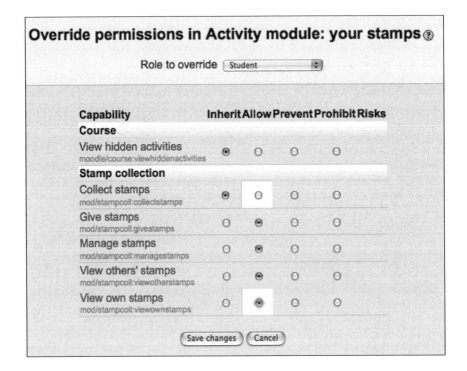

Workshop

This is not strictly an add-on, but it is hidden by default, so you'll need to get your administrator to unhide it by going to **Site Administration | Modules | Activities | Manage Activities**.

Workshop allows students to be assessed by themselves, their peers, and by teachers. It can be used to help students develop their writing and speaking (if you add the sound recorder, NanoGong, to your HTML editor). Since the preparation of writing and speaking presentations is often an iterative process, feedback from peers and teachers, as well as the opportunity to judge your own work according to clear criteria, can be tremendously helpful. Workshop allows you to fine-tune weighting of peer and teacher assessments to make the overall assessment as fair as possible; for example, you can increase the teacher's weighting if you think that peers have given marks which are too low.

Workshop has a large number of variables to take into consideration, so you need to think carefully about how you want to use it, but once set up, it's easy to use. See Chapter 10, *Extended Activities* for an example of Workshop in which students go through the following process:

- Read and assess a film review posted by the teacher

- Write draft 1 of their own review of a film

- Assess their peers' first draft reviews of a film

- Submit a final draft review

- Receive a final assessment from the teacher

Afterword

There's a lot to take in in this chapter. We've reviewed the pros and cons of using Moodle for assessing and looked in some detail at the various tools available. We've also looked at some of the interesting add-ons that are available for Moodle. You don't need to know all of this to start assessing, but it's worth checking this chapter before you start a new assessment project with your students.

Once you're familiar with the basics, it's worth exploring the help documents on the Moodle site, too:

- Quiz: http://docs.moodle.org/en/Quizzes

- Assignment: http://docs.moodle.org/en/Assignment

- Lesson: http://docs.moodle.org/en/Lesson_module

- Workshop: http://docs.moodle.org/en/Workshop_module

- Questionnaire: http://docs.moodle.org/en/Questionnaire_module

10
Extended Activities

Extended activities reinforce the key features of **communicative language teaching** outlined in Chapter 1, *What Does Moodle Offer Language Teachers?*. In particular, they:

- Allow us to set up **integrated skills** work
- Create more opportunities for **iterative work**, which, with appropriate feedback from teachers, can further develop language skills
- Create more opportunities for peer-to-peer **interaction**
- Allow us to incorporate a variety of **feedback** types
- Can lead to a greater sense of achievement in students

Many of the activities in earlier chapters illustrate integrated activities in that they combine two or more skills. Here are just a few examples:

Chapter	Activity	Skills
3	Activity 3: Using comments in Glossary module for students to comment on their keywords	Reading and writing
4	Activity 4: Learning by repeating—poems	Listening and speaking
5	Activity 2: Using the Lesson module to get students to notice grammar points	Listening and analyzing grammar
6	Activity 2: Reading and listening simultaneously	Reading and listening

This chapter goes one step further by suggesting two ways of creating a **sequence** of such activities using Moodle. The first approach is for you to plan and link activities yourself. The next section provides suggestions on how to do this. The second approach is to use pre-structured Moodle extended tasks. This chapter looks at four of these extended activities.

Planning a sequence of activities

It's quite normal for teachers to create a sequence of activities which reflect a range of skills.

A task-based or **content-based approach** is a good example of this. In their book, *Doing Task-based Teaching*, Oxford University Press, 2007, Dave and Jane Willis show how you might combine the following related activities:

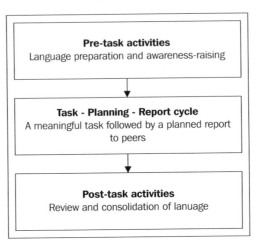

The easiest way to provide navigation for learners to follow a sequence of tasks is to set the course view page to topics or weekly format. To do this, go to your course page, and select **Administration | Settings | Format**. Then choose **Topics format** or **Weekly format**.

Using the **Topics format** you could organize activities according to a given topic. You can hide topics you don't want users to see by clicking on the eye icon in the right-hand corner of the topic. By choosing **Weekly format** you can organize activities chronologically by weeks.

Once you have chosen your course format, you can set up a sequence of activities. A simple way would be to use Moodle Web page to list the activities that you want students to do.

To do this, make sure you're in editing mode, then go to **Add a resource...** and select **Compose a web page**. Your page could look something like this:

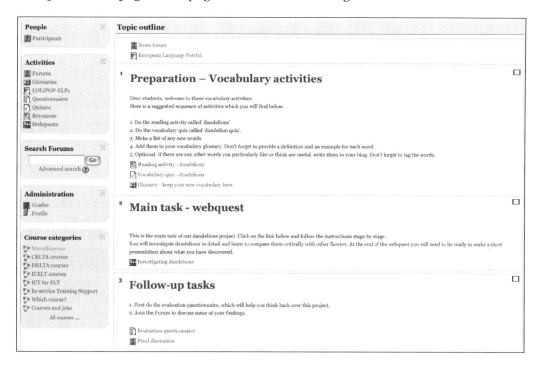

You could also use the calendar to indicate deadlines for certain tasks. See Chapter 2, *Getting Started with Moodle* for help with setting up calendar events.

If you want to have more control of your learners, you can restrict availability of many activities on the activity set-up page. To do that, change the dates available section, or click on the **Hide** option at the bottom of the set-up page. Moodle 2.0 will have a conditional activities module, which will make completion of one activity a condition for going on to further activities in a sequence set by the teacher.

Other possible integrations with Moodle

The extended activities in this chapter are just a few examples of the many integrations possible. Below are a few more ideas, and for yet more, go to `http://moodle.org`.

LAMS (Learning Activity Management System): This is a feature-rich, external product with a drag-and-drop authoring system which allows you to sequence a range of e-learning tools. It can be integrated into Moodle. Go to `http://Moodle.org` | **Downloads | Modules and plugins**, and search for "LAMS". There is also more information at `http://lamsfoundation.org/`.

 SLOODLE: This is an integration of the virtual world, Second life, with Moodle. Go to `http://moodle.org` | **Downloads | Modules and plugins**, and search for "sloodle".

Mahoodle: This is a more sophisticated e-portfolio than Exabis e-portfolio, used in this chapter. Go to `http://mahara.org`, and do a search for "Moodle".

Wiziq: This is a free web-conferencing program which has a Moodle plugin. Go to `http://wiziq.com` for more information. All users need an account. To get the Moodle plugin, `http://moodle.org` | **Downloads | Modules and plugins**, and search for "wiziq".

Dimdim: This is also a free web-conferencing program which has a Moodle plugin. Go to `http://dimdim.com` for more information. All users need an account. To get the Moodle plugin, go to `http://moodle.org` | **Downloads | Modules and plugins**, and search for "dimdim".

What this chapter covers

The extended, integrated activities in this chapter are based on pre-structured modules which provide a framework for your activities and help you plan them. This gives you a standardized approach, which makes it easier for teachers to plan the activities. It also makes it easier for students to follow the activities, because they become familiar with them through repetition.

A lot of variation is possible within these modules, as the following examples will show.

We will focus on four modules:

- Webquest
- E-portfolio
- Workshop
- Reader

Let's review each module so that you can get an idea of the range of possibilities each offers.

Webquests

These have become a popular way of guiding students to find out information on the Web. They follow the spirit of Moodle in that they encourage individual thinking and a constructivist approach to learning (`http://docs.moodle.org/en/Philosophy`). They could be simple knowledge hunts in which students gather some information and report back. Or they could be more engaging webquests in which students raise their critical awareness by evaluating different sorts of information they find. Here's an example of each:

Knowledge hunt about London

Students are asked to find out some basic information about London: population, ethnic makeup, and interesting facts about the transport system. They are given some useful websites to visit, like `http://www.londoncouncils.gov.uk/londonfacts/keyfacts/default.htm`. They then present this information to their class.

Webquest about having a sixth runway at London Heathrow Airport

Students are asked to evaluate the viability of a sixth runway at London's Heathrow Airport. The teacher gives them links to a variety of websites with different, possibly contradictory, information. Students need to evaluate the information and then present their own views.

There's a fuller definition of a webquest at `http://webquest.org`.

 The Moodle Webquest allows you to upload resources, too. This may be useful if you want to save students' time or if access to certain websites is limited in your organization.

Webquest components

The Moodle add-on Webquest has the following components:

- Introduction
- Task
- Process
- Evaluation
- Conclusion
- Teams

The role of the **Introduction** part is to explain what the overall aim of the webquest is. It's an opportunity to motivate and engage students, make them aware of key issues, and set the scene for some investigative work. The introduction can include appropriate and appealing graphics, and you could also embed a voice introduction using the voice recorder, NanoGong (see Chapter 2, *Getting Started with Moodle* for help with using NanoGong).

The **Task** part describes the *goal* of the webquest and not how to do it. That comes in the process section. Task helps students understand what they'll be doing and why, and mentions how they'll present the results of the task. The default presentation mechanism at the end of the webquest comes in the evaluation stage. You could also have students prepare any of the following:

- Face-to-face presentation
- Classroom wall display
- A posting in a Moodle Forum
- A portfolio page like Exabis, described later in this chapter
- A web page

Students will need to know whether to include graphs, maps, essays, fact sheets, timelines, presentations, wall displays, and diagrams, for example. So we need to make that clear in the instructions.

The **Process** is a set of questions that students need to answer to complete the task. It's also where teachers include hyperlinks to useful web resources for students to use. It's in this section that you distinguish between a knowledge hunt and a webquest, according to the type of questions you set. If you need help grading the complexity of your questions, Bloom's Taxonomy, which is mentioned in Chapter 6, *Reading Activities*, should be a useful tool.

The **Evaluation** section is where students upload their webquest response for the teacher to evaluate. They can upload their work as an individual or as part of a team. The current version allows students to see each other's work once the deadline for submissions has passed. The Webquest set-up page allows teachers to set the evaluation criteria for students' work, which will appear to teams or individuals under evaluation.

Teams allows you to appoint students to a given team. The first named person in the team list becomes the team leader. When you build a team, make sure that you transfer the team leader's name first. That person's submission should represent the whole group's submission. Once it is submitted, other team members can't add to it. The team leader can, however, delete and resubmit their webquest response. This feature can also be suppressed.

Limitations to the Webquest module

- No teacher's page to make it clear to other teachers how they should use your webquest. Teachers can make a separate information document for other teachers, which they can hide.

- The Moodle groups feature is not available, though teachers can put students into teams who submit a joint webquest. These teams could be individual students or groups of students.

- No role settings override available.

In spite of these limitations it's a useful basic tool. The module's author is working on an improved version for Moodle 2.1. See *Activity 1* for an example of how to use the Webquest module.

See `http://webquest.org/` for more information on webquests.

 There is also a WebQuest SCORM add-on which can be used to create webquests.

E-portfolio

E-portfolios are an exciting way of collating, organizing, and presenting Moodle users' work. A variety of document types can be included; for example, word-processed documents, recordings, videos, and images. Users have control over who sees which parts of the portfolio, and the portfolio can be exported or viewed outside Moodle. Here is a list of the key features of the Moodle Exabis e-portfolio copied from `http://docs.moodle.org/en/Exabis_e-portfolio_block`.

- *An individual starting page which may contain one's curriculum vitae or similar*
- *A manageable category-system on two levels (main category and sub category)*
- *File-management within the category-system (i.e. for publication of one's best work-efforts)*
- *Publication of interesting links within Moodle or into the web via weblink*
- *Self-reflection and documentation of one's personal learning-style by using private notes (with the option for publication within Moodle or into the web via weblink)*
- *Commenting-functionality for published links, files and notes*
- *Export-functionality into a SCORM-zip-format*
- *Cross-course usage of eportfolio-module*
- *Import of assignments from within all Moodle-courses into an individual portfolio*
- *Import of previously SCORM-packages exported from eportfolio-module*

Notes on features

- The category system allows you to make one type of information a sub-category of another. For example:
    ◦ Work experience (top category)
    ◦ Retail work (sub-category)
    ◦ Office work (sub-category)

- **SCORM** stands for **Shareable Content Object Reference Model**. The SCORM export feature archives the whole portfolio as a ZIP file. It can then be read by a wide range of other programs, including other **Learner Management Systems (LMSs)**. SCORM files do for programs what PDFs do for documents.

And here are a few ideas for using **Student e-portfolios**:

- **Resumes**, which include direct links to web pages and other documents
- **Collection of work documents** to meet course criteria
- **Project display**, which features the final product of a project

- **Evaluation of courses**
- **Repository of documents**
- **Presentation of work** for parents

There are useful presentations of portfolios in language teaching at:

- `http://www.teachingenglish.org.uk/think/articles/portfolios-elt`
- `http://iteslj.org/Techniques/Ali-Portfolios.html`

See *Activity 2* for an example of using the Moodle E-portfolio to display a collection of students' work. It will include peer and teacher comments on the work.

Note that only the portfolio owner can edit their portfolio, so you need to make sure the instructions for doing that are clear to your students. You could also consider using the Book module to provide instructions. Also, each Moodle user can have only one portfolio per Moodle, but that portfolio can include lots of different collections of artifacts, including resume, project work, and evaluation reviews. Users can make different categories to organize different types of documents and notes, and they can make different views to limit what can be seen and by whom.

Limitations

- If the course is deleted, the e-portfolio is deleted. To get round this, you can export e-portfolios as SCORM files, and then re-import them to new courses.
- You cannot delete portfolios in one go: each element has to be deleted separately.

Other portfolios

Lolipop, which is discussed in Chapter 9, *Assessment,* and the add-on Mahara are also worth exploring. The Mahara website also has useful information on using portfolios: `http://mahara.org/about/eportfolios`.

Workshops

The example activity shows how you can extend an activity to include different skills which are practiced over a period of time. The key features we are interested in are how a student's piece of work, spoken or written, can be evaluated by teachers, other students, and by students themselves as part of a developmental process so that the original draft benefits and improves.

An additional attractive feature of this module is that before students even begin to write their own work, you can force them to evaluate other work. That work can be by other students, or can be chosen by the teacher to exemplify good or bad practice. That way students become sensitized to the language and structure of the writing or speech they should be emulating, or not.

Two advantages of this approach are that it saves the teacher time and attunes students to the criteria for producing a good final product. It can save the teacher time, because once the students become more critically analytical, they reduce the amount of evaluation that the teacher has to do.

Reader

This add-on activity helps you set up an online library. The way it works is that you make books or texts available online or offline. Students read the books. They then do a quiz on the books. If students get an appropriately high mark in the quiz, they are awarded a star. They then go on to the next book or text. And so on.

Activity 1: Supporting student investigation of knowledge or issues using the Webquest module

Aim: Help students read and evaluate issues using web materials

Moodle modules: None

Extra programs: Add-on Webquest

Ease of setup: ***

In this webquest students will write a critical evaluation. We'll need to choose the subject and questions carefully, according to the age and interests of the students and their level of language. Our example is a webquest for teenagers to investigate the film "Slumdog Millionaire" and the situation it describes. They'll need a general introduction which sensitizes them to the film and then some guiding questions. Finally, they'll need some resources which help them evaluate the slum situation in India. This is what the first page of the webquest will look like when it's finished:

Here's how to do it

1. In editing mode on your course, select **Add an activity...** from the drop-down menu.

2. Choose **Webquest**.

3. Complete the set-up page, paying attention to the information below:

Settings	Details
Name	Let's call it **Slumdog Millionaire**.
Introduction	This is an important step. It's often motivating to be upbeat to make the webquest as enticing as possible. We could write something like this: ### Mumbai slums **This is a picture of a slum in Mumbai – or Bombay. Can you imagine what it's like to live there? Dirty conditions. No water, no sewage facilities, no public transport, pollution, housing shortages. 7 million people live in conditions like this in Mumbai, but why and what can be done about it? This webquest will help you answer just those questions – and through the film, 'Slumdog Millionaire'.** We can also add an image as in the screenshot above. See Chapter 2, *Getting Started with Moodle* for help with adding images.
Grade	We'll have four questions worth ten points each, so let's put **40** as our grade.

Settings	Details
Number of tasks to perform	We have four questions, so select **4**.
Number of attachments in each post	We'll write **0,** as we're not attaching any documents.
Evaluation by teams	This means will each team designated by the teacher submit one task to be evaluated. I want students to do the task individually and be graded individually, so I'll select **No**.
Grading strategy	This is the same as the **Grading strategy** for the Workshop module, which is set out in *Activity 3*. We want to grade four separate questions, and we want the score to build up for each answer. So we'll choose **cumulative**.
Maximum size	This refers to the attachment size. We're not allowing attachments. So we can leave it on **10 kb**, the lowest setting.
Beginning of post and End of post	Make sure you put real dates here. Otherwise, when you press **Save changes,** you'll get an error message and all your description will disappear.
Visible	Select **Show** to make the webquest available to students. Alternatively, we could click on **Hide** for now, and change it to **Show** later, when it's ready for students to use.

4. Click on **Save changes**.

5. The **Editing tasks** page will now appear. We'll write the task descriptions afterwards. The four questions we wrote in the description now appear as four separate tasks, which can be evaluated at the end of the webquest. The format for the task evaluation will vary according to the grading strategy you chose in Step 3.

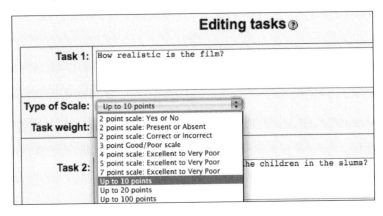

There is a choice of scales in the drop-down menu.

Let's choose **Up to 10 points**, so that we can give up to ten points for each question.

6. Next, we need to add the task description for the tasks we've just written. To do that, click on **Tasks** in the left-hand column. Then click on **Edit task description**. The editing box will then appear. This is where you describe the task and prepare the students for the presentation they will make. You could write something like this:

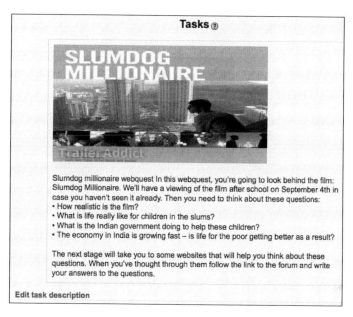

The movie trailer is embedded in the text and comes from `http://www.` `traileraddict.com/trailer/slumdog-millionaire/trailer`.

See Chapter 2, *Getting Started with Moodle* if you need help with embedding videos.

7. Click on **Save changes** again.

8. The next stage of the webquest is the **Process**. Click on **Process** in the left-hand column. Again, it is divided into two parts. In the top part you should write specific guidelines and questions for students to follow. Make this page as clear as possible so that students don't come back for you for clarification. Also, other teachers need to be able to follow this easily in case they want to use it.

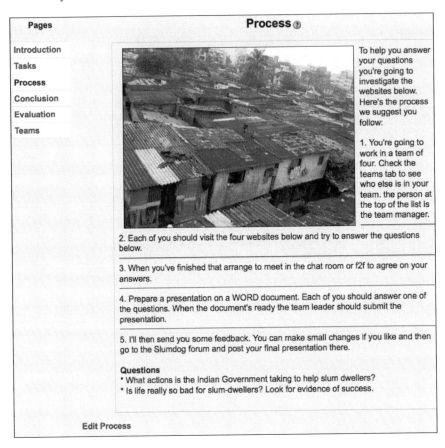

9. Click on **Save changes**. Below you should add the resources you want the students to use. As you can see from the screenshot next, there's a choice between uploading a file or naming a URL. We'll put in `http://www.planetizen.com/node/35269` as one of our resources and `http://news.bbc.co.uk/2/hi/business/6970800.stm` as the other one. Click on **Edit Process** to add these resources.

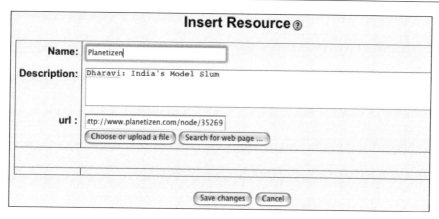

This is what the **Resources** section of the page will look like after you click on **Save changes**.

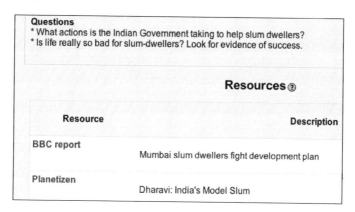

10. Next, click on the **Conclusion** tab on the left. This is a good place to remind students what they have learned and point to other similar situations that they might think about. Here's what we could write:

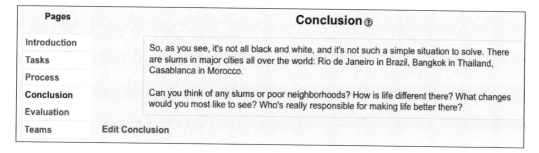

11. The **Evaluation** button is what we click on to evaluate students' responses to the tasks. If we click on it now, we'll see the **No answer has been submitted yet** message. Once students start submitting their answers, we'll see their names here and be able to write comments and grade their work. If you chose to create teams in Step 3, you'll need to allocate students to the teams now. Press the **Teams** tab. If you get the **Evaluation by teams is not activated** warning, you'll have to click on the **Update this Webquest** button in the top right-hand corner. Once you're there, change **Evaluation by teams** to **Yes**. This doesn't work the other way round, however. In other words, if you've already set up teams which have submitted work, you can't disable them.

Creating teams

12. You only need to read the next two sections if you do want teams to submit joint assignments. You'll need to click on **Insert teams**. Then you'll need to give a name to each team you want to create. Let's call them **red** team and **blue** team. You can have as many teams as you need.

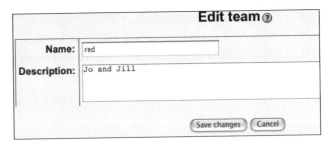

We can write the names of the people in the team in the **Description** box for easy identification.

13. Press **Save changes**. Then press the **red** label in the **Teams** column.

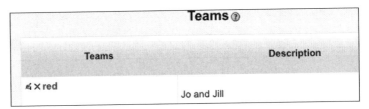

Now we can add **Jo** and **Jill** to the team by selecting their names in the right-hand column and clicking on the arrow so that they move into the left-hand column and join the team. N.B. The first person you transfer will be the team leader. I want Jill to be the red team leader. So I'll transfer her name first.

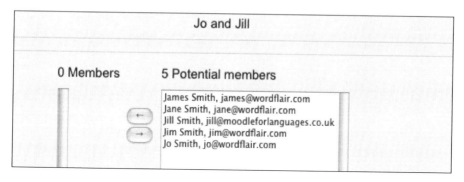

The webquest is now ready for students to use. Once they have submitted their presentations, you can click on the **Evaluation** tab to see their work and award a grade for each of the tasks according to the grading strategy that you chose on the set-up page. Once the deadline for submissions has passed, students will be able to view each other's work.

Optional

Create a forum so that students can continue discussing issues related to the webquest. See Chapter 4, *Speaking Activities, Activity 1* if you need help with setting up a Forum.

Activity 2: Creating a display of student work using the E-Portfolio block

Aim: Help students organize a range of work documents

Moodle modules: None

Extra programs: Add-on Exabis E-Portfolio block

Ease of setup: ***

In this scenario, students have to display their best language work for a given period. The fact that their work will be on display should motivate them to produce the best work possible. It will remind them of the work they've done and help them reflect on it. It's also a chance for students to benefit from each other's work.

Here's how to do it

First of all, make sure the add-on block has been installed. The following example is for a portfolio for the fictitious Jill Smith, so I'll write the instructions as if I were telling her what to do. Remember that teachers can't edit students' portfolios. You might find it useful to set up a dummy student and log on as that student to try out the procedure. You can delete the dummy student later on, if necessary.

First, though, we need to make sure that the Exabis E-Portfolio block is available. To do that:

1. Click on **Turn editing on.**

2. Go to the **Blocks** drop-down menu. Click on **Add....**

3. Select **Exabis E-Portfolio.**

4. Instructions from now on relate to what Jill (or any other student) needs to do.

   Click on **My Portfolio** in the Exabis E-Portfolio block on your course page and you will be able to start building your portfolio. This is what you'll see:

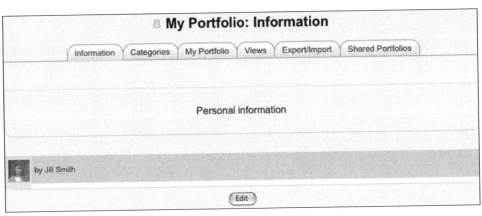

Here you can write an introduction to your portfolio. The **Information** section can contain any information you want. If it's the introduction to a resume, you would include personal data, perhaps. In this case, it's the introduction to your work over the last term.

5. Click on **Edit**, and write something like the following:

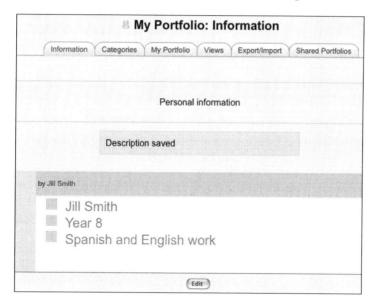

If you need help with the colors and graphics, see Chapter 11, *Formatting and Enhancing Your Moodle Materials*.

6. Now you need to create at least one category for your portfolio. To do that, click on the **Categories** tab. You can make as many different categories as you want. This will be useful if you collect a lot of different documents that aren't related to each other in your portfolio.

Right now we want one main category, **Languages**, and two sub-categories called **Spanish** and **English**. Click on the **Edit** button, and add each of those categories.

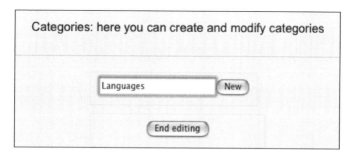

When you've written in the main category label, press **New**. Now create two sub-categories: one called **English** and the other one called **Spanish**. Press **New** to save them each time.

7. When you have all the categories you want, click on **End editing**. Your categories should look like this:

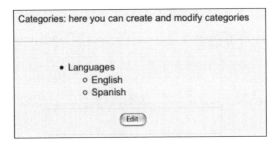

8. Now press the **My Portfolio** tab. You'll see the following:

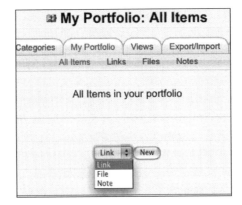

This is where you create the content for your portfolio. You have a choice between:

- º   **Link** — these are hyperlinks to web pages that you have created, either within Moodle or on the Web.

- º   **File** — here you can upload files to your portfolio.

- º   **Note** — here you can write a note that explains the contents of your portfolio. You could also use this function to write parts of your resume, or write questions that you want others to answer.

You're going to add some artifacts to the English category: one link to a blog you've written about fashion in English, one file with a project description you wrote, and one note that explains what work you've been doing.

First, let's add a link. You can either do this by clicking on the **Links** tab and then selecting **Add a new link**, or you can click on the **All items** tab, select **Link** from the drop-down menu in the bottom box, and then click on **New**. The following screenshot shows the **Link** set-up page:

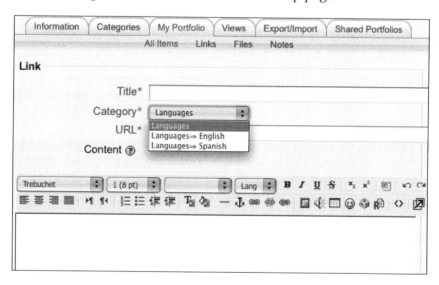

Complete the boxes along the following lines:

Settings	Details
Title	Let's write **Jill's blog about NY fashion in English**.
Category	Select **Languages => English** from the drop-down menu, where you will see the two categories that we created earlier.
URL	Write in the full web address of your link: `http://blog.jill/english`.
Content	Give a brief description of the link. For example:
	This is a blog I've been writing about fashion in New York. It has pictures of latest fashions and some interesting information about latest trends. Take a look!
	You can also add images, embed videos, or add audio recordings here.

9. Next, you are going to add a file. The file you want to include is already on Moodle, because you submitted it as an assignment. To access it, click on the **Export/Import** tab. Then click on **Import** from Moodle-assignments. Then click on **Add this file** next to the file you want to import. Again, you can write a title, choose the category, and write a description for the file. As with all HTML boxes, you can include a spoken comment if you have NanoGong in the HTML editor.

If you want to include a file from your computer, click on the **Files** link. Then click on **Add new file**. Finally, browse to the file on your computer that you want to upload.

10. Now you are going to add some notes. To do that, click on the **Notes** tab and provide information in the same way as you did for **Links** and **Files**. When the **My Portfolio** section is finished, it will look something like this.

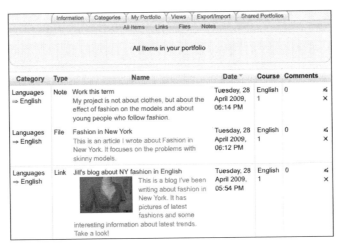

If you click on the edit icons in the **Comments** column, you can edit the content of any of your portfolio artifacts.

11. Now click on the **Views** tab. This is where you decide which parts of your portfolio you want other people to see. You can have different views for different people. You can also make your portfolio visible as a web page for people to see outside Moodle.

    Click on **Add View**. As you can see, there are five elements to the view page: **View Information**, **Your Items**, **Special Items**, and **View Design**. At the bottom of the page there's a button for sharing your portfolio, too. First complete the **View Information**. Give the view a title. Let's call this **Jill's fashion project**. Next provide a short description.

12. Next, you're going to design your view. To do that, you drag items from the **Your Items** block and the **Special Items** block into the **View Design** block. The **Special Items** elements allow you to add other bits of text to your portfolio. Let's add the personal information that you wrote earlier. And let's use the headlines to create section headers. In the screenshot below, we've added a **Personal information** section, and we've created headlines for **Blogs** and **Articles**. Then we've dragged across items from **Your Items** into the appropriate section of the **View Design**.

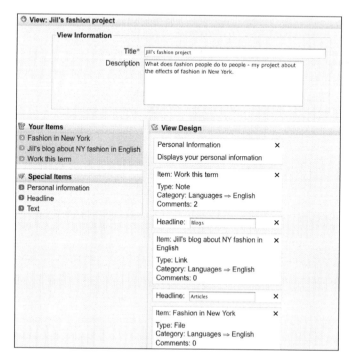

You can also change the order of the artifacts if you want, by dragging them up or down. As soon as you click on an object in the **View Design**, a hand icon appears, which indicates it's ready to be dragged.

13. Before you leave this page, you need to decide who you want to see your view. Let's imagine you want just two of your fellow course members to see your portfolio for now. So click on the **Sharing** arrow at the bottom of the page, and select **Internal Access**. Then select the names of the students you want to be able to see you portfolio.

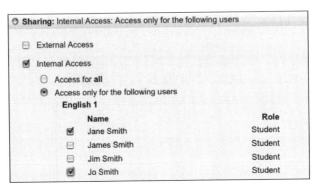

Views provide a lot of flexibility, and you can edit existing ones or add new ones for different audiences whenever you want. The view named **Jill's fashion project** is now visible to **Jo** and **Jane**. When Jane logs on and clicks on the **Shared Portfolios** link in the portfolio block, she'll find a link to your portfolio. By clicking on the link, she'll see this:

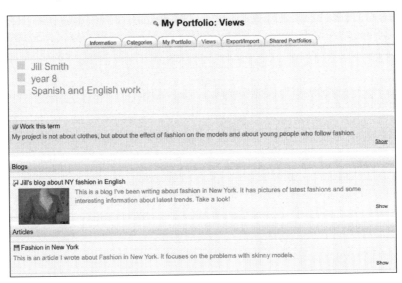

She can click on any item and write a comment on it. When you go back to your portfolio, you'll be able to see that comment and any others that have been written. You can also reply to other people's comments. Note that course teachers can only see the view if the student gives them access.

Activity 3: Using Workshop to support iterative writing

Aim: Help students develop their writing though reflection and evaluation from peers and teachers

Moodle modules: Workshop

Extra programs: None

Ease of setup: ***

Since the Workshop module can seem a bit daunting with all its variations, I suggest you follow a recipe first. Then once you get the hang of it, you should find it easy to adjust it to suit your own needs.

In the following scenario, students are going to practice writing a film review. The workflow will look like this:

1. Students review and evaluate three film reviews provided by the teacher.
2. Students then write their own first draft.
3. Three peers review the drafts.
4. Students produce their final drafts.
5. The teacher finally evaluates each final product.

Workshop is flexible. You could miss out Stage 1 if you want students to go straight to draft submission. You could miss out Stage 3, but then the activity would be more like the regular Assignment module. You could miss out Stage 5 if you're more interested in this as a peer review exercise.

There are three steps involved in creating a Workshop:

1. Adding the course.
2. Setting grading criteria.
3. Adding examples for students to practice on.

Here is how to do it

1. Click on **Turn on editing**. Go to the **Add an activity** drop-down menu and select **Workshop**.

2. Let's go through the set-up page step by step. Take a deep breath: it's a long set-up page!

Settings	Details
Submission Title	Let's call it **workshop – Writing a film review**.
Description	Write something like this:
	FILM REVIEW
	In this activity you're going to write a review of a film you've seen recently.
	First you'll access 3 reviews written by someone else. In each case decide whether you think the reviews were well written or not. You'll need to pay attention to the following:
	• key themes
	• strengths
	• weaknesses
	• background music
	• photography
	• general recommendations
	After the evaluations, you will write your own review of a film you saw recently.
	To help you along, you will make helpful suggestions on each other's work. Then when you're ready you can submit your final version for me to mark. I'll then give you feedback on your language.
	Your teacher
Grade for assessments and Grade for submissions	Here we are introduced to an important distinction in the Workshop jargon. An assessment is the draft that a student or peer sees. A submission is what finally goes to the teacher to mark. In the **Grade for assessments**, you decide what percentage of the total mark comes from student evaluations. Let's say **25** in this case. In the **Grade for submissions**, write **75**. The total mark for the submission will be 25 + 75 = 100. The teacher can readjust this balance at any time. If more than one peer provides a **grade for assessment**, the average of the grades is given.

Settings	Details
Grading Strategy	This strategy applies to the grades that both students and teachers give. Exception: If **Not graded** is chosen, students don't grade, but the teacher can still give a final grade. Let's choose **Error-banded**, because we want it to be easy for peers to evaluate each other's work at this stage. We can move on to a more detailed grading strategy later on when students are more used to the system.

Grading strategies available in Workshop

Type of strategy	Description	Comments
Not graded	No grade is given by the students. They can still make comments. The teacher can grade the student comments and can still give a final grade.	Useful for getting students to contribute ideas on each other's work, maybe point out possible language errors.
Accumulative	This is the default type of grading. The grade is divided into different elements which cover different aspects of the student's work. For example, did they mention a, b, and c? Did they see the difference between X and Y? The final mark is based on the cumulative grades from peers and teacher based on these elements.	Useful for students to understand the importance of specific elements in their work.
Error-banded	The submission is graded according to a set of yes/no statements. The grade depends on the number of correct elements. Peer reviewers only have to decide if something is there or not.	Makes reviewing simpler for peers.
Criterion	This is similar to accumulative, except that peers and teachers evaluate according to broader criteria; for example, content, language, and organization.	Good for developing skills to evaluate overall qualities of a piece of work.
Rubric	This is similar to criterion grading, except that each criterion is broken down into a set of statements.	Harder to set up that criterion grading, but may lead to more precise marking.

Settings	Details
Number of Comments, Assessment Elements, Grade Bands, Criterion Statements or Categories in a Rubric	This relates directly to the grading strategy you chose. So if you chose **Not graded,** for example, and then put a **10** in this box, up to ten comments can be made by different peers. Again, the following table should make this clearer. Let's choose **6,** because we're going to create six yes/no statements for students to answer when they review each other's work. This is a simplistic way of evaluating work, but it helps teachers and students get used to the system.

Grading elements

Number of Comments	The number of comments peers can make on an assessment
Assessment Elements	The number of key elements peers and teachers will evaluate
Grade Bands	The number of yes/no statements peers will have to answer to evaluate the work
Criterion Statements	The number of general criteria to evaluate against
Categories in a Rubric	The number of sets of criteria to include

Settings	Details
Number of Attachments expected on Submissions	This indicates the maximum number of attachments that students can attach. The number you give indicates how many upload boxes will be shown to the student, but they will not need to upload to send in a final submission of their assignment if it is not necessary. Let's put **3,** in case students need to attach several documents.
Allow Resubmissions	This means that students can benefit from an iterative writing process. Their final grade will be based on their best score. Note that when submissions are selected for peer review, it is likely that the newest one will be selected for peer review, but if students submit several pieces of work in quick succession, they are all equally likely to be chosen for peer review. Let's put **Yes.** This means that students will be able to learn from each other and resubmit their work.

Settings	Details
Number of Assessments of Examples from Teacher	As mentioned in the description, students can assess some examples before they write their own work, and, of course, before they assess each other's work. This will help them become more critical and maybe produce better work.
	Let's select **1**. This means students won't be able to submit their own work until they have reviewed the example. There are some reports on `moodle.org` that multiple submissions do not always work, so test this out first if you want to include more than one example.
Comparison of Assessments	The choice is between **very lax**, **lax**, **fair**, **strict**, and **very strict**.
	This looks at the amount of agreement between peers' evaluations and the teacher's evaluation. If it's set to **very lax** and there is quite a big difference between the marks, the student's mark will still count quite a lot. If it's set to **very strict** and there's a big difference, the student's mark won't count at all. This is a way of eliminating random-guessing on the part of the peer reviewer.
	Let's choose **fair** to try to rule out random-guessing.
Number of Assessments of Student Submissions	Remember, assessments are the draft versions. We want our students to review three different assessments, so let's write **3** here. Note that once the peers have reviewed the work, the student who wrote it can see the comments and the grade. This can be disputed—see the **Agreements must be agreed** setting in a bit.
Weight for Teacher Assessments	The default is **1**. That means the teacher's assessment has the same weighting or value as the students'. You can set it to a higher weighting if you think that students are over grading each other's work. The weighting can be changed at any time, and it's worth changing it to see what a difference, if any, it makes to the final mark. Let's leave it at 1 for now.
Over Allocation	This determines whether there is a balanced allocation of peer assessments. If you leave it at **0**, each assessment will be reviewed exactly the same number of times. If you put **1**, then some assessments may be allocated once more than others.
	Ideally, all peer assessments should be balanced. There is a problem when some students have to wait for their full quota of assessments until the last student has submitted his/her work. If you set the **Over Allocation** level to **1**, most students will not have to wait.
	Let's set ours to **1** for this activity.

Settings	Details
Self Assessment	If you set this to **yes**, students will also assess their own work. Let's set this to **yes**, as we want students to apply the assessment criteria to their own work. As we set the **Number of Assessments of Student Submissions** to **3**, they will now have a total of 4 submissions to evaluate. Note that if the **Number of Assessments of Student Submissions** is set to **0** and **Self Assessment** is turned on, this becomes a self-graded assignment.
Assessments must be agreed	If you select **no**, then there is no discussion about grades, just one-way feedback from peers.
	If you select **yes**, then students can agree or disagree about the grades. There is an option to revise grades and the discussion continues until an agreement is reached or the deadline is reached. If there is no final agreement, the disputed mark is not used in the final grades.
	We want to raise our students' awareness of criteria in this exercise. So let's select **yes**.
Hide Grades before Agreement	If you hide the grades in peer assessments, only the comments are visible. This may be more helpful for students wanting to improve their work and avoids potential arguments over grades if the grades are not hidden. For that reason, let's hide grades.
League Table of Submitted Work	The number you choose decides how long the list of best assignments is. Let's avoid having a league and leave the setting at **0**.
Hide Names from Students	There is a danger of bias in gradings if students know who graded them. So this option to hide names is quite useful. Let's set it to **yes**.
Use Password and Password	This allows you to set a password to enter the workshop. Let's put in a password to reduce the risk of illicit grading.
Maximum Size	This is the maximum size of submissions. If it's not high enough, you'll need to speak to your website administrator about increasing it. The administrator will need to adjust the `php.ini` file on the server.
Start of submissions, Start of assessments, End of submissions, End of assessments, Release Teacher Grades	Enter these dates carefully, as they determine when students can start and end each stage. Let's allow about 3 days between each stage.

Settings	Details
Group mode	As with other activities, you can set the **Group mode** to **No groups** in which all students work together, **Separate groups** in which students can only see their own group, or **Visible groups** in which students work in their own group but can see other groups. On this occasion, we don't want any groups.
Visible	We want students to see the activity now, so let's choose **show**.

3. Click on **Save changes**.

4. This will bring you to the **Editing Assessment Elements** page.

    At the top-half of the page write the yes/no statements you want to use to review the piece. Below each one, include the weighting for the statement. Ours are all set to **1**, except **general recommendations**, which we've set to **2**, because it's a key point. This is what the top-half of my **Editing Assessment Elements** looks like:

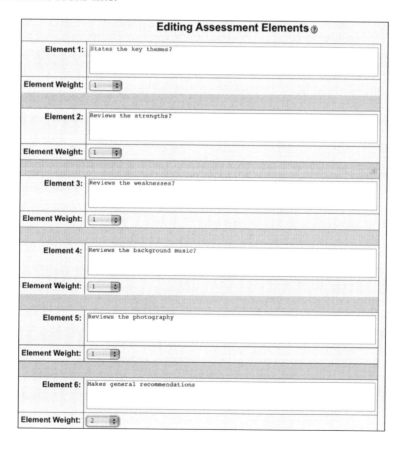

The bottom-half of the screen matches the number of errors with the score that the student will get.

Grade Table

Number of Negative Responses	Suggested Grade
0	75
1	65
2	55
3	45
4	35
5	25
6	0

Save changes   Cancel

In other words, if we can answer "yes" to all the assessment criteria, and if students meet all the assessment criteria, they will get the maximum **75**, which we set in **Suggested Grade** above. If students omit two of the criteria, they will get a mark of 55, and so on.

5. Click on **Save changes**.

You'll now be presented with an administrative overview.

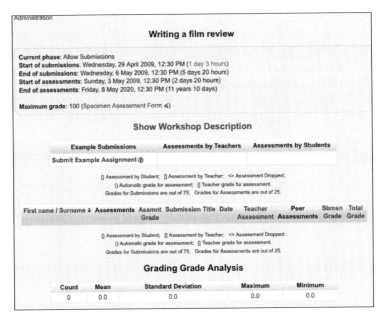

Administration

Writing a film review

Current phase: Allow Submissions
Start of submissions: Wednesday, 29 April 2009, 12:30 PM (1 day 3 hours)
End of submissions: Wednesday, 6 May 2009, 12:30 PM (5 days 20 hours)
Start of assessments: Sunday, 3 May 2009, 12:30 PM (2 days 20 hours)
End of assessments: Friday, 8 May 2020, 12:30 PM (11 years 10 days)

Maximum grade: 100 (Specimen Assessment Form ⚄)

Show Workshop Description

Example Submissions	Assessments by Teachers	Assessments by Students
Submit Example Assignment ⑦		

() Assessment by Student; [] Assessment by Teacher; <> Assessment Dropped;
() Automatic grade for assessment; [] Teacher grade for assessment.
Grades for Submissions are out of 75; Grades for Assessments are out of 25.

First name / Surname ↓	Assessments	Assmnt Grade	Submission Title	Date	Teacher Assessment	Peer Assessments	Sbmsn Grade	Total Grade

() Assessment by Student; [] Assessment by Teacher; <> Assessment Dropped;
() Automatic grade for assessment; [] Teacher grade for assessment.
Grades for Submissions are out of 75; Grades for Assessments are out of 25.

Grading Grade Analysis

Count	Mean	Standard Deviation	Maximum	Minimum
0	0.0	0.0	0.0	0.0

6. Now we need to add some example reviews for students to assess. To do that, click on **Submit Example Assignment**, as seen in the previous screenshot. Write in the **Submission Title**, and give the instructions for this step to your students as below. Don't forget to add the actual example by clicking on the **Browse...** button and uploading it from your computer. As in many other activities, you can also include a spoken introduction by clicking on the NanoGong icon.

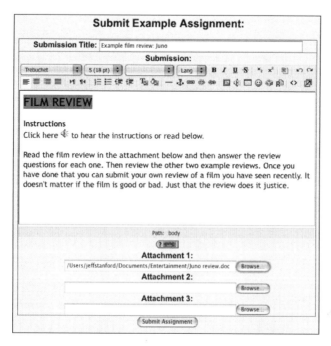

7. Click on **Submit Assignment**. You should then get an **Upload Successful** message. If you don't, it could be that your file size exceeds the limit. This is usually only the case if it contains very large graphics.

8. You can now review the example by clicking on the **Example film review: Juno** that we've just created.

9. Next, assess the example review yourself by clicking on **Assess** in the **Assessments** column.

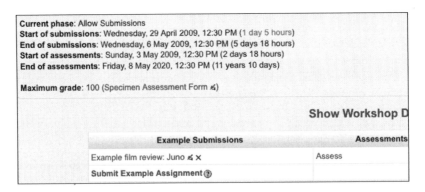

10. Now start answering the questions yourself. Make sure you add comments in the **Feedback** column, as they will be useful for your students to read.

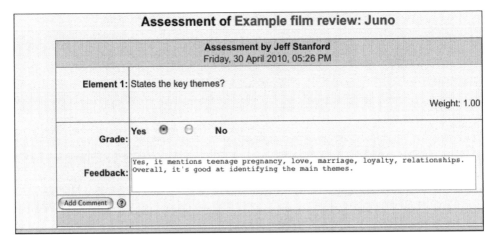

 Can't see the other questions?

Afterwards, you'll need to scroll down to answer the other five questions that you set in Step 4 earlier.

After the last question you'll notice there's an **Optional Adjustment** drop-down menu. Use this if you want to increase or decrease the score by up to 20 points. The text box allows you to say why you've made this adjustment. When you've finished, press **Save my assessment**.

11. You've now finished setting up the Workshop. Students can start using it. First they'll need to evaluate the example review. Then they can submit their own for peer assessment. When students first open the activity this is what they'll see:

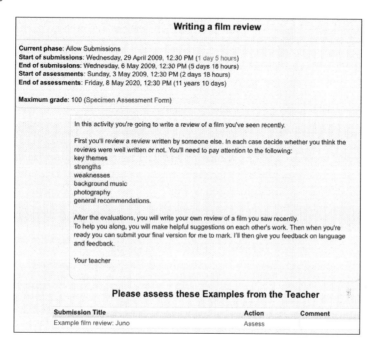

12. They should open the film review in the **Submission Title** column and then click on **Assess** to make their own assessment of it. After they save their assignment, they'll be presented with an assignment submission screen. If you want to keep the assignments anonymous, get the students to write a non-personal submission title, like "review of Titanic film". Students can either write their submission in the text box, where they can include sound and graphics if necessary, or they can attach a document with the review.

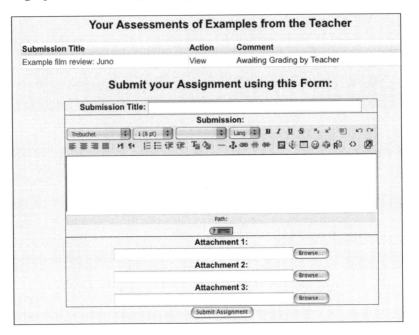

13. Once they have done that, they can see the useful overview of activities that the Workshop module provides. As we can see in the next screenshot:

   ○ They've submitted their review of the example, and they are waiting for the teacher to evaluate their review

   ○ They've submitted their own review of the film and can now do a self-assessment

   ○ They have the option of editing or deleting their own assessment

Show Workshop Description

Your Assessments of Examples from the Teacher

Submission Title	Action	Comment
Example film review: Juno	View	Awaiting Grading by Teacher

Please assess your Submission(s)

Submission Title	Action	Comment
review of Titanic film	Assess	Own Work

Your assessments of work by your peers

No Assessments Done

Your Submissions

Submission Title	Action	Submitted	Assessments
review of Titanic film	Edit | Delete	Thursday, 30 April 2009, 06:29 PM	0

An important point here is that the Moodle site **cronjob** must have run for you to see the updated interface. Ask your administrator about this if you don't get an updated interface quickly enough.

14. This is what the teacher will see once students **Jill** and **James** have both reviewed the example review and submitted their own reviews:

Show Workshop Description

Example Submissions	Assessments by Teachers	Assessments by Students
Example film review: Juno ✎ ✗	[55] ✎ ✗	{55 (25)}
Submit Example Assignment ⑦		

{} Assessment by Student; [] Assessment by Teacher; <> Assessment Dropped;
() Automatic grade for assessment; [] Teacher grade for assessment.
Grades for Submissions are out of 75; Grades for Assessments are out of 25.

First name / Surname ↓	Assessments	Assmnt Grade	Submission Title	Date	Teacher Assessment	Peer Assessments	Sbmsn Grade	Total Grade
Jill Smith	{55 (-)}	4.2	review of Titanic film ✎ ✗	30/04/09 18:29	Assess		0.0	4.2
James Smith	{65 (-)}	4.2	Review of Mad Max ✎ ✗	30/04/09 18:48	Assess		0.0	4.2
Jeff Stanford	{55 (25)}	4.2	Example film review: Juno ✎ ✗	30/04/09 17:29	[55] ✎ ✗	{55 (25)}	55.0	59.2

{} Assessment by Student; [] Assessment by Teacher; <> Assessment Dropped;
() Automatic grade for assessment; [] Teacher grade for assessment.
Grades for Submissions are out of 75; Grades for Assessments are out of 25.

The teacher should now assess Jill's and James' assessments by clicking on **Assess** to the right of their names.

The details on both the teacher's and the student's views will gradually in-crease in number as they complete various stages of the process. The teacher has a record of the work submitted by all students and the grades awarded to them. Don't forget that we set strict deadlines for start and end times for submissions in Step 3 earlier. If necessary, you can go to the set-up page and change dates. This might be necessary, for example, if all the students have already submitted their review of the example and are ready to review each other's submissions but the time for reviewing hasn't arrived yet.

15. When the final deadline for submissions has passed, students will not be able to access their grades until the deadline for the final grades has been reached. It is during that gap that the teacher has the chance to review and alter the final grades if necessary. This is what the final grade tally might look like:

First name / Surname ↓	Assessments	Assmnt Grade	Submission Title	Date	Teacher Assessment	Peer Assessments	Sbmsn Grade	Total Grade
James Smith	{65 (16)} {74 (-)} {75 (-)}	11.0	Review of Mad Max ✎ ✗	30/04/09 18:48	[75] ✎ ✗	{75 (25)}	75.0	86.0
Jim Smith	{65 (25)} {61 (-)}	8.3	review of film Batman ✎ ✗	30/04/09 19:10	[57] ✎ ✗	{57 (25)}	57.0	65.3
Jill Smith	{55 (25)} {65 (-)} {45 (-)}	12.5	review of Titanic film ✎ ✗	30/04/09 18:29	[55] ✎ ✗	{55 (25)}	55.0	67.5
Jane Smith	{65 (25)} {75 (-)} {75 (-)}	12.5	review of Star Trek ✎ ✗	30/04/09 19:02	[75] ✎ ✗	{75 (25)}	75.0	87.5
Jeff Stanford	{55 (25)} {55 (25)} {75 (25)} {75 (25)} {57 (25)}	20.8	Example film review: Juno ✎ ✗	30/04/09 17:29	[55] ✎ ✗	{65 (16)} {55 (25)} {55 (25)}	58.3	79.1

{} Assessment by Student; [] Assessment by Teacher; <> Assessment Dropped;
() Automatic grade for assessment; [] Teacher grade for assessment.
Grades for Submissions are out of 75; Grades for Assessments are out of 25.

The total grades are in the final column. Teachers can review the submissions by clicking on the title in the **Submission Title** column. It's also possible to click on the grades in the **Teacher Assessment** column and adjust them if necessary. For example, if you decide that the grade for Jill Smith's review was too low, you could re-read it, click on the **Teacher Assessment** mark, and adjust your marks. The easiest way to do this would be by using the **Optional Adjustment** drop-down menu at the bottom of the score sheet.

Workshop tips

- Examples of model texts — both good and bad — help students understand the assessment criteria and therefore the things to take on board with their writing.

- Make the assessment criteria as clear as possible.

- Tell students to come to you if they are confused by the comments from their peers.

- This may be a new process, so evaluate the whole exercise afterwards — that will help you improve the activity the next time round.

- There is more support and examples of Workshop in use at:

  ○ `http://www2.oakland.edu/elis/traindocs/Moodle/Workshop/index.html`

  ○ `http://docs.moodle.org/en/Workshops`

Activity 4: Using Reader to create an extended reading program

Aim: Set up a reading program with end-of-book quizzes using the Reader module

Moodle modules: Quiz

Extra programs: Reader

Ease of setup: ***

Sometimes students need or want to read a whole string of books — or we want them to! Thomas Robb has come up with a great way of organizing this sort of extended reading in an add-on module called Reader. It allows teachers to set up reading programs for long-term, extended reading, and helps organize key aspects of the program.

The module includes a database with the following sorts of information:

- Book name — this must be the same as the quiz name
- Publisher
- Reading level
- Length of book
- Image of book cover

It allows teachers to associate quiz with each book. Students read a book, do the associated quizzes, then, optionally, receive a token as a reward. The token is designed to be the book cover, but you can use any image. The teacher decides how many questions students need to answer at the end of each book.

So, in preparation, you need to have the following:

- A set of books for students to read — online or offline.
- A list of those books.
- A quiz for each book.
- The publisher's name.
- The level of difficulty of the books — you can decide how many levels you have and how you label them.
- The quizzes that you want to include — see Chapter 3, *Vocabulary Activities, Activity 11* for help with setting up a Quiz.
- Images of the front cover on your computer — see Chapter 11, *Formatting and Enhancing Your Moodle Materials* for help with preparing images. Most front cover images can be saved from `http://amazon.com`.

This will take some time to compile, but once it is ready, the teacher does not need to intervene, and the module can last for an extended period. Good sources of online books are `http://scribd.com` and `http://gutenberg.org`. An Internet search for "online books" will bring up other possibilities.

To save you much of the preparation work, Thomas Robb has made available a list of books and quizzes which you can use at `http://moodlereader.org/moodle/course/view.php?id=14`.

Here's how to do it

1. Before you set up the activity, check the default settings for Reader. To do that, on the home page, go to **Site Administration | Modules | Activities | Reader**. You will see the following page:

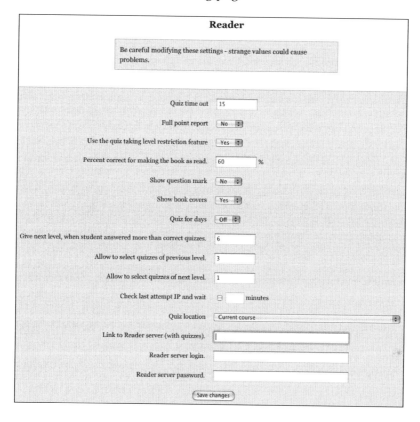

You can leave most of these settings as they are. If you want to take advantage of Thomas Robb's extensive database of quizzes, you'll need to complete the **Link to Reader server (with quizzes)**, the **Reader server login**, and the **Reader server password** settings. To get these, you need to write to Thomas Robb at `admin@moodlereader.org`, explaining how you intend to use them.

2. In editing mode on your course, click on **Add an activity....**

3. Select **Reader** from the drop-down menu.

4. Complete the introductory page as follows. Pay particular attention to the following items:

Settings	Details
Name	Let's call this **Your books**.
Summary	Write something simple, like:
	This Module allows you to select books, and do quizzes based on those books. You will get a score for the quiz and will receive a token for each book you read, which you can see in your book report.
Timing	Here we can set time limits for the availability of the quiz and the duration of each quiz. Let's check **Open the quiz** and **Close the quiz** for now. That will enable permanent access. Let's leave the **Time limit** on **15 minutes**, so that students don't have enough time to find the answer without reading the whole book.
Show exact score	Let's leave this on **Yes** for now. That means that students will see the exact overall score they get on the quizzes. If we set it to **No**, they'll just know whether they've passed or not.
Percent correct for marking the book as read	Here we decide what percentage of the total mark students need to get for the book to be considered read. Let's put **60%**.
Hide individual question values	Let's set this to **No**, so that students know what mark they're getting for each item in the quiz.
Show book covers	Let's put **Yes,** as this makes the activity more attractive. It does give you the extra work of making sure you have images of book covers available, though.
Quiz for days	Let's set this to **Off** for now. There is also the option in the drop-down menu to make each book quiz available for **1, 2,** or **3** days.
Total point goal for the entire term	Let's leave this at **0**.
Give next level, when student answered more than correct quizzes	Let's put **3**. That means that students have to read at least three books at one level before they are automatically advanced to the next level.
Allow to select quizzes of previous level	Let's put **2**. That means that students can choose up to two quizzes at the previous level.
Allow to select quizzes of next level	Let's put **2**. That means students can take up to two quizzes at the next level.
No promotion after level	Let's leave this at **0**. That means that students can be promoted to any level that we have set. If we put a level number here, students cannot be promoted beyond that level.

Settings	Details
Ignore quizzes taken before	Let's set this to the date we want students' quiz scores to be valid from. Let's put today's date.
Teacher-made quizzes for this module can be found in this course, which is not open for students access.	This is a handy way of accessing quizzes that you may have created on other courses which are not otherwise available to students. Select other course quizzes you want to use from the drop-down menu.
Security	Let's set these on **Off** for now. These security measures are explained in Chapter 2, *Getting Started with Moodle*.
Common module settings	Here we can decide if we want to use groups. Let's leave it at **No groups** for now. These settings are explained in Chapter 2, *Getting Started with Moodle*.

5. Click on **Save and display.**

6. This brings you to the **Reading Report** page. It's empty at the moment, because we haven't entered any quizzes and I haven't read any books.

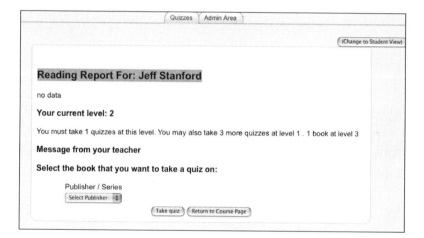

Some teachers wonder how you add books and look for a button to do that: don't! It doesn't exist. As mentioned before, you add books by adding the quiz that is about the book. In other words, you can't add a book if you haven't prepared a quiz for it. To make things simpler, the quiz should have the same name as the book.

To add our first book (quiz), we should click on the **Admin Area** tab.

7. This is the menu you'll be presented with:

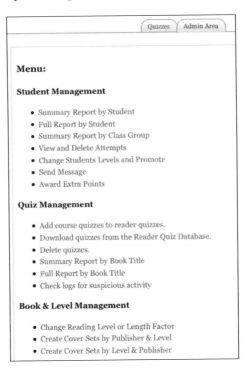

Click on **Add course quizzes to reader quizzes**. It's on this page that you enter details of the new book and where you choose the quiz you want to attach to the reader.

In the **Select Quizzes** section we must select a quiz and select or give details of the book.

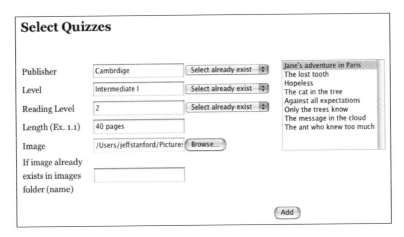

In the previous screenshot we have chosen the quiz based on the book **Jane's adventure in Paris** and completed the details for it.

Enter the book information in the left-hand column. Note that this is the only chance you have to add the book cover image, so make sure you have it ready. It's worth spending the time doing this, because when students have read their books and passed the associated quiz, they will be rewarded with a token, which is the book cover image, or any other image you decide on. This may motivate some learners to read more. As an alternative, you could use one book image for all books. There's a downloadable one at `http://moodleforlanguages/images/books.gif`. It looks like this:

The right-hand column lists all of the quizzes you have produced so far. If the quiz you want isn't there, you will need to write it first, then come back to this page to select it for the Reader module. To set up a Quiz, follow the instructions in Chapter 3, *Vocabulary Activities, Activity 11*. You could include a variety of question types: true/false, multiple-choice, short-answer, and ordering questions work well. Here are some suggestions for what you can focus on in your questions:

- ° Multiple-choice questions on specific details in the story
- ° Multiple-choice questions like "Who said 'X'?"
- ° True/false questions about events in the story
- ° Ordering questions which test knowledge of the order of events in the story

Only automatically gradable questions can be included. So we can't include essay questions that need to be manually graded. The **Manual grading** tab that appears on some pages is, in fact, redundant.

A book evaluation is automatically included in each quiz as the final question, so that you know whether students enjoy the books on the list.

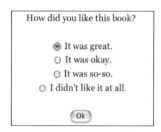

The results are not currently built into the system. This is on the author's to-do list.

8. Once you have set up the readers and quizzes you want the students to have access to, the module is ready to use. When students click on the reader activity, they will be presented with their reading report (see Step 6 above) and a choice of books to read.

9. Teachers can use the **Admin Area** to review the progress of students, to promote them, and to get summaries of students' work or use of different books. Here are some extra notes on the menu items available in the **Admin** menu. Many of them are self-explanatory. The punctuation is copied from the original.

Student Management

Summary Report by Student	This lists books students have read, the level of difficulty of the books, and the marks obtained by each student.
Full Report by Student	This includes information on all the books read by students. S-level stands for the Student's level. B-level stands for Book level. It's possible that the Student's level is 2, but he or she read a book at level 1.
Summary Report by Class Group	This provides averages for groups. You need to have set up groups on the set-up page for this to work.
View and Delete Attempts	You can delete attempts, if necessary.
Change Students Levels and Promote	You can change students' levels according to the progress they're making.
Send Message	This displays a message on the Moodle Reader page. It doesn't send an email, as you might think.
Award Extra Points	This allows you to award extra points to students for manually graded questions (essays) on their quizzes.

Quiz Management

Add course quizzes to reader quizzes	Here you can add quizzes that you have set up for your course. Remember that you can expand the source of quizzes on the set-up page.
Download quizzes from the Reader Quiz Database	You can write to Thomas Robb at `admin@ moodlereader.org` and request a username and password to download the many quizzes he has created on his site.
Delete quizzes	To remove quizzes you no longer want in the Reader module.
Summary Report by Book Title	Gives basic book information and a summary of pass marks obtained for each book.
Full Report by Book Title	This gives basic book information and individual student marks for each book. There are further links to the Moodle Gradebook, where all Reader quiz marks are stored, too.
Check logs for suspicious activity	If you click on **Go**, you can see whether students have used a different IP address (that's the unique address of their computer) to the ones in your security setting. You can also monitor the delay time between attempts at different quizzes.

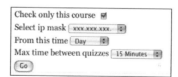

See Chapter 2, *Getting Started with Moodle* for more information on security settings.

Book & Level Management

Change Reading Level or Length Factor	The length factor assumes that books at the same level are of a similar length. If a book is significantly shorter, you can reduce the length factor, or if a book is significantly longer, you can increase the length factor.
Create Cover Sets by Publisher & Level	This allows you to view the cover sets available, sorted by publisher then by level. Cover sets are the book cover images.
Create Cover Sets by Level & Publisher	This allows you to see the same cover sets, but sorted first by level, then by publisher.

[You could also use the Reader module for students to listen to audio books.]

Index

F

G

X

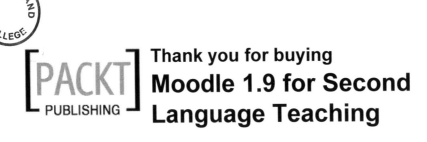

Moodle 1.9 for Second Language Teaching

Packt Open Source Project Royalties

When we sell a book written on an Open Source project, we pay a royalty directly to that project. Therefore by purchasing Moodle 1.9 for Second Language Teaching, Packt will have given some of the money received to the Moodle project.

In the long term, we see ourselves and you—customers and readers of our books—as part of the Open Source ecosystem, providing sustainable revenue for the projects we publish on. Our aim at Packt is to establish publishing royalties as an essential part of the service and support a business model that sustains Open Source.

If you're working with an Open Source project that you would like us to publish on, and subsequently pay royalties to, please get in touch with us.

Writing for Packt

We welcome all inquiries from people who are interested in authoring. Book proposals should be sent to author@packtpub.com. If your book idea is still at an early stage and you would like to discuss it first before writing a formal book proposal, contact us; one of our commissioning editors will get in touch with you.

We're not just looking for published authors; if you have strong technical skills but no writing experience, our experienced editors can help you develop a writing career, or simply get some additional reward for your expertise.

About Packt Publishing

Packt, pronounced 'packed', published its first book "Mastering phpMyAdmin for Effective MySQL Management" in April 2004 and subsequently continued to specialize in publishing highly focused books on specific technologies and solutions.

Our books and publications share the experiences of your fellow IT professionals in adapting and customizing today's systems, applications, and frameworks. Our solution-based books give you the knowledge and power to customize the software and technologies you're using to get the job done. Packt books are more specific and less general than the IT books you have seen in the past. Our unique business model allows us to bring you more focused information, giving you more of what you need to know, and less of what you don't.

Packt is a modern, yet unique publishing company, which focuses on producing quality, cutting-edge books for communities of developers, administrators, and newbies alike. For more information, please visit our website: www.PacktPub.com.

Moodle 1.9 E-Learning Course Development

ISBN: 978-1-847193-53-7   Paperback: 360 pages

A complete guide to successful learning using Moodle

1. Updated for Moodle version 1.9

2. Straightforward coverage of installing and using the Moodle system

3. Working with Moodle features in all learning environments

4. A unique course-based approach focuses your attention on designing well-structured, interactive, and successful courses

Moodle Teaching Techniques

ISBN: 978-1-847192-84-4   Paperback: 200 pages

Creative Ways to Use Moodle for Constructing Online Learning Solutions

1. Applying your teaching techniques through Moodle

2. Creative uses for Moodle's standard features

3. Workarounds, providing alternative solutions

4. **Abundantly illustrated with screenshots of the solutions you'll build**

5. Especially good for university and professional teachers

Please check **www.PacktPub.com** for information on our titles

994320

Printed in Great Britain by
Amazon.co.uk, Ltd.,
Marston Gate.